T0228026

IET COMPUTING SERIES 37

Handbook of Big Data Analytics

IET Book Series on Big Data–Call for Authors

Editor-in-Chief: Professor Albert Y. Zomaya, University of Sydney, Australia
The topic of big data has emerged as a revolutionary theme that cuts across many technologies and application domains. This new book series brings together topics within the myriad research activities in many areas that analyse, compute, store, manage, and transport massive amounts of data, such as algorithm design, data mining and search, processor architectures, databases, infrastructure development, service and data discovery, networking and mobile computing, cloud computing, high-performance computing, privacy and security, storage, and visualization.
Topics considered include (but not restricted to) IoT and Internet computing; cloud computing; peer-to-peer computing; autonomic computing; data centre computing; multi-core and many core computing; parallel, distributed, and high-performance computing; scalable databases; mobile computing and sensor networking; Green computing; service computing; networking infrastructures; cyber infrastructures; e-Science; smart cities; analytics and data mining; big data applications, and more.
Proposals for coherently integrated International co-edited or co-authored handbooks and research monographs will be considered for this book series. Each proposal will be reviewed by the Editor-in-Chief and some board members, with additional external reviews from independent reviewers. Please email your book proposal for the IET Book Series on Big Data to Professor Albert Y. Zomaya at albert.zomaya@sydney.edu.au or to the IET at author_support@theiet.org.

Handbook of Big Data Analytics

Volume 1: Methodologies

Edited by
Vadlamani Ravi and Aswani Kumar Cherukuri

The Institution of Engineering and Technology

Published by The Institution of Engineering and Technology, London, United Kingdom

The Institution of Engineering and Technology is registered as a Charity in England & Wales (no. 211014) and Scotland (no. SC038698).

© The Institution of Engineering and Technology 2021

First published 2021

The Institution of Engineering and Technology
Michael Faraday House
Six Hills Way, Stevenage
Herts, SG1 2AY, United Kingdom

www.theiet.org

British Library Cataloguing in Publication Data
A catalogue record for this product is available from the British Library

ISBN 978-1-83953-064-7 (hardback Volume 1)
ISBN 978-1-83953-058-6 (PDF Volume 1)
ISBN 978-1-83953-059-3 (hardback Volume 2)
ISBN 978-1-83953-060-9 (PDF Volume 2)
ISBN 978-1-83953-061-6 (2 volume set)

Typeset in India by MPS Limited
Printed in the UK by CPI Group (UK) Ltd, Croydon

Contents

About the editors	**xiii**
About the contributors	**xv**
Foreword	**xxi**
Foreword	**xxiii**
Preface	**xxv**
Acknowledgements	**xxvii**
Introduction	**xxix**

1 The impact of Big Data on databases   1
Antonio Sarasa Cabezuelo

1.1	The Big Data phenomenon	2
	1.1.1 Big Data Operational and Big Data Analytical	3
	1.1.2 The impact of Big Data on databases	5
1.2	Scalability in relational databases	6
	1.2.1 Relational databases	6
	1.2.2 The limitations of relational databases	7
1.3	NoSQL databases	9
	1.3.1 Disadvantages of NoSQL databases	11
	1.3.2 Aggregate-oriented NoSQL databases	12
	1.3.3 MongoDB: an example of documentary database	13
	1.3.4 Cassandra: an example of columnar-oriented database	14
1.4	Data distribution models	15
	1.4.1 Sharding	15
	1.4.2 Replication	17
	1.4.3 Combining sharding and replication	18
1.5	Design examples using NoSQL databases	19
1.6	Design examples using NoSQL databases	19
	1.6.1 Example 1	19
	1.6.2 Example 2	21
	1.6.3 Example 3	26
	1.6.4 Example 4	29
1.7	Conclusions	30
	References	31

2   Big data processing frameworks and architectures: a survey   37
Raghavendra Kumar Chunduri and Aswani Kumar Cherukuri

2.1   Introduction   37
2.2   Apache Hadoop framework and Hadoop Ecosystem   39
       2.2.1   Architecture of Hadoop framework   39
       2.2.2   Architecture of MapReduce   39
       2.2.3   Application implemented using MapReduce: concept
                generation in formal concept analysis (FCA)   46
2.3   HaLoop framework   53
       2.3.1   Programming model of HaLoop   54
       2.3.2   Task scheduling in HaLoop   54
       2.3.3   Caching in HaLoop   55
       2.3.4   Fault tolerance   55
       2.3.5   Concept generation in FCA using HaLoop   56
2.4   Twister framework   56
       2.4.1   Architecture of Twister framework   57
       2.4.2   Fault tolerance in Twister   58
2.5   Apache Pig   59
       2.5.1   Characteristics of Apache Pig   59
       2.5.2   Components of Apache Pig   59
       2.5.3   Pig data model   60
       2.5.4   Word count application using Apache Pig   60
2.6   Apache Mahout   61
       2.6.1   Apache Mahout features   61
       2.6.2   Applications of Mahout   61
2.7   Apache Sqoop   62
       2.7.1   Sqoop import   62
       2.7.2   Export from Sqoop   63
2.8   Apache Flume   63
       2.8.1   Advantages of Flume   63
       2.8.2   Features of Flume   64
       2.8.3   Components of Flume   64
2.9   Apache Oozie   66
2.10   Hadoop 2   66
2.11   Apache Spark   67
       2.11.1   Spark Core   69
       2.11.2   Driver program   69
       2.11.3   Spark Context   69
       2.11.4   Spark cluster manager   70
       2.11.5   Spark worker node   70
       2.11.6   Spark resilient distributed datasets (RDDs)   70
       2.11.7   Caching RDDs   71
       2.11.8   Broadcast variables in spark   71
       2.11.9   Spark Datasets   72

	2.11.10	Spark System optimization	73
	2.11.11	Memory optimization	73
	2.11.12	I/O optimization	74
	2.11.13	Fault tolerance optimization	74
	2.11.14	Data processing in Spark	75
	2.11.15	Spark machine learning support	78
	2.11.16	Spark deep learning support	79
	2.11.17	Programming layer in Spark	80
	2.11.18	Concept generation in formal concept analysis using Spark	82
2.12	Big data storage systems		85
	2.12.1	Hadoop distributed file system	86
	2.12.2	Alluxio	88
	2.12.3	Amazon Simple Storage Services—S3	88
	2.12.4	Microsoft Azure Blob Storage-WASB	88
	2.12.5	HBase	88
	2.12.6	Amazon Dynamo	88
	2.12.7	Cassandra	89
	2.12.8	Hive	89
2.13	Distributed stream processing engines		90
	2.13.1	Apache Storm	90
	2.13.2	Apache Flink	92
2.14	Apache Zookeeper		94
	2.14.1	The Zookeeper data model	95
	2.14.2	ZDM—access control list	96
2.15	Open issues and challenges		97
	2.15.1	Memory management	97
	2.15.2	Failure recovery	97
2.16	Conclusion		98
References			98

3 The role of data lake in big data analytics: recent developments and challenges   105
T. Ramalingeswara Rao, Pabitra Mitra and Adrijit Goswami

3.1	Introduction		105
	3.1.1	Differences between data warehouses and data lakes	107
	3.1.2	Data lakes pitfalls	108
3.2	Taxonomy of data lakes		108
	3.2.1	Data silos	108
	3.2.2	Data swamps	109
	3.2.3	Data reservoirs	109
	3.2.4	Big data fabric	109
3.3	Architecture of a data lake		110
	3.3.1	Raw data layer	110
	3.3.2	Data ingestion layer	111

		3.3.3	Process layer	111
		3.3.4	Ingress layer	112
		3.3.5	Responsibilities of data scientists in data lakes	112
		3.3.6	Metadata management	113
		3.3.7	Data lake governance	113
		3.3.8	Data cataloging	114
	3.4	Commercial-based data lakes		114
		3.4.1	Azure data lake environment	114
		3.4.2	Developing a data lake with IBM (IBM DL)	115
		3.4.3	Amazon Web Services (AWS) Galaxy data lake (GDL)	115
	3.5	Open source-based data lakes		116
		3.5.1	Delta lake	116
		3.5.2	BIGCONNECT data lake	116
		3.5.3	Best practices for data lakes	117
	3.6	Case studies		118
		3.6.1	Machine learning in data lakes	120
		3.6.2	Data lake challenges	120
	3.7	Conclusion		120
	References			121

4   Query optimization strategies for big data   125
Nagesh Bhattu Sristy, Prashanth Kadari and Harini Yadamreddy

	4.1	Introduction		126
		4.1.1	MapReduce preliminaries	127
		4.1.2	Organization of the chapter	127
	4.2	Multi-way joins using MapReduce		127
		4.2.1	Sequential join	129
		4.2.2	Shares approach	130
		4.2.3	SharesSkew	132
		4.2.4	Θ-Join	135
	4.3	Graph queries using MapReduce		138
		4.3.1	Counting triangles	138
		4.3.2	Subgraph enumeration	140
	4.4	Multi-way spatial join		147
	4.5	Conclusion and future work		153
	References			153

**5   Toward real-time data processing: an advanced approach
    in big data analytics**   157
Shafqat Ul Ahsaan, Harleen Kaur and Sameena Naaz

	5.1	Introduction		157
	5.2	Real-time data processing topology		159
		5.2.1	Choosing the platform	159
		5.2.2	Entry points	159
		5.2.3	Data processing infrastructure	159

5.3   Streaming processing   160
5.4   Stream mining   161
        5.4.1   Clustering   161
        5.4.2   Classification   161
        5.4.3   Frequent   162
        5.4.4   Outlier and anomaly detection   162
5.5   Lambda architecture   162
5.6   Stream processing approach for big data   163
        5.6.1   Apache Spark   163
        5.6.2   Apache Flink   164
        5.6.3   Apache Samza   167
        5.6.4   Apache Storm   167
        5.6.5   Apache Flume   168
        5.6.6   Apache Kafka   169
5.7   Evaluation of data streaming processing approaches   172
5.8   Conclusion   172
Acknowledgment   172
References   173

6   **A survey on data stream analytics**   **175**
    Sumit Misra, Sanjoy Kumar Saha and Chandan Mazumdar

6.1   Introduction   175
6.2   Scope and approach   177
6.3   Prediction and forecasting   178
        6.3.1   Future direction for prediction and forecasting   179
6.4   Outlier detection   180
        6.4.1   Future direction for outlier detection   182
6.5   Concept drift detection   183
        6.5.1   Future direction for concept drift detection   187
6.6   Mining frequent item sets in data stream   187
        6.6.1   Future direction for frequent item-set mining   190
6.7   Computational paradigm   191
        6.7.1   Future direction for computational paradigm   196
6.8   Conclusion   197
References   198

7   **Architectures of big data analytics: scaling out data mining**
    algorithms using Hadoop–MapReduce and Spark   **209**
    Sheikh Kamaruddin and Vadlamani Ravi

7.1   Introduction   209
7.2   Previous related reviews   211
7.3   Review methodology   214
7.4   Review of articles in the present work   217
        7.4.1   Association rule mining/pattern mining   217

	7.4.2	Regression/prediction/forecasting	224
	7.4.3	Classification	227
	7.4.4	Clustering	237
	7.4.5	Outlier detection/intrusion detection system	246
	7.4.6	Recommendation	248
	7.4.7	Others	249
7.5	Discussion		252
7.6	Conclusion and future directions		260
	References		270

8 A review of fog and edge computing with big data analytics   297
Ch. Rajyalakshmi, K. Ram Mohan Rao and Rajeswara Rao Ramisetty

8.1	Introduction		298
	8.1.1	What is big data?	298
	8.1.2	Importance of big data in cloud computing	299
	8.1.3	Merits and demerits	299
8.2	Introduction to cloud computing with IoT applications		299
	8.2.1	Cloud computing importance	302
	8.2.2	Cloud offloading strategies	303
	8.2.3	Applications of IoT	303
	8.2.4	Merits and demerits of IoT application with cloud	305
8.3	Importance of fog computing		305
	8.3.1	Overview of fog	306
	8.3.2	Definition for fog	307
	8.3.3	Description of fog architecture	307
	8.3.4	Research direction in fog	310
8.4	Significance of edge computing		310
	8.4.1	What is edge computing	310
	8.4.2	Benefits of edge computing	310
	8.4.3	How edge computing used in IoT applications	311
	8.4.4	Future of edge computing	312
8.5	Architecture review with cloud and fog and edge computing with IoT applications		312
	8.5.1	How IoT applications meeting the challenges at edge	312
	8.5.2	Review on cyber threats, latency time and power consumption challenges	313
	8.5.3	Applications and future scope of research	314
8.6	Conclusion		314
	References		314

9 Fog computing framework for Big Data processing using cluster management in a resource-constraint environment   317
Srinivasa Raju Rudraraju, Nagender Kumar Suryadevara and Atul Negi

| 9.1 | Introduction | | 317 |

9.2   Literature survey   319
    9.2.1   Cluster computing   320
    9.2.2   Utility computing   321
    9.2.3   Peer-to-peer computing   321
    9.2.4   Distributed computing frameworks   321
    9.2.5   Gaps identified in the existing research work   323
    9.2.6   Objectives of the chapter   323
9.3   System description   323
9.4   Implementation details   324
    9.4.1   Using resource constraint device (Raspberry Pi)   324
    9.4.2   Spark fog cluster evaluation   326
9.5   Results and discussion   329
9.6   Conclusion and future work   332
References   332

10 **Role of artificial intelligence and big data in accelerating
     accessibility for persons with disabilities**   335
     Kundumani Srinivasan Kuppusamy

10.1   Introduction   335
10.2   Rationale for accessibility   336
10.3   Artificial intelligence for accessibility   337
    10.3.1   Perception porting   337
    10.3.2   Assisting deaf and hard of hearing   338
    10.3.3   AI-based exoskeletons   339
    10.3.4   Accessible data visualization   339
    10.3.5   Enabling smart environment through IoT for
                 persons with disabilities   339
10.4   Conclusions   340
References   340

Overall conclusions   345
Vadlamani Ravi and Aswani Kumar Cherukuri

Index   347

About the editors

Vadlamani Ravi is a professor in the Institute for Development and Research in Banking Technology (IDRBT), Hyderabad where he spearheads the Center of Excellence in Analytics, the first-of-its-kind in India. He holds a Ph.D. in Soft Computing from Osmania University, Hyderabad and RWTH Aachen, Germany (2001). Earlier, he worked as a Faculty at the National University of Singapore from 2002 to 2005. He worked in RWTH Aachen under DAAD Long Term Fellowship from 1997 to 1999. He has more than 32 years of experience in research and teaching. He has been working in soft computing, evolutionary/neuro/fuzzy computing, data/text mining, global/multi-criteria optimization, big data analytics, social media analytics, time-series data mining, deep learning, bankruptcy prediction, and analytical CRM. He published more than 230 papers in refereed international/national journals/conferences and invited chapters. He has 7,891 citations and an *h*-index of 42. He also edited a book published by IGI Global, USA, 2007. He is a referee for 40 international journals and an Associate Editor for Swarm and Evolutionary Computation, Managing Editor for Journal of Banking and Financial Technology, and Editorial Board Member for few International Journals of repute. He is a referee for international project proposals submitted to European Science Foundation, Irish Science Foundation, and book proposals submitted to Elsevier and Springer. Further, he is listed in the top 2% scientists in the field of artificial intelligence and image processing, as per an independent study done by Stanford University scientists (https://journals.plos.org/plosbiology/article?id=10.1371/journal.pbio.3000918). He consults for and advises various Indian banks on their Analytical CRM, Fraud Detection, Data Science, AI/ML projects.

Aswani Kumar Cherukuri is a professor of the School of Information Technology and Engineering at Vellore Institute of Technology (VIT), Vellore, India. His research interests are machine learning, information security. He published more than 150 research papers in various journals and conferences. He received Young Scientist fellowship from Tamil Nadu State Council for Science & Technology, Govt. of State of Tamil Nadu, India. He received an inspiring teacher award from The New Indian Express (leading English daily). He is listed in the top 2% scientists in the field of artificial intelligence and image processing, as per an independent study done by Stanford University scientists (https://journals.plos.org/plosbiology/article?id=10.1371/journal.pbio.3000918). He executed few major research projects funded by several funding agencies in Govt. of India. He is a senior member of ACM and is associated with other professional bodies, including CSI, ISTE. He is the Vice Chair of IEEE taskforce on educational data mining. He is an editorial board member for several international journals.

About the contributors

Shafqat Ul Ahsaan is working as a research scholar in the Department of Computer Science, School of Engineering Sciences and Technology, Jamia Hamdard, New Delhi, India. He received his Master's degree in Computer Science from Jamia Hamdard New Delhi, India. His research interests include big data analytics and machine learning.

Antonio Sarasa Cabezuelo received the Ph.D. degree in Computer Science from the Complutense University of Madrid. He is currently an associate professor with the Computer Science School, Complutense University of Madrid, and a member of the ILSA Research Group. He has authored over 150 research papers in national and international conferences and journals. His research is focused on big data, artificial intelligence, e-learning, markup languages, and domain-specific languages.

Aswani Kumar Cherukuri is a professor at School of Information Technology and Engineering, Vellore Institute of Technology, Vellore, India. He holds a Ph.D. degree in Computer Science from Vellore Institute of Technology, India. His research interests are information security, machine learning, and quantum computing.

Raghavendra Kumar Chunduri is currently a research student at School of Information Technology and Engineering, Vellore Institute of Technology, Vellore, India. His research interests are big data, machine learning, and software engineering.

Adrijit Goswami received his M.Sc. and Ph.D. degrees from Jadavpur University, India, in 1985 and 1992 respectively. In 1992, he joined the Indian Institute of Technology Kharagpur, India, where at present he is a professor in the Department of Mathematics. He has published articles in JORS, EJOR, Computers and Mathematics with Applications, Production Planning and Control, OPSEARCH, International Journal of Systems Science, the Journal of Fuzzy Mathematics, Journal of Information and Knowledge Management, International Journal of Uncertainty, Fuzziness and Knowledge-Based Systems, Journal of Applied Mathematics and Computing, International Journal of Data Analysis Techniques and Strategies, Knowledge and Information Systems, Expert Systems and Applications, International Journal of Production Economics, etc. His research interests include data mining, big data, cryptography, distributed and object-oriented databases, inventory management under fuzzy environment, optimization, database systems, data mining techniques under fuzzy environment, and information security. He has published more than 115 papers in international journals and conferences in these areas.

Prashanth Kadari is currently a research scholar in the Department of Computer Science and Engineering, National Institute of Technology, Andhra Pradesh, India. His research areas of interest include machine learning, deep learning, big data analytics, distributed computing.

Sk Kamaruddin is a Ph.D. scholar at Institute for Development and Research in Banking Technology, Hyderabad and University of Hyderabad. He did his MCA from Utkal University, Bhubaneswar in 2000. He has 14 years of teaching experience. He published 6 conference papers which have a total citation count of 47. His research interests are machine learning, data mining, natural language processing, big data analytics, distributed and parallel computation.

Harleen Kaur is a faculty at the Department of CSE, School of Engineering Sciences and Technology at Jamia Hamdard, New Delhi, India. She recently worked as a research fellow at United Nations University (UNU), Tokyo, Japan in IIGH-International Centre for Excellence, Malaysia to conduct research on funded projects from South-East Asian Nations (SEAN). She is working on Indo-Poland bilateral international project funded by Ministry of Science and Technology, India and Ministry of Polish, Poland. In addition, she is working on a national project catalysed and supported by National Council for Science and Technology Communication (NCSTC), Ministry of Science and Technology, India. Her key research areas include information analytics, applied machine learning, and predictive modelling. She is the author of various publications and has author/editor of several reputed books. She is a member to international bodies and is a member of editorial board of international journals on data analytics and machine learning. She is the recipient of the Ambassador for Peace Award (UN Agency) and is a funded researcher by external groups.

K.S. Kuppusamy is an assistant professor in the Department of Computer Science, School of Engineering and Technology, Pondicherry University, Pondicherry, India. His research interest includes accessible computing, human–computer interaction, machine learning. He has published 95+ papers in indexed international journals, international conferences, and technical magazines. His articles are published by reputed publishers such as Oxford University Press, Elsevier, Springer, Taylor and Francis, World Scientific, Emerald and EFY. He is the recipient of Best Teacher award from Pondicherry University six times. He is serving as the Counsellor for Persons with Disabilities at HEPSN Enabling Unit, Pondicherry University.

Chandan Mazumdar obtained his Master of Engineering in Electronics & Telecommunication from Jadavpur University, India in 1983. He has been teaching computer science and engineering. For the last 35 years. He has contributed to various organizations like DRDO, MEITY, IDRBT, and industries through R7D and consultancies. His current research interests are information and network security, fault tolerance, and big data analytics.

Sumit Misra obtained his B.E. in Electronics and Communication Engineering from BIT Mesra in 1988 and M.E. in Electronics and Telecommunication Engineering from Jadavpur University in 1991. He is pursuing his Ph.D. in the Department of Computer Science and Engineering, Jadavpur University. He is currently working as Associate Vice President in RS Software (India) Limited. Data analytics and industry domain of electronic payment systems are his areas of interest.

Pabitra Mitra is currently working as an associate professor in the Department of Computer Science and Engineering, Indian Institute of Technology Kharagpur, India. He received his Ph.D. degree in Computer Science from Indian Statistical Institute, India, in 2003. He received his B.Tech. degree from the Indian Institute of Technology Kharagpur, India in 1996. He was honoured with Royal Society Indo-UK Science Network Award 2006, INAE Young Engineer Award 2008, IBM Faculty Award 2010. His current research areas include data mining, pattern recognition, machine learning, and information retrieval. He has published more than 219 papers in international journals and conferences in these areas.

Sameena Naaz is working as an associate professor in the Department of CSE, Jamia Hamdard, New Delhi, India. She has a total experience of about 20 years with 1-year overseas experience. She received her B.Tech. and M.Tech. degrees from Aligarh Muslim University, in 1998 and 2000, respectively. She received Ph.D. from Jamia Hamdard in the field of distributed systems and has published several research articles in International Journals and Conferences. Her research interests include distributed systems, big data, cloud computing, data mining, and image processing. She is on the reviewer and editorial board of various international journals and has served as a program committee member of several international conferences.

Atul Negi is working as a professor in the School of CIS at UoH. His research interests include pattern recognition, machine learning, and IoT.

Ch. Rajyalakshmi is presently working as Assistant Professor in the Department of Computer Science & Engineering (CSE), B V Raju Institute of Technology, Narsapur, Hyderabad. She is having 15+ years of teaching experience in the field of computer science and engineering. She is a member of CSI. Her areas of interest are big data, remote sensing, machine learning, and artificial intelligence.

Rajeswara Rao Ramisetty is presently working as a professor in the Department of Computer Science & Engineering (CSE), JNTUK-UCEV, Vizianagaram. He did his Postdoctoral Research from the University of Missouri (UOM), Columbia, USA. Dr. R. Rajeshwara Rao is having 18+ years of teaching experience in the field of computer science and engineering. He is a state-level committee member for Curriculum Development for the state of *Andhra Pradesh appointed by AP-State Council for Higher Education (APSCHE)* for Computer Science and Engineering. To his credit, he had published papers in *ACM, Elsevier, Springer*, and other reputed journals. He received *Dr. Abdul Kalam Award* for Teaching Excellence-2019 from Marina Labs, Chennai. *Best Researcher* Award from JNUK,

Kakinada on 28 December, 2018. He received the *VIDYA RATAN* award from T.E. H.E.G, New Delhi for the year 2011. He is an academic advisor to National Cyber Safety and Security Standards (NCSSS). He is a member of CSI and Sr. Member of IEEE. His areas of interest are artificial intelligence, speech processing, pattern recognition, NLP, and cloud computing.

K. Ram Mohan Rao is presently working as a senior scientist, National Database for Emergency Management, National Remote Sensing Centre, ISRO, Balanagar, Hyderabad. He is having total 15 years of experience in research and development at ISRO. He had 10 years of teaching experience in the field of computer science and geoinformatics at P.G. level at the Indian Institute of Remote Sensing, Indian Space Research Organization, Dehradun. To his credit, he had published papers in *various national and international* reputed journals. He is a member of CSI, Indian Society of Remote Sensing and Indian Society of Geomatics. His area of Interest are remote sensing and geoinformatics.

Vadlamani Ravi has been the professor at the Institute for Development and Research in Banking Technology, Hyderabad since June 2014. He obtained his Ph. D. in the area of Soft Computing from Osmania University, Hyderabad and RWTH Aachen, Germany (2001). He authored more than 230 papers that were cited in 7891 publications and has an h-index 42. He has 32 years of research and 20 years of teaching experience.

Srinivasa Raju Rudraraju is a research scholar in the School of CIS at the University of Hyderabad (UoH). His research interests include IoT, fog computing.

Sanjoy Kumar Saha obtained his Bachelor and Master in Engineering degrees in Electronics and Tele-Communication from Jadavpur University, India in 1990 and 1992, respectively. He obtained his Ph.D. from Bengal Engineering and Science University, Shibpur (now IIEST, Shibpur), India in 2006. Currently, he is working as a professor in the Computer Science and Engineering Department of Jadavpur University, India. His research area includes signal processing, pattern recognition, and data analytics.

Nagesh Bhattu Sristy is an assistant professor in the National Institute of Technology, Andhra Pradesh, India. He received his Master of Technology from Indian Institute of Science, Bangalore and Doctor of Philosophy from National Institute of Technology, Warangal. His research interests include Bayesian machine learning, deep learning, distributed computing, database systems, blockchain systems, and privacy preserving data-mining.

Nagender Kumar Suryadevara received the Ph.D. degree from Massey University, New Zealand. His research interests include wireless sensor networks, IoT, and time-series data mining.

Ramalingeswara Rao Thottempudi submitted his Ph.D. thesis from Theoretical Computer Science Group, the Department of Mathematics, Indian Institute of Technology Kharagpur, India. He received his M.Tech. degree in Computer

Science and Data Processing from Indian Institute of Technology Kharagpur, India, in 2010. His research interests include big data analytics, large-scale distributed graph processing, and machine learning with big data.

Harini Yadamreddy is an assistant professor in the Vignan's Institute of Information and Technology, Visakhapatnam, Andhra Pradesh, India. She received her Master of Technology from University of Hyderabad, Hyderabad. Her research interests include distributed computing, machine learning, computer networks.

Foreword

The *Handbook of Big Data Analytics* (edited by Professor Vadlamani Ravi and Professor Aswani Kumar Cherukuri) is a two-volume compendium that provides educators, researchers, and developers with the background needed to understand the intricacies of this rich and fast-moving field.

The two volumes (Vol. 1: Methodologies; Vol. 2: Applications in ICT, Security and Business Analytics) collectively composed of 26 chapters cover a wide range of subjects pertinent to database management, processing frameworks, and architectures, data lakes, query optimization strategies, towards real-time data processing, data stream analytics, fog and edge computing, artificial intelligence and big data, and several application domains. Overall, the two volumes explore the challenges imposed by big data analytics and how they will impact the development of next-generation applications.

The Handbook of Big Data Analytics is a timely and valuable offering and an important contribution to the big data processing and analytics field. I would like to commend the editors for assembling an excellent team of International contributors that managed to provide a rich coverage of the topic. I am sure that the readers will find the handbook useful and hopefully a source of inspiration for future work in this area. This handbook should be well received by both researchers and developers and will provide a valuable resource for senior undergraduate and graduate classes focusing on big data analytics.

Professor Albert Y. Zomaya
Editor-in-Chief of the *IET Book Series on Big Data*

Foreword

I have the pleasure of writing the foreword for this excellent book on Big Data Analytics – Frameworks, Methodologies and Architectures. This handbook is the first volume in the two-volume series on Big Data Analytics.

Big data is pervading every sphere of human activity and applying entire gamut of analytics on large-scale data gathered by organisations is only a logical step. There are vast panoramas of applications of Big Data Analytics across different disciplines, industries, and sectors. Numerous publications have appeared in reputed journals/conferences dealing with this exciting field and its ever-increasing applications in innumerable domains. The publications of this volume is timely and warranted because under one roof readers can find all that is needed to learn and implement big data analytics architectures, frameworks, and methodologies.

The book is a collection of chapters on foundations of big data analytics technologies ranging from data storage paradigms like data lake, frameworks (subsuming Hadoop and Apache Spark paradigms), methodologies, and architectures involving distributed and parallel implementation of statistical and machine learning algorithms. Some chapters dwell on cloud computing, fog computing, edge computing, and how big data analytic is relevant over there as well. Few chapters have addressed the analytics over data streams. The editors of this volume, Professors Vadlamani Ravi and Aswani Kumar Cherukuri are well known academics and researchers in this field. The exposition in the book is near complete, comprehensive, and lucid. The contributors of this volume have compiled a wealth of knowledge. I must congratulate the authors of the individual chapters as well as the Editors for putting together such an interesting collection of chapters and sharing their expertise. That the Editors have taken painstaking efforts is very much evident in the selection of the diverse yet well-connected chapters.

In nutshell, this volume of *Handbook of Big Data Analytics* is an important contribution to the literature. Therefore, I have no hesitation in recommending this book as a textbook or a reference book for undergraduate, graduate students, and research scholars. Even, practitioners from various service industries stand to benefit from this book alike.

Rajkumar Buyya, Ph.D.
Redmond Barry Distinguished Professor
Director, Cloud Computing and Distributed Systems (CLOUDS) Lab
School of Computing and Information Systems
The University of Melbourne, Australia

Preface

In the current era of Industry 4.0, mobility, IoT, cloud and fog, etc. massive volumes of a variety of data are being created/generated $365 \times 24 \times 7$ with a rapid velocity. When we are inundated by so much data, the veracity of data (source of data) has also become a critical issue. It is estimated that more than 2.5 quintillion bytes of data are being generated every day. Almost all organizations and enterprises are trying to leverage the big data to derive valuable and actionable insights. The process of unravelling hidden nuggets of knowledge, latent patterns, and trends in this big data is known as big data analytics (BDA). There are several heterogeneous architectures, frameworks, methodologies which are mostly open sourced that are designed to ingest, store, process, and analyse the big data. There are several data mining and machine learning techniques that work on top of these frameworks in order to unearth knowledge value from the big data. However, there exist several inherent research challenges that need to be addressed in these frameworks in order to improve the effectiveness and efficiency of BDA life cycle. These challenges are posed by the different characteristics of the big data.

This edited volume of the *Handbook of Big Data Analytics – Architectures and Frameworks* contains a varied and rich collection of ten contributions illustrating different architectures, frameworks, and methodologies. Chapter 1 provides a detailed analysis on the impact of big data on databases. Further, this chapter illustrates how new types of databases are different from relational models and the problem of application scalability. Chapter 2 presents a detailed discussion on MapReduce, HaLoop, Twister, Apache Mahout, Flame, Spark, storage architectures like HDFS, Dynamo, Amazon S3. Data lakes are an emerging technology to ingest and store massive data repositories originated from heterogeneous data sources at a rapid pace. Chapter 3 introduces data lakes, big data fabric, data lake architecture, and various layers of data lakes. The authors of Chapter 4 present query optimization strategies for big data with a focus on multi-way joins. The-state-of-the-art algorithms such as MR sequential join, shares algorithm, SharesSkew, Θ-Join, graph-based query processing algorithms are all discussed. Each of the algorithms is analysed for communication cost of various alternatives. Chapter 5 provides an in-depth analysis of real-time data-processing topology, various big data streaming approaches like Hive, Flink, Samza. The authors of Chapter 6 present a survey on data stream processing systems. Their survey considered four areas of data stream analytics: forecasting, outlier detection, drift detection, and mining frequent itemsets. Chapter 7 presents a comprehensive review of the extant big data processing platforms. Further, this chapter addresses the research question, viz. how to scale the extant statistical and machine learning algorithms for five data mining tasks – classification, clustering, association rule mining, regression/forecasting, and recommendation system. Chapter 8 discusses the current trends of fog and edge computing architectures with a focus on big data analytics. Chapter 9 presents the implementation aspects of big data sets storage and processing in fog computing clustering environments. Experimental results demonstrate the feasibility of the proposed framework in resource-constrained environments. Chapter 10 analyses the impact of AI and big data on human–computer interaction with a focus on accessibility for the individuals with disabilities.

This volume will provide students, scholars, professionals, and practitioners an extensive coverage of the current trends, architecture, frameworks, and methodologies that help them not only to understand but also implement and innovate. It also throws to open a number of research questions and problems.

Vadlamani Ravi
Aswani Kumar Cherukuri

Acknowledgements

At the outset, we express our sincere gratitude to the Almighty for having bestowed us with this opportunity, intellect, thoughtfulness, energy, and patience while executing this exciting project.

We are grateful to all the learned contributors for reposing trust and confidence in us and submitting their scholarly, novel work to this volume and their excellent co-operation in meeting the deadlines in the whole journey. It is this professionalism that played a great role in the whole process enabling us to successfully bringing out this volume. We sincerely thank Valerie Moliere, Senior Commissioning book editor, IET and Olivia Wilkins, Assistant Editor, IET for their continuous support right from the inception through the final production. It has been an exhilarating experience to work with them. They provided us total freedom with little or no controls, which is necessary to bring out a volume of this quality and magnitude.

We are grateful to the world-renowned expert in big data analytics and cloud computing, Dr. Rajkumar Buyya, Redmond Barry Distinguished Professor and Director of the Cloud Computing and Distributed Systems (CLOUDS) Laboratory at the University of Melbourne, Australia for being extremely generous in writing the foreword for these two volumes, in spite of his busy academic and research schedule.

Former Director IDRBT, Dr. A.S. Ramasastri deserves thanks for his support to the whole project.

Last but not least, Vadlamani Ravi expresses high regard and gratitude to his wife Mrs. Padmavathi Devi for being so accommodative and helpful throughout the journey as always. Without her active help, encouragement, and cooperation, projects of scale cannot be taken up and completed on schedule. He owes a million thanks to her. He acknowledges the support and understanding rendered by his sons Srikrishna and Madhav in the whole project.

Aswani Kumar Cherukuri sincerely thanks the management of Vellore Institute of Technology, Vellore for the continuous support and encouragement towards scholarly works. He would like to acknowledge the affection, care, support, encouragement, and understanding extended by his family members. He is grateful to his wife Mrs Annapurna, kids Chinmayee and Abhiram for always standing by his side.

Vadlamani Ravi, IDRBT, Hyderabad
Aswani Kumar Cherukuri, VIT, Vellore

Introduction

Vadlamani Ravi[1] and Aswani Kumar Cherukuri[2]

Riding on the new wave, the fourth paradigm of science, viz. data-driven approaches, the decade of 2010 witnessed a spectacular growth in the data generation in every field and domain both with and without human intervention. It can metaphorically be termed 'Data Deluge' or 'Data Tsunami'. It is appropriately termed big data.

The 'quint' essential (pun intended) character of big data is succinctly captured by five dimensions: volume, velocity, variety, veracity, and value. While volume dimension connotes the humungous size of the data, velocity refers to the high speed with which the data comes in; variety dimension refers to the presence of structured, semi-structured, and unstructured data; veracity indicates the certainty of thee sources of data, and finally value dimension connotes the value versus noise present in the voluminous data.

Numerous studies on this exciting topic of big data from the perspective of data engineering, data science have appeared in the literature. In other words, frameworks and methodologies for ingestion, storage, distribution, parallelisms, and analysis have been propounded. Data parallelization, algorithm parallelization, and compute parallelization have been addressed in these efforts. Data and compute parallelization have been accomplished by Hadoop–MapReduce paradigm and reached a mature stage through Hadoop 2.0. A myriad of applications catering to ingestion, distributed data/file storage, database, data warehouse, querying, data administration, data streaming, machine learning, visualization, etc. have formed the ecosystem of Hadoop under Apache license, and these efforts have been accentuated by the advent of Apache Spark, which is touted to be 100 times faster than the MapReduce paradigm. Further, the acceptance and growth of the concept of a data lake which can accommodate structured, semi-structured, and unstructured data in their native format contributed to the tremendous proliferation of big data implementations in all science, engineering, and other fields. Concomitantly, the machine learning libraries also started getting enriched in Apache Spark though MLlib. While this trend of data parallelization is referred to as horizontal, wherein multiple commodity hardware is used in master–slave architecture, vertical parallelization also bursts into the scene with the proliferation of GP-GPU programming and CUDA environment within a single server. Finally, a hybrid of horizontal–vertical parallelization in the form of a cluster of GPU machines has also been

[1]Center of Excellence in Analytics, Institute for Development and Research in Banking Technology, Hyderabad, India
[2]School of Information Technology & Engineering, Vellore Institute of Technology, Vellore, India

designed and exploited for complex problems. However, the algorithm parallelization threw up another interesting area of research wherein extant algorithms were
checked whether they are amenable to parallelization. This line of research
spawned applied statistical and machine learning algorithms. Consequently, it
turned out that many extant algorithms are intrinsically parallel, by accident, and
they were immediately exploited to come out with the parallel and distributed
counterparts. Simultaneously, the in-memory and in-database computation also
trigger many innovations on the memory and compute side of the innovation called
big data analytics. Companies like Teradata, Oracle, SAP, Vertica, IBM, etc.
contributed to this dimension of the growth. Furthermore, cloud computing further
added to the prominence and use of big data paradigm. Thus, in essence, a convergence and confluence of a myriad of technologies came together, collaborated,
and cooperated to the successful adoption of big data analytics in many domains.

Further, the service companies like Yahoo, Google, eBay, and Amazon fuelled
the growth of big data analytics-both by churning out new data storage, querying,
distributed architectures, and putting them to effective use within their businesses.
Interesting it is then, the traditional work-horse IT companies such as IBMs
Microsofts, Teradatas, Oracles, Nvidias have started contributing to this exciting
field. This trend is unlike the one observed in other IT advancements, wherein
traditional IT companies propound, prove, and propagate a new technology.
Nevertheless, the field of big data analysis grew phenomenally over the past
decade.

Chapter 1

The impact of Big Data on databases

Antonio Sarasa Cabezuelo[1]

The last decade, from the point of view of information management, is character-ized by an exponential generation of data. In any interaction that is carried out by digital means, data is generated. Some popular examples are social networks on the Internet, mobile device apps, commercial transactions through online banking, the history of a user's browsing through the network, geolocation information gener-ated by a user's mobile, etc. In general, all this information is stored by the com-panies or institutions with which the interaction is maintained (unless the user has expressly indicated that it cannot be stored).

The Big Data arises due to the economic and strategic benefits that could be obtained from the exploitation of the stored data [1]. However, the practical implementation of Big Data has required the development of new technological tools, both hardware and software, that are adequate to exploit the data under the established conditions. Essentially these conditions can be summarized in [2]:

1. Availability of huge amounts of data with different degrees of structure (structured, semi-structured or unstructured) and formats (videos, photos, documents and so on).
2. Need to process large amounts of data in a short time, efficiently and in real time.
3. Need to interpret the results with the aim of making decisions that allow obtaining a strategic or economic benefit.

These requirements directly affect the way to store and process the information [3]. In this chapter, it is analyzed how the Big Data phenomenon has affected some characteristics of databases.

The structure of the chapter is as follows. In Section 1.1, it is presented an introduction to the Big Data phenomenon, showing its main characteristics, the objectives to be achieved and the technologies that are required. Section 1.2 describes the problem of the scalability of applications and their influence on the way infor-mation is stored. Section 1.3 introduces the NoSQL databases. In Section 1.4, are

---

[1]Departamento de Sistemas Informáticos y Computación, Universidad Complutense de Madrid, Madrid, Spain

discussed the models of data distribution. Section 1.5 introduces the issue about the consistency of information. In Section 1.6, some examples are presented in order to illustrate the concepts discussed in the previous sections. Finally, Section 1.7 presents a set of conclusions.

1.1   The Big Data phenomenon

Formally, Big Data can be defined as a set of technologies that allow the collection, storage, processing and visualization, potentially under real-time conditions, of large data sets with heterogeneous characteristics [4]. In this sense, there are five characteristics known as the "5Vs" (speed, volume, variety, truth and value) that define the type and nature of the data that is processed and the purposes that are sought with their processing [5]:

- Volume. It refers to a large volume of information handled (magnitudes of the order of petabytes or exabytes of information are considered). In addition, the data that needs to be managed increases with an exponential growth, which forces continuous extensions of the storage capacity of the machines.
- Velocity. It refers to the enormous speed with which information data is generated, collected and processed. In this sense, it is necessary to be able to store and process in real-time millions of data generated in seconds. Many of these data come from information sources such as sensors, social networks, environmental control systems and other information gathering devices. Observe that it is the processing speed that allows obtaining a profit from the exploitation, before the data becomes obsolete.
- Variety. This characteristic refers to the need to be able to manage information that comes from very heterogeneous information sources in which the data use different structuring schemes, different types of data, etc. So to be able to add all the data and be able to manage them as a unit, you need information storage that is flexible enough to host heterogeneous data.
- Value. This aspect refers to the ability to exploit stored information in order to take advantage of it for different purposes such as obtaining an economic return, optimizing production, improving the corporate image, better approaching the needs and preferences of customers or predicting how an advertising or sales campaign for a specific product can be developed well. This feature is basic so that a company or entity may be interested in investing in processing such amounts of information.
- Veracity. This characteristic refers to the need to adequately process the large volumes of information, so that the information obtained is true and allows one to make appropriate decisions based on the results of its processing. This aspect together with the previous one constitutes two important reasons that give meaning to the massive processing of the information.

On the other hand, from the technological point of view, a set of new needs that previously did not exist arise [6]:

- Need for a decentralized and flexible data architecture [7].
- Need to use distributed computing models that allow managing and processing the type of data specific to these environments (semi-structured or non-structured data). In this sense, they will be required to carry out very intensive processing tasks in a massive way [8].
- Need to analyze large amounts of data in real time in distributed execution environments [9].

1.1.1 Big Data Operational and Big Data Analytical

In order to describe the technological developments produced in the field of Big Data, it is possible to differentiate between Big Data Operational [10] and Big Data Analytical [11]. The Big Data Operational refers to the set of tools that have been developed to solve some of the technological problems discussed. In a schematic way by areas, we have the following tools [12]:

- Mass processing systems to be able to work with huge amounts of data in real time. These systems require being able to work in parallel to obtain sufficient computing power and use new computing paradigms such as the map-reduce algorithm. Some examples of these processing systems are Spark [13] or Hadoop [14].
- Data visualization tools that aim to help interpret the results of the processed data through visual representations that intuitively and simply show the data. In this way the analysts can make decisions and take advantage of the information obtained from the processing of the data. Some examples of these tools are Tableau or QlickView.
- Specific programming languages to perform data analysis and process information. Data structures are required to facilitate the manipulation of data and operations on them. Some examples are the R programming language, a specific language for data analysis, or the scientific libraries of the general purpose Python programming language.
- New systems of persistence of the information more adapted to the new needs of storage and data processing. This is the case of the so-called NoSQL databases [15].
- Algorithms for processing information from the area of statistics and the area of artificial intelligence that work very efficiently when used on a large amount of data. For example, machine learning algorithms or deep learning algorithms.

Observe that in order to take advantage of the benefits that the described technologies can bring, it is necessary to know the characteristics of the information sources, to know the nature of the data that will be obtained, to know the type of questions to answer and to know the characteristics of the available tools so that they can select the most appropriate one to be able to answer the questions posed.

In this sense, choosing the right tool is a critical step in the application of Big Data to a specific problem and domain.

On the other hand, the Big Data Analytical [16] refers to the types of analysis and processing of the information that you want to perform. In general, these are predictive processing models [17] that aim to answer questions about the future behavior of a process, an individual or a human group based on the known behaviors of the past and other complementary data available related [18]. Thus, in this type of models, it is sought to achieve objectives of the following style [19]:

- Predict certain behaviors from the data generated by an individual [20]. For this, the probability that an individual has to show a specific behavior in the future is evaluated based on the previous behaviors, as well as other adjacent data.
- To look for regularities in the information [21]. In this sense, information is processed in order to find repetitive patterns that allow information to be discriminated. These patterns can be used to answer questions that arise about the behavior of an individual, human group or institution.
- Determine a risk or opportunity [22]. To do this, real-time calculations are carried out on the data collected with the aim of being able to evaluate a certain risk or opportunity, which will guide the taking of an appropriate decision. For this, some factors are important [23], such as the speed at which it is processed, the amount of data that is processed and the quality of the data regarding its generation and processing time.
- To discover relationships between the data in order to classify individuals in groups [24]. This type of analysis is often very useful in business areas to distinguish business segments, so for example the type of product that can be offered to a young person is not the same as an elderly person or adult. In this way, you can know common information of each group and be able to make specific decisions for each segment.
- Identify relationships between different individuals [25]. This allows predicting the consequences that a decision can have on a group of individuals, as well as planning different types of actions and effects on the related individuals or being able to infer information implicitly from existing relationships. A typical example may be the search for relationships and information from people who are in contact through a social network.
- To describe the relationship that may exist between all the elements that must be taken into account in order to make a decision [26], be able to obtain the decision to be taken that is the most optimal of the possible ones based on the known information and know the variables and values that determine the decision itself. All in order to predict the results by analyzing many variables. This type of analysis has an especially important application in the decision-making of a company where there are many variables to be taken into account, there is an economic risk, and certain results are expected to be obtained.

Therefore, the Big Data phenomenon appears due to the business opportunities [27] that arise from having huge amounts of data to be processed and exploited. This is why new information processing needs arise that give rise to a technological change with the appearance of a set of new technologies, algorithms, programming languages and computing paradigms.

1.1.2   The impact of Big Data on databases

The question this chapter tries to answer is how the Big Data phenomenon effects on databases. In this sense, there are three aspects to analyze:

1. The scalability of the application. In the context of Big Data, large amounts of data must be processed, which are characterized by their exponential and very rapid growth. In this sense, processing needs will be important and applications must adapt to these needs. This is a challenge for the developer to be able to scale the application dynamically to the evolution of the needs and not become obsolete. To solve this scaling problem, two types of solutions are proposed: vertical scaling and horizontal scaling. The vertical scaling focuses on having a single machine with the necessary features to meet the needs raised, while horizontal scaling proposes the use of a cluster of machines whose joint operation in parallel will cover the processing needs. Economic and maintenance aspects make the horizontal solution more suitable for this context. This situation directly influences the persistence systems used, since the relational databases behave well in centralized but not distributed environments such as the one involving a horizontal scaling solution. It is for this reason that as a consequence of the use of solutions based on the execution in clusters of machines, new models of persistence of the information that receive the generic name of NoSQL databases appear.

2. The distributed architecture of the information. The horizontal scaling makes it necessary for the developed applications to distribute the information in different nodes of a cluster of machines. There are different models to distribute and maintain information in a cluster. The most optimal way is to make a partition of the information between the machines and a replication of the parts obtained in order to ensure that failures in some of the machines will not leave the system invalidated. It should also be borne in mind that these distribution models are aimed at optimizing access to information, and in this sense, some characteristics regarding the consistency and availability of the information (ensured by ACID transactions in relational model) will not be maintained. For example, there will be a concept of lighter information consistency (even there will be cases where consistent information cannot be assured) and in the same way with respect to the availability of information.

3. Consistency. This aspect refers to the ability of the application to recover from machine failures of the cluster in which it is running, ensuring the availability of data in different execution scenarios and failure of the cluster. Thus, the design of the application should take into account this type of situation in such a way that the availability of the data is assured, although not the consistency as indicated previously. Situations of weak consistency will be admitted.

In the following sections, the aspects mentioned earlier will be discussed in greater depth.

1.2   Scalability in relational databases

The need for scalability in applications that are used in the context of Big Data has directly influenced databases. In this sense, the large amount of data that is necessary to manage and the exponential increase in data (and with a very fast generation speed since in many cases they come from sensors or vital signs control devices, nature phenomena, etc.) makes it necessary for the systems to be scalable according to the different needs that arise. In this sense, machines with an important processing capacity are required. There are two ways to scale a system: horizontal scaling or vertical scaling [28]. Vertical scaling is based on using a single machine with high performance that covers the necessary computational features required. However, from the economic and strategic point of view, it is a bad solution given that the exponential growth of the data and its speed of generation means that, in a relatively short time, the machines become obsolete and small with respect to the processing needs required, making it necessary to purchase a new machine with higher performance. Likewise, we must unite the fact of the strategic weakness of a centralized solution, given that a failure in the machine that contains the storage system will have as a consequence a loss of information and therefore all the applications that exploit the stored data. (Normally there are security copies that are made periodically so that the impact of an event of this nature has limited effects.)

The horizontal scaling is based on using a set of machines that work collaboratively in parallel in the processing of information called machine cluster [29]. In this way the joint work of all of them allows one to reach the required processing capacity. In addition, when you need to increase the processing capacity at a given time, just increase the number of machines that make up the cluster. Likewise, the types of machines used in the clusters are usually of inferior quality in terms of performance and cheaper than the machines used in a vertical scaling solution. A requirement in this type of solution is that the data that is being managed is distributed among the machines in the cluster. This requirement, in certain conditions, constitutes an advantage with respect to a vertical solution since, if any machine in the cluster fails, the system does not have to stop working since the rest of the machines will continue to work (and if they have also been replicated the data in several machines, it will be enough to redirect the system to the replicated machine). In the field of Big Data, and taking into account the exponential growth of the data that must be managed, horizontal scaling will be more optimal than vertical scaling. In this sense, the design and development carried out by a software engineer for a Big Data context will have to be oriented to support horizontal scaling solutions. Thus an aspect that is directly influenced by this type of horizontal solutions is the persistence of information.

1.2.1   Relational databases

In the last decades, the most extended persistence mechanism has been the relational databases. This type of database is based on a formal model called relational model that uses tables as a storage unit [30]. A table is an information structure formed by columns that represent the information fields from which you want to store information and rows that are the actual information of each column. A set of columns represent the information that you want to store from an abstract relationship such as a student, a company, an employee, and each row represents a specific instance of the abstract relationship [30].

Relational databases present a set of characteristics that make them very efficient in the processing of stored information, such as [31]

- Concurrence [32].[*] This aspect refers to situations in which a set of stored data needs to be processed by more than one application at a time.
- Integration.[†] This aspect refers to those situations in which several computer applications share data in some way such that one of the applications uses the data that is generated by other applications.
- Standard model.[‡] Another basic aspect offered by relational databases refers to the standard elements on which it is based.

1.2.2 The limitations of relational databases

If it is considered the problem of scaling applications using relational databases, then the following solutions are recommended:

- In a vertical scaling solution, the relational databases are an ideal solution, since these are designed to run in centralized environments on a single machine.

---

[*]Processing operations involve sequential tasks of access, modification, deletion or insertion of data. The order in which these tasks are carried out can be important in some cases, since it can change the final state of the data depending on the order of execution of the tasks, and therefore the consistency of the information. These situations make necessary the existence of some mechanism that allows to coordinate the applications in an appropriate way that access the data. It could be done manually and implemented directly in the application code. However, this solution is complicated in a number of problems that arise in an incremental way as the number of applications involved increases. In this sense, a fundamental characteristic of relational databases is the availability of a mechanism already implemented in them to deal with this problem. It is about the use of the transaction concept, as a processing unit. Thus, transactions allow the programmer to manage the access and processing concurrency in a relational database system in an efficient and transparent manner.

[†]In these cases, it is necessary to coordinate the collaborating applications so that inconsistencies do not occur in the exchanged data, and that they are synchronized so that the consuming application knows when it can recover data, and the production application knows when it can add new data. In this sense, the storage of data in a relational database is a very interesting solution, since it can act as a mediator between the applications involved and can also guarantee that the information synchronization and consistency needs will be fulfilled again by the concept of ACID transactions and the concurrency control system implemented in the relational databases (since one of the consequences of using the ACID model is to ensure proper functioning in these situations).

[‡]On the one hand, the relational model is found to be a formal conceptual on which these databases are based. On the other hand, the language of SQL relational databases. In this sense, anyone who wants to design, create or manage a relational database will use the same terminology and concepts, as it is standard. Likewise, in the case of SQL, although there are different implementations of the language with some differences, the fundamental and basic constructions of the language are the same in all SQL dialects. This factor of standardization has been one of the reasons that have driven its use and expansion, since it allows working with unknown development groups with a common language and terminology.

- In a horizontal scaling solution. A requirement in this type of solution is that the data that is being managed is distributed among the machines in the cluster [33]. However, this feature conflicts with a natural scope of execution of a relational database that is centralized in a single machine [34]. Thus, in general, relational databases are not designed or prepared for implementation in distributed environments. Problems of the type such as knowing how to decompose the tables of a relational database and deciding which tables are stored in one machine and which in another, or how to execute the queries on the tables, in the case of being distributed, are considered. You would have to know where each table is located. Other problems also occur about the type of queries that are possible to perform in a distributed environment, referential integrity, transaction management or concurrency control. On the other hand, there is an economic factor that must also be taken into account, if a relational database is distributed, and this is due to the fact that this type of executions would require the execution of several different instances of the databases, which would increase its economic cost. To solve these limitations, solutions have emerged within the scope of relational databases that have tried to add some of the necessary requirements for distributed execution. These solutions are generically called NewSQL databases [35]. They maintain the main characteristics of a relational database, as well as the use of the standard SQL language [36]. However, none of them has achieved sufficient implantation to become a distributed solution of the relational model [37]. Thus, the relational databases are still used for the areas for which they were created.

  Note that relational databases present other disadvantages in the field of Big Data with respect to cost and efficiency [38]:

- The fixed data schema used by the relational databases. In the relational model, a task prior to the storage of the data consists of creating a schema of the type of information to be stored. In this way, they fix the types of data that are admitted. If you want to store other types of data you will have to make changes to the scheme. However, these changes often introduce anomalies in the stored data (e.g., in terms of the relational model there will probably be rows with many columns with null values). In this sense, it is said that the information stored in a relational database is structured because it follows a previously defined scheme. In the field of Big Data, the information that needs to be stored can be very diverse, from structured, semi-structured data or even data without structure. In addition, in general it is not known a priori how the type of data will be. For these reasons, you cannot fix a fixed structure for the information you want to store. Thus, the characteristics of the data that needs to be stored in a Big Data environment are incompatible with the need to set a previous scheme in the relational model, since its use would make it necessary to make changes in the schema for each new type of data that is stored, introducing anomalies in the database or having to make changes in the tables and relationships defined.

- The data structures that are used in the field of relational databases and those that are used in the programs that exploit the data of these storage systems [39].

In the case of relational databases, the stored data corresponds to simple data such as numbers, strings or Booleans. They do not support any type of complex structured data such as a list or record. Likewise, the unit of storage and exchange of information are the rows of the tables that serve as storage. However, programming languages manipulate data with greater richness and structural complexity such as stacks, tails, lists, etc. This supposes a problem of communication of the information between the databases and the programs [40], since it forces to implement a translation process between both contexts. Thus every time information is retrieved from a relational database for use in a program; it is necessary to decompose it and transform it into the data structures that are being used in it. And likewise, when a program needs to store information in a relational database, it requires another process of transforming the information stored in the data structures managed by the program into simple data and grouped into sequences that constitute rows, which is what supports storing a relational database. These transformations constitute an additional computational cost to the information processing that is carried out in the programs, which can have a significant impact on both code lines with execution time, depending on the amount of data and transformations that are necessary to carry finished. This problem treats the difference in the nature of the data managed by a relational database and by the programming languages. To alleviate this problem, some solutions have been created such as frameworks that object-oriented databases or frameworks that map the information stored in the database to an object-oriented model such as Hibernate. However, these solutions are not entirely effective although they solve part of the problem described. They introduce other problems such as reduction in the performance of the database due, among other reasons, to the implementation of operations and queries that obviate the existence of a database below the object-oriented model.

1.3 NoSQL databases

Given the limitations present in the relational databases to cover the needs arising in the field of Big Data, some companies such as Amazon and Google began to develop alternative persistence systems that fit better with these requirements (Big Tables of Google and Dynamo de Amazon). These databases have the common characteristic of being able to manage and process huge amounts of data through a distributed system. From that moment, other databases emerged with the same objective of solving the problems and limitations that the relational databases were not able to cover. The databases that emerged in this process were called NoSQL databases [41] and share some characteristics as follows:

- They do not use the SQL language to make queries [42] (there are some databases that use languages with a very similar syntax as is the case of the Cassandra database with the CQL language). However, they all have query languages with a similar purpose.

- Most NoSQL databases include among its features the possibility of running in distributed environments [43], thus responding to the needs of distributed processing. It is a success factor since it allows one to process large amounts of data in a cheaper and more efficient way to run the databases in distributed solutions of a cluster type of machines that allow one to scale the systems by adding new machines to the cluster. This feature influences the underlying data models in how to manage data consistency or concurrency. Not all NoSQL databases comply with this characteristic, as is the case of graph-oriented databases that are not designed for execution in a distributed environment.

- They do not use predefined information structuring schemes [44]. One of the characteristics of the NoSQL databases that represent a major change with respect to the relational databases is the lack of need to define a schema of the structure of the information that will be stored in it. The origin of this characteristic is found in the conditions of information processing that occur in the Big Data field. In this context, the type of data generated can be semi-structured or unstructured. It is necessary to aggregate together data that is heterogeneous; in many cases, the data that needs to be stored may have errors or there may be empty information fields. Data are generated at great speed and in huge quantities. Therefore, no schemas are used in the NoSQL databases, the information to be stored is simply added, and there is no verification process about the structure and types of data used. The only requirement is that the data be compatible with the data model underlying the type of NoSQL database being used. These conditions are incompatible with the type of information for which a relational database is designed, given that data is expected that responds to a structure of previously fixed information, homogeneous data will be added, the expected amounts of data are not so enormous and its inclusion in the tables is generally done in a planned manner. Note that in relational databases the first thing to do is define a schema of the information to be stored, indicating how the information will be structured and what type of data will be used. In this way, the information that is stored must comply with this definition (not admitting data that does not comply with it). It is true that relational databases could be used for these situations; however, the implications would be that tables with many fields would be needed to store any type of information, and that the resulting tables after storing the information would have many empty fields (specifically the rows of heterogeneous data). That is why it is not a good idea [45]. This dissonance with the relational model gave rise to this characteristic that is present in the NoSQL databases, and that represents the need to have unlimited flexibility to be able to store what is necessary, since it cannot be predicted what the information will be like. It must be managed. However, this feature has precisely the advantage of being able to store any information element without being subject to any type of restrictions, being able to adapt to different situations, which is very useful in the context of Big Data (which is by nature dynamic) as previously argued. Likewise, it represents a solution to the problem of impedance. The possibility of storing data with any type of structure eliminates the need for information transformations to adapt the information managed by the applications that process the information in the database and the data structures used by the databases to store it. As already mentioned, this involved a cost to be taken into account, since part of the application code had to be dedicated to this task.

- In most cases, NoSQL databases are open source projects [46].

Table 1.1 shows a comparison between relational databases and NoSQL databases.

Although the NoSQL databases share the general characteristics mentioned, there are other characteristics that allow one to differentiate them and use them to make a classification [47]. Although there is no single classification, however, it is possible to differentiate them according to the underlying data model. So it is possible to consider the following types of families [48]:

- Key-value databases [49]: Riak, Redis, Dynamo and Voldemort.
- Document-oriented databases [50]: MongoDB, CouchDB.
- Database based on columns [51]: Cassandra, Hypertable, HBase, SimpleDB.
- Graph databases [50]: Neo4J, Infinite Graph.

It should be noted that this classification is artificial because many of the databases that are classified into different families, however, share characteristics, so it would have been just as well that they were classified in one family or another. For example, MongoDB is a documentary type database; however, one of the ways to access information is through the key of the information fields [52], so it would be correct to classify it as a key-value database.

1.3.1 Disadvantages of NoSQL databases

Note that the NoSQL databases also have some disadvantages that are summarized in the transfer of responsibilities that were previously carried out by the database management systems to the programmer [53]. Thus, some operations that were done in a transparent manner such as maintaining the consistency of the data when they are updated or deleted, ensuring that the data entered are of the expected types, managing the concurrency of data access, as well as others, now they must be made directly from the programs that process the information. This also has a problem that, in order to access the data, it is necessary for the programmer to know what type of information and how it is structured in the database.

Table 1.1   Relational databases vs NoSQL databases

Feature	NoSQL databases	Relational databases
Performance	High	Low
Reliability	Poor	Good
Availability	Good	Good
Consistency	Poor	Good
Data Storage	Optimized for huge data	Medium sized to large
Scalability	High	High (but more expensive)

Likewise, this situation has another direct consequence that is the implicit representation of the information scheme in the code of the programs that process the information (with the difference that this scheme in the relational world is automatically managed by the base management system of data, while the programmer must manually manage the global NoSQL with the negative implications of this situation) [54]. Some consequences of this situation are [55], for example, that changes in the content of the database will produce changes in the code (i.e., a strong dependence will be created between the code and the persistence system). This dependence on the code has a negative effect on the quality of the code, given that the degree of reuse of the programming codes decreases because they are particularized to a specific situation. Also, when it is necessary to know what information is stored and how it relates, you should consult the application code. The consistent elimination is another of the main problems that occur [56], since it can happen that the execution of an operation of this nature deletes related information between which there is dependency with which the consistency of the information is reduced, and in the same way, the successive eliminations can leave isolated information that cannot be accessed (garbage), which requires a cleaning of the database to eliminate these information elements that are no longer useful. Other consequences are the impossibility of creating scheduled procedures to verify the restrictions of the information that is stored.

1.3.2   *Aggregate-oriented NoSQL databases*

The most widely used data models in the Big Data field correspond to the families of documentary, key-value and column-oriented NoSQL databases. This set of families is called aggregate-oriented models [57]. In this context, an aggregate represents a complex data structure that maintains a set of data related to each other. This structure can correspond to typical data structures of programming languages such as lists, nested data records, etc. Aggregates are treated as a non-decomposable unit for the purpose of processing or consistency management [58]. Thus, the operations carried out on an aggregate are considered atomic, and from the operational point of view the operations take aggregates and give as aggregate results.

This organization of information has some advantages such as the management of the clusters where the aggregates are used as a unit of replication and distribution of the data, or the manipulation of the information from the programs since, being structures similar to those used in programming languages, they are easier to manipulate and manage from the programs [59].

Regarding the management of the consistency of the information, it should be noted that, although this type of databases do not support ACID-style transactions on a set of aggregates, nevertheless the operations on individual aggregates are performed in an atomic manner of an added every time. In this sense, if you want to perform atomic operations on a set of aggregates, it would be necessary to implement it from the programs that manage them.

From a semantic point of view, when you have a complex information element, if a relational database is used, then it is necessary to decompose that information into simpler information elements with basic types, in order to be stored in a database relational. And in the same way to return the information, it will be necessary to reconstruct the existing relations in the information. However, in an aggregate-oriented model, this process of decomposition of information will not be necessary, given that aggregates are directly managed, that is, aggregates are recovered, aggregates are processed and aggregates are returned [60]. However, it must be borne in mind that the use of aggregates makes it difficult to define aggregates that can be used in different contexts.

Next, by way of example, it will be described the data models of two representative databases of the documentary and columnar families.

1.3.3   MongoDB: an example of documentary database

To illustrate the documentary data model, MongoDB will be used. It is a document-oriented NoSQL database. It is characterized by the fact that it stores the data in JSON documents with a dynamic schema called BSON. Conceptually, a document is a set of allowed structures and types that can be stored, and it is possible to access the structure of the aggregate. In this sense, you can make queries based on the aggregate fields, being able to recover parts of the aggregate instead of the complete aggregate, and you can also create indexes based on the aggregate content. Since each aggregate has an associated identifier, then it is possible to search for the key-value style.

In MongoDB [61], documents are the basic unit of organization of information and play a role equivalent to a row in relational databases. A document is an ordered set of keys that have associated values such as {"Name": "Juan", "Country": "Spain"}. The values correspond to some typical data structures such as arrays of values, basic types (Booleans, integers, strings, etc.) or embedded documents. The documents can be used as values of a key to organize the data in the most natural way possible. For example, if you have a document that represents a person and you want to store your address could be created by nesting a document "address" to the document associated with a person such as

```
{
   "Name": "John",
   "Address": {
            "Street": "George Washington 3",
            "City": "Boston",
            "Country": "USA"
}}
```

MongoDB is able to navigate the structure of embedded documents and perform operations with their values such as creating indexes, queries or updates. The main disadvantage of embedded documents is due to the repetition of data. In certain situations, this is a disadvantage as in the case of modifications, since it will have to be modified in all places where there is repeated information.

Conceptually, above the documents, are the collections. A collection is a group of documents that plays the role analogous to the tables in the relational databases.

The collections have dynamic schemes, which means that within a collection there can be any number of documents with different structures. Although any document can be put in any collection and it is not necessary to have different schemes for different types of documents, it is interesting to use more than one collection and have documents separated by collections because of the following [62]:

- If different types of documents are kept in the same collection, problems will occur to ensure that each query only retrieves documents of a certain type or that the code of the application implements queries for each type of document.
- It is faster to obtain a list of collections than to extract a list of the types of documents in a collection.
- The grouping of documents of the same type together in the same collection allows the location of the data.
- When creating indexes, certain structure is imposed on the documents (especially on the unique indexes). These indexes are defined by collection so that by placing documents of a single type in the same collection then the collections can be indexed more efficiently.

Finally, the collections are grouped into databases, so that a single instance of MongoDB [63] can manage several databases each grouping zero or more collections. A good rule of thumb is to store all the data in an application in the same database.

1.3.4   Cassandra: an example of columnar-oriented database

In relational databases, the row is used as a storage unit, which helps one to perform the writings with performance. However, there are scenarios where scripts are rare, and what you need to do is read a couple of columns of many rows at a time. In this situation, it is better to store groups of columns for all rows called families of columns as a basic storage unit, so these databases are said to be based on columns [64]. In this model, you can think of a structure added to two levels, so the first key is a row identifier that allows access to a second level aggregate that is what is called columns. Access to the row is complete, but there are operations that allow you to select a particular column.

To illustrate this model, Cassandra's case will be discussed. It was created to be integrated into the Facebook search engine. Conceptually, it is based on three elements [65]: KeySpace, family of columns and the primary key for the family of columns.

A family of columns stores the data in the form of rows and columns. A row can contain one or more logical rows and is uniquely identified by a primary key in the family of columns. A logical row is composed of columns, and each column has two parts: name and value. In addition, the columns are ordered by their names.

A family of columns can have two types of rows: static and wide. A static row has a fixed number of columns (e.g., a family of columns without grouping columns will always have a fixed number of rows for each partition key). And a broad row is one that has a variable number of columns (e.g., a family of columns with grouping columns can have a variable number of rows for each partition key).

In a family of columns, a row is uniquely identified by a primary key. In this sense, it is mandatory for all families of columns to define a primary key. A primary key of a family of columns must be unique and consists of a partition key and a set of grouping columns. The partition key establishes in which node the logical rows of a row will be stored (this means that rows with different partition keys can reside in different nodes), and the grouping columns are used to store and sort the rows. In addition, these databases have the following properties [66]:

- The primary key for a single column is only a partition key.
- All rows of a partition key are stored in a single node, and they are stored arranged according to the grouping columns.
- The order of the columns in the definition of a primary key of a row identifies which columns act as a partition key and which act as grouping columns.
- A partition key can be made up of more than one column.
- A family of columns can have multiple grouping columns, so that the values of the columns of each row are sorted according to the order in which the grouping columns are defined.

A KeySpace is a namespace that contains a set of families of columns.

1.4   Data distribution models

The use of horizontal scaling solutions not only affects the persistence models that should be used but also affects the distribution of information. When using a cluster of machines, the information must be partitioned between the different machines that make up the cluster in such a way that a load balance is maintained between them. Likewise, it must be ensured that the readings and writings of information are carried out in the most optimal way avoiding response latencies or the loss of information. Other aspects that are influenced are the consistency and availability of information. In a distributed environment the consistency of the information is complicated to guarantee. In this sense, we will use a weaker concept of consistency that admits that inconsistencies may exist during time ranges, which will be corrected a posteriori. Regarding the availability of information, to ensure it, we choose to carry out a process of replication of the information partitioned in the different nodes of the cluster. In this way, failures that may occur in any machine in the cluster should not affect the access of information, because it will be replicated in another machine. So, the need to manage large amounts of data makes it necessary to use different models of data distribution [67].

1.4.1   Sharding

In some cases, the databases are very busy since there are many users who are accessing different parts of the data set. In these circumstances, you can think of performing horizontal scaling by putting the different parts of the data on different servers. This technique is called sharding [68]. In the ideal case, there would be different users that would consult different server nodes. In this way, when each user interacts with a different server, then quick responses could be obtained from each server and the workload would be balanced between the servers. In order to implement it, it is necessary to guarantee that the data that will be accessed together is grouped in the same node and that these groups are arranged in the nodes to provide the best access to the data. The first problem that arises is how the data can be agglutinated so that the user retrieves their data from a single server. To organize the data in the nodes, certain factors must be taken into account as follows [69]:

1. If it is known that most access to information is made based on a physical location, then the data should be stored near where they are going to be accessed.
2. Another factor to keep in mind is to maintain the workload. In this sense, you must store the information so that it is distributed evenly across the nodes, getting equal amounts of load. This organization could vary with time if, for example, it is observed that certain data tends to be more visited on certain days, for which specific rules of the domain can be defined to be used in these cases.
3. In some cases, it may be useful to keep certain data together if it is expected that they will be read in sequence.

The sharding can be implemented at the level of the logic of the application by dividing the data into the fragments that are necessary. However, this complicates the programming model since the code must ensure that queries are distributed across the different fragments, and any rebalancing of the sharding will require changes in the application code and data migrations. To solve this problem, many NoSQL databases offer autosharding where it is the database itself that has the responsibility to assign the data to different fragments and ensure that access to the data is carried out in the correct fragment. The sharding technique is particularly valuable with respect to performance, since it improves performance in both reading and writing. In this sense, sharding provides a way to horizontally scale the scriptures. With respect to failure recovery, sharding does not achieve significant improvements when used alone. Thus, if the data is in different nodes and a failure occurs in a node, the impossibility of accessing the data to the corresponding fragment will only affect the users of the data of that fragment since they will not be able to access their data. However, it is not a good solution to have a part of the database not accessible. Note that sharding tends to decrease the ability to recover from failures since there is a tendency in clusters to use less reliable machines, which increases the probability of failure in the nodes. That is why sharding tends to decrease the capacity of Fault recovery. When using sharding you have to take into account the original design of the database. So if it was originally designed to use sharding then it is best to run them directly on a cluster, and if they were designed to run on a single server, then it is better to start running them on a single server, and in the case of problems with loading, then use sharding.

1.4.2   Replication

There are two types of replication [70]: master–slave and peer-to-peer. The master–slave distribution consists in replicating the data through multiple nodes, so that there is a node that acts as a primary or master node, which represents the valid source of the data and is responsible for processing any modification thereof. The rest of the nodes are slaves or secondary, an existing process that synchronizes them with the primary node. The main advantages of this model are as follows [71]:

1. It is very useful for scaling when you have to perform intensive readings on the data. This can be scaled horizontally to maintain many read requests, adding more secondary nodes and ensuring that all requests are directed to the secondary nodes. The only limitation is the ability of the primary node to process the updates and move them to the slave nodes. In this sense, it is not a good scheme in situations where there is a large writing traffic, although the downloading of the reading traffic helps one to handle the writing load.

2. Another advantage is the ability to recover from failures [72]. If the primary node fails, then at least the slave nodes can handle the read requests. This situation is useful when most of the accesses are readings. When the primary node fails, it is not possible to write scripts until the node is recovered or a new primary node is chosen from among the secondary ones (this situation is fast in this case, since there are secondary nodes that are replicas of the primary node). Note that this possibility of being able to replace the primary node with a secondary one is not only useful when you want to scale, it can also be useful in other situations. For example, you can design a single-server solution with a large recovery capacity before failures, so that all read and write traffic goes to the primary node while the secondary nodes act as backup copies.

The primary node can be chosen manually or automatically. Manual selection means that when the cluster of nodes is configured, there is a node that is chosen as primary. In the automatic election, the cluster of nodes is created and it is the nodes themselves that choose between them the primary node. This option is simpler and also allows the cluster to choose a new primary node when a failure occurs, reducing downtime. In order to achieve a recovery in the event of failures in the readings, it is necessary to ensure that the paths of the readings and the writings are different, so that a fault in the writing can be handled and readings can still be made. This means that readings and writings have to be made in separate connections to the database. The main disadvantage of this model is inconsistency. There is a danger that different clients will read different secondary nodes and the data will be different because certain changes have not yet been propagated to the secondary nodes. In the worst case, it means that a client cannot read a script he has just made. Even this can be a problem in a single-server configuration with nodes that are backup copies, because if the primary node fails, some updates will be lost by not passing to the secondary nodes.

The master–slave model [73] facilitates scalability at the reading level, but not scalability at the writing level. In addition, it provides failover recovery for a secondary node, but not for the primary node. However, the primary node is still the only point of failure. In this sense, peer-to-peer replication eliminates this problem, eliminating the figure of the primary node. All replicas are equally important and can accept scripts, and if any of the replicas fail, it does not prevent access to the database. In addition, it is possible to add new nodes to improve performance. The biggest problem with this model is consistency. So when you can write in two different places, then there is a risk that two processes are trying to update the same record at the same time, producing a writing–writing conflict. In this sense, to observe that inconsistencies in the reading will lead to transitory problems, however, inconsistencies in the scriptures are permanent. To avoid these problems we have two approaches [74]:

1. Each time data is written, replicas are coordinated to avoid conflicts. The main disadvantage is the cost of network traffic to coordinate writes. Observe that it is not necessary that all the replies reach an agreement, only the majority. In this approach, consistency over availability is valued.
2. Another option is to consider an inconsistent writing. There are situations in which a policy of merging inconsistent writes can be followed. The maximum performance of the writing on any replica is obtained as a benefit. In this case, the availability on the consistency is valued.

1.4.3   Combining sharding and replication

Replication and sharding are strategies that can be combined. If both techniques are used, then there will be multiple primary nodes, but for each data item there will be only one primary node. Depending on the configuration, you can choose that a node is primary for some data and secondary for others or have dedicated primary or secondary nodes for certain jobs. The combination of techniques is a common strategy in column-type NoSQL databases [75]. In this context, you could have tens or hundreds of nodes in a cluster with fragmented data about them. In relation to the data distribution models, it exists the CAP theorem [76]. This theorem formalizes some properties that are fulfilled in a distributed system running in a cluster of machines. In this sense, it establishes that, given a system under the previous conditions, only two of the following possible properties can be fulfilled at the same time: consistency of the managed data, availability of access to the data stored in the machines that make up the cluster and tolerance to system partitioning. The theorem can be analyzed in several cases [77]:

1. If the system consists of a single machine. In this case, if the machine works correctly, the information will be available and the consistency of the stored information can be guaranteed. In addition, it is not possible for partitioning of the system to occur.
2. If the system consists of more than one machine. In this case, if a partitioning of the system occurs, it is interpreted that availability is maintained whenever a request is made to a machine that is in operation then a response is received. Thus, the partitions have consequence as a compensation between the consistency and

the availability of the system, that is, some inconsistencies of the system will be maintained in exchange for increasing the availability of the system. Note that this balance between consistency and availability is directly related to the latency of a system. So the more machines exist in a system, the better the consistency, but the availability is worse since the latency of the system increases.

1.5 Design examples using NoSQL databases

In relation to consistency, we must observe that the more machines are involved in a request, the greater the possibility of avoiding an inconsistency.

In this context, the concepts of "writing quorum" and "reading quorum" are defined [78]. The "writing quorum" indicates that the number of machines participating in the writing must be greater than half the number of machines involved in a replication (N). The number of replicas is often known by the replication factor. Similarly, the reading quorum is defined as the number of machines that need to be contacted in order to be sure that the most up-to-date data is available. This case is more complicated because it depends on how many machines need to confirm a writing.

Note that it is easy to confuse the number of machines in the cluster with the replication factor, and these values are often different. In fact, it is generally suggested that a replication factor of 3 is sufficient, since it allows a single node to fail while still maintaining the quorum for readings and writes. If you have automatic rebalancing, it will not take long to create a third replica, and the chances of losing the second replica before being replaced are very small.

The number of machines involved in an operation may vary with the operation. When writing, quorum might be required for some types of updates, but not for others depending on how much the consistency and availability are valued. Similarly, a reading needs speed, but it can tolerate lack of updating if it contacts fewer machines.

It is often necessary to take both aspects into account. If rapidity is needed strongly consistent readings, then the writings may be required to be recognized by all the machines, allowing the readings to contact only one machine. That would mean that the writings are slow, since they have to contact all the machines and they would not be tolerant of the loss of a machine.

1.6 Design examples using NoSQL databases

In this section, it will show several examples that illustrate what was described in the previous sections. In this sense, several scenarios are going to be proposed, and we will discuss how to solve them.

1.6.1 Example 1

Consider a car rental company with driver of the Uber type. The company has an app for mobile devices that allows you to request a trip in any city in the world where the company operates. When the user requests the path in the app, the system searches for all available vehicles that are close to the customer's current position and can choose one of them. Each vehicle shows the type, the comments of other users about their experience with the driver of the vehicle, as well as an offer on the price of the requested journey. In addition, the app allows the user to enter comments on the service received, score the driver, as well as make the payment of the service. Likewise, the app has a loyalty system, so that for each trip that the user makes, this one receives a number of points equivalent to meters that can travel for free. The user can use the accumulated points in any journey.

It is known that the number of users registered in the app is huge, that the number of times the app is used is also very large and that the app can be used in any city in the world. For these reasons, it is necessary that the volume of data that will be necessary to manage will also be enormous.

Considering the given description of the application, the distribution architecture will be analyzed in terms of partitioning and replication of the data, and the transactional system that is most suitable for the application described. Likewise, a design for the distribution architecture will be proposed.

First, it will be analyzed the types of data that need to be managed in the app:

- Information about the vehicles and drivers registered in the system. Regarding a vehicle, it will be interesting to have information about the type of car, brand, geolocation, accidents that the vehicle has had, etc. And on the driver should be stored information about their personal data, experience in the service, comments and ratings that have made users about it, etc. Likewise, information should be stored on the journeys made with the vehicle and with the driver.
- Information about the users registered in the system. The personal data, the journeys you have made, the accumulated points, the comments you have made about drivers and services, etc.
- Information generated in real time about vehicles such as breakdowns or accidents that occur in the vehicle, incidents related to the driver or user, incidents along the way, etc.
- Information on the availability status of a vehicle at any given time.

According to the description, the information that must be managed is heterogeneous with each other and may vary depending on the type of vehicle and for each user of the app. Thus, the most appropriate solution to manage this type of information would be one based on an aggregation model. Note that a solution based on a relational model would not be very appropriate in this context given the variability and heterogeneity of the data. In order to refine the solution, it must take into account the nature of the types of data that will be managed, the frequency of access necessary to them and how fast access should be. In this sense, a solution is proposed in which several types of aggregation models are combined:

- It is proposed to use a documentary model to store the information referring to vehicles, drivers and users. Each of these data sets could be kept in different collections, one for each type of data. This solution allows an efficient organization of the variable data and facilitates its consultation and optimal storage without the need of having a standard or complex structure. It also allows maintaining redundant information that can be interesting to have grouped according to the type of data that is consulted. For example, the comments made about a vehicle (driver) and those who make those comments. In this sense, it is important to add the comments that have been made on a specific vehicle (driver) by the users, as well as to add all the comments made by a user on the different vehicles (drivers) that he has used.

- It is proposed to use a model of key-value type to maintain the availability status of vehicles. Since it is atomic information, the proposed solution allows an efficient recovery of information if an identifier that could be a unique composite key is used to represent the corresponding state.

- Finally, it is proposed to use a columnar model to store all the information that is generated in real time about the vehicles (drivers). In this sense, an identifier formed by the city and the registration of the car (driver's ID) could be used as a key. In addition, this solution would allow the data to be partitioned by city of reference, which would make access and retrieval of information more efficient. Note that another advantage of this solution is that access to data in this model does not require recovering all the attributes (which could be many and varied).

- With respect to the model of distribution and synchronization of the different databases, we propose the replication of data in different server clusters grouped by continent, country or region depending on the number of cities in which the app operates. In this way, efficient access to information is facilitated based on the proximity of the user. In particular, it is proposed to create at least two clusters per country with at least six servers physically located in different places, so as to guarantee high availability in the case of an incident in one of the clusters. Likewise, in order to scale the writings that are made, it is proposed that the replication strategy be of the peer-to-peer type or a master–slave replication with several master servers, where the replication is performed asynchronously.

With respect the transactional system, the most suitable system should guarantee a final consistency in time that even if certain data are not consistent or accurate, it has the advantage that it allows one to reduce the latencies in the updates with asynchronous replication and improves the robustness of the system, since it will be able to continue to work even in situations of network partitions.

Finally, it must be noted that the system will require high transactionality; so to achieve high performance, it is necessary to avoid the use of indexes on the stored information. To meet this objective, additional collections could be defined with the information that will be most consulted. For example, collection could be created with all the information about the vehicles available in a specific city, or by countries. In this way, access to the most used information is accessed directly.

1.6.2 Example 2

A very common model in computer companies is to offer a product with different services depending on the type of customer. For example, they offer personal solutions, integrated solutions and services in the cloud. Personal solutions are sold through licenses for entire periods of years, and it is a product exclusively for private customers. On the other hand, integrated solutions and services in the cloud are business-oriented products and are contracted for entire periods of months. Regardless of the type of product, it is required to store the following data: product identifier, product name, version and price. In addition, on personal solutions you want to store your functionality, on the integrated solutions your functionality and number of users will be saved, and finally on the services in the cloud the purpose will be saved, and compatible systems. Regarding the clients, the NIF, the name, a bank account number, a telephone number and a contact email must be stored. Observe Figure 1.1 [79] that illustrates the situation.

A solution will be analyzed to store the required information using a document-oriented NoSQL database that guarantees the atomicity of inserts and updates operations for the sale of the described products. To finalize the analysis, the queries will be designed for the case that access to purchases is made through customers, and another solution for the case in which access is made through the products.

In general, document-oriented NoSQL databases have the document as the minimum unit of exchange; therefore, operations on the document are executed atomic. For this reason, if you want to simulate the atomicity of the operations for the two proposed cases then aggregates must be designed that meet two conditions: (a) the aggregate must include all the necessary information that must be processed in the operation, and (b) it must be organized the aggregate information according to the type of processing that you want to perform. As you do not specify the type of queries you want to make about the aggregate, there are different solutions. Here are two possible solutions:

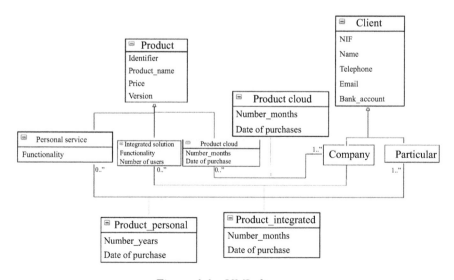

Figure 1.1   UML diagram

1. Assuming that information is accessed through the products sold. In this case, the aggregate should contain the attributes of the product sold, an additional attribute that will indicate the type of product and a list of sub-aggregates with the information of each customer that has purchased that product and all the attributes of the corresponding association. The key to the aggregate will be the product identifier. The following example shows an aggregate for a product of the individual program type:

```
{
    "Identifier": "P678333",
    "Product_name": "MegaWord",
    "Version": "3.5",
    "Price": 200,
    "Functionality": "Word processor",
    "Type": "Individual program",
    "Customers": [
        {
        "NIF": "T35352344",
        "Name": "Walter Priece",
        "Account_banking": "ES4556939300943",
        "Telephone": + 494583999330,
        "Email": "walterpriece@gmail.com",
        "Purchase date": "12-04-2018",
        "Number_years": 1,
        "Type": "Particular"
        },
        {
        "NIF": "T38343900",
        "Name": "Melissa Clevers",
        "Account_banking": "ES4510992309333",
        "Telephone": 49309473822,
        "Email": "melclevers@gmail.com",
        "Number_years": 2,
        "Purchase date": "03-24-2018",
        "Type": "Particular"
        }
    ]}
```

The following example corresponds to an integrated solution:

```
{
    "Identifier": "I999348834",
    "Product_name": "OfficePlusPremiun"
    "Version": "4.1",
    "Price": 900,
    "Functionality": "Office package",
    "User_number": 50,
    "Type": "Integrated solution",
```

```
"Customers":[
   {
   "NIF": "R663472883",
   "Name": "Berlin University",
   "Account_banking": "ES334353553433",
   "Telephone": 4988347939,
   "Email": "office@berlinuniversity.org",
   "Purchase date": "12-03-2018",
   "Number_month": 14,
   "Type": "Company"
   },
   {
   "NIF": "M88347834",
   "Name": "John and Brothers, S.A.",
   "Account_banking": "ES9997447228883",
   "Telephone": 4438892030,
   "Email": "johnbrothers@hotmail.com",
   "Purchase date": "10-02-2018",
   "Number_month": 48,
   "Type": "Company"
   }
]}
```

The following example corresponds to cloud services:

```
{
   "Identifier": "N433533",
   "Product_name": "DesktopPremium",
   "Version": "4.3",
   "Price": 700,
   "Purpose": "Virtual Desktop",
   "Systems_compatibles": ["Linux", "Windows"],
   "Type": "Services in the cloud",
   "Customers":[
      {
      "NIF": "5465757564T",
      "Name": "Balay, S.A.",
      "Account_banking": "ES67885443344",
      "Telephone": 47348834939,
      "Email": "balaycompany@hotmail.com",
      "Purchase_date": "12-02-2018",
      "Number_month": 23,
      "Type": "Company"
      },
      {
      "NIF": "T8888349",
      "Name": "Harrods, S.A.",
```

```
          "Account_banking": "ES4567897676",
          "Telephone": 5039488394,
          "Email": "harrodscompany@hotmail.com",
          "Purchase_date": "11-03-2018",
          "Number_month": 24,
          "Type": "Company"
       }
    ]}
```

2. Assuming that information is accessed through customers. In this case, the aggregate will contain the attributes of a client, an additional attribute that will indicate the type of client and a list of subdocuments with the information of the products purchased and all the attributes of the corresponding association. The key of the aggregate will be the customer's NIF. The following example shows an aggregate for a company-type client:

```
{
   "NIF": "T8888349",
          "Name": "Harrods, S.A.",
          "Account_banking": "ES4567897676",
          "Telephone": 5039488394,
          "Email": "harrodscompany@hotmail.com",
          "Type": "Company"
   "Products": [
       {
"Identifier": "N433533",
"Product_name": "DesktopPremium",
"Version": "4.3",
"Price": 500,
"Purpose": "Virtual Desktop",
"Systems_compatibles": ["Linux", "Windows"],
"Purchase_date": "11-03-2018",
"Number_month": 24,
"Type": "Services in the cloud"
             }
      ]}
```

And the following example corresponds to a particular client:

```
{
          "NIF": "T35352344",
          "Name": "Walter Priece",
          "Account_banking": "ES4556939300943",
          "Telephone": +494583999330,
          "Email": "walterpriece@gmail.com",
   "Type": "Private",
   "Products": [
       {
```

```
    "Identifier": "P3456",
    "Product_name": "PlusWord",
    "Version": "3.5",
    "Price": 200,
    "Functionality": "Word processor",
    "Purchase date": "12-04-2018",
    "Number_years": 1,
    "Type": "Individual program"
}
    ]}
```

1.6.3   Example 3

Consider a company that distributes Rubik's cubes. Each cube is characterized by the name, the shape of the cube, the number of elements it has, the type of games that can be made, the manufacturer and the type of competitions that are carried out on that cube. In addition, each type of game is characterized by a difficulty of performance between 1 and 10, and each competition is characterized by the minimum age to participate and by the nature of the competition (local, national or international). The company sells to individuals and stores, having information about the sales it has made of each type of cube. Specifically, it is known when the sale was made, and to whom it was made. To properly plan the stock of cubes, the company is interested in making statistics on the cubes sold each year and on the type of customers and their preferences. The domain described is summarized in Figure 1.2.

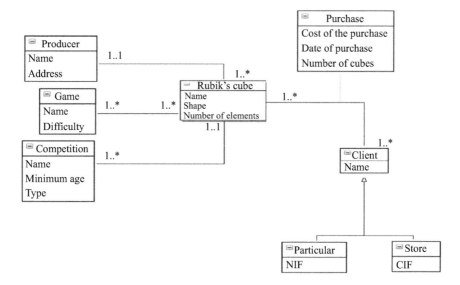

Figure 1.2   UML class diagram

A solution will be analyzed to store the required information using a NoSQL database oriented to documents and how to carry out the fragmentation of the data in order to make the described queries as efficient as possible. According to the restrictions given, the queries will be made on the cubes that are sold and the customers that make the purchases of the cubes. That is why you will need two collections of documents, a collection called Cubes that will contain one document for each type of cube and another collection called Clients that will contain one document for each customer that has made a purchase of a cube. An example of a document in the Cubes collection could be as follows:

```
{
    "Name": "Walter Warrior",
    "Shape": "Square",
    "Dimensions": "3 * 3",
    "Maker":{
     "Name": "Games and cubes",
     "Address": "Main Street, 3. London 50001"},
      "Games": [{"Name": "Colors", "Difficulty": 5},
               {"Name": "Numbers", "Difficulty": 4}],
      "Competition": [{"Name": "Pin-Yu Championship", "Minimum Age": 10,
                      "Character": "International"}],
    "Purchases":[
    {
      "Name": "Supergames",
      "CIF": "Q23223834",
      "Purchase date": "02/10/2018",
      "Type": "Store",
      "Number of cubes": 3,
      "Cost of purchase": 24
    },
    {
      "Name": "Peter Brown",
      "NIF": "R34335343",
      "Purchase date": "01/20/2018",
      "Type": "Private",
      "Number of cubes": 1,
      "Cost purchase": 8
    }
  ]
}
```
An example of a document in the Customers collection could be as follows:
```
{
    "Name": "Games and books S.L.",
    "CIF": "Q23223834",
    "Type": "Store",
    "Purchases": [
```

```
      {
        "Purchase date": "10/02/2017",
        "Cost purchase": 24,
        "Number of cubes": 3,
        "Cube":{
           "Name": "Big Warrior",
           "Shape": "Square",
           "Dimensions": "3 * 3",
           "Manufacturer": {"Name": "More cubes",
             "Address": "Main Street, 8. London 50001"},
           "Games": [{"Name": "Colors", "Difficulty": 5},
               {"Name": "Numbers", "Difficulty": 4}],
         "Competition": [{"Name": "Pin-Yu Championship", "Minimum Age": 10,
                          "Character": "International"}]
      }
   },
      {
   "Purchase date": "03/10/2017",
   "Cost of purchase": 20,
   "Number of cubes": 4,
   "Cube":{
      "Name": "MoFang JiaoShi",
      "Shape": "Square",
      "Dimensions": "3 * 3",
      "Manufacturer": {"Name": "Cubes and games",
        "Address": "Trafalgar Square, 14. London 40009"},
      "Games": [{"Name": "Colors", "Difficulty": 6},
           {"Name": "Letters", "Difficulty": 3}],
      "Competition": [{"Name": "Competition of British gamers",
                       "Minimum age": 18, "Character": "Local"}]
      }
    }
   ]
 }
```

Regarding the fragmentation of data, it will be fragmented at the collection level, defining a different type of shard keys and distribution policy for each collection:

- Cubes document. The planned consultations about this collection require recovering the information per year. In this sense, it would be interesting to distribute the documents according to the range of values of the year. For this, the best solution is to take the year value of the "Purchase date" field as the shard key for the Cubes collection and use a distribution policy based on the range of the same. This solution facilitates a more efficient recovery of documents as they are sequential accesses.

- Client document. The planned consultations on this collection do not require a sequential recovery or other restrictions, so it would be sufficient to establish a distribution that ensures a balanced load of the system nodes. This objective can be achieved by using a hash function on the shard key that is chosen. It could be chosen as such, the identifier of each document associated with each client.

Likewise, if the queries to be made were specifically known, indexes could be defined on the affected fields in each collection to speed up the recovery operations.

1.6.4   Example 4

It is necessary to store purchases of video games. The information required is the following:

- Users: user name (identifies the user), Facebook account (unique), nationality, date of birth, date of registration.

- Purchases: user who makes the purchase, date of purchase and purchased video game. Each purchase is made by a single user and can be done on a video game.
- Video games: unique identifier, video game title, description, launch date, minimum age of the user to buy the game and gender (optional). A video game can be classified in zero or several genres. The genres are not defined a priori.
- About this information, it is necessary to make the following queries:
- User data based on your username or your Facebook account.
- Titles of video games purchased by a specific user and ordered descending by date of purchase.
- Video games launched every month ordered by launch date and by the minimum user age (in years) ascending.

A solution will be analyzed to store the required information using a NoSQL database oriented to columns (Figure 1.3). To make queries efficient, a family of columns appropriate for each of them will be defined.

Because it will be done frequent queries based on the username or the Facebook account, it will be necessary to create two families of columns, with the same information.

The partition key of the family of columns of "users_fac" will be "facebook", and this will be the family of columns on which the queries will be executed based on the Facebook account, which is unique.

In the case of queries based on the username, by not ensuring their uniqueness in the conditions of the problem, we will have "user" as the partition key, and we will also add "facebook" (which is unique) as a clustering key, in order to guarantee uniqueness and avoid upserts.

Because queries are going to be executed to obtain the titles of the games purchased by a specific user, the partition key of the family of columns "purchases"

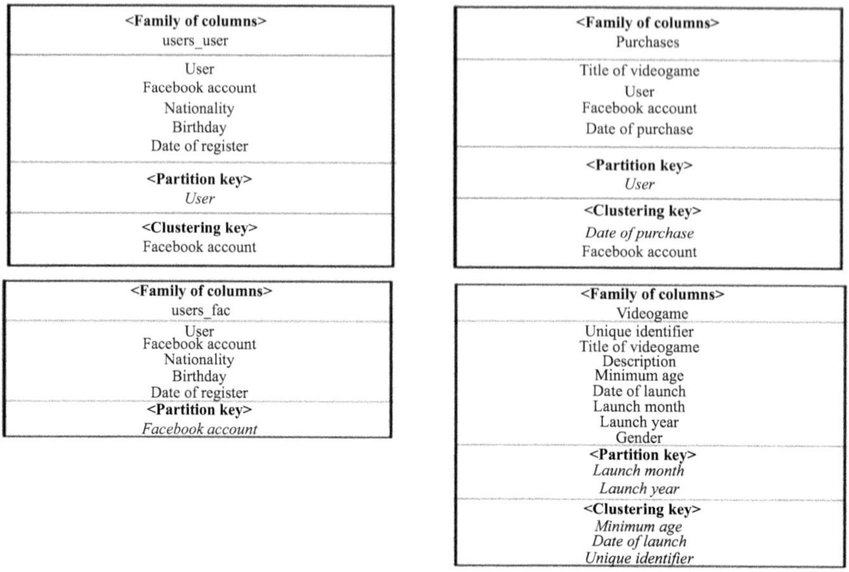

<Family of columns> users_user	<Family of columns> Purchases
User Facebook account Nationality Birthday Date of register	Title of videogame User Facebook account Date of purchase
<Partition key> *User*	<Partition key> *User*
<Clustering key> Facebook account	<Clustering key> *Date of purchase* Facebook account

<Family of columns> users_fac	<Family of columns> Videogame
User Facebook account Nationality Birthday Date of register	Unique identifier Title of videogame Description Minimum age Date of launch Launch month Launch year Gender
<Partition key> *Facebook account*	<Partition key> *Launch month* *Launch year*
	<Clustering key> *Minimum age* *Date of launch* *Unique identifier*

Figure 1.3   NoSQL database oriented to columns

will be "user", but as "user" is not guaranteed the uniqueness, we will add "face-book" as one of the clustering keys to avoid upsets when entering data.

As the purchase data are ordered in descending order at the purchase date, you must also add "purchase date" as the grouping key, specifying in addition that it is desired in descending order.

Because they are going to consult the video games released every month, we will use the "month" and "year", as a tuple of partition key, since if not requesting the data per month the video games launched in the different years would overlap.

Because "month" and "year" do not guarantee uniqueness, "identifier" is added as grouping key, to achieve uniqueness and avoid upserts when entering data.

"Age" and "date" are also added as a grouping key since the data is requested to be returned in ascending order.

1.7   Conclusions

In this chapter it has been analyzed how the phenomenon of Big Data has influenced in the development of the databases. For it, first of all, an introduction to the Big Data phenomenon has been made in order to describe the fundamental changes that occurred in terms of technologies, work tools, execution conditions or types of applications that are normally developed. Next, it has been discussed about aspects of the design and development of a database that it must be considered in the context of Big Data. Next, the chapter has focused on developing each aspect: the problem of scalability, data distribution models and consistency. In the first case, it has been described the need of horizontal scaling solutions and how this influences the way information is stored. In this sense, the model of relational persistence is not the most appropriate, and it is necessary to use other alternative persistence models that receive the generic name of NoSQL databases. The horizontal scaling solutions on machine clusters are required to use new models of data distribution on these machines. In this sense, the models used to partition the information between the different machines and replicate the information (in order to ensure the availability to failures of any cluster machine) have been shown. Next, it has been introduced the issue of consistency of information. The chapter ends with the presentation of a set of use cases where it is necessary to design a solution in order to store data. Also, the solutions of each case are presented. Each solution uses the concepts described in the chapter. This chapter is a starting point in order to the reader can investigate in each of the aspects described.

References

[1]   Shah, M. (2016). Big data and the Internet of Things. In Big Data Analysis: New Algorithms for a NewSociety (pp. 207–237). Springer, Cham.

[2]   Khan, N., Yaqoob, I., Hashem, I. A. T., *et al.* (2014). Big data: Survey, technologies, opportunities, and challenges. The Scientific World Journal, 2014.

[3]   Jacobs, A. (2009). The pathologies of big data. Communications of the ACM, 52(8), 36–44.

[4]   Assunção, M. D., Calheiros, R. N., Bianchi, S., Netto, M. A., and Buyya, R. (2015). Big Data computing and clouds: Trends and future directions. Journal of Parallel and Distributed Computing, 79, 3–15.

[5]   Ivanov, T., Korfiatis, N., and Zicari, R. V. (2013). On the inequality of the 3V's of Big Data Architectural Paradigms: A case for heterogeneity. arXiv preprint arXiv:1311.0805.

[6]   Khosla, P. K., and Kaur, A. (2018). Big Data technologies. In Data Intensive Computing Applications for Big Data, 29 (p. 28). IOS Press, Amsterdam, Netherlands.

[7]   Bakshi, K. (2012). Considerations for big data: Architecture and approach. In Aerospace Conference, 2012 IEEE (pp. 1–7). IEEE.

[8]   Chen, C. P., and Zhang, C. Y. (2014). Data-intensive applications, challenges, techniques and technologies: A survey on Big Data. Information Sciences, 275, 314–347.

[9]   Russom, P. (2011). Big data analytics. TDWI Best Practices Report, fourth quarter, 19(4), 1–34.

[10] Gandomi, A., and Haider, M. (2015). Beyond the hype: Big data concepts, methods, and analytics. International Journal of Information Management, 35(2), 137–144.

[11] Demchenko, Y., De Laat, C., and Membrey, P. (2014). Defining architecture components of the Big Data Ecosystem. In Collaboration Technologies and Systems (CTS), 2014 International Conference on (pp. 104–112). IEEE.

[12] Zicari, R. V. (2014). Big data: Challenges and opportunities. In Big Data Computing (p. 564). Chapman and Hall/CRC, London, UK.

[13] Dholakia, A., Venkatachar, P., Doshi, K., *et al.* (2017). Designing a high performance cluster for large-scale SQL-on-Hadoop analytics. In Big Data (Big Data), 2017 IEEE International Conference on (pp. 1701–1703). IEEE.

[14] Huang, W., Meng, L., Zhang, D., and Zhang, W. (2017). In-memory parallel processing of massive remotely sensed data using an apache spark on Hadoop yarn model. IEEE Journal of Selected Topics in Applied Earth Observations and Remote Sensing, 10(1), 3–19.

[15] Corbellini, A., Mateos, C., Zunino, A., Godoy, D., and Schiaffino, S. (2017). Persisting big-data: The NoSQL landscape. Information Systems, 63, 1–23.

[16] Chen, M., Mao, S., and Liu, Y. (2014). Big data: A survey. Mobile Networks and Applications, 19(2), 171–209.

[17] Minelli, M., Chambers, M., and Dhiraj, A. (2012). Big data, big analytics: Emerging business intelligence and analytic trends for today's businesses. John Wiley & Sons, Hoboken, New Jersey.

[18] Kasun, L. L. C., Zhou, H., Huang, G. B., and Vong, C. M. (2013). Representational learning with extreme learning machine for big data. IEEE Intelligent Systems, 28(6), 31–34.

[19] Zhou, L., Pan, S., Wang, J., and Vasilakos, A. V. (2017). Machine learning on big data: Opportunities and challenges. Neurocomputing, 237, 350–361.

[20] Power, D. J. (2016). Data science: Supporting decision-making. Journal of Decision Systems, 25(4), 345–356.

[21] Provost, F., and Fawcett, T. (2013). Data science and its relationship to big data and data-driven decision making. Big Data, 1(1), 51–59.

[22] Witten, I. H., Frank, E., Hall, M. A., and Pal, C. J. (2016). Data Mining: Practical machine learning tools and techniques. Morgan Kaufmann, San Francisco, USA.

[23] Nadal, S., Herrero, V., Romero, O., *et al.* (2017). A software reference architecture for semantic-aware Big Data systems. Information and Software Technology, 90, 75–92.

[24] Wu, X., Zhu, X., Wu, G. Q., and Ding, W. (2014). Data mining with big data. IEEE Transactions on Knowledge and Data Engineering, 26(1), 97–107.

[25] Suthaharan, S. (2014). Big data classification: Problems and challenges in network intrusion prediction with machine learning. ACM SIGMETRICS Performance Evaluation Review, 41(4), 70–73.

[26] Ratner, B. (2017). Statistical and machine-learning data mining: Techniques for better predictive modeling and analysis of big data. Chapman and Hall/CRC, London, UK.

[27] Marjani, M., Nasaruddin, F., Gani, A., *et al.* (2017). Big IoT data analytics: Architecture, opportunities, and open research challenges. IEEE Access, 5, 5247–5261.

[28] Gudivada, V., Apon, A., and Rao, D. L. (2018). Database systems for big data storage and retrieval. In Handbook of Research on Big Data Storage and Visualization Techniques (pp. 76–100). IGI Global, Hershey, Pennsylvania.

[29] Sabegh, M. A. J., Lukyanenko, R., Recker, J., Samuel, B., and Castellanos, A. (2017). Conceptual modeling research in information systems: What we now know and what we still do not know. In Proceedings of the 16th AIS SIGSAND Symposium.

[30] Elmasri, R., and Navathe, S. (2010). Fundamentals of database systems. Addison-Wesley Publishing Company, Boston, USA.

[31] Kunda, D., and Phiri, H. (2017). A comparative study of NoSQL and relational database. Zambia ICT Journal, 1(1), 1–4.

[32] Coronel, C., and Morris, S. (2016). Database systems: Design, implementation, & management. Cengage Learning, Kentucky, USA.

[33] Gessert, F., Wingerath, W., Friedrich, S., and Ritter, N. (2017). NoSQL database systems: A survey and decision guidance. Computer Science-Research and Development, 32(3–4), 353–365.

[34] Sharma, S., Tim, U. S., Wong, J., Gadia, S., and Sharma, S. (2014). A brief review on leading big data models. Data Science Journal, 13, 138–157.

[35] Pavlo, A., and Aslett, M. (2016). What's really new with NewSQL?. ACM SIGMOD Record, 45(2), 45–55.

[36] Kumar, R., Gupta, N., Maharwal, H., Charu, S., and Yadav, K. (2014). Critical analysis of database management using NewSQL. International Journal of Computer Science and Mobile Computing, 3, 434–438.

[37] Stonebraker, M. (2012). NewSQL: An alternative to NoSQL and old SQL for new OLTP apps. Communications of the ACM. Retrieved, 07-06.

[38] Stonebraker, M. (2010). SQL databases v. NoSQL databases. Communications of the ACM, 53(4), 10–11.

[39] Li, Y., and Manoharan, S. (2013). A performance comparison of SQL and NoSQL databases. In Communications, Computers and Signal Processing (PACRIM), 2013 IEEE Pacific Rim Conference on (pp. 15–19). IEEE.

[40] Jatana, N., Puri, S., Ahuja, M., Kathuria, I., and Gosain, D. (2012). A survey and comparison of relational and non-relational database. International Journal of Engineering Research & Technology, 1(6).

[41] Zakhary, V., Agrawal, D., and Abbadi, A. E. (2017). Caching at the web scale. Proceedings of the VLDB Endowment, 10(12), 2002–2005.

[42] Tiwari, S. (2011). Professional NoSQL. John Wiley & Sons, Hoboken, New Jersey.

[43] Vaish, G. (2013). Getting started with NoSQL. Packt Publishing Ltd, Birmingham, USA.

[44] Melton, J., and Simon, A. R. (1993). Understanding the new SQL: A complete guide. Morgan Kaufmann, San Francisco, USA.

[45]   Tauro, C. J., Aravindh, S., and Shreeharsha, A. B. (2012). Comparative study of the new generation, agile, scalable, high performance NOSQL databases. International Journal of Computer Applications, 48(20), 1–4.

[46]   Oussous, A., Benjelloun, F. Z., Lahcen, A. A., and Belfkih, S. (2017). NoSQL databases for big data. International Journal of Big Data Intelligence, 4(3), 171–185.

[47]   Han, J., Haihong, E., Le, G., and Du, J. (2011). Survey on NoSQL database. In Pervasive Computing and Applications (ICPCA), 2011 6th International Conference on (pp. 363–366). IEEE.

[48]   Davoudian, A., Chen, L., and Liu, M. (2018). A survey on NoSQL stores. ACM Computing Surveys (CSUR), 51(2), 40.

[49]   Perkins, L., Redmond, E., and Wilson, J. (2018). Seven databases in seven weeks: A guide to modern databases and the NoSQL movement. Pragmatic Bookshelf, New York, USA.

[50]   Pethuru R., and Ganesh C. (2018). A deep dive into NoSQL databases: The use cases and applications. Academic Press, Cambridge, USA.

[51]   Kalid, S., Syed, A., Mohammad, A., and Halgamuge, M. N. (2017). Big-data NoSQL databases: A comparison and analysis of "Big-Table", "DynamoDB", and "Cassandra". In Big Data Analysis (ICBDA), 2017 IEEE 2nd International Conference on (pp. 89–93). IEEE.

[52]   Pokorný, J. (2015). Database technologies in the world of big data. In Proceedings of the 16th International Conference on Computer Systems and Technologies (pp. 1–12). ACM.

[53]   Hecht, R., and Jablonski, S. (2011). NoSQL evaluation: A use case oriented survey. In Cloud and Service Computing (CSC), 2011 International Conference on (pp. 336–341). IEEE.

[54]   Haseeb, A., and Pattun, G. (2017). A review on NoSQL: Applications and challenges. International Journal of Advanced Research in Computer Science, 8(1).

[55]   Nayak, A., Poriya, A., and Poojary, D. (2013). Type of NOSQL databases and its comparison with relational databases. International Journal of Applied Information Systems, 5(4), 16–19.

[56]   Gupta, S., and Narsimha, G. (2017). Efficient query analysis and performance evaluation of the NoSQL data store for Big Data. In Proceedings of the First International Conference on Computational Intelligence and Informatics (pp. 549–558). Springer, Singapore.

[57]   Atzeni, P., Cabibbo, L., and Torlone, R. (2018). Data modeling across the evolution of database technology. In A Comprehensive Guide Through the Italian Database Research Over the Last 25 Years (pp. 221–234). Springer, Cham.

[58]   Wu, D., Sakr, S., and Zhu, L. (2017). Big data storage and data models. In Handbook of Big Data Technologies (pp. 3–29). Springer, Cham.

[59]   Zheng, K., Gu, D., Fang, F., Zhang, M., Zheng, K., and Li, Q. (2017). Data storage optimization strategy in distributed column-oriented database by considering spatial adjacency. Cluster Computing, 20(4), 2833–2844.

[60]   Zhao, G., Lin, Q., Li, L., and Li, Z. (2014). Schema conversion model of SQL database to NoSQL. In P2P, Parallel, Grid, Cloud and Internet Computing (3PGCIC), 2014 Ninth International Conference on (pp. 355–362). IEEE.

[61]   Jose, B., and Abraham, S. (2017). Exploring the merits of NoSQL: A study based on MongoDB. In Networks & Advances in Computational Technologies (NetACT), 2017 International Conference on (pp. 266–271). IEEE.

[62]   Kumar, K. S., and Mohanavalli, S. (2017). A performance comparison of document oriented NoSQL databases. In Computer, Communication and Signal Processing (ICCCSP), 2017 International Conference on (pp. 1–6). IEEE.

[63]   Parmar, R. R., and Roy, S. (2018). MongoDB as an efficient graph database: An application of document oriented NOSQL database. Data Intensive Computing Applications for Big Data, 29, 331.

[64]   Branch, S., Branch, B., and Boroujen, I. (2017). A novel method for evaluation of NoSQL databases: A case study of Cassandra and Redis. Journal of Theoretical and Applied Information Technology, 95(6).

[65]   Anand, S., Singh, P., and Sagar, B. M. (2018). Working with Cassandra database. In Information and Decision Sciences (pp. 531–538). Springer, Singapore.

[66]   Abdelhedi, F., Brahim, A. A., and Zurfluh, G. (2018). Formalizing the mapping of UML conceptual schemas to column-oriented databases. International Journal of Data Warehousing and Mining (IJDWM), 14(3), 44–68.

[67]   Hao, Z., Novak, E., Yi, S., and Li, Q. (2017). Challenges and software architecture for fog computing. IEEE Internet Computing, 21(2), 44–53.

[68]   Bagui, S., and Nguyen, L. T. (2015). Database sharding: To provide fault tolerance and scalability of big data on the cloud. International Journal of Cloud Applications and Computing (IJCAC), 5(2), 36–52.

[69]   Valentini, G. L., Lassonde, W., Khan, S. U., *et al.* (2013). An overview of energy efficiency techniques in cluster computing systems. Cluster Computing, 16(1), 3–15.

[70]   Sadalage, P. J., and Fowler, M. (2013). NoSQL distilled: A brief guide to the emerging world of polyglot persistence. Pearson Education, New York, USA.

[71]   Debski, A., Szczepanik, B., Malawski, M., Spahr, S., and Muthig, D. (2018). A scalable, reactive architecture for cloud applications. IEEE Software, 35(2), 62–71.

[72]   Gorton, I., and Klein, J. (2015). Distribution, data, deployment: Software architecture convergence in big data systems. IEEE Software, 32(3), 78–85.

[73]   Hu, H., Wen, Y., Chua, T. S., and Li, X. (2014). Toward scalable systems for big data analytics: A technology tutorial. IEEE Access, 2, 652–687.

[74]   Pokorny, J. (2013). NoSQL databases: A step to database scalability in web environment. International Journal of Web Information Systems, 9(1), 69–82.

[75]   Hsieh, M. J., Ho, L. Y., Wu, J. J., and Liu, P. (2017). Data partition optimisation for column-family NoSQL databases. International Journal of Big Data Intelligence, 4(4), 263–275.

[76] Abadi, D. J. (2012). Consistency tradeoffs in modern distributed database system design: CAP is only part of the story. Computer, (2), 37–42.

[77] Stonebraker, M. (2010). Errors in database systems, eventual consistency, and the cap theorem. Communications of the ACM, BLOG@ ACM.

[78] Ghomi, E. J., Rahmani, A. M., and Qader, N. N. (2017). Load-balancing algorithms in cloud computing: A survey. Journal of Network and Computer Applications, 88, 50–71.

[79] Shin, K., Hwang, C., and Jung, H. (2017). NoSQL database design using UML conceptual data model based on Peter Chen's framework. International Journal of Applied Engineering Research, 12(5), 632–636.

Chapter 2

Big data processing frameworks and architectures: a survey

Raghavendra Kumar Chunduri[1] and Aswani Kumar Cherukuri[1]

In recent times, there has been rapid growth in data generated from autonomous sources. The existing data processing techniques are not suitable to deal with these large volumes of complex data that can be structured, semi-structured or unstructured. This large data is referred to as Big data because of its main characteristics: volume, variety velocity, value and veracity. Extensive research on Big data is ongoing, and the primary focus of this research is on processing massive amounts of data effectively and efficiently. However, researchers are paying little attention on how to store and analyze the large volumes of data to get useful insights from it. In this chapter, the authors examine existing Big data processing frameworks like MapReduce, Apache Spark, Storm and Flink. In this chapter, the architectures of MapReduce, iterative MapReduce frameworks and components of Apache Spark are discussed in detail. Most of the widely used classical machine learning techniques are implemented using these Big data frameworks in the form of Apache Mahout and Spark MLlib libraries and these need to be enhanced to support all existing machine learning techniques like formal concept analysis (FCA) and neural embedding. In this chapter, authors have taken FCA as an application and provided scalable FCA algorithms using the Big data processing frameworks like MapReduce and Spark. Streaming data processing frameworks like Apache Flink and Apache Storm is also examined. Authors also discuss about the storage architectures like Hadoop Distributed File System (HDFS), Dynamo and Amazon S3 in detail while processing large Big data applications. The survey concludes with a proposal for best practices related to the studied architectures and frameworks.

2.1 Introduction

In the present era of data explosion, with the increase in users on various application domains like social networking [1] and e-commerce [2] platforms, the data is

[1]School of Information Technology and Engineering, Vellore Institute of Technology, Vellore, India

being collected at an unprecedented scale. This large amount of data being collected is called "Big data." The characteristics of Big data are known as the Vs of Big data [3,4]. There are many characteristics of Big data, but in this survey, the focus is on a selected number of the Big data characteristics.

- Volume is the primary characteristic and it determines the amount of the data that is generated and stored. The size of the data decides whether the data can be considered as Big data or not.
- Velocity describes the speed at which the data is generated and processed.
- Veracity refers to the quality and value of the data that is captured.
- Variety determines the type of the data, i.e., whether it is structured, unstructured or semi-structured along with the nature of the data.
- Value is another important characteristic. Although data is produced in larger volumes, it is not useful until this turns into something useful, i.e., value that is added to the companies/organizations after collecting and extracting the useful information from large datasets.

There are several traditional data processing frameworks discussed in the literature, but these frameworks are not generally suitable for large volumes of data because of their architectural complexity [5]. So parallel processing frameworks are needed to store and process the massive amounts of data effectively and efficiently. Various parallel processing frameworks are developed to process Big data by supporting most of its characteristics. Of these, Hadoop [6] is the most widely used distributed processing framework for solving problems that involve massive amounts of data and computations [5]. It provides distributed storage to organize the large amounts of data and to process Big data using the MapReduce programming model. Spark is another most widely used general purpose cluster computing framework for processing Big data [7]. Storm [8] and Flink [9] are used for real-time streaming applications that take real-time streaming data as an input. Caffe [10] and Deep learning for java (DL4j) [11] are deep learning frameworks used for model training and they are primarily used in natural language processing, computer vision and speech recognition applications. Table 2.1 represents the overview of the various characteristics of the Big data.

The goal of this survey is to provide timely study on existing Big data processing frameworks. Section 2.2 discusses Hadoop architecture and the

Table 2.1   Characteristics of Big data

Big data characteristics	Description	Purpose
Volume	Size of data	Amount of data stored and collected. Data size is in TB, PB
Velocity	Speed of data	Data generation frequency: the speed at which the data is generated and processed
Variety	Type of data	Different forms of the data like structured, semi-structured and unstructured
Veracity	Data quality	Data needs to be accurate It is worthless if not accurate
Value	Business value	The business value of the data collected

MapReduce programming model. Sections 2.3 and 2.4 discuss about iterative MapReduce frameworks like HaLoop and Twister. Sections 2.5–2.10 describes about the components of Hadoop Ecosystem like Apache Pig, Mahout, Sqoop, Flume, Oozie and briefly Hadoop 2. In Section 2.11, authors detail about Apache Spark and its components. Section 2.12 looks Big data storage systems like HDFS, Amazon S3, Dynamo and many more. Section 2.13 discusses about stream processing engines. In Section 2.14, we detailed Apache Zookeeper, a distributed system coordination service provider. Section 2.15 presents the open challenges in Big data processing frameworks followed by findings and the conclusion in Section 2.16.

2.2   Apache Hadoop framework and Hadoop Ecosystem

Apache Hadoop is an open-source framework that offers storage and processing of large datasets in a distributed manner on a network of commodity computers [12]. In Hadoop, the cluster of commodity computers ranges from a few machines and servers to thousands of machines with each machine having its own local computation and storage facilities. Hadoop was developed and programed using Java language. Hadoop contains two parts, HDFS and MapReduce. HDFS [13] is a distributed file system used for storing large volumes of data, whereas programming model of the MapReduce is used to process large datasets. Figure 2.1 represents the Hadoop Ecosystem which is discussed in later sections.

2.2.1   Architecture of Hadoop framework

For data storage and processing, Hadoop adopts the master–slave architecture design. The master node in Hadoop consists of NameNode for data storage, and JobTracker is used to process data using MapReduce. The slave nodes are the machines that contain TaskTrackers and DataNodes which are used to perform complex computations and to store data [14].

Figure 2.2 represents the high-level master–slave architecture of the Hadoop framework where the master and slave nodes of a cluster are presented. The JobTracker is always communicating with all the TaskTrackers and similarly, the NameNode is communicating with the DataNodes in the cluster [5].

2.2.2   Architecture of MapReduce

There are many distributed programming models that bring several issues like granularity of the tasks, reliability of the hardware and platforms where the execution is taking place. MapReduce addresses most of these issues. MapReduce is a generic framework used for processing and generating large datasets with a parallel and distributed algorithm on a cluster [15,97]. Hadoop is a widely used framework implemented in Java and is used for distributed storage and distributed processing of very large datasets on a cluster which is built from commodity hardware. MapReduce is a programming model for large-scale data processing. MapReduce is being used in various fields including machine learning [16–18], textual retrieval [19], content pattern analysis [20] and click stream

Hadoop Ecosystem

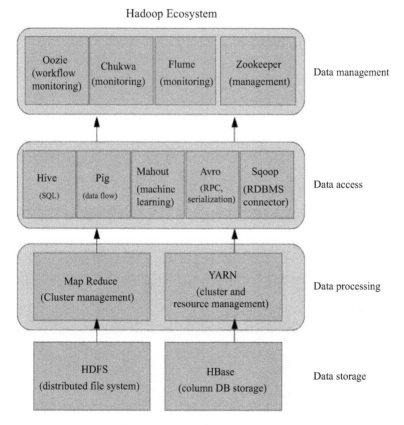

Figure 2.1   Hadoop Ecosystem

sessionization [21]. Furthermore, MapReduce is adopted by numerous fields like mobile environments [22], cloud environments [23], grid computing [24] and multi-core many-core systems [25]. The MapReduce framework is based on two basic operations, map and reduce, which are applied to the data. These two operations gave the name MapReduce framework.

For MapReduce, programmers have to design map functions for processing key–value pairs, which generates intermediate outputs in the form of key–value pairs [26]. The reduce function will merge all the intermediate keys that are generated at the map output level. Both the map function and reduce function work to maintain the MapReduce workflow. The execution of the reduce function will start after the completion of the map function or once the map function output is available. MapReduce assumes that maps execute in parallel and that they are independent in nature. The key perspective of the MapReduce algorithm is, if each map and reduce are independent of all the other maps and reducers that are operating in the network, the operation will keep running in parallel on various keys and lists of data [27]. Figure 2.3 gives a pictorial representation of the MapReduce

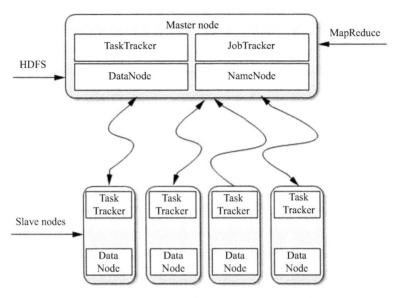

Figure 2.2   Mater–slave architecture of Hadoop framework

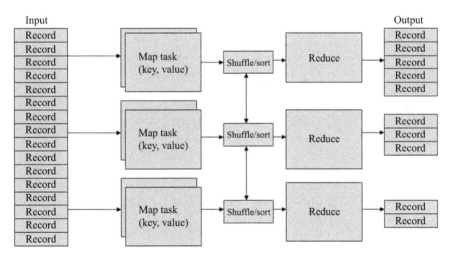

Figure 2.3   Pictorial representation of MapReduce

process. The shuffle/sort phase is an intermediate phase that automatically starts after the completion of the map phase. The output of map phase is shuffled and sorted to optimize the work of the reducer. Figure 2.4 provides the flow of MapReduce job execution. The client submits a MapReduce job and the job tracker receives the job and then assigns a JobId and puts into an internal queue. Then the job scheduler picks the job from a queue and initializes it and uses an

MR Job Process

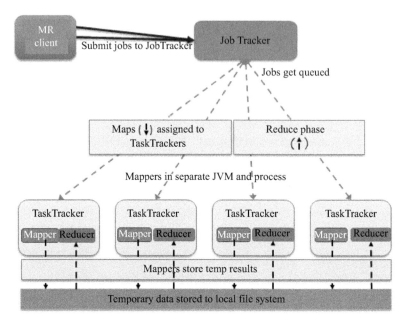

Figure 2.4   MapReduce job execution process

internally scheduling algorithm that determines which job's task should be processed first and then, JobTracker assigns tasks to TaskTracker that is ready to
available to run the task. All the responsibilities of the MapReduce jobs, such as
the execution of jobs, the scheduling of map tasks, reduce tasks and combiners,
monitoring success as well as failure of individual job tasks and the completion of
the batch job will be taken care by the JobTracker. During the MapReduce job
execution phase, the JobTracker monitors the TaskTrackers, while the map or
reduce tasks are executing. If the JobTracker does not receive any heartbeat
messages from the TaskTracker within a specified time (10 min by default), it
understands that the TaskTracker has failed and it will reschedule all pending
tasks or the tasks in progress to another available TaskTracker. The failed
TaskTracker will be blacklisted by the JobTracker, but it remains in communication with the JobTracker. The TaskTracker heartbeat messages contain
information such as the available physical and virtual memory, information about
CPU usage. The response from the JobTracker contains the next action that has to
be performed by the TaskTracker.

2.2.2.1   Executing the map phase
After the initialization of the map phase, first the resources that are required for the job
are copied from HDFS. Then the JobTracker will be requested to execute the Job. The
JobTracker initializes the job then reads and splits the input and creates a map task for

each job. The JobTracker will then call the TaskTrackers. The TaskTrackers will run the map tasks on the data that is assigned to them. The map task reads the input, splits the data as input (key, value) pairs and provides the mapper method and produces (key, value) pairs as output [28]. The output of the map is used as an intermediate output in between map and reduce tasks. The InputFormat creates InputSplits, and the RecordReader is used to present a record-oriented view for the mapper.

- Input files: Input file contains input data for the MapReduce job. The input files can reside in HDFS or Amazon S3 buckets if they are large.
- InputFormat: The format of the input for the MapReduce job. InputFormats are used to define how input files are split and read. MapReduce accepts three types of input formats. The input formats are inherited from FileInputFormatClass. When a MapReduce job starts, the FileInputFormat is provided with a path to input files and reads all files in the directory. Then the input is split into one or more InputSplits. Table 2.2 shows the standard input formats that can be used in InputFormats in MapReduce.
- InputSplit: The data that has to be processed by an individual map task is called as InputSplit. It is the logical representation of the data present in the HDFS blocks.
- RecordReader: The RecordReader class is used to load the data from the input files and converts into (key, value) pairs for the mapper.

Figure 2.5 shows the pictorial representation of map phase as explained. In map phase, for every input (key, value) pair, there shall be at least one output. While generating the list of (key, value) pairs, the key attribute will be repeated many times. The key attribute is reused in the reduce stage for aggregating the values based on the key. In the MapReduce, input of the reduce function must be the same as the output of the map function. Once the map function execution is completed, the results will be stored in buffer storage by the corresponding task trackers.

2.2.2.2 Shuffling and sorting

The intermediate phase is very important in optimizing the MapReduce program. As presented in Figure 2.2, once the output from the map function is available, the intermediate phase will start automatically [29]. After the map function completes its execution, the output will be sorted on the basis of the key attribute of the map

Table 2.2 InputFormat in MapReduce

InputFormat	Description	Key	Value
TextInputFormat	Default format; reads lines of text files	The byte offset of the line	Contents of the line
KeyValueInputFormat	Parses lines into key, value pairs	Everything up to the first tab character	The remainder of the line
SequenceFileInputFormat	A Hadoop-specific high-performance binary format	User defined	User defined

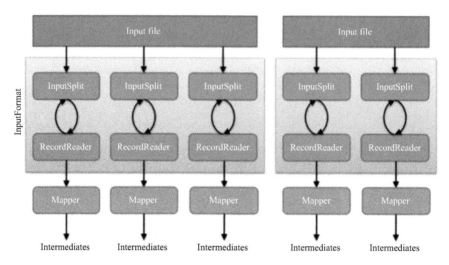

Figure 2.5   Map phase execution

function and then initiates the sorting phase. The buffer memory presented at the TaskTracker is used for storing the output from the sorting operation. By default, the buffer memory stores the map function output, and if the size of the output is more than the threshold value, it will be stored to a local disk and will be available through Hypertext Transfer Protocol (HTTP). Partitioners and combiners in MapReduce are responsible for dividing up the intermediate key space and assigning intermediate key–value pairs to reducers.

- The partitioner at the map stage will start partitioning the emitted intermediate (key, value) pairs. Partitioning will take place only if the partitioner is present. The partitioner specifies the task to which an intermediate key–value pair must be copied.
- The combiner is often the reducer itself is used when it is configured in the job class. The combiner function is used to compress and speed up the data transmission of the map function output to the reduce phase.

The partitioner in MapReduce can be configured using

```
job.setPartitionerClass(LogPartitioner.class);
```

The combiner in MapReduce can be configured using

```
job.setCombinerClass(LogReducer.class);
```

Figure 2.6 shows the MapReduce execution flow when a partitioner and a combiner are configured in the configuration class.

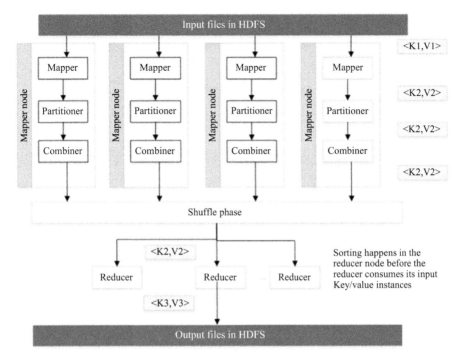

Figure 2.6   MapReduce execution flow with the presence of partitioner and combiner

2.2.2.3   Reduce phase execution

As soon as the output of the map phase is available, the reduce node running on the TaskTracker will collect and group the map output. Then the output is merged into a single file and sorted before it is taken by the reducer. The reduce task receives a list of input values from an input (key, list (value)) which will be aggregated on the basis of custom logic and produces the output (key, value) pairs [30,31]. Once the reduce function execution is completed, it writes the output directly into HDFS in the same format that is specified in the MapReduce job configuration class. Figure 2.7 represents the reducer phase execution in MapReduce job.

OutputFormat: OutputFormat is used to specify the output format of the MapReduce job. Typically, it is configured in the reducer phase and writes the output to files on HDFS as specified by the OutputFormat. Both the InputFormat and the OutputFormat functions are important for every MapReduce job. The instances of OutputFormat provided by Hadoop write files onto the local disk. Each reducer writes a separate file in a common output directory. These files will typi-cally be named **partnnnnn**, where **nnnnn** is the partition id associated with the reduce task. The output directory can be set using

FileOutputFormat.setOutputPath()

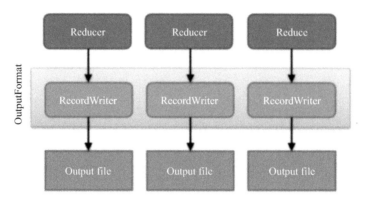

Figure 2.7   Reduce phase execution

Table 2.3   OutputFormats in MapReduce

OutputFormat	Description
TextOutputFormat	Default; writes lines in "key, value" form
SequenceFileOutputFormat	Writes binary files suitable for reading into subsequent MapReduce jobs
NullOutputFormat	Disregards its inputs

Table 2.3 shows the output formats in the MapReduce.

• RecordWriter: RecordWriter writes the output (key, value) pairs to an output file. The output files can be saved to disks or HDFS.

2.2.3   Application implemented using MapReduce: concept generation in formal concept analysis (FCA)

In this section, authors discuss about applying MapReduce in the domain of FCA. FCA is a widely used unsupervised machine learning technique for knowledge representation and data analysis. The challenge in FCA is to identify the formal concepts and construct a concept lattice for knowledge representation from the identified formal concepts. So this section gives a detailed note on how MapReduce can be used to FCA for efficient data analysis and knowledge representation, i.e., identification of formal concepts and constructing the concept lattice. The following is the code overview for the identification of formal concepts in FCA using MapReduce. Any MapReduce application requires three types of functions/ classes. The job class also called the configuration class or client class is the starting point of the execution where all the parameters required for executing the MapReduce application are configured. The map class or map method is the implementation of the map phase, and the reduce class or the reduce method is the implementation of the reduce phase.

The Job configuration class:LatticeJob.java

```
package com.hadoop.mr.lattice;
import org.apache.hadoop.conf.Configuration;
import org.apache.hadoop.fs.Path;
import org.apache.hadoop.io.IntWritable;
import org.apache.hadoop.io.LongWritable;
import org.apache.hadoop.io.NullWritable;
import org.apache.hadoop.io.Text;
import org.apache.hadoop.mapreduce.Job;
import org.apache.hadoop.mapreduce.lib.chain.ChainMapper;
import org.apache.hadoop.mapreduce.lib.chain.ChainReducer;
import org.apache.hadoop.mapreduce.lib.input.FileInputFormat;
import org.apache.hadoop.mapreduce.lib.output.FileOutputFormat;
import org.apache.hadoop.mapreduce.lib.output.TextOutputFormat;
public class LatticeJob {
public static void main(String[]args) throws Exception {
    Configuration configuration = new Configuration();
    Job job = new Job(configuration, "latticejob");
       FileInputFormat.addInputPath(job,hdfs/fcainput);
    job.setJarByClass(LatticeJob.class);
    ChainMapper.addMapper(job,LatticeMapper.class,
         LongWritable.class,Text.class,
            IntWritable.class,Text.class,
         configuration);
    ChainReducer.setReducer(job,LatticeReducer.class,
         IntWritable.class,Text.class,
         IntWritable.class,Text.class,configuration);
    ChainReducer.addMapper(job,LatticeMapper.class,
         IntWritable.class,Text.class,
         Text.class,NullWritable.class,
         configuration);
    job.setOutputFormatClass(TextOutputFormat.class);
    FileOutputFormat.setOutputPath(job,hdfs/fcaoutput);
    intcode=job.waitForCompletion(true)?0:1;
       System.exit(code);
  }
}
```

The previous source code is the configuration class for the formal concept identification in large formal contexts and the explanation is given in detail. The standard imports required for the job are declared as

```
import org.apache.hadoop.conf.Configuration;
import org.apache.hadoop.fs.Path;
import org.apache.hadoop.mapreduce.lib.chain.ChainMapper;
import org.apache.hadoop.mapreduce.lib.chain.ChainReducer;
import org.apache.hadoop.io.Text;
import org.apache.hadoop.io.IntWritable;
import org.apache.hadoop.mapreduce.Job;
import org.apache.hadoop.io.LongWritable;
import org.apache.hadoop.mapreduce.lib.input.FileInputFormat;
import org.apache.hadoop.mapreduce.lib.output.TextOutputFormat;
import org.apache.hadoop.mapreduce.lib.output.FileOutputFormat;
import org.apache.hadoop.io.NullWritable;
```

The name of the job is configured as the lattice job and passed as an argument in the job class instance.

```
Job job = new Job(configuration, "latticejob");
```

The input is read from the following path

```
FileInputFormat.addInputPath(job, hdfs/fcainput);
```

Identifying formal concepts is an iterative job and requires the concepts that are generated in the earlier map task. Hence, the mapper and reducer are implemented as ChainMapper and ChainReducer that allow one to use multiple maps and reduce classes in a single map task. In ChainMapper, the classes are invoked in a chained (or piped) fashion, so that the output of the first map task becomes the input to the second map task, and so on until the output of the last map task is written to the buffer storage. The mapper class takes long and text values as an input and provides integer and text as an output. The reducer class accepts integer and text as input and provides the integer and text as output.

```
ChainMapper.addMapper(job, LatticeMapper.class, LongWritable.class,
Text.class, IntWritable.class, Text.class, configuration);

    ChainReducer.setReducer(job, LatticeReducer.class,
IntWritable.class, Text.class, IntWritable.class, Text.class, configuration);
```

The output format of the job is the TextOutput format and the output is written into the following path of HDFS.

```
job.setOutputFormatClass(TextOutputFormat.class);
FileOutputFormat.setOutputPath(job, hdfs/fcaoutput);
```

A sample pseudo code for the mapper class is provided here.
The Mapper class:LatticeMapper.java
package com.hadoop.mr.lattice;

```
import java.io.IOException;
import java.util.HashSet;
import java.util.Map.Entry;
import java.util.Set;
import java.util.StringTokenizer;

import org.apache.hadoop.io.IntWritable;
import org.apache.hadoop.io.LongWritable;
import org.apache.hadoop.io.Text;
import org.apache.hadoop.io.Writable;
import org.apache.hadoop.mapreduce.Mapper;

import com.google.common.collect.ArrayListMultimap;
import com.google.common.collect.ListMultimap;
import com.google.common.collect.Lists;
import com.google.common.collect.Multimap;
import com.google.common.collect.Sets;

public class LatticeMapper extends
        Mapper<LongWritable,Text,IntWritable,Text>{
@Override
    protected void map(LongWritable key, Text value,
        Context context)
                throws IOException,
                InterruptedException {
            Set<Text>attributeSet=newHashSet<Text>();
            Set<Text>objectSet=newHashSet<Text>();
            Set<Text>comparisionSet=objectSet;
            Set<Text>minimumSet=newHashSet<Text>();
    ................
            ................
    }
}
```

The LatticeMapper class extends the mapper class of Hadoop MapReduce and
overrides the map method by taking the inputs using the input format that is specified in the configuration class.

```
public class LatticeMapper extends Mapper
< LongWritable, Text, IntWritable, Text > {

    @Override
protected void map(LongWritable key, Text value,
Context context){
... }
}
```

Similarly, the LatticeReducer class is provided here.
The Reducer class:LatticeReduce.java
package com.hadoop.mr.lattice;
import java.io.IOException;
import java.util.HashSet;

import java.util.Map.Entry;
import java.util.Set;
import org.apache.hadoop.io.IntWritable;
import org.apache.hadoop.io.LongWritable;
import org.apache.hadoop.io.NullWritable;
import org.apache.hadoop.io.Text;
import org.apache.hadoop.io.Writable;
import org.apache.hadoop.mapreduce.Reducer;
import org.apache.log4j.Logger;

import com.google.common.collect.ArrayListMultimap;
import com.google.common.collect.Lists;
import com.google.common.collect.Multimap;
import com.google.common.collect.Sets;

public class LatticeReducer extends
            Reducer<IntWritable,Text,IntWritable,Text> {
        int finalKey = 1;
        //private NullWritable finalKey = NullWritable.get();
        private Text finalValue = newText();
        @Override
        protected void reduce(IntWritable key,
            Iterable <Text> values,
                Context context)
                Throws IOException,
                InterruptedException {
                ....
                ....
            }
}
```
```

The LatticeReducer class extends the reducer class of Hadoop MapReduce and overrides the reduce method by taking the input from the output format of the map class and then writes the output according to the output format that is specified in the configuration class.

```
public class LatticeReducer extends Reducer
< IntWritable, Text, IntWritable, Text > {
@Override
protected void reduce(IntWritable key,
Iterable <Text> values,
Context context)
throws IOException, InterruptedException {
... } }
```

In Table 2.4, an example formal context called the number context is taken as input and the MapReduce job is executed on this context to identify the formal concepts. The formal concepts in Table 2.5 are identified after the execution of the MapReduce job. Figure 2.8 represents the programming model of concept generation in FCA using MapReduce architecture; however, this approach later proved to be inefficient when compared with the FCA implementations using distributed frameworks like Apache Spark and iterative MapReduce framework HaLoop that are discussed in later sections.

The execution of the MapReduce job for the concept generation as shown in Figure 2.8 is given as follows:

- The formal context is read from the HDFS and the least formal concept is calculated.
- The least formal concept and each object are supplied to the mapper; the map phase finds the set of concepts, and the reduce phase processes these concepts to generate the unique concepts and passes on to the ChainMapper.
- The ChainMapper again will calculate some more concepts, and this process will be continued until the greatest formal concept is obtained or the least extent formal concept is found.

Table 2.4 Example formal context for selected numbers between 1 and 10

	Even	Odd	Prime	Perfect square
1		X		X
2	X		X	
3		X	X	
4	X			X
5		X	X	
9		X		X

Table 2.5   Formal concepts generated for the earlier context with its extent and intent

Concept no.	Extent	Intent
1	1,2,3,4,5,9	ϕ
2	2,4	Even
3	1,4,9	Perfect square
4	2,3,5	Prime
5	1,3,5,9	Odd
6	4	Even, perfect square
7	2	Even, prime
8	1,9	Odd, perfect square
9	3,5	Odd, prime
10	ϕ	Even, odd, prime, perfect square

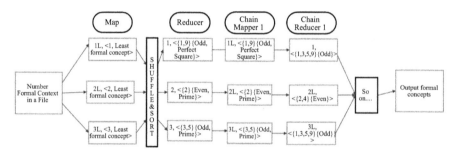

Figure 2.8   Programming model of ConceptGeneration using MapReduce

Every formal context induces a pair of operators, called concept-forming operators. For a formal context (G, M, I) we define concept-forming operators $\uparrow:2^G \rightarrow 2^M$ and $\downarrow:2^M \rightarrow 2^G$ are defined for every $P \in G$ and $Q \in M$ as
$P\uparrow = \{m \in M \mid$ for each $g \in P$ $(g, m) \in I\}$
$Q\uparrow = \{g \in G \mid$ for each $m \in Q$ $(g, m) \in I\}$
$P \uparrow$ represents a set of all attributes shared by all objects from set P and $Q\downarrow$ represents a set of all objects which share all attributes from Q.

A formal concept of formal context (G, M, I) is a pair (P, Q) with $P \subseteq G$, $Q \subseteq M$, $P\uparrow = Q$, $Q\downarrow = P$. For a formal concept (P, Q) in (G, M, I) the sets P and Q are called the extent and the intent of concepts respectively.

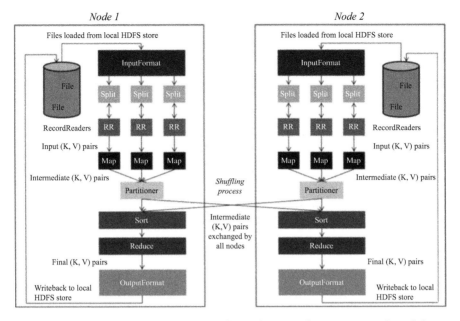

Figure 2.9   Overview of the execution flow of MapReduce in two nodes of the cluster

The least extent containing $A \subseteq X$ is $A^{\uparrow\downarrow}$. The least intent containing $B \subseteq Y$ is $B^{\downarrow\uparrow}$

From the above definition, the least formal concept can be defined as LeastFormalConcept = (LeastIntent, B) = $(B^{\downarrow\uparrow}, B)$

Similarly the least extent formal concept is defined as LeastExtentFormalConcept = $(A, A^{\uparrow\downarrow})$

Figure 2.9 represents the overview of the MapReduce job execution on the TaskTrackers of the Hadoop cluster.

2.3   HaLoop framework

MapReduce is a distributed programming model used for processing large datasets on the data that is in the hundreds of computers without managing concurrency, robustness and scalability as discussed in Section 2.2. Many algorithms can be implemented using the MapReduce framework, but data analysis algorithms that require iterative computations do not work well with MapReduce architecture [32]. Hence, there are some iterative MapReduce frameworks developed to handle iterative applications, the HaLoop framework is one among them. It extends the MapReduce framework and handles the iterative applications efficiently [33]. The cache in the HaLoop is used to

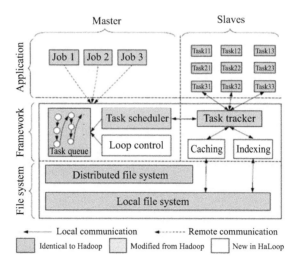

Figure 2.10   Architecture overview of HaLoop framework

cache the data during the first iteration and reuses it in later iterations. Figure 2.10 represents the architecture of HaLoop; it adopts the architecture and distributed computing model from Hadoop. In HaLoop, the existing Hadoop programs can be reused without any modifications and makes them work iteratively with additional simple configurations. The user-defined map and reduce functions can be used as it is HaLoop without any major changes. HaLoop also uses HDFS for storing input and output. HaLoop follows the same process as Hadoop while executing the job by utilizing the JobTracker, MasterNode, DataNodes and TaskTrackers during the execution of the map and reduce phases. Some of the extensions of HaLoop over Hadoop are discussed next.

2.3.1   Programming model of HaLoop

To support iterative applications, HaLoop adopts the same programming model of Hadoop MapReduce. The map and reduce phase execution in HaLoop takes place exactly the same way as they do in Hadoop except that the map and reduce function computations will take place in a loop. The loop will continue until the user-specified termination condition becomes true. In HaLoop, the user has to define map and reduce functions, and both the map and reduce functions take a (key, value) pair as an input. Like in Hadoop, the output of the map function will be input to reduce functions and produce final output. The loop controller in HaLoop will take care of the execution of map and reduce functions in a loop body. Every iteration comprises one or more MapReduce steps and constructs a loop body.

2.3.2   Task scheduling in HaLoop

The task scheduler in HaLoop is designed to perform potentially better than the schedulers in Hadoop. The main focus of HaLoop scheduler is to take care of scheduling the tasks that require the same data to be executed on the same node. While processing iterative applications, HaLoop scheduler locates the tasks that require data which is cached locally and this feature is called the inter-iteration locality. The scheduler in HaLoop will maintain a track of data partitions that are processed by the map and reduce functions on each slave node and use the information for scheduling subsequent tasks to accomplish inter-iteration locality. Every slave node in HaLoop will have a fixed number of slots for executing map and reduce tasks. The slave nodes will send the heartbeat messages to the master about the availability of the slave node, the master then decides whether to schedule a task or not on the slave nodes based on the availability status in heartbeat messages. If all the slots are occupied by map or reducer tasks, then JobTracker will consider that slave node as fully loaded and reassign the tasks to the slave nodes that are available. Task execution, managing cache and indices are taken care by the TaskTrackers in HaLoop.

2.3.3   Caching in HaLoop

One of the prominent features in HaLoop is caching. During the first iteration of every application, HaLoop creates indexed local caches. The indexed local caches will contain the data that is required across various iterations of the application execution. This will help one to reduce loading of I/O cost, shuffling and grouping of data in later iterations. HaLoop supports three types of cache: mapper input cache, reducer input cache, reducer output cache. During initial iterations, the mapper input cache is used to avoid nonlocal data reads. If a mapper performs nonlocal data read during its first iteration, the input split will be cached in the disk of the mapper's physical machine. Then the inter-iteration locality takes place and all mappers will read the data from local. The reducer input cache is designed to avoid reprocessing of the same data with the same mapper in multiple iterations. The reducer inputs will cache across all the reducers and create a local index for the cache data. The local caches at both map and reduce phase decrease the data transfer and data shuffling significantly and improve the overall performance of the MapReduce job.

2.3.4   Fault tolerance

HaLoop's fault tolerance is the same as Hadoop fault tolerance with an extra care for supporting iterative applications. Computational failures in iterative programming models introduce the risk of recursive recovery, where a failure in one step in a particular iteration leads to re-execution of all the preceding steps in the same iteration or all previous iterations. HaLoop fault tolerance is designed to handle recursive recovery efficiently. Upon a failure, the inter-iteration cache will be reconstructed again from intermediate outputs, and this will be helpful to re-execute the failed tasks from the step where the failure occurred instead of starting the iteration from the first step. Also the failures of DataNodes and TaskTrackers in HaLoop are the same as failure in Hadoop. Chunduri and Cherukuri used HaLoop approach to one of the widely used unsupervised machine learning technique FCA to generate the formal concepts [34] which is discussed in later sections.

2.3.5   Concept generation in FCA using HaLoop

The concept generation in FCA is an iterative task, and adoption of MapReduce did not give enough benefit since MapReduce has few limitations while executing iterative applications. Hence, HaLoop is used to generate formal concepts in FCA and the algorithm is named as HaLoopUNCG algorithm. The fundamentals to implement HaLoopUNCG algorithm using HaLoop framework is to design map and reduce functions for concept generation.

- Initially the least formal concept $(B^{\downarrow\uparrow},B)$ and the relative complement set (O-$B^{\downarrow\uparrow}$) (where O is the total number of objects in FCA) are computed, and the map function is called with each element in relative complement set and least concept as key and value pair.
- Set relative complement set to RC.
- Set least formal concept to (A,B), from second iteration concepts generated (the extent and intent) in first iteration which will be considered as least formal concept.
- The HaLoopUNCG map function is applied on each key, value pair to generate its concepts in each iteration.
- The HaLoopUNCG reduce function aggregates all the generated concepts for all iterations, the desired output.

Figure 2.11 represents the first two iterations of the concept generation algorithm using HaLoopUNCG algorithm. The first iteration starts from least formal concept, for every element in relative complement set; the algorithm finds the neighbors for the least formal concept. The algorithm will cache the concepts generated in this iteration. From the next iteration, relative component set of objects in each concept which is stored in cache will be the key and concept itself is the value. The corresponding neighbor concepts for the taken input concept will be computed and cached. This process will be repeated for *n*-iterations until all the concepts are found or till the least extent is calculated. The UNCG implementations reuse the map and reduce functions of MapReduce approach with slight modifications.

2.4   Twister framework

Twister is another iterative processing framework used to process the iterative tasks using MapReduce efficiently. Twister follows a publisher/subscriber message model for computations and data transfers. By adding programming extensions to the MapReduce model, Twister supports multiple types of data transfers such as broadcast and scatter [35]. Also Twister has a configuration phase called config, where configuration parameters are set for one time and then it uses the same parameters iteratively. This helps in efficient execution of time-consuming MapReduce applications. Iterative MapReduce applications operate on two types of data: static and variable. The static data is used during the start of the each iteration, and the data remains until the execution is completed. The variable data is the output of each iteration and used in the next iterations. During the execution, reading of static data from disk for each iteration is highly inefficient and time-consuming, as the data

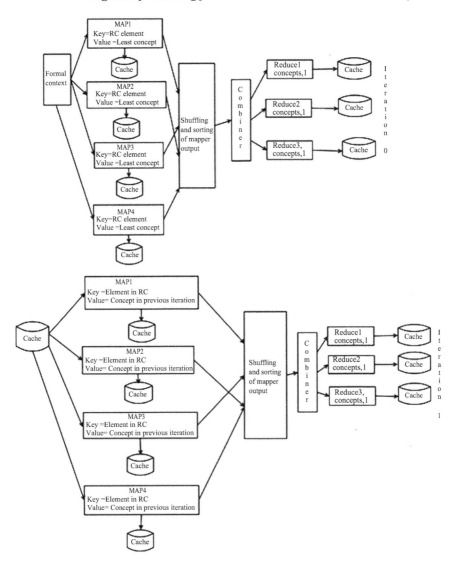

Figure 2.11 Programming model of HaLoop concept generation algorithm

needed for each iteration has to be read from disk every time. Twister addresses this issue by formulating long-running cacheable map and reduces tasks. This reduces the requirement of loading static data every time during each iteration.

2.4.1 Architecture of Twister framework

Twister is a distributed in-memory MapReduce run time. It is an improved version of Hadoop MapReduce and is suitable for iterative applications. It loads blocks of data from local disks of the worker nodes and handles the intermediate data in the worker's distributed memory. The communication and the transfer of data in the form of blocks between nodes are performed via publish/subscribe messaging model. The Twister architecture comprises three main entities:

- client-side driver called Twister driver that is responsible to drive the entire MapReduce computations;
- Twister Daemon running on all of the worker nodes in the cluster;
- a broker network responsible for establishing the messaging.

Figure 2.12 represents the architecture of the Twister framework. Twister initially launches and creates a daemon process on each worker node in the cluster then establishes a link between worker node and broker network to receive data and communication commands. The daemons of workers take care of controlling map and reduce tasks, preserving a pool for workers to perform any map or reduce tasks, informing status, and finally answering any control actions. The Twister driver client offers an API to users for translating the generated calls, and to manage the set of instructions and forwarding the input data messages to the daemons running on the workers using the broker network.

2.4.2   *Fault tolerance in Twister*

The fault tolerance mechanism in Twister is almost similar to that in Hadoop. Like Hadoop, Twister assumes that the failure of that master node is very rare and so there is no support for applications if the master node fails. The communication

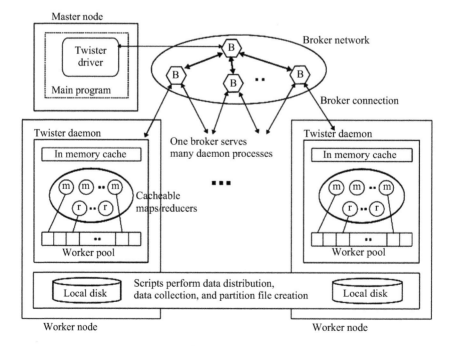

Figure 2.12   Architecture of Twister framework

infrastructure in Twister is independent of fault tolerance. Also, data replication in Twister provides high availability of data during any stage of large MapReduce applications execution.

2.5 Apache Pig

Apache Pig [36] is a high-level platform for creating programs that run on Hadoop. It is an abstraction over MapReduce used to analyze large sets of data represented as data flows. The language that Pig uses is called Pig Latin that helps Pig to execute its jobs in MapReduce and Apache Spark. Pig Latin abstracts the MapReduce programming and makes MapReduce similar to that of SQL. Pig can be extended by implementing user-defined functions (UDFs) using Java, Python and Ruby to support customization. The Pig Latin script is compiled into MapReduce jobs that run on Hadoop. Pig was developed by Yahoo in the year 2006 which is an ad hoc method for creating and executing MapReduce jobs on huge datasets without having the knowledge of Java programming and mainly used for rapid development.

2.5.1 Characteristics of Apache Pig

- **Pigs eat anything:** Pig can process any type of data; it may be structured, relational, flat, nested or unstructured. Pig is also capable of reading data from other sources like Hive and Cassandra.
- **Pigs live anywhere:** Although Pig was first implemented on Hadoop, Pig can be easily integrated with any other frameworks and they can be run on local.
- **Pigs are domestic animals:** Pig is designed to be easily understandable and modifiable by users. Pig Latin programming language is easy to wrap one's head around. In addition, its capabilities can be easily extended by importing various UDFs.
- **Pigs fly:** This motto speaks to the speed with which Pig can process data. It also embodies the ability to help users express complex logic in just a few lines of Pig Latin code.

2.5.2 Components of Apache Pig

- Parser: Parser will handle the Pig scripts initially and do type checking, syntax checking of the script and other miscellaneous checks. The output of the Pig parse will be a directed acyclic graph (DAG) representing Pig Latin statements and logical operators. In the Parser output DAG, the logical operators of the script represent as nodes and data flows represent edges.
- Optimizer: The optimizer takes the logical plan (DAG) to carry out the logical optimizations such as pushdown and projection.
- Compiler: The compiler is used to compile the optimized logical plan to a series of MapReduce jobs.
- Execution engine: The MapReduce jobs are submitted in a sorted order and executed on Hadoop to produce desired results.

2.5.3   Pig data model

Pig supports the following four complex data types:

- Atom: a simple atomic value (int, long, double, string)
- Tuple: a sequence of fields that can be any of the data types
- Bag: a collection of tuples of potentially varying structures

    A bag is an unordered collection of tuples with a possibility of duplicate data models present in Pig. While grouping, bags are used to store collections. Typically the size of the bag is almost the size of the local disk, which means the size of the bag is limited. When a bag is full, then Pig will spill the bag into local disk and keep only some parts of the bag in memory. There is no necessity that the complete bag should fit into memory. We represent bags with "{}".
- Map: An associative array. The key of the map must be a char array and the value can be of any type.

    Pig supports all the widely used data types. Table 2.6 shows the data types that are supported in Apache Pig.

2.5.4   Word count application using Apache Pig

The next Pig Latin script is the word count script implemented using Apache Pig. The MapReduce word count program requires the implementation of JobConfiguration, mapper and reducer class, but the Pig Latin script does not require all of them.

```
–To Load input from the file named "words", and call the single field in the
record 'line'.
input = load 'words' as (line);
– TOKENIZE splits the line into a field for each word.
– flatten will take the collection of records returned by ToKENIZE and
produce a separate record for each one, calling the single
– field in the record word.
words = foreach input generate flatten(TOKENIZE(line)) as word;
– Now group them together by each word.
grpd = group words by word;
– Count them.
cntd = foreach grpd generate group, COUNT(words);
– Print out the results.
dump cntd;
```

```
Input: Apple is a fruit
Apple is a company
Hadoop is a framework
```

Output:
Apple, 2
is, 3
a, 3
fruit, 1
company, 1
Hadoop, 1
framework, 1

2.6   Apache Mahout

Apache Mahout [37] is a scalable machine learning library implemented on top of Hadoop that has capabilities of distributed fitness function for evolutionary programming. Mahout libraries are scalable to support applications that require large volumes of data.

2.6.1   Apache Mahout features

In this section, the primary features of Apache Mahout are listed.

- For performing data mining tasks on huge volumes of data, Mahout has a ready-to-use framework that lets the developers to develop applications and to analyze large volumes of data in a fast pace.
- The Mahout library has implementations of several MapReduce-enabled implementations for clustering, classification, collaborative filtering algorithms, matrix and vector libraries.

Some examples are as follows: *k*-means, fuzzy *k*-means, frequent item-set mining, complementary naïve Bayes and naïve Bayes.

2.6.2   Applications of Mahout

Mahout is used in several domains for various applications. All the big technology giants like Facebook, Microsoft, Twitter are using Mahout for various Big data use cases.

Table 2.6 Pig data types

Data type	Description	Example
Int	Signed 32-bit integer	10
Long	Signed 64-bit integer	20l
Float	32-bit floating point	10.2f
Double	63-bit floating point	10.2
Chararray	Character array in unicode UTF-8 format	Big data
Bytearray	Byte array	Even, perfect square
Boolean	Boolean	True/false (case insensitive)

- Mahout recommender engine algorithm is used by Foursquare to find out entertainment and food places available in a given area.
- Twitter is using Mahout libraries for interest modeling applications.
- Yahoo is using Mahout libraries for pattern mining applications.

2.7   Apache Sqoop

Apache Sqoop [38] is an interface used to transfer data between Hadoop and structured data sources such as RDBMS. Sqoop is implemented in Java and can be easily integrated with Big data processing frameworks like MapReduce, Hive and Pig. Generally, Sqoop is called **SQL to Hadoop and Hadoop to SQL**. These are called Sqoop import and Sqoop export.

2.7.1   *Sqoop import*

The import in Sqoop is used to import tables from RDBMS to HDFS. Each row in a table is treated as a record in HDFS and all records are stored as text data in text files or as binary data in Avro or Sequence files.

```
The command used to import data from database to sqoop is
$ sqoop import
–connect jdbc:mysql://localhost/userdb
–username root
–table emp –m 1
```

The previous command is used to import the employee table from MySQL local database to HDFS. The following argument can be passed to the previous command if we want to export data to a specific directory.

```
–targetdir < new or exist directory in HDFS >
```

To import only certain rows of the data, the following argument can be passed.

```
where < condition >
eg: $ sqoop import
–connect jdbc:mysql://localhost/userdb
username root
table emp
m 1
where "salary >'10000'"
target-dir /wherequery
```

The previous example imports employee data from the emp table whose salary is greater than 10,000.

2.7.2 Export from Sqoop

The export in Sqoop is used to export files from HDFS to database tables. In order to export the data, the tables in the target database must exist. The input files are read and parsed into set of records with a user-provided delimiter. The next command will export the emp table from HDFS to SQL:

```
$ sqoop export
connect jdbc:mysql://localhost/db
username root
table employee exportdir emp_data
```

Table 2.7 shows the list of databases that Apache Sqoop is currently supporting, and Figure 2.13 shows the pictorial representation of imports and exports in Sqoop.

2.8 Apache Flume

Apache Sqoop is used to transfer structured data between data sources and Hadoop but it does not have the capability to handle unstructured data or streaming data. To address this limitation, Apache Flume [39] is developed. Flume is a simple, robust, reliable, fault tolerant and flexible tool for data ingestion from various data sources and stream engines like web servers, Twitter streaming and social media data.

2.8.1 Advantages of Flume

There are many advantages of Flume and some of them are listed in this section.

- Using Apache Flume, data can be stored into centralized data stores like HBase and HDFS.
- When data producers are producing excess data then Flume controls the flow and provides a steady flow of data to the data destination, i.e., centralized data stores.
- Flume supports the feature of contextual routing.

Table 2.7   Databases that support Sqoop import and exports

Database	Version	Direct support?	Connect string matches
HSQLDB	1.8.0+	No	jdbc:hsqldb:*//
MySQL	5.0+	Yes	jdbc:mysql://
Oracle	10.2.0+	No	jdbc:oracle:*//
PostgreSQL	8.3+	Yes (import only)	jdbc:postgresql://
CUBRID	9.2+	No	jdbc:cubrid:*

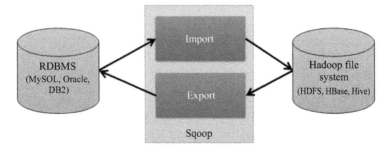

Figure 2.13   Imports and exports in Sqoop

- Flume guarantees the reliable message delivery. The Flume transactions are channel-based. For every message, two transactions, one sender and one receiver are maintained.

2.8.2   Features of Flume

Some of the features of Flume are given in this section.

- Flume collects the log data from multiple web servers and ingests into centralized data stores like HBase and HDFS efficiently in batch mode, as well as in real time.
- Using Flume, one can import larger volumes of event data generated from various social networking applications like Facebook, Twitter and e-commerce applications like Amazon.
- Flume supports multi-hop flows, fan-in fan-out flows and large set of sources and destinations types.
- Flume scales horizontally.

2.8.3   Components of Flume

As shown in Figure 2.14, the data is generated by the data generators and the Flume agents running on each data generator collect the data. The collected data is aggregated and transferred into centralized data stores like HDFS, HBase. Figure 2.15 describes the components of Apache Flume.

- Flume event: An event is the basic unit of the data transported inside Flume. It contains a payload of byte array that is to be transported from the source to the destination accompanied by optional headers.
- Flume agent: An agent is an independent daemon process (JVM) in Flume. It receives the data (events) from clients or other agents and forwards it to its next destination (sink or agent). Flume may have more than one agent. Following diagram represents a Flume agent.
- Source: Source collects the data from the data generators and sends it to one or more channels in the form of events. Source is a component of Flume agent. Apache Flume supports several types of sources and each source receives events from a specified data generator.

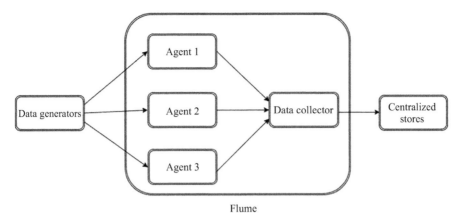

Figure 2.14   *Architecture of Apache Flume*

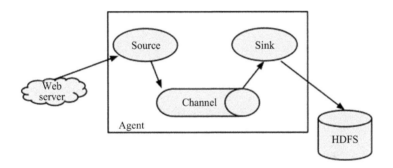

Figure 2.15   *Data flow model in Apache Flume*

   Some examples are as follows: Avro source, Thrift source, Twitter 1% source, etc.

- Channel: A channel is a transient store used to receive the events from the source and buffers them till they are consumed by sinks. It acts as a bridge between the sources and the sinks. These channels are fully transactional and they can work with any number of sources and sinks.

   Some examples are as follows: JDBC channel, File system channel, Memory channel, etc.

- Sink: A sink is used to store the data into centralized stores like HBase and HDFS. It consumes the data (events) from the channels and delivers it to the destination. The destination of the sink might be another agent or the central stores.

   An example is as follows: HDFS sink

- Interceptors: Interceptors are the components of Flume used to inspect/alter the Flume events that are transferred between source and channel.

- Channel selectors: If multiple channels are available, channel selectors in Flume are used to decide which channel can be opted for data transfer. Flume supports the following two types of channel selectors:
  - Default channel selectors: Default channel selectors replicate all the events in a channel; hence, they are also called replicating channel selectors.
  - Multiplexing channel selectors: Multiplexing channel selectors are used to send events based on the address specified in the header of the event.
- Sink processors: Sink processors are used to create load balance events across multiple sinks from a channel. Sink processors are also used to create fail over paths for the sinks and used to invoke a particular sink from the selected group of sinks.
  Flume can be configured in many types of topologies:
- Single-agent topology: In single-agent topology, a Flume agent can directly send data to its final destination, HDFS.
- Multi-agent topology: In multi-agent topology, a Flume agent sends data to intermediate Flume agents that may later send the data to the final destination HDFS (e.g., web services and intermediate agents).
- Replicating topology: In replicating topology, the events can be replicated by Flume. Data can be sent to batch processing systems or archival or storage or even real-time systems.

2.9   Apache Oozie

Apache Oozie [40] is a server-based workflow scheduling system used to run and manage Hadoop jobs in a distributed environment. Oozie combines multiple complex jobs and run sequentially to accomplish a bigger task. The control flow nodes in Oozie workflow defines the start and end of the workflow and controls the execution path of the workflow. Action flow nodes in the workflow are used to start the task execution. Oozie is implemented in Java and supports different types of actions like MapReduce job execution, Pig execution and HDFS. Following three types of Oozie obs are created:

- Oozie Workflow jobs: Oozie Workflow jobs are used to specify the sequence of actions to be executed. They are represented as DAGs.
- Oozie Coordinator jobs: Oozie Coordinator jobs contain workflow jobs triggered by availability of time and data.
- Oozie Bundle: Oozie Bundle can be referred to as a package of multiple coordinator and workflow jobs.

Figure 2.16 shows an example Oozie workflow that has MapReduce, Spark and Pig jobs along with Hive query.

2.10   Hadoop 2

Apache Hadoop 2 [5] is the second version of Hadoop framework used for distributed data processing. In Hadoop 1, MapReduce programming model is used to

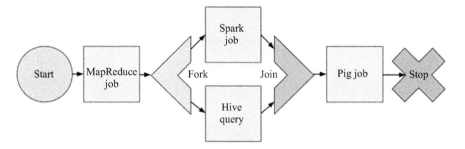

Figure 2.16   Oozie workflow with MapReduce and Spark jobs

take care of both Hadoop cluster resource management along with data processing, because Hadoop 1 is limited to work only with applications that can be implemented only in MapReduce. Hadoop 2 overcomes this problem by separating the cluster resource management with distributed data processing. Hadoop 2 introduces a new layer called yet another resource negotiator (YARN) that will take care of cluster resource management and allow Hadoop 2 to work with different data processing frameworks like MapReduce, Apache Spark and message passing interface (MPI). Figure 2.17 shows the difference between architecture of both Hadoop 1 and Hadoop 2. Table 2.8 gives an overview of the Hadoop Ecosystem components.

2.11   Apache Spark

There are many distributed computing frameworks with Hadoop MapReduce being one of the most widely used frameworks for Big data processing. However, MapReduce is not well suited for applications that require real-time data processing and applications that require iterative computations. MapReduce needs a lot of data shuffling over the network which increases in communication cost and results in high execution times while working on large datasets [32,41,42]. Apache Spark addresses the bottlenecks in MapReduce with its underlying architecture. Apache Spark is well-suited applications that work iteratively and require access to the same data multiple times. The in-memory computations of Apache Spark increase the execution time ten times faster than Hadoop MapReduce. The architecture and components of Apache Spark are discussed in the next. Apache Spark [7] is an open-source cluster computing framework that enables batch and real-time data processing and supports flexible data processing in memory. Spark provides an interface for programming entire clusters with inherent data parallelism and fault tolerance. Apache Spark is a distributed computing framework used to write programs that run in parallel across many nodes in a cluster of computers. Spark efficiently extends the MapReduce framework to support additional types of computations. Speed is an important factor for processing large datasets, to achieve the required speed, and it performs in memory computations. Spark is also more

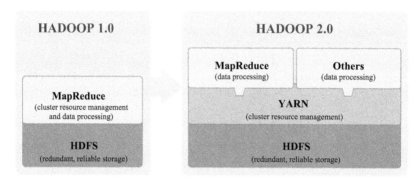

Figure 2.17   Comparison of Hadoop 1 and Hadoop 2

Table 2.8   Hadoop Ecosystem components

Data management	Data access	Data processing	Data storage
Oozie;(workflow monitoring)	Hive(SQL)	MapReduce(cluster management)	HDFS(distributed file System)
Flume;(monitoring)	Pig(dataflow)	YARN(cluster and resource management)	HBase;(column DB storage)
Zookeeper;(management)	Mahout;(machine learning) Sqoop;(RDBMS connector)		

efficient than MapReduce for applications running on disks. Spark is integrated closely with Big data processing frameworks like Hadoop and can access any Hadoop resources and data sources while running. Hence, Spark is widely used in applications of several domains like machine learning [43–47,95–96,99–103], geospatial applications [48], security applications [49] and mobile applications [50]. Spark abstracts the tasks of job submission and execution, resource scheduling, tracking and communication between nodes and the low-level operations that are inherent in parallel data processing. Spark is similar to other distributed processing frameworks like Apache Hadoop as it provides higher-level API for working with distributed data. The idea behind the implementation of Spark is to develop a computing framework for distributed machine learning algorithms and later it is extended to graph processing and stream processing applications. Hence, it is designed to achieve high performance of iterative application, where the same data needs to be accessed multiple times [53]. The high performance of Spark is achieved through data caching in memory, combined with low latency and overhead to launch parallel computational tasks. Spark is used for a wide range of large-scale data processing tasks in machine iterative analytics and machine learning. Spark Core, Spark streaming real-time, Spark MLlib, Spark SQL and Spark GraphX are the main components of Apache Spark. Figure 2.18 represents the Spark Ecosystem.

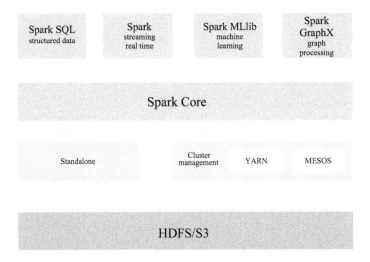

Figure 2.18   Spark Ecosystem

2.11.1   Spark Core

The basic functionality of the Spark is provided by Spark Core. Spark Core includes the components for memory management, task scheduling, interacting with storage systems and fault recovery. It also incorporates other features like resilient distributed dataset (RDD), a fault tolerance collection of elements that operate in parallel. RDDs are the Spark's main programming abstraction. RDDs are a collection of elements that are distributed across many computer nodes and perform the tasks in parallel.

2.11.2   Driver program

The driver program is the heart of Spark job execution process. The driver runs the application code that creates RDDs. The driver program creates Spark Context called the driver. The driver program splits the Spark applications into tasks and schedules the tasks to run on executors in various worker nodes.

2.11.3   Spark Context

Spark Context is another important component of the Spark application and is used as a client in Spark's execution environment. Spark Context is used to get the current status of the application, it creates and manipulates the distributed datasets and manages the Spark execution environment, including running Spark jobs, accessing services such as task scheduler and block manager.

```
val sc = new SparkContext(masternode, applicationName)
```

2.11.4   Spark cluster manager

Spark cluster manager plays a vital role in Spark execution environment. The Spark Context interacts with the cluster manager and gets the resources. It acts like a NameNode in Hadoop. Spark cluster manager keeps track of all the resources and then allocates the resources as per the need, manages the worker nodes and the driver program. Figure 2.19 represents the detailed architecture of Apache Spark.

2.11.5   Spark worker node

Every worker node has executors running inside of them. Each executor will run multiple tasks. The tasks are the fundamental units of the execution. Every worker node also maintains the cache memory that plays a key role to improve the speed of Apache Spark. Each worker node caches the data, and the cached data is used for in-memory computations.

2.11.6   Spark resilient distributed datasets (RDDs)

RDDs are the core components of Apache Spark, primary task of which is to collect the data from data sources and then distribute, partition the collected data across all the nodes in a cluster [92]. Spark RDDs are fault tolerant; this means that if a given node or task fails, the RDD can be reconstructed automatically on the remaining nodes and complete the job. RDDs in Spark operate in parallel on its data. RDDs in Spark can be created using the next snippets.

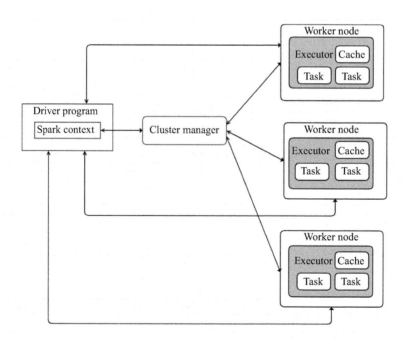

Figure 2.19   Architecture of Apache Spark

```
val datainput RDD=sparkcontext.textFile(inputFilePath)
val datainput RDD=sparkcontext.parallelize(dataList)
```

RDDs in spark support two types of operations: transformations and actions. Information about transformations and actions is given next. Examples of some of the important transformations and actions are given next.

Transformations: Map, FlatMap, Reduce
Actions: count, reduce, saveAsTextFile

Once the RDDs in spark are created, the transformations and actions can be performed on the distributed dataset. A transformation operation in Spark is used to create a new dataset from an existing dataset, whereas an action operation performs some computation on the dataset and returns a value to the driver program. Spark transformations are lazy, meaning that they do not compute their results right away. The transformations are computed when an action requires a result that needs to be sent to driver program. Each RDD maintains a pointer to one or more parents along with the metadata about it, i.e., the type of relationship it has with its parent. When a transformation is called on RDD, the RDD keeps a reference to its parent, which is called lineage. Spark creates a lineage graph with all the series of transformations that are applied. When the driver submits the job, the lineage graph is serialized to the worker nodes. Each of these worker nodes applies the transformations on different nodes and allows an effective fault tolerance by logging all the transformations that are used to build the dataset. If a partition of RDD is lost, the RDD has enough information from the lineage graph to recompute the failed partition, thus lost data can be recovered quickly without requiring the costly recomputation.

2.11.7 Caching RDDs

RDD caching is the most important feature of the Spark. The data will be cached in memory across the cluster. The cache method is used to cache the data and tell Spark that the RDD should be kept in memory. The first time, an action is called on RDD that initiates a computation; the data is read from the disk and stored into memory. This means that the first time an operation is initiated; the time it takes to run the task will be longer because the input is being read from disk. The second time, when the same data is being accessed, the data will be read directly from cache memory. This avoids expensive I/O operation and speeds up the processing time and improves the performance of the algorithm significantly.

2.11.8 Broadcast variables in spark

A broadcast variable in Spark is a read-only variable that is made available from the driver program that runs the Spark Context object in the nodes that perform the computations. In iterative applications, sometimes, every iteration requires the same data multiple times; in such cases, broadcast variables are used to store the data that is required by every iteration.

2.11.9   Spark Datasets

A Spark Dataset is a strongly typed immutable collection of objects that are mapped to a relational schema. The encoders in Dataset API are responsible for converting between JVM objects and tabular representations [51]. The tabular representations in Spark are stored using the Tungsten Binary format [52]. Spark Datasets understand the structure of the data in datasets and help Spark to create more optimal layout while caching datasets. The latest API releases of Spark automatically generate encoders for a wider variety of primitive data types. The usage of Dataset API looks similar to RDD API.

```
Creation of RDD for wikipedia data
val inputLines = sparkcontext.textFile("/wikipedia")
val inputWords = inputLines.flatMap(_.split(" ")).filter(_ != "")
Creation of Dataset from wikipedia data
val inputLines = sqlContext.read.text("/wikipedia").as[String]
val inputWords = inputLines.flatMap(_.split(" ")).filter(_ != "")
```

Datasets in Spark also support most of the transformations that can be performed on RDD. Datasets in Spark take the advantage of built-in functions which is helpful to represent the computational logic with lesser code. Also with the support of built-in functions, the execution will be significantly faster. Figure 2.20 shows the execution time of distributed word count in Spark when executing using RDDs and Datasets. In this example, the Datasets are proven to be faster because of the built-in aggregate count function. And in Figure 2.21, we showed the comparison of the usage of cache memory while executing the distributed word count program using RDDs and Datasets.

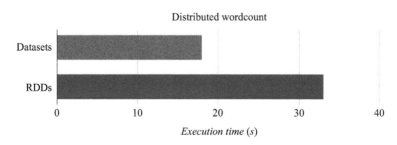

Figure 2.20   Comparison of distributed word count execution times while using RDD and Datasets in Spark

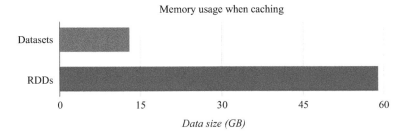

Figure 2.21 Comparison of distributed word count cache memory usage while using RDD and Datasets in Spark

2.11.10 Spark System optimization

The most important concern for Spark System is performance. Many optimization techniques are studied on top of Spark for performance tuning. The major optimization techniques proposed on Spark System are used in this survey.

2.11.10.1 Scheduler optimization

Spark has a centralized schedule that takes care of allocating available resources to the pending tasks according to policies like FIFO, and Fair. The existing policies are not well suitable for the current data analytics [52]. So other scheduling mechanisms are proposed that can handle the task of scheduling efficiently for large-scale distributed application processing.

2.11.10.2 Decentralized task scheduling

With the increase in demand for Big data analytics, the large degree of parallelism and shorter task durations to provide low latency are important factors to any scheduler while scheduling. The existing scheduler in Spark is a centralized scheduler and it is not well suited to achieve low latency and high availability. Sparrow [54] is a decentralized scheduler proposed on top of Spark that provided attractive stability and availability. Sparrow uses the power of two choices technique while running jobs in parallel on a cluster. Sparrow makes efficient scheduling of tasks with the help of these three techniques:

- batch sampling: it reduces the time of the tasks response that is decided by the finishing time of the last task, by placing the tasks in a batch manner instead of placing each task individually;
- late binding is used to provide delays during allocation of tasks, because the length of the server (job) queue results in a poor norm of latency time;
- global policies are enforced on worker machines to support placement constraints of each job and task.

2.11.11 Memory optimization

For the processing frameworks that support in-memory computations, efficient memory usage is one of the most important metrics. Most in-memory computing frameworks are designed using languages that support garbage collection like Java and Scala. There will be a performance overhead while using these languages because of the garbage-collector-induced pause and can be addressed by improving the performance of the garbage collector. The application tasks run on different worker nodes in the Spark cluster, every worker node has its own garbage collection and all the worker nodes communicate data among them. If one node is stuck in garbage collection phase, all other worker nodes have to wait until the computation of the garbage collection at that node. This pause in garbage collection leads to long wait times and has a great impact on the performance of the application. So, Mass *et al.* [55,56] proposed a holistic runtime system that collectively manages the garbage collector across all the nodes, instead of performing garbage collection at each individual node. The holistic garbage collector system is allowed to perform the centralized garbage collection for every node by considering the application-level optimizations.

2.11.12 I/O optimization

For data-intensive applications in Spark, efficient optimization techniques are required for loading massive amounts of data and then transmitting data among worker nodes during task execution. Following are the optimization techniques that are used for I/O optimization in Spark.

2.11.12.1 Data compression and sharing

Spark supports in-memory data sharing for tasks within an application, but not for the tasks within different applications. This leads to reading of the same data from the disk for each new task. Li *et al.* [57,58] proposed Tachyon to address this issue. Tachyon is a distributed in-memory file system that achieves reliable data sharing among tasks from different applications. Also, to enable more data storage in memory, Rachit *et al.* [59] proposed Succinct in Tachyon that compresses input data and increases memory storage. Succinct also provides a facility to execute queries on the compressed data and reduces decompression time.

2.11.12.2 Data shuffling

Network I/O and disk I/O are two performance bottlenecks for Spark applications. Shuffle phase enables many-to-many data transfer for tasks across machines in a worker node. However, this consumes more network bandwidth and degrades performance. Zhang *et al.* [93] figured that the bottlenecks in shuffle phase are large-disk I/O operations and proposed Riffle to address the I/O issues. Riffle merges fragmented intermediate shuffle files into large block files and converts small and random disk I/O operations into large and sequential ones.

2.11.13 Fault tolerance optimization

Yu *et al.* [60] proposed an algorithm for fault tolerance optimization in spark. Being an in-memory computing a framework, Spark may lose data when a node failure occurs and increases the execution time. The checkpoint algorithm by Yu *et al.* [60] considers the computational cost, the operation complexity, length of the RDD lineage and the size.

2.11.14 Data processing in Spark

As a data processing framework, Spark supports various data computations like Stream processing, graph processing, machine learning and deep learning models.

2.11.14.1 Spark streaming

Spark streaming is one of the components of the Spark Ecosystem that allows processing of scalable, high-throughput, fault-tolerant stream processing of live data streams from various data sources like Amazon Kinesis, Flume and Kafka. Spark streaming transforms streaming computations into a series of micro batch computations and divides the live data streams into batches of a predefined interval and then considers each batch of data as RDD. This makes Spark streaming integration easy with the other components in the Spark Ecosystem. Also Spark streaming provides fault tolerance characteristics. There are three phases in Spark streaming:

1. Gathering: It is the process of gathering streaming data. The data is gathered from
   i. basic sources: these are the sources that are available in streaming context API such as socket connections and file system;
   ii. advanced sources: these are the sources like Flume, Amazon Kinesis and Kafka from which data can be gathered.

2. Processing: during the processing phase, computations are performed on the gathered data.
3. Data storage: the processed data is pushed into a file system. Spark streaming provides a high level of data abstraction known as discretized stream or DStream. DStream in Spark signifies the continuous stream of data. It can be created in two ways, either from high-level operations on other DStreams or from sources like Kafka, Flume and Kinesis.

The next lines of code show the SparkStreaming Context configuration to read data from data streams.

```
import org.apache.spark.streaming._
import org.apache.spark._
val configuration = new SparkConf().setAppName("WordCount")
val ssc = new StreamingContext(configuratio5, Seconds(5))
```

Using this context, the DStream that represents streaming data from a TCP source is specified with a hostname and port. In the next example, localhost is used.

```
val inputLines = ssc.socketTextStream("localhost", 9000)
```

After the configuration of the StreamingContext, it has to be started to begin the computation. The context can be initialized using

```
ssc.start()
```

Similarly, the context can be terminated using

```
ssc.awaitTermination()
```

2.11.14.2   Spark GraphX

Spark supports large graph processing using an API called Spark GraphX [61]. Most of the computing problems concern processing large graphs, as the graph grows larger in scale, the complexity in processing the graphs will become complex. Spark GraphX is a distributed framework proposed for large graph processing developed on top of Spark with the help of optimization techniques proposed. Few of the optimization strategies are mentioned as follows:

- GraphX comes with a wide range of built-in partitioning functions. The vertex collection is hash partitioned by vertex ids and edge collection is partitioned by UDFs. GraphX adopts a vertex cut approach for distributed graph partitioning. GraphX partitions the graph along vertices rather than splitting along edges. The vertex partitioning reduces both communication and storage overhead. Logically, the vertex partitioning corresponds to assigning edges to machines and allowing the vertices to span across multiple machines. The key challenge in efficient graph-parallel computation is when a graph is edge partitioned, joining of vertex attributes with the edges has to be processed efficiently. Because not all partitions will contain edges adjacent to all vertices, GraphX maintains an internal routing table that identifies where to broadcast vertices when implementing the joining required for operations like triplets and aggregate messages. Figure 2.22 represents the vertex and edge cut partitioning of graph in Apache GraphX.
- GraphX uses JVM byte code analysis to determine what properties a UDF can access. This byte code analysis reduces join operations in GraphX.
- There are many specialized graph processing frameworks like Pregel [62] which are implemented on top of GraphX for iterative computations of graphs.

GraphX inherits the fault tolerance techniques from Spark which generally overlooked in most of the graph processing frameworks. Studies also prove that GraphX is one of the most widely used and faster graph processing system when compared to all the existing graph processing frameworks.

2.11.14.3   Features of Spark GraphX

The following features of Spark GraphX are discussed in this section.

- Flexibility: Spark GraphX works with both graphs and computations. GraphX unifies ETL (extract, transform and load), exploratory analysis and iterative graph computation within a single system. We can view the same data as both

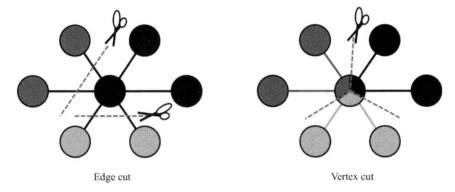

Edge cut   Vertex cut

Figure 2.22   Vertex and edge cut partitioning in GraphX

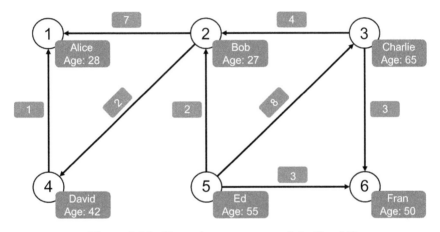

Figure 2.23   Example property graph in GraphX

graphs and collections, transform and join graphs with RDDs efficiently and
write custom iterative graph algorithms using the Pregel API.

- Speed: Spark GraphX provides comparable performance to the fastest specialized graph processing systems. It is comparable with the fastest graph systems while retaining Spark's flexibility, fault tolerance and ease of use.
- Growing algorithm library: GraphX provides access for growing library of graph algorithms. Some of the popular algorithms that one can use are connected components, triangle count, page rank, SVD++, label propagation and strongly connected components.

2.11.14.4   Example of GraphX

Looking at the graph represented in Figure 2.23, we can extract information about
the people (vertices) and the relations between them (edges). The graph here
represents the Twitter users and their followers. For example, Bob follows Davide
and Alice on Twitter.

```
/Importing the necessary classes
import org.apache.spark._
import org.apache.spark.util.IntParam
import org.apache.spark.rdd.RDD
import org.apache.spark.graphx.util.GraphGenerators
import org.apache.spark.graphx._

    //To Display graph vertices:
users (vertices).
val graphVertexRDD: RDD[(Long, (String, Int))] = sparkcontext.parallelize
(vertexArray)
val graphEdgeRDD: RDD[Edge[Int]] = sparkcontext.parallelize(edgeArray)
val   graph:   Graph[(String,   Int),   Int]   =   Graph(graphVertexRDD,
graphEdgeRDD)
graph.vertices.filter case (id, (name, age)) = > age > 40
.collect.foreach case (id, (name, age)) = > println(s"$name is $age")
```

The output for the previous code is as follows:

```
David is 42
Fran is 50
Ed is 55
Charlie is 65
```

2.11.15   Spark machine learning support

Machine learning is a scientific study of algorithms and statistical models used to develop personalized, predictive insights and recommendations without using explicit instructions. Most machine learning models and algorithms are iterative applications; Spark is an efficient in-memory computing system well suited for processing iterative applications. Recently, a lot of research has been done to build effective machine learning libraries on top of Spark. Some of the most widely used Spark libraries for machine learning are discussed next.

2.11.15.1   Spark MLlib

MLlib [63] is a common distributed machine learning library in Spark. It provides many types of scalable implementations of common machine learning algorithms for regression, prediction, classification, clustering and collaborative filtering. MLlib also provides fewer lower-level machine learning optimization primitive APIs.

MLlib supports the implementation of various classic machine learning algorithms, including linear models like support vector machines, logistic and linear regressions [64]. MLlib also provide implementations for naïve Bayes and decision trees for classification and regression problems, FP Growth for frequent pattern mining, *k*-means clustering and principal component analysis for dimensionality reduction. MLlib also provides spark.ml library for practical machine learning pipelines. The implementation of MLlib provides tight and seamless integration of other components within the Spark Ecosystem.

2.11.15.2 Example of MLlib

The example provided here is the uses of the FP-Growth model of the MLlib library, to identify the frequent patterns and association rules in a given input dataset. Authors are using the FP-Growth model in their future works to find the attribute implications and construct an implication in a given formal context, by treating the context as an FP-Growth model.

```
import org.apache.spark.rdd.RDD
import org.apache.spark.SparkContext
import org.apache.spark.sql.SQLContext
import org.apache.spark.SparkConf
import org.apache.spark.sql.SparkSession
import org.apache.spark.ml.fpm.FPGrowth
//import org.apache.spark.mllib.fpm.FPGrowth.FreqItemset
import sqlContext.implicits._
val inputFile ="/hdfs/datafile";
implicit val sc = new SparkContext("local", "attribute-implication")
val data = spark.read.textFile(inputFile)
val dFAttributes = data.map(f => f.trim().split(' ')).toDF("items").cache()
dFAttributes.show(1000)
val fpg = new FPGrowth().setMinSupport(0.0)
val model = fpg.fit(dFAttributes)
println("pritning association rules")
val associationRules = model.associationRules
associationRules.show(20)
```

2.11.15.3 Keystone ML

Keystone ML [89] is an open-source machine learning framework implemented in Scala by AMP labs of UC Berkeley. Keystone ML is designed to simplify the construction of large-scale machine learning applications with Apache Spark. Keystone ML supports high-level logical operators and allows users to specify end-to-end machine learning applications in a single system. The keystone ML is a framework that can be easily scalable depending on the data and problem complexity. Keystone ML has automatic optimization features using the library of ML operators and computing resources [65]. Keystone ML framework is widely used for genomics and solar physics applications.

2.11.16 Spark deep learning support

Deep learning is another class of machine learning algorithms that have been widely used in many fields, including in image processing, natural language

processing and bioinformatics. There are many deep learning frameworks implemented on top of Spark like Deeplearning4j and CaffeOnSpark.

2.11.16.1   Deeplearning4j (DL4j)

DL4j is a deep learning library written in Java and Scala. DL4j implemented a
package called dl4j-spark-ml [11] that integrates Apache Spark and provides the
implementations of deep learning algorithms like restricted Boltzmann machines,
deep belief networks, deep autoencoders, recurrent Nets/LSTMs, convolutional
Nets, Word2Vec, Doc2vec and Glove.

2.11.16.2   CaffeOnSpark

CaffeOnSpark [28] is a deep learning framework implemented in C++ developed
by Yahoo and brings deep learning to Spark clusters by combining features of deep
learning framework Caffe and large-scale data processing framework, Spark.
CaffeOnSpark [66] enables distributed deep learning on a cluster of GPU and CPU
servers. CaffeOnSpark is a distributed extension of Caffe that supports feature
extraction, neural network model training and testing. It also supports distributed
learning using the existing Lightning Memory-Mapped Database files. The Caffe
computing engines are launched on GPU or CPU devices within the Spark executor
by invoking the JNI layer with fine grain memory management. Moreover,
CaffeOnSpark takes Spark + MPI architecture in order to achieve similar performance as dedicated deep learning clusters by using MPI all-reduce style interface
via RDMA network communications.

2.11.17   Programming layer in Spark

Spark is implemented in Scala [67], an object-oriented functional programming
language running on Java virtual machine and calls Java libraries directly in Scala
code. Most of the users working in data science are not very well familiar with
Scala and Java. Hence, Spark also supports languages like R, Python and also high-
level declarative languages like SQL.

2.11.17.1   PySpark

PySpark [68] is a Python API for Spark, which exposes Spark programming model
to Python. It allows users to write Spark applications using Python language a
dynamically typed language that enables RDDs in Spark to have the capability to
store objects of multiple data types. The RDDs in PySpark also support same
functions as that of Scala API, by taking Python collection types as inputs and
returns the Python collection types as output. The PySpark API supports anonymous functions that can be passed as arguments by using lambda functions.

2.11.17.2   SparkR

R [69] is a most popular programming language widely used in numeric analysis
and machine learning domains. Data scientists widely use R for statistical computing and data analysis. SparkR is a light-weight front-end system that incorporates R into Spark and enables R programmers to perform large-scale data analysis.

SparkR [70] supports distributed dataframe implementations for large datasets. SparkR is implemented on the basis of Sparks parallel dataframe abstraction and supports all Spark dataframe analytical operations and functions like aggregation, grouping, mixing in SQL queries and filtering [90].

2.11.17.3   Spark SQL

Spark SQL [71] is a package for working with structured data. It allows data querying via SQL and Hive, a variant of SQL called Query Language (HQL). Spark SQL provides Spark with more information about the structure of both data and computations being performed. This information is mainly used in different ways, such as by using SQL and dataframe API. Figure 2.24 represents the programming interface to Spark SQL. Spark SQL exposes interfaces using JDBC/ODBC, command line interfaces and dataframe API's implemented in Spark supported programming languages.

2.11.17.4   DataFrames in Spark SQL

A spark DataFrames [72] is a distributed immutable collection of data organized in a two-dimensional labeled data structure with named columns like a table in relational database and provides operations to filter, group, process and aggregate the available data. DataFrames are designed to make large datasets processing easier by imposing a structure onto a distributed collection of data and allow high-level abstraction. DataFrame supports reading of data from most popular formats, including JSON, S3, HDFS and many more. DataFrames in Spark supports query optimizer called Catalyst optimizer that is responsible for execution optimization. The Catalyst optimizer in dataframe compiles the operation before any computation starts and builds a physical plan for execution. The optimizer understands the structure and semantics of the data to make intelligent decisions to speed up the computation. Spark applications that use DataFrames with optimization has proven to be more efficient than the applications that use RDDs.

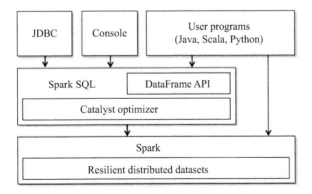

Figure 2.24   Interfaces to Spark SQL and interaction with Spark

Creation of DataFrames from JSON file stored in Amazon S3 bucket
logs = sparkcontext.load("s3n://path/to/data.json", "json")
Creation of DataFrames from Hive table
users = sparkcontext.table("users")

The chart represented in Figure 2.25 shows the runtime performance of the group by aggregation on a 10 million integer pairs on a single machine using both Python and Scala languages. Because of the Catalyst optimizer that enables the optimized execution, applications using Spark DataFrames are faster when compared to the applications that use RDDs.

Table 2.9 represents the comparison of various Big data processing systems based on its various characteristics.

2.11.18 Concept generation in formal concept analysis using Spark

FCA also benefited from Spark while handling large datasets [44]. The concept generation algorithm implemented using Spark is named SparkConceptGeneration algorithm. The SparkConceptGeneration algorithm is a distributed algorithm formalized by a recursive function NeighborConcept (), which lists all the formal concepts starting from the least formal concept [45]. The recursive function NeighborConcept() takes a tuple called a concept as an input that has five parameters. The five parameters are the extent and intent of the concept, isValidNeighbor a Boolean flag, size of the intent and parent index. The parameter isValidNeighbor is used to determine whether a particular input concept can generate the neighbor concept. This parameter is useful for the first step in the canonicity test. The parameter parent index determines the level of the concept in the lattice graph. The value of the parent index is set to "1" for the least formal concept and the value gets incremented for the neighbor concepts that are generated from every concept. The NeighborConcept () function generates all the upper neighbor concepts in different iterations and stops after the greatest formal

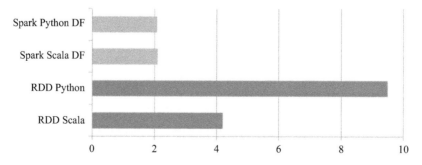

Figure 2.25   Performance of aggregating 10 million into pairs in seconds

Table 2.9   Comparison of Big data processing systems

Framework	Architecture	Execution model	Characteristics	File system	Cache support
Hadoop	Parallel MapReduce tasks	Batch processing	Efficient replication mechanism and fault tolerance	HDFS, S3	No
Twister	Iterative MapReduce tasks	Iterative processing	Designed for long running MapReduce tasks, efficient fail over mechanisms	Local disks	Yes
HaLoop	Iterative MapReduce tasks	Iterative processing	Caching for loop-invariant data, efficient scheduling	HDFS, S3	Partial cache
Apache Spark	Distributed computation using distributed data stores	Batch, iterative and real-time streaming	In memory computation and efficient data recovery using DAGs	HDFS, S3	Yes

concept is found. Every iteration of the recursive process undergoes a two-step cano-nicity test to make sure that the generated concepts are not considered for processing again. The concepts generated in each iteration are saved into Spark's RDD and persist in the cache. The second step of the canonicity checks the cache before processing the concept and decides whether or not to process the concept where the first step is to check whether a concept can have neighbors or not. The SparkConceptGeneration algorithm along with the two-step canonicity test is defined as IsCanonicalMethod in Algorithm 2. Algorithms 3 and 4 implement the concept-forming operators ↑ and ↓. The SparkConceptGeneration algorithm starts by creating a Spark Context and takes a formal context file as an input. The objects and attributes in the input file are separated by a character, a runtime parameter determined on the basis of the type of data. The programming model of SparkConceptGeneration is shown in Figure 2.26.

Algorithm 1 IsCanonical

---

1   Function: isCanonical(concept.intent)
2   Input: intent of the concept, neighbors RDD
3   Output:true/false
4   val neighbors=getPersistentRDDs()
5   val count=neighbors.filter(._2.contains(concept.intent)).count()
6   **if** *count > 0* **then**

7   false
8   **else**
9   true
10 **end**

Algorithm 2 SparkConceptGeneration

Input: *Concept concept*
Output: *neighbor*
1   NeighborConcept(Concept concept){
2   val minSet=Set(contextObjectsRDD)−Set(concept.extent)
3   val minRDD=contextObjectsRDD−concept.extent
4   val neighbors=ϕ
5   **if** *concept:isValidNeighbor* **then**
6   **if** *isCanonical(concept:intent)* **then**
7   parent_index=parent_index+1
8   **for** *x in (contextObjectsRDD−(concept.extent))* **do**
9   B_1=concept.extent $\cup$ (objectConceptFormingOperator(x))
10   A_1=attributeConceptFormingOperator(B_1)
11   **if** *minRDD $\cap$ ((A1−(concept.extent))−(x)) == ϕ* **then**
12   neighbors=neighbors $\cup$ (Concept(A1, B1,
                        true,B1,size,parent_index))
13   neighbors.cache
14   **else**
15   minSet= minSet−x.toSet
16   neighbors=neighbors $\cup$ (Concept(A1, B1,
                        false,B1,size,parent_index))
17   neighbors.cache
18   **end**
19   **end**
20   **end**
21   **for** *neighbor in neighbors* **do**
22   NeighborConcept(Concept concept)
23   **end**
24   }
25 **end**

Algorithm 3 AttributeConceptFormingOperator

---

1   Function: attributeConceptFormingOperator(concept.object)
2   Input: attribute

3 Output:all objects sharing the attribute
4 val objectRDD=sc.parallelize(contextAsMap.get(concept.attribute).toSeq)
5 return objectRDD

Algorithm 4 ObjectConceptFormingOperator

---

1 Function: objectFormingOperator(concept.attribute)
2 Input: object
3 Output:all attributes sharing the object
4 val attributeRDD=sc.parallelize(contextInverseAsMap.get(concept.attribute).
toSeq)return attributeRDD

2.12 Big data storage systems

In the Big data era, data is generally stored and managed in distributed file systems, cloud storages and databases. These storage systems should be highly available during the application processing. This section gives an overview on widely used Big data storage systems.

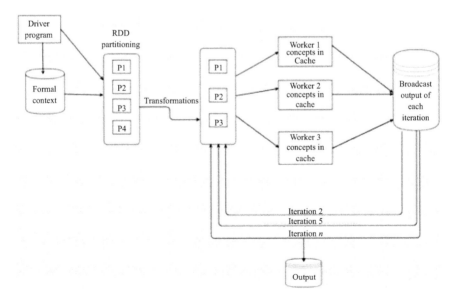

Figure 2.26 Programming model of Spark ConceptGeneration algorithm

2.12.1   Hadoop distributed file system

A distributed file system called HDFS distributes multiple copies of data across various machines (DataNodes) which offers fault tolerance and reliability. If a machine having the copy of the file crashes, another replicated data source will provide the same data. HDFS stores file system metadata and application data separately. Hadoop HDFS architecture is a master–slave architecture in which NameNode is called the master node that stores metadata, i.e., number of data blocks, replicas of the data and other details. The slave nodes or DataNodes contain actual data. The HDFS architecture consists of one NameNode and other nodes, called DataNodes. The main aim of HDFS is to achieve high throughput when large sets of data are introduced. The data in HDFS is always consistent because of the data replication mechanism where each block of data is replicated for high availability and address fault tolerance issues [13]. The block replication in HDFS is a three-way replication, where each block of data is always consistent and available in three data nodes at any time. Figure 2.27 represents the architecture of HDFS. The application data is stored in DataNodes and HDFS stores metadata on NameNode. The HDFS namespace is a hierarchy of files and directories that are represented by inodes on NameNode. The metadata information contains file type, permissions on the file, modifications and access times recorded by inode. The content of the file is split into blocks (typical size of a block is 128 MB) and each block is independently replicated across multiple DataNodes in the cluster. The mapping of blocks to DataNodes and the namespace trees is maintained by the NameNode. Each replica of the block in DataNode is represented by two files.

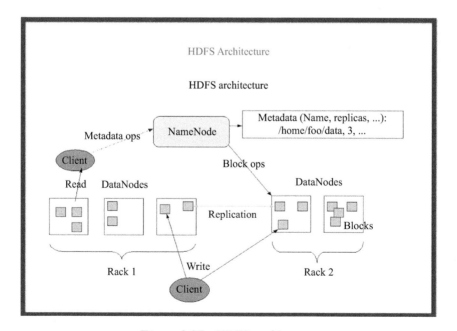

Figure 2.27   HDFS architecture

The first file contains data and the other file contains the metadata of the blocks; these metadata are checksums for the data in it and the generation time stamp. During start-up, each DataNode connects to NameNode and performs a handshake which is used to verify namespace ID and the version of the software the DataNode uses. If the namespace ID of the DataNode does not match with the NameNode, the DataNode shuts down automatically. The namespace ID is stored on all nodes of the cluster. A newly initialized DataNode is permitted to join the Hadoop cluster and receive the cluster's namespace ID; this happens after a handshake and the DataNode registers with the NameNode. A DataNode identifies block replicas in its possession to the NameNode by sending a block report that contains block id, generation time stamp and length of each block replica. The first block report is sent immediately when the DataNode is registered with the NameNode, subsequent block reports are sent every hour. This provides an up-to-date view of the block to NameNode regarding where it is located on the cluster. The DataNodes send heartbeat to the NameNode once every 3 s.

If the NameNode does not receive a heartbeat in 10 min, it will consider that the DataNode is out of service and will decide that all block replicas are unavailable. The NameNode will schedule the creation of new replicas of these blocks on the other available DataNodes. Heartbeats from DataNode carry information about total storage, fraction of storage that is used and remaining empty storage. These statistics collected by NameNode are used for block allocation and load balancing decisions. The NameNode does not send requests to DataNodes directly, instead it uses the replies of heartbeats to send instructions to the DataNode which include commands to replicate blocks to other nodes, remove local block replicas, shutdown the node, reregister and for sending an immediate block report. These commands are used for maintaining the overall system integrity. The NameNode can process thousands of heartbeats per second without effecting its other operations. The following are some of the widely used HDFS commands:

To create directory:
hdfs dfs -mkdir /user/vituser/dir1
To list all the files
hdfs dfs -ls /user/vituser/dir1
To save data in hdfs
hdfs dfs -put /home/vituser/Desktop/sourcedir /user/vituser/targetdir
to get data from HDFS
hdfs dfs -get /user/vituser/targetdir/sourcedir /home/vituser/Desktop
To copy data from local to HDFS
hdfs dfs -copyFromLocal /home/vituser/Desktop/sourcedir /user/vituser/targetdir
To copy data to local from HDFS
hdfs dfs -copyToLocal /home/vituser/Desktop/sourcedir /user/vituser/targetdir

2.12.2   *Alluxio*

Alluxio [73] is an open-source virtual distributed file system that lies between computation and storage in Big data analytics stack. It provides a data abstraction layer for computation frameworks and enables applications to connect to numerous storage systems through a common interface. Alluxio was developed as Tachyon, at AMP labs in UC Berkeley. Alluxio is fault tolerant and uses the lineage graph to recover from failures and to reimplement the tasks [73].

2.12.3   *Amazon Simple Storage Services—S3*

Amazon Simple Storage Services called S3 [75] in short is a cloud-based storage [75] system that stores data in cloud using the techniques of cloud computing and virtualization. This web-based storage service allows users to store and fetch data from the cloud using a rest-style HTTP interface. S3 manages the data in the form of objects with object storage architecture. Objects are organized into buckets and the buckets are owned by AWS accounts. Users can access the data in S3 buckets from Big data processing frameworks by providing S3 URI formats [76].

2.12.4   *Microsoft Azure Blob Storage-WASB*

Azure Blob Storage is a cloud data storage [75] developed by Microsoft to store and fetch data from the cloud. In WASB, data is stored in the form of Binary Large Objects (BLOBs). WASB [77] supports the following three types of blobs:

- the block blobs are used to store streaming cloud objects;
- append blocks, which are the blobs that are optimized for append operators;
- page blobs are used for random writes.

The data in the WASB can be accessed using the URI format is given as **WASB://path**.

2.12.5   *HBase*

HBase [78] is an open-source distributed database system developed from the idea of Google's Bigtable [79] with the features of data compression and in-memory computations. HBase runs on top of Hadoop and leverages the high scalability of HDFS and batch processing capabilities of MapReduce and supports large-scale data analytics by providing real-time data access. HBase is a column-oriented key–value database in which each data table is stored as multidimensional sparse map having time stamp for each cell tagged by column name, column type, start key and the end key.

2.12.6   *Amazon Dynamo*

Developed by Amazon, Dynamo [80] is a decentralized key–value storage system that offers high availability and scalability for Amazon applications. Dynamo adopts the characteristics of both databases and distributed hash tables [81] and supports efficient optimization techniques to achieve high performance. Dynamo uses consistent hashing to divide and replicate data across various machines to overcome in homogeneous data and workload distribution. It also adopts a technology that enables arbitration and decentralized replication synchronization protocols to ensure data consistency during data updates.

2.12.7 Cassandra

Apache Cassandra [82] is open-source highly scalable NoSQL database designed to handle large amounts of data across commodity computers, providing high availability with no single point failure. Cassandra is initially developed by Facebook and later open sourced in 2008. Cassandra adopts the data model from Google Bigtable and Amazon Dynamo. The data in Cassandra is automatically replicated on multiple machines with the configured replication factor [83]. Cassandra also offers an adjustable level of consistency by allowing users to balance trade-off between reads and writes under different circumstances.

Table 2.10 is a comparison of different storage systems that are used to store Big data based on the characteristics of the storage systems. We summarize the storage systems in different ways based on its storage types, where the data is stored, how the data is stored and the license required to use them.

2.12.8 Hive

Apache Hive [84] is a data warehouse software built on top of Apache Hadoop that is used to facilitate reading, writing and managing large datasets stored in distributed data storage systems using SQL. Hive gives SQL-like interface to query data stored in various storage systems like HDFS and HBase. The HiveQL provides the necessary SQL abstractions to integrate SQL-like queries with Java. Apache Hive is initially developed by Facebook and later it is open sourced to Apache.

Table 2.10   Comparison of Big data storage systems

Storage name	File system	Storage location	Data store format	License type
HDFS	Distributed file system	Memory, disk	Document-oriented store	Open source by Apache
Alluxio	Distributed file system	Memory, disk	Document-oriented store	Open source by Apache
Amazon S3	Cloud storage	Disk	Object store	Commercial
Microsoft WASB	Cloud storage	Disk	Object store	Commercial
HBase	Distributed database	Disk	Key–value store	Open source by Apache
Dynamo	Distributed database	Disk	Key–value store	Commercial
Cassandra	Distributed database	Memory, disk	Key–value store	Open source by Apache

Apache Hive supports analysis to data stored in storage systems like Hadoop HDFS, Amazon S3 and Alluxio. The following are the features of Apache Hive:

- Hive introduces data indexing to provide acceleration, index type includes bitmap index and compaction.
- It supports storage types such as plain text, HBase, RCFil and ORC.
- Operations on compressed data using algorithms DEFLATE, Snappy and BWT.
- It supports built-in user-defined function for data manipulations. UDF's in Hive can be extended to support the business use cases.
- Hive Query Language (HiveQL) that can easily integrate with MapReduce and Apache Spark.

2.13   Distributed stream processing engines

Distributed stream processing engines have been on the rise over the last few years resulting from the increase in data production from various sources. Initially, Hadoop [92] became popular as batch processing engine then users started focusing on stream processing with the increase in demand for real-time data analytics. Spark streaming, Storm and Flunk are the most widely used stream processing frameworks that are discussed in this section.

2.13.1   Apache Storm

2.13.1.1   Architecture of Apache Storm

Apache Storm [8] is reliable and flexible distributed stream processing framework that supports many programming languages. Storm is used to process large real-time data streams in horizontally scalable and fault-tolerant methods with the capability of high ingestion rates. Storm's highly scalable framework adds computing resources linearly to keep up its performance even if the load is increased. Storm also supports master–slave architecture. It contains two main components, nodes and components. Storm supports two types of nodes, a master node and worker node. A master node executes a daemon called Nimbus that is responsible for assigning tasks to the machine and monitor performance. Worker nodes run the daemon called Supervisor. Supervisor assigns tasks to other nodes and operates them as per the need. Supervisors start one or more worker processes called workers that run in parallel to process the input. Figure 2.28 represents the architecture of Apache Storm with one master node and five worker nodes. The Nimbus process will run on the master node and a supervisor process will run on each worker node. The worker nodes read the input from database or a file system and similarly write the output to a database.

Apache Storm contains four components that are shown in Figure 2.29.

1. Tuple: The primary data structure in Storm. Tuples are the list of ordered elements that support all data types.
2. Stream: Stream is the unordered sequence of Tuples.

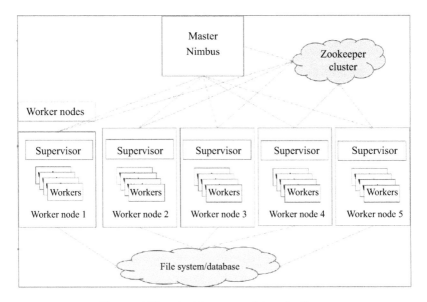

Figure 2.28   Architecture of Apache Storm

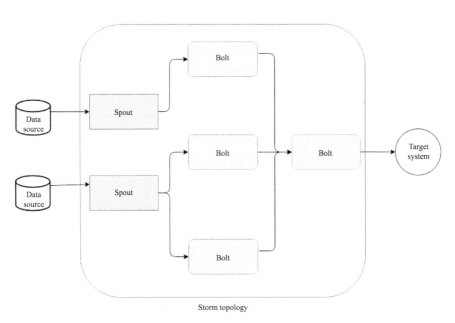

Figure 2.29   Components of Apache Storm

3. Spouts: Spouts are the sources of data streams, e.g.: Twitter streaming API, Kafka queues and many more.
4. Bolts: These are the logical processing units that get data from spouts. Bolts process the data received from spouts or other bolts and produce new output streams. Bolts support operations such as filter, aggregation and joins.

2.13.2   Apache Flink

Apache Flink [9] is a distributed streaming dataflow engine developed by Apache and implemented in Scala and Java for high performance, scalable and accurate real-time applications. Flink is a high-throughput and low-latency engine that executes arbitrary data flow programs in a pipelined and data-parallel manner. Flink supports batch, stream processing programs and iterative applications. Flink works on Kappa architecture that has a single processor stream that treats input as a stream and processes the data in real time. The key concept in Kappa architecture is to handle both batch and real-time data through a single stream processing engine. The architecture of the Apache Flink is presented in Figure 2.30. Program is the code that runs on the Flink cluster. The client is responsible for taking programs, to construct the job dataflow graph and then passing it to the JobManager and retrieve the job results. The JobManager is responsible for creating the execution graph after receiving the job dataflow graph from the client. JobManager also assigns tasks to TaskManager and supervises the job execution. Every TaskManager has allocated with slots to run their tasks in parallel and sends the status of the tasks to the JobManager.

Apache Flink supports the fault tolerance mechanism based on distributed checkpoints and savepoints. A checkpoint is an automatic, asynchronous snapshot of the state of an application and its position in a source stream. When a failure occurs, the Flink program will automatically recover and resume processing from

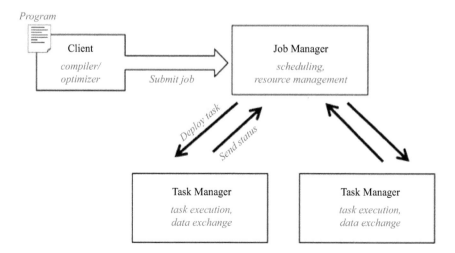

Figure 2.30   Apache Flink architecture

the last completed checkpoint, ensuring that Flink maintains "exactly-once" state semantics within an application, i.e., each incoming event affects the final result only once. Savepoints are manually triggered checkpoints. A user can generate a savepoint, stopping a running Flink program, and then resume the program from the same application state and position in the stream. Savepoints enable updates to a Flink program or a Flink cluster without losing the application's state.

2.13.2.1 Apache Kafka

Initially developed by Linkedin and later open sourced to Apache Software Foundation, Apache Kafka [27] is a reliable, durable and scalable open-source distributed publish–subscribe messaging framework with high throughput. Apache Kafka contains a robust queue that can let users to pass messages from one end point to other and can handle large volumes of data.

2.13.2.2 Architecture of Kafka

Figure 2.31 represents the architecture of Apache Kafka and the following are the main components in the Kafka system:

1. Topics: Topics store the data and generally topics in Kafka are split into partitions.
2. Partition: Partitions in Kafka are a set of equal size segment files that contain sequence of messages in immutable order. Each topic in Kafka is assigned with at least one partition to handle any volume of data.
3. Partition offset: Each data partition have unique sequence id called offset.
4. Replicas of partition: Replicas are the copies of the data partitions used to prevent data loss. Partition replicas cannot read or write data.
5. Brokers: Brokers are systems responsible for maintaining the data that is published. Each broker can be assigned with 0 or more partitions per topic. Let the number of brokers be N and number of partitions in a topic be N, then each broker will get one partition. If the number of brokers N is more than the number of partitions in a topic, then the N first brokers will have one partition

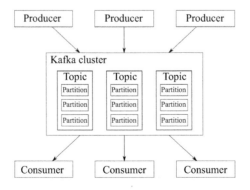

Figure 2.31   Architecture of Apache Kafka

and the remaining brokers will not have any partitions for a particular topic. If the number of partitions is less than the number of brokers, each broker will have more than one partition. This is not recommended due to unequal load distribution among brokers.

6. Kafka cluster: Kafka systems with more than one broker are called Kafka clusters.
7. Producers: Producers are the systems that publish messages onto topics. Every time a producer publishes a message to a broker, the broker simply appends the message to the last segment file. Producers can also send messages to partitions of their own choice.
8. Consumers: Consumers are the systems that consumers message from the topics. Consumers can be subscribed to one or more topics.
9. Leader: Leader node is responsible for all read and write operations within a partition. Each partition has one leader.
10. Follower: Followers are the nodes that follow the leader. If a leader fails, then one of the followers will become leader. A follower acts as normal consumer, pulls messages and updates its own data store Kafka that can be easily integrated with external stream processing frameworks like Apache Storm and Apache Flink. Kafka system guarantees no downtime and no data loss while using it to process large datasets.

Table 2.11 represents the comparison of various stream processing frameworks based on its architectures.

2.14   Apache Zookeeper

Zookeeper is a distributed coordination service that helps one to manage large distributed systems [85]. Zookeeper follows client–server architecture where server nodes provide services and clients are the nodes that make use of those services.

Table 2.11   Comparison of stream processing systems

Streaming engine	Data processing	Stream processing	Flow of data	Scalability	Latency
Spark	Batch and stream processing	Micro batch streaming	DAG	Highly scalable	Low latency
Storm	Stream processing	One by one event processing	DAG	Supports scalability	Extremely low latency
Flink	Batch and stream processing	Process streams for workloads like batch, micro batch and SQL stream	Cycle dependency graphs	High scalability	Low latency and high throughput

Zookeeper exposes client libraries using the applications that make calls to use Zookeeper services. Every client should import the client library to communicate with the Zookeeper nodes. In Zookeeper, all systems store a copy of the data. Zookeeper servers run in stand-alone and quorum modes. When the server is running in stand-alone mode, it means that there is only a single server and Zookeeper state is not replicated. Quorum mode supports a group of Zookeeper servers known as the Zookeeper ensemble; the ensemble replicates the state and serves the client requests together. Zookeeper helps to maintain naming, group services for distributed applications and configuration information. Zookeeper imposes different protocols on cluster so that the applications cannot implement on its own. It provides a single coherent view of multiple machines. Figure 2.32 shows the architecture of Zookeeper. It contains three types of machines:

1. Servers: The servers monitor the clients. When a new client is connected, it sends an acknowledgment. When a client communicates with the server and if the server does not respond, then the client will automatically redirect the message to another server.
2. Client: Clients are the nodes in distributed application cluster used to access information from the server. Each client in the cluster sends a message to server at frequent intervals of time to inform server that it is alive and available.
3. Leader: One of the servers in the architecture is named Leader. It passes all the information to clients and also acknowledges that the server is alive. The Leader is a fault-tolerant server that automatically recovers if any of the connected nodes failed.

2.14.1   The Zookeeper data model

The Zookeeper data model in Figure 2.33 follows a hierarchical namespace where each node is called ZNode. Each node in the namespace contains the data and the child nodes. It is like a file system that allows a file also to be a directory. The paths to ZNodes in Zookeeper data model are always expressed as canonical, slash separated and absolute paths. Every ZNode in Zookeeper maintains a stat structure

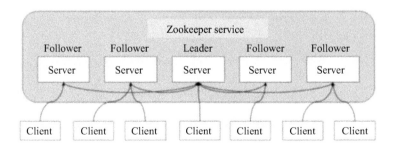

Figure 2.32   Apache Zookeeper architecture

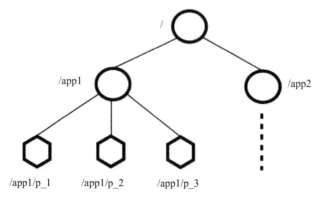

Figure 2.33   Zookeeper data model

that includes the time stamps and version number of data changes. The version number along with time stamps allow Zookeeper to validate the cache and to coordinate updates. For every data change in ZNode, the version number will be increased. Whenever a client retrieves data from ZNode, it also receives the version number of the data. Also, when a client is trying to update or delete the data, the version of the data of ZNode it is updating or deleting has to be supplied; if the version of the data that is supplied does not match the actual version, the update will fail. ZNodes have the following characteristics, as they are the main entities that a program access:

- Watches: Clients will set watches on the ZNodes, and these watches will be triggered when there is a data change on the ZNode and then the watch will be cleared. Zookeeper will send a notification to the client when a watch is triggered. A watch is a onetime trigger that is sent to the client.
- Access to data: The data stored at each ZNode in a namespace is read and written atomically. Reads get all the data in a ZNode and write replaces all the data.
- Ephemeral nodes: As long as the session that created the ZNode is active, Ephemeral ZNodes exist and they will be deleted when the session ends. Because of this behavior, Ephemeral nodes are not allowed to have child ZNodes.
- Sequential nodes: These are the ZNodes that can be accessed by assigning the path to the ZNode by adding a 10-digit sequence number to the original name.

2.14.2   ZDM—access control list

ZNodes in Zookeeper are controlled by access control lists (ACLs) in Zookeeper. ACL is made up of pair of (Scheme: id, permission). The following are the built-in schemes in Zookeeper.

Zookeeper schemes:
world has a single id, anyone that represents anyone.
auth represents any authenticated user, doesn't use any id.
digest uses a **username:password** string to generate MD5 hash which is then used as an ACL ID identity. Authentication is done by sending the username: password in clear text.
When used in the ACL the expression will be the following
username:base64 encoded SHA1 password digest.
host uses the client host name as an ACL ID identity. The ACL expression is a hostname suffix. For example, the ACL expression,
host:corp.com matches the ids host:hosta.corp.com and host:hostb.corp.com, but not host:hostb.store.com.
ip uses the client host IP as an ACL ID identity. The ACL expression is of the form addr/bits where the most significant bits of address are matched against the most significant bits of the client host IP.
ACL Permissions:
READ: To get data from a node and also lists all of its children
ADMIN: Admin is used to set permissions
WRITE: To set or write data for a node
CREATE: Used to create a child node
DELETE: Used to delete a child node

The Zookeeper client libraries are available in two languages: Java, C and users can use the services offered by Zookeeper using the Java or C client libraries.

2.15 Open issues and challenges

In this section, we discuss the research challenges and opportunities for Big data processing systems.

2.15.1 Memory management

Memory is an important resource while dealing with large-scale applications. The proper configuration of memory required to run large-scale applications is non-trivial for performance improvement. Since most of these frameworks use JVM's, the overhead of JVM garbage collection is an overhead. Mass *et al.* [54,55] have detailed a study of GC's impact on distributed environment. The proper GC tuning plays an important role in performance optimization. There is a lot of research in early stages on efficient memory management usage for distributed frameworks and applications like Tungsten are developed to address these issues.

2.15.2 Failure recovery

MapReduce provides fault tolerance through replication and checkpoints where as Spark achieves failure recovery via lineage recomputation [94]. Both of these failure recovery techniques are cost inefficient as both depend on data replication across network and data storage or for storing the lineage information. It thus remains as an open issue on how to enhance fault tolerance for Big data processing systems. Yu *et al.* [59] proposed a checkpoint-based failure recovery in Spark, but still it is not enough to address the challenges with respect to all the existing Big data processing frameworks. Also, Samuel *et al.* [86] proposed some of the open issues and challenges while adopting Big data.

2.16   Conclusion

Big data analytics has garnered significant interests and contributions from academia and industry because of its ability to process very large datasets. The existing Big data platforms support processing and analytical tools for decision-making through recommendations and automatic detection of abnormal behavior, new trends or anomalies and many more. In this chapter, we have studied various Big data characteristics and the emerging Big data processing frameworks, storage systems and examined the roles they play in Big data analysis. Authors have categorized Big data processing systems based on their features and services provided. Thus, this chapter provides a detailed insight into the architectural strategies and practices that are currently followed in Big data computing. Authors first reviewed the Hadoop Ecosystem in detail, including the MapReduce, iterative MapReduce frameworks. The other components of the Hadoop Ecosystem like Apache Pig, Mahout and data processing tools like Sqoop and Avro are discussed. Then the information about Apache Spark and its components are discussed in detail. Streaming frameworks, storage systems and Zookeeper coordination within distributed systems are also examined. It is expected that this work can be a useful resource for the users of Big data analytics and to users of Big data processing frameworks. In spite of the important developments in the field of Big data, there are also some short comings in the Big data processing frameworks. Most of the time, the short comings are related to framework architecture and techniques. Hence, further research needs to be carried out in various areas, including data organization, domain-specific tools and platform tools in order to create next-generation Big data infrastructures. Hence, issues in the technology and framework architectures in many Big data areas can be further studied and constitute an important research topic.

References

[1]   Pujol, JM., Erramilli, V., Siganos, G., *et al.*: The little engine(s) that could: Scaling online social networks. In Proceedings of the ACM SIGCOMM 2010 Conference, 2010, pp 375–386.

[2]   Wang, L., Lu, L., Prasad, S., Anand, R., Zoheb, V., and AnHai, D.: Muppet: MapReduce-style processing of fast data. Proceedings of the VLDB Endowment, 2012, 5(12), pp 1814–1825.

[3]   Emani, KC., Cullot, N., and Nicolle, C.: Understandable big data: A survey. Journal Computer Science Review, 2015, 17(c), pp 70–81.

[4] Gandomi, A. and Haider, M.: Beyond the hype: Big data concepts, methods, and analytics. International Journal of Information Management, 2015, 35 (2), pp 137–144.

[5] Apache Hadoop. In http://hadoop.apache.org.

[6] Prabhu, C., Chivukula, A., Mogadala, A., Ghosh, R., and Livingston, L.: Big data tools—Hadoop ecosystem, Spark and NoSQL databases. In Big Data Analytics: Systems, Algorithms, Applications, Springer, Singapore, 2019, pp 83–165.

[7] Apache Spark. In https://spark.apache.org/, 2015.

[8] Apache Storm. In https://storm.apache.org/, 2015.

[9] Apache Flink. In https://flink.apache.org/.

[10] Jia, Y., Shelhamer, E., Donahue, J., *et al.*: Caffe: Convolutional Architecture for Fast Feature Embedding. arXiv preprint arXiv:1408.5093, 2014.

[11] Spark package – dl4j-spark-ml. In https://github.com/deeplearning4j/dl4j-spark-ml, 2016.

[12] Amer, A.B., Mohammad, A., and Harb, S.: A Survey on MapReduce Implementations. International Journal of Cloud Applications and Computing, 2016, 6(1), pp 59–87.

[13] Chansler, R., Kuang, H., Radia, S., Shvachko, K., and Srinivas, S.: The Hadoop distributed file system. The Architecture of Open Source Applications, 2012.

[14] White, T., Hadoop: The Definitive Guide. O'Reilly Media, Yahoo! Press, 2009.

[15] Dean, J. and Ghemawat, S.: MapReduce: Simplified data processing on large clusters. In Proceedings of the 6th Symposium on Operating System Design and Implementation, 2004, pp 137–150.

[16] Chu, CT., Kim, SK., Lin, Y., *et al.*: Map-Reduce for machine learning on multicore. In B. Schölkopf, J.C. Platt, and T. Hoffman (Eds.), Proceedings of 19th Conference on Advances in Neural Information Processing Systems, 2010, pp 281–288.

[17] Chunduri, RK., Kumar, CA., and Tamir, M.: Concept generation in formal concept analysis using MapReduce framework. In: International Conference on Big Data Analytics and Computational Intelligence (ICBDAC 2017), 2017.

[18] Reza, BZ. and Gunnar, C.: Dimension Independent Matrix Square Using MapReduce. In http://arxiv.org/pdf/1304.1467v3.pdf, 2014.

[19] Elsayed, T., Lin, J., and Oard, DW.: Pairwise document similarity in large collections with MapReduce. In Proceedings of the 46th Annual Meeting of the Association for Computational Linguistics: Human Language Technologies, 2008, pp 265–268.

[20] Guo, L., Tan, E., Chen, S., Zhang, X., and Zhao, Y.: Analyzing patterns of user content generation in online social networks. In Proceedings of the 15th ACM SIGKDD International Conference on Knowledge Discovery and Data Mining, 2009, pp 369–378.

[21] Friedman, E., Pawlowski, PM., and Cieslewicz, J.: SQL/MapReduce a practical approach to self-describing, polymorphic, and parallelizable user-defined functions. Proceedings of the VLDB Endowment, 2009, 2(2), pp 1402–1413.

[22] Dou, A., Kalogeraki, V., Gunopulos, D., Mielikäinen, T., and Tuulos, V.: Misco: a MapReduce framework for mobile systems. In F. Makedon, I. Maglogiannis, and S. Kapidakis (Eds.), Proceedings of the 3rd International Conference on PErvasive Technologies Related to Assistive Environments, 2010, 32, pp 1–8.

[23] Marozzo, F., Talia, D., and Trunfio, P.: P2P-MapReduce: Parallel data processing in dynamic cloud environments. Journal of Computer and System Sciences, 2012, 78(5), pp 1382–1402.

[24] Tang, B., Moca, M., Chevalier, S., He, H., and Fedak, G.: Towards MapReduce for desktop grid computing. In F. Xhafa, L. Barolli, H. Nishino, and M. Aleksy (Eds.), Proceedings of International Conference on P2P, Parallel, Grid, Cloud and Internet Computing, 2010, pp 193–200.

[25] Chen, R., Chen, H., and Zang, B.: Tiled-MapReduce: Optimizing resource usages of data-parallel applications on multicore with tiling. In Proceedings of the 19th International Conference on Parallel Architectures and Compilation Techniques, 2006, pp 523–534.

[26] Lee, K.H., Lee, Y.J., Choi, H., Chung, Y.D., and Moon, B.: Parallel data processing with MapReduce: A survey. CM SIGMOD Record, 2011, 40(4), pp 11–20.

[27] Apache Kafka. In https://kafka.apache.org/.

[28] Caffeonspark. In https://github.com/yahoo/CaffeOnSpark, 2016.

[29] Vaidya, M.: Survey of parallel data processing in context with MapReduce. Computer Science and Information Technology, 2011, 3, pp 69–80.

[30] Varsha, B.B.: Survey paper on big data and Hadoop. International Research Journal of Engineering and Technology, 2016, 3(1), pp 861–863.

[31] Vibhavari, C. and Rajesh, N.P.: Survey paper on big data. International Journal of Computer Science and Information Technologies, 2014, 5(6), pp 7932–7939.

[32] Pavlo, A., Paulson, E., Rasin, A., *et al.*: A comparison of approaches to large-scale data analysis. In Proceedings of the ACM SIGMOD, 2009, pp 165–178.

[33] Bu, Y., Howe, B., Balazinska, M., and Ernst, M.D.: HaLoop: Efficient iterative data processing on large clusters. Proceedings of the VLDB Endowment, 2010, 3(1), pp 285–296.

[34] Chunduri, R.K. and Kumar, C.A.: HaLoop approach for concept generation in formal concept analysis. Journal of Information & Knowledge Management, 2018, 17(3), pp 1–24.

[35] Ekanayake, J., Li, H., Zhang, B., *et al.*: Twister: A runtime for iterative MapReduce. In Proceeding of the 19th ACM International Symposium on High Performance Distributed Computing, 2010, pp 810–818.

[36] Apache Pig. In https://pig.apache.org/, 2016.

[37] Apache Mahout: Scalable Machine-Learning and Data-Mining Library. In http://mapout.apache.org, 2010.

[38] Apache Sqoop. In https://sqoop.apache.org/.

[39] Apache Flume. In https://flume.apache.org/.

[40] Apache Oozie. In https://oozie.apache.org/.

[41] DeWitt, D. and Stonebraker, M. MapReduce: A major step backwards. The Database Column, 2008, 1.

[42] Stonebraker, M., Abadi, D., DeWitt, D.J., *et al.*: MapReduce and parallel DBMSs: friends or foes?. Communications of the ACM, 2010, 53(1), pp 64–71.

[43] Agarwal, S., Liu, D., and Xin, R.: Apache spark as a compiler: Joining a billion rows per second on a laptop. In https://databricks.com/blog/2016/05/23/apache-spark-as-a-compiler-joining-a-billion-rows-per-second-on-a-laptop.html, 2016.

[44] Chunduri, R.K. and Kumar, C.A.: Scalable Algorithm for Generation of Attribute Implication Base using FP-Growth and Spark Springer Soft Computing, 2021 (Accepted).

[45] Chunduri, R.K. and Kumar, C.A.: Scalable formal concept analysis algorithms for large datasets using Spark. Journal of Ambient Intelligence and Humanized Computing, 2019, 10(11), pp 4283–4303.

[46] Domoney, W.F., Ramli, N., Alarefi, S., and Wlaker, D.S.: Smart city solutions to water management using self-powered, low-cost, water sensors and Apache Spark data aggregation. In Proceedings of the 3rd International Renewable and Sustainable Energy Conference (IRSEC)-2015, 2015.

[47] Shanahan, J. and Dai, L.: Large Scale distributed data science using Apache Spark. In Proceeding KDD '15 Proceedings of the 21st ACM SIGKDD International Conference on Knowledge Discovery and Data Mining, 2015, pp 2323–2324.

[48] Yu, J., Wu, J., and Sarwat, M.: A demonstration of GeoSpark: A cluster computing framework for processing big spatial data. In: 32nd IEEE International Conference on Data Engineering, ICDE, 2016, pp 1410–1413.

[49] Gupta, G. and Manish K.: A framework for fast and efficient cyber security network intrusion detection using Apache Spark. Procedia Computer Science, 2016, 93, pp 824–831.

[50] Alsheikh, M., Niyato, D., Lin, S., Tan, H., and Han, Z.: Mobile big data analytics using deep learning and Apache Spark. IEEE Networks, 2016, 30(3) pp 22–29.

[51] Armbrust, M., Fan, W., Xin, R., *et al.*: Introducing Apache Spark Datasets. In https://databricks.com/blog/2016/01/04/introducing-apache-spark-data-sets.html, 2016.

[52] Rosen, J. and Xin, R.: Project Tungsten: Bringing Apache Spark Closer to Bare Metal. In https://databricks.com/blog/2015/04/28/project-tungsten-bringingspark-closer-to-bare-metal.html, 2015.

[53] Tang, S., He, B., Yu, C., *et al.*: A Survey on Spark Ecosystem for Big Data Processing. In https://arxiv.org/abs/1811.08834, 2018.

[54] Ousterhout, K., Wendell, P., Zaharia, M., *et al.*: Sparrow: Distributed, low latency scheduling. In Proceedings of the Twenty-Fourth ACM Symposium on Operating Systems Principles, 2013, pp 69–84.

[55] Maas, M., Asanovi, K., Harris, T., *et al.*: Taurus: A holistic language runtime system for coordinating distributed managed-language applications. In Proceedings of the Twenty-First International Conference on Architectural Support for Programming Languages and Operating Systems, 2016, pp 457–471.

[56] Maas, M., Asanovi, K., Harris, T., *et al.*: Trash day: Coordinating garbage collection in distributed systems. In 15th Workshop on Hot Topics in Operating Systems (HotOS XV), 2015.

[57] Li, H., Ghodsi, A., Zaharia, M., *et al.*: Tachyon: Memory throughput i/o for cluster computing frameworks. In 7th Workshop on Large-Scale Distributed Systems and Middleware, 2013.

[58] Li, H., Ghodsi, A., Zaharia, M., *et al.*: Tachyon: Reliable, memory speed storage for cluster computing frameworks. In Proceedings of the ACM Symposium on Cloud Computing, 2014, 6, pp 1–15.

[59] Rachit A., Anurag K., and Ion S.: Succinct: Enabling queries on compressed data. In 12th Symposium on Networked Systems Design and Implementation, 2015, pp 337–350.

[60] Yu, J., Ying, C., and He, J.: Towards fault tolerance optimization based on checkpoints of in-memory. Journal of Ambient Intelligence and Humanized Computing, 2018.

[61] Gonzalez, J.E., Xin, R.S., Ankur, D., *et al.*: GraphX: Graph processing in a distributed dataflow framework. In Proceedings of the 11th USENIX Conference on Operating Systems Design and Implementation, 2014, pp 599–613.

[62] Malewicz, G., Austern, M.H., Bik, A., *et al.*: Pregel: A system for large-scale graph processing. In Proceedings of the 2010 ACM SIGMOD International Conference on Management of Data, 2010, pp 135–146.

[63] Meng, X., Bradley, J., Yavuz, B., *et al.*: MLlib: Machine Learning in Apache Spark. arXiv preprint arXiv:1505.06807, 2015.

[64] Spark Machine learning library (MLlib) guide. In MLlib: https://spark. apache.org/docs/latest/mllib-guide.html, 2015.

[65] Luszczak, A., Szafranski, M., Switakowski, M, *et al.*: Databricks Cache Boosts Apache Spark Performance—Why NVMe SSDs Improve Caching Performance by 10x. In https://databricks.com/blog/2018/01/09/databricks-cache-boostsapache-spark-performance.html, 2018.

[66] Caffeonspark open sourced for distributed deep learning on big data clusters. In http://yahoohadoop.tumblr.com/post/139916563586/caffeonsparkopen-sourced-for-distributed-deep, 2016.

[67] Scala language. In https://spark.apache.org/docs/latest/api/scala/index.html, 2016.

[68] Spark Python api. In http://spark.apache.org/docs/latest/api/python/index. html, 2016.

[69] The r project for statistical computing. In https://www.r-project.org/, 2016.

[70] SparkR (R on Spark). In https://spark.apache.org/docs/latest/sparkr.html, 2016.

[71] Michael, A., Reynold, S., Cheng, L., *et al.*: Spark SQL: Relational data processing in spark. In Proceedings of the 2015 ACM SIGMOD International Conference on Management of Data, 2015.

[72] Armbrust, M., Liu, D., and Xin, R.: Introducing DataFrames in Apache Spark for Large Scale Data Science. In https://databricks.com/blog/2015/02/17/introducing-dataframes-in-spark-for-large-scale-data-science.html, 2015.

[73] Alluxio, formerly known as tachyon, is a memory speed virtual distributed storage system. In http://www.alluxio.org/, 2016.

[74] Amazon s3. In https://en.wikipedia.org/wiki/Amazon S3, 2016.

[75] Cloud storage. In https://en.wikipedia.org/wiki/Cloud storage, 2016.

[76] S3 support in apache Hadoop. In http://wiki.apache.org/hadoop/AmazonS3, 2016.

[77] Introduction to Microsoft Azure storage. In https://azure.microsoft. com/en-us/documentation/articles/storageintroduction/, 2016.

[78] Apache HBase. In http://hbase.apache.org/, 2015.

[79] Chang, F., Dean, J., Ghemawat, S., *et al.*: Bigtable: A distributed storage system for structured data. In Proceedings of the 7th USENIX Symposium on Operating Systems Design and Implementation, 2006, 7, pp 1–15.

[80] DeCandia, G., Hastorun, D., Jampani, M., *et al.*: Dynamo: Amazon's highly available key-value store. SIGOPS Operating Systems Review, 2007, 41(6), pp 205–220.

[81] Distributed hash table. In https://en.wikipedia.org/wiki/Distributed_hash_table, 2016.

[82] Apache Cassandra. In https://en.wikipedia.org/wiki/Apache Cassandra, 2016.

[83] Lakshman, A. and Malik, P.: Cassandra: A decentralized structured storage system. SIGOPS Operating Systems Review, 2010, 44(2) pp 35–40.

[84] Apache Hive. In https://github.com/apache/hive, 2016.

[85] Apache Zookeeper: https://zookeeper.apache.org/.

[86] Samuel, S.J., Kounidnya, R.V.P., Sashidhar, K., and Bharathi, C.R.: A Survey on Big data and its research challenges. ARPN Journal of Engineering and Applied Sciences, 2015, 10(8), pp 3343–3347.

[87] Sameer, A., Mozafari, B., Panda, A., *et al.*: BlinkDB: Queries with bounded errors and bounded response times on very large data. In Proceedings of the 8th ACM European Conference on Computer Systems, EuroSys'13, 2013, pp 29–42.

[88] Sparks, E.R., Venkataraman, S., Kaftan, T., *et al.*: KeystoneML: Optimizing pipelines for large-scale advanced analytics. In 2017 IEEE 33rd International Conference on Data Engineering, 2017, pp 535–546.

[89] Venkataraman, S., Yang, Z., Davies, E.L., *et al.*: SparkR: Scaling r programs with spark. In SIGMOD'16 Proceedings of the 2016 International Conference on Management of Data, 2016, pp 1099–1104.

[90] Venner, J., Pro Hadoop. Apress, 2009.

[91] Zaharia, M., Chowdhury, M., Das, T., *et al.*: Resilient distributed datasets: A fault-tolerant abstraction for in-memory cluster computing. In Proceedings of the 9th USENIX Conference on Networked Systems Design and Implementation (NSDI), 2012.

[92] Zhang, H., Cho, B., Seyfe, E., Ching, A., and Freedman, M.J.: Riffle: Optimized shuffle service for large-scale data analytics. In Proceedings of the Thirteenth EuroSys Conference, EuroSys '18, 2018.

[93] Shaikh, E., Mohiuddin, I., Alufaisan, Y., and Nahvi, I.: Apache spark: A big data processing engine. In 2nd IEEE Middle East and North Africa COMMunications Conference (MENACOMM), 2019, pp 1–6.

[94]   Sidiropoulos, G., Kiourt, C., and Moussiades, L.: Crowd simulation for crisis management: The outcomes of the last decade. Machine Learning with Applications, 2020.

[95]   Berges, I., Julio, V., Durán, R., and Illarramendi, A.: A semantic approach for big data exploration in industry 4.0. big data research, 2021.

[96]   Kalia, K., and Neeraj Gupta.: Analysis of hadoop MapReduce scheduling in heterogeneous environment, Ain Shams Engineering Journal, 2021, 12(1).

[97]   Juez-Gil, M., Arnaiz-González, A., Rodríguez, J., López-Nozal, C., and García-Osorio, C.: Rotation forest for big data. Information Fusion, 2021, 74, pp 39–49.

[98]   Sleeman IV, W. and Krawczyk, B.: Multi-class imbalanced big data classification on Spark, Knowledge-Based Systems, 2021, 212.

[99]   Ahmed, N., Barczak, A.L.C., Susnjak, T., and Rashid, M.A.: A comprehensive performance analysis of Apache Hadoop and Apache Spark for large scale data sets using HiBench. Journal of Big Data, 2020, 7(1).

[100]   Zhang, X. and Wang, Y.: Research on intelligent medical big data system based on Hadoop and blockchain. EURASIP Journal on Wireless Communications and Networking, 2021, 7(1).

[101]   Mostafaeipour, A., Jahangard Rafsanjani, A., Ahmadi, M., and Arockia Dhanraj, J.: Investigating the performance of Hadoop and Spark platforms on machine learning algorithms. The Journal of Supercomputing, 2021, 77(2).

[102]   Qin, W., Liu, F., Tong, M., and Li, Z.: A distributed ensemble of relevance vector machines for large-scale data sets on Spark. Soft Computing, 2021.

[103]   Bose, R. and Frew, J.: Lineage retrieval for scientific data processing: A survey. ACM Computing Surveys, 2005, 37(1), pp 1–28.

Chapter 3

The role of data lake in big data analytics: recent developments and challenges

T. Ramalingeswara Rao[1], Pabitra Mitra[2] and Adrijit Goswami[1]

Big data analytics has brought a new revolution in the modern data world to process massive datasets across various fields of science and technology. The main tasks in processing big data are data acquisition, data storage, data management, data processing and applying data analytics. The earlier generations of data repositories are data warehouses that store the structured datasets and enable customers to view and mine data in different dimensions. Data warehouses and data marts are assumed to provide solutions to end-users for making decisions from the data. However, data warehouses store only structured data and unable to maintain massive repositories of different types of heterogeneous datasets. The most recently developed technologies are *data lakes* (DLs) that store a voluminous amount of datasets with heterogeneous kinds of data from diverse sources. In this chapter, we explore the concept of a DL, big data fabric, DL architecture and various layers of a DL. We also present various components of each of the layers that exist in a DL. We compare and contrast the notion of data warehouses and DLs concerning some key characteristics. Moreover, we explore various commercial- and open-source-based DLs with their strengths and limitations. Also, we discuss some of the key best practices for DLs. Further, we present two case studies of DLs: Lumada data lake (LDL) and Temenos data lake (TDL) for digital banking. Finally, we explore some of the crucial challenges that are facing in the formation of DLs.

3.1 Introduction

One of the significant challenges in the current trend of big data is the efficient storage of data at a massive scale. Massive datasets that are difficult to acquire, store, ingress, manage, refine, analyze and visualize using traditional data

[1]Theoretical Computer Science Group, Department of Mathematics, Indian Institute of Technology Kharagpur, Kharagpur, India
[2]Department of Computer Science and Engineering, Indian Institute of Technology Kharagpur, Kharagpur, India

management systems causes to big data [1,2]. DLs are upcoming new-generation data management environment that effectively handles massive data challenges and provides new levels of real-time data. DLs maintain massive volumes of data and allow the data in its original format from diverse data sources. The earlier generation of storing data uses data warehouses. The concept of DL works in contrast to data warehouses that provide complete structured, decision-oriented and subject-oriented databases [3] and have a drawback of partitioning the data into silos. The data preprocessing in data warehouses is expensive. In data warehouses, the data is frequently updated through extraction, transformation, loading (ETL) process (schema-on-write) that is very expensive. In contrast to data warehouses, DLs quickly allow one to access data using schema-on-read. DLs govern data with diverse on-request, ad hoc query analysis, whereas data warehouses govern structured data and do querying according to industry needs. The word DL was initially used by James Dixon in 2010 [4]. Dixon compared the concept of data mart and DLs as follows. A data mart is alike to cleaned, packaged water in a bottle and available in a structured format for easy utilization. However, a DL comprises raw data similar to a pool of water in its natural form. DLs decompose the data silos and allow industries to view data in multiple dimensions and perform various types of analytics. A DL is a fully maintained storehouse that enables us to store large-scale structured and unstructured data at low cost. A DL comprises raw data irrespective of data source and data structure. A DL stores unprocessed raw data, whereas data warehouse stores processed data [5]. The raw data which loads into the DL has no schema. However, the schema is defined while utilizing the data in the DL. A data warehouse is an extremely designed data model before data is loaded. The maintenance of data warehouses is expensive due to its required software, infrastructure and additional manpower. The DLs permit a combination of different types of data into a single repository. Some of the significant advantages of DLs are as follows [6]: (i) since the data is stored in raw form, DLs greatly minimize the data preparation time, (ii) multiple types of users can access the DL, including business users, data scientist and developers and (iii) a DL with sufficient tools allows for real-time querying and saves time and data-processing cost. DLs facilitate to consume raw data from diverse sources, store data in its native form, refine the data, assure the data availability and permit data scientists, business intelligence experts, analysts to ingress and govern data to maintain quality of data and security services [7]. The word "data lake" is closely associated with big data technologies, and they have a wide range of possibilities for storing several key use cases. The DL concept has its foundation in big data technology and is closely integrated with Hadoop ecosystem [8]. A DL comprises many layers, including the raw data layer, data ingestion layer (DIL), process layer and ingress layer. Each layer employs a variety of big data tools and technologies to perform the functionalities in the DL. Data scientists play a key role to look at the datasets, build data models, perform exploratory data analysis and test the models [9]. Data scientists enable a DL useful by allowing accessibility to total data, create scripts in various languages like python and process the data on a cluster environment for quick response in hours than in multiple days.

According to Nick Heudecker, in a broad sense, "data lakes are represented as organization-wide data management platforms that analyze data from diverse sources by storing it in its native (raw) form" [10,11]. In other words, rather than storing data in a specifically developed data store, move the raw data into a DL in its original format. Keeping data in its raw form avoids the predetermined costs of ingesting the data. Once if the data is stored into the DL, it is available for every person of a particular organization. The notion of a DL is a centralized system of data from diverse sources in a single location. A DL is not a product to buy, rather it is a referential architecture of an integrated technology that represents how an organization stores large-scale data, enables data access for users by maintaining data governance, data quality and provides services through various kinds of analytics [12]. One can build useful applications that allow smarter recommendations to the customers based on historical data.

3.1.1   Differences between data warehouses and data lakes

In this section, we present the key differences between data warehouses and DLs. Table 3.1 shows the difference between a data warehouse and a DL concerning some significant characteristics. Each of the comparisons of the characteristics is explained as follows. (i) A data warehouse allows only homogeneous data (structured), whereas a DL stores heterogeneous data, including structured, unstructured data from diverse data sources [13]. (ii) Data warehouses work based on the concept of *schema-on-read* (late binding) that is required before loading the data. DLs work based on *schema-on-read* and the data is accessible at the time of usage rather than predefined schema. (iii) A data warehouse stores the data in the form of files

Table 3.1   Major differences between data warehouses and data lakes

Characteristic	Data warehouse	Data lake
Data type	Homogeneous, structured, processed	Heterogeneous, unstructured
Schema	Schema-on-write (ETL process)	Schema-on-read (data is accessible at the time of usage)
Data storage	Stores in files and folders, expensive for storing massive datasets	Flat architecture, stores raw data
		HDFS, low cost, stores massive data at large scale
Scalability	Highly expensive for storing massive datasets	Highly scalable, stores massive data at large scale
Agility	low agility	High agility
Data processing	OLAP	Big data processing using Hadoop, Spark, Flink, Storm
Users	Business analysts	Data scientists
Reporting	Visualizations, business intelligence	Machine learning tasks, real-time analytics, streaming analytics

and folders. A DL can store the data in the Hadoop distributed file system (HDFS) at a large scale. (iv) The cost of storing large-scale datasets in data warehouses is very high, whereas DLs are highly scalable and store the raw data at any scale. (v) The data can be processed using OLAP in multidimensional views in data warehouses. However, in DLs, the data can be processed using big data frameworks such as Hadoop, Spark, Flink and Storm [2]. (vi) The major users for data warehouses are business professionals, business analysts. The users for DLs are data scientists and developers [14]. (vii) In a data warehouse, various kinds of analytics can be applied to uncover intuitive insights through visualization. In DLs, apply machine learning (ML) tasks to get the required predictions. Also, streaming data can be processed using distributed streaming systems such as Kafka and Apache Storm [15].

3.1.2   Data lakes pitfalls

Following are some of the limitations of DLs:

- A DL stores any kind of data without proper governance, metadata managing mechanism; the DL has a risk of turning into a data swamp.
- Another issue is security and access control. The security issues of a centralized DL still have to improve as the DL stores all kinds of data without proper observations [11].
- Many efforts are required to develop and maintain a DL from data ingestion to reporting. Integrating various tools for storing and analysis of massive datasets is a difficult task.
- The current DL works do not fully solve the issues relevant to security and quality of data.
- More advanced metadata management techniques have to be developed in order to maintain proper file management.
- Since a DL consists of various kinds of tools, the performance of all tools is not the same when compared to a general-purpose infrastructure.

3.2   Taxonomy of data lakes

In this section, we discuss some significant taxonomy of DLs, particularly, data silos, data swamps, data reservoirs and data fabric.

3.2.1   Data silos

The data that exists in the raw form of a repository before processing in an organization is known as *data silos* [16]. Data silos control information sharing and collaboration between various groups and results in low-quality decision-making that causes fewer business profits. Silos are isolated data islands, and they make it exceedingly expensive to obtain data that can be utilized for other purposes [17]. The following are some of the significant points to break up the data silos. (i) Data silos do not break down themselves. Industries have to make top priority in eliminating data silos. Design a complete plan of removing silos and convey the employees about organization challenges and goals. (ii) By 2020, the majority of the industries are using public clouds to manage their data subjecting to *vendor lock-in*, a very expensive and long-delayed process to shift data from one platform to another [18]. Eliminate data silos by employing appropriate platforms, databases that provide you the capability to forward your data to your choice. (iii) Most of the data silos are formed as there is no proper communication among various teams of different departments. Avoid data silos by motivating employees of organizations to maintain proper communication among different groups continuously. (iv) Form a simple environment by integrating the required tools and technologies. (v) Develop more storage facilities of data. Train the employees to understand the nature of the data and know the processing methods with appropriate processing environments.

3.2.2   Data swamps

A DL without applying proper data governance transforms into a risky *data swamp* [19], from which business outcome cannot be obtained.

3.2.3   Data reservoirs

A data swamp consists of overflowed data and is not secure to use it. In data swamps, nobody knows from where the data is coming; there is no guarantee for the reliability and security of the data. A DL with proper data governance is known as a data reservoir and adds value to analytics projects [20]. A data reservoir explores valuable information to users who can accomplish the following tasks. (i) Examine and understand the specific status of a task. (ii) Construct analytical models for that task and (iii) evaluate the analytical solution of the task for generating successful production to enrich it. A data reservoir with proper abilities guarantees that the data is appropriately cataloged and secured so that the subject matter experts have data access for their works. Subject matter experts play a crucial role in using proper analytics and obtaining valuable insights at suitable points of an organization. Business teams take advantage of data from the data reservoir to turn the data into value.

3.2.4   Big data fabric

The enormous amount of data relevant to distinct users and enterprises will flow from various sources to different destinations. Massive amounts of data related to customers are stored in public clouds, private clouds and on-premises. The goal is to leverage the connectivity between public cloud, private cloud and on-premises and manage the data for easy use of customers. A data fabric is a hybrid cloud management solution for freedom, control and movement of data [21]. That is, a data fabric is a distributed environment along with a set of data services that maintain persistent abilities over a choice of end-points covering on-premises and several cloud environments. A data fabric is a blend of architecture and technology that is configured for effective management of various kinds of data to avoid complexities among data utilizing different database management systems and deployed over a wide range of platforms [22]. Many data-driven enterprises construct data fabrics to drive business consequences. A data fabric is not a centralized hub but handles data and refining as virtual resources over a common architectural platform. A data fabric is an architectural pattern that responds to the requirement to bridge the data and application silos in most of the enterprises [23]. The fabric traverses along the stages of storage and processing of data and minimizes the need for replicating or movement of data to the consumption point and eliminates the restrictions between the batch, interactive and real-time processing. The fabric serves data and refining as utility that is capable of accommodating data at a large scale with diverse types of data and content and allows multiple data access modes.

3.3 Architecture of a data lake

In this section, we present the architecture of a DL, different layers in a DL and components of each layer. A DL mainly comprises four layers: the *raw data layer*, the *DIL*, *process layer* and *ingress layer* [7,24]. Figure 3.1 illustrates various components of distinct layers of a DL.

3.3.1 Raw data layer

The role of the *raw data layer* is to ingest raw data effectively and quickly. This layer consists of data in its native form, and modifications to the data are not allowed at this stage. Also overriding of the data is not accepted in this layer [7]. The raw data can be organized based on the data source, type of subject, object, month, year and day of the raw data. Initially, the data in this layer is not ready to use and requires many steps to use the relevant data. The data that exists in the raw

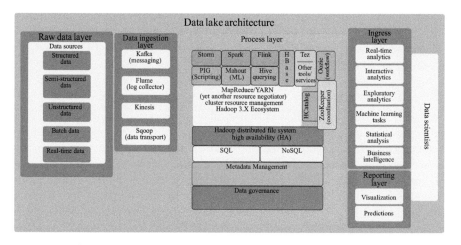

Figure 3.1 Components of different layers of a data lake

data layer is of the type structured, semi-structured and unstructured. Also, this layer acquires data from various sources both batch and streaming data.

3.3.2 Data ingestion layer

The process of acquiring and importing data into a data storage system is known as data ingestion. Data ingestion aims to ensure the method of acquiring data into a DL for instantaneous use or to store in a database [25]. The responsibility of DIL is to consume the messages from the messaging system and accomplishing the necessary transformation for ingesting the data into the lambda layer and the transformed out-turn satisfies the expected computing formats. The data ingestion phase assures that the message consumption rate is superior to or equal to the rate of message ingestion without any latency in message processing. The DIL handles a variety of data types, including structured, semi-structured and unstructured datasets. Also, this layer works well with batch processing data, streaming data and real-time data. Moreover, the DIL supports various storage systems. The popular data ingestion tools are Kafka [26], Sqoop [27], Flume [28], Kinesis [29] and Chukwa [30] that pull/receive the data from external sources and forward data into storage systems of a DL.

- Apache Kafka [31] is a distributed streaming system that handles a massive amount of log data, stores, processes stream of records. Kafka provides a log aggregation service that acquires physical log files from servers, forwards them into a storage system like HDFS and processes the log data.
- Flume is a distributed, reliable log service that efficiently collects, aggregates and moves large-scale data from various applications into HDFS [28].
- Amazon kinesis captures, processes and analyzes video, streaming data and provides a cost-effective stream-processing mechanism at any scale [29]. Kinesis ceaselessly captures data and stores terabytes of data for every hour from diverse sources like social network feeds, location-based events, weblog data, online banking transactions.
- Sqoop is a distributed data ingestion tool that transports bulk volume of structured data between different databases and Hadoop [27]. Sqoop allows data import and export from outermost sources to HDFS. It coordinates with Oozie by automating the import and export mechanisms.

3.3.3 Process layer

In this layer, customers can modify the data according to their necessities and store intermediary modifications. This layer processes the batch, streaming data by coordinating with big data tools such as Hadoop and Spark. This layer enables end-users to perform operations such as selection, projection, join, aggregation, for various kinds of data analysis [32]. According to the current trend of the data world, a better choice to process the data in DLs is to use the Hadoop 3.x ecosystem. Hadoop ecosystem is an integrated environment that consists of a collection of tools and technologies, including data-processing tools like MapReduce, streaming tools, ML tools, distributed message systems. Hadoop MapReduce performs efficiently to process massive amounts of batch data [33]. The process layer in Figure 3.1 consists of HDFS for the storage of large-scale data. Also, YARN works as a cluster resource manager. The best tools for handling the streaming data are Spark streaming, Apache Flink and Apache Storm [2]. However, adopting the most recent big data technologies through the Hadoop 3.x ecosystem to process both batch and streaming data by data scientists and researchers is an added advantage of DLs in transforming data into value.

3.3.4   Ingress layer

This layer facilitates to keep the prepared information and allows users to ingress the data. The ingress layer enables users to access the data and to apply various kinds of analytics, including ML tasks, statistical analysis, business intelligence tasks and reporting [32]. From the processed data, the data scientists can view the intuitive insights of data using statistical analysis, real-time analytics through visualizations.

3.3.5   Responsibilities of data scientists in data lakes

A data scientist has to perform a wide range of operations starting from data collection, data cleaning, data profiling, data preparation, data managing, data mining, data modeling, data analysis and data visualization. The following are some of the key aspects of the responsibilities of a data scientist. Data scientists have a good background in statistics, data mining, ML, deep learning and work closely with various departments of an organization [34].

- A data scientist must have end-to-end knowledge from the raw data layer to the data ingress layer of a DL. Data scientists must know the process of data capturing, data management, data processing, data analysis and data visualization. Data capture includes acquiring data from web servers, banking transactions, sensors, search engines, machines. Data scientists must also be aware of various distributed file systems such as HDFS to store the petabytes of data, if the data is stored, managing the data using traditional and NoSQL databases.
- Data scientists have sound knowledge in NoSQL databases, including document-based, key-value, column-oriented, in-memory and various graph databases to load the data from distributed file systems.
- They must have good practical knowledge of distributed computing frameworks that include Hadoop, Spark, Flink, Storm to process the batch and streaming data. They also need to be familiar with interactive analytical tools such as Hive, Impala, to provide an interactive environment for users so that they can easily access and analyze data.
- Data scientists create models, train the models, apply the ML algorithms, visualize the insights of data and make collaborations with business teams. In data analysis, model the data using ML algorithms and apply statistical, data/graph mining techniques to detect the intuitive insights of data. Data scientists need to have practical knowledge in ML libraries such as Mahout, Spark MLlib, FlinkML, Orange, H_2O.

- Data scientists use data cataloging to detect required data for developing novel analytics. After the detection of the required data, data scientists copy the data into a sandbox environment and start for data preparation and analysis.
- A good background of statistics is helpful to discover trends in various kinds of business applications.
- Practical skills of visualizing the data after applying various kinds of analytics are required. Neo4j Bloom, Tableau, Cytoscape, NodeXL, Pajek, and Gephi are some of the visualization tools [2].

3.3.6 Metadata management

The purpose of metadata management in DLs is to provide an effective mechanism that provides easy access and invisibility of data to end-users [7]. Metadata is useful to retrieve the data relevant to user's requirements, quick access to data, verification of data source, refining archives to get belief and detect concerned data to improve data analyzation. The metadata management in DLs can be classified into three ways: (i) technical, (ii) operational and (iii) business. The technical metadata comprises the schema of the data relevant to data type, the structure of the data and data format. The operational data consists of information about data processing that captures lineage, quality, profile and origin of the data. The business metadata comprises the business entities and relevant representations such as business names, descriptions, tags and masking rules. Another significant metadata classification that DLs support is intra-metadata and inter-metadata. Intra-metadata provides information about each dataset relevant to data properties, definitional metadata, navigational activities, data life cycle, data rating and evaluation [35]. We present a brief introduction to the previous characteristics.

- Data properties consist of details about name, data size, identity, structural type and formation date of a dataset.
- Definitional metadata discusses the semantic and schematic properties of a dataset.
- Navigational activities consist of dataset location paths and navigational URLs.
- Lineage represents the life cycle of data that includes data sources and data-processing details.

The method of organizing metadata properly is crucial in maintaining the DLs. A unified DL management system facilitates metadata formation and preservation, an intrinsic part of the DL mechanisms. Without proper metadata mechanism, data dropped into DLs may not be visible again [36]. The primary component of DLs that play a vital role is *metadata catalog* that allows searching across the metadata. The metadata catalog does not permit the DLs to transform into data swamps.

3.3.7 Data lake governance

The purpose of data governance is to shape business information in unique ways to satisfy customer's needs. Data governance differentiates between various forms of metadata, including business metadata, technical metadata [37]. Data governance has to apply on all layers to ensure data security, quality of the data, data ingress, data life cycle and metadata management. A governed DL comprises clean, concerning data from unstructured and structured data sources. A DL with proper data governance provides cleaned data, easy accessibility of data and maintains high security for data.

3.3.8   Data cataloging

An enterprise data catalog unified with a governance environment can serve customers to quickly detect, curate, classify, govern, analyze and distribute purpose-ready data. The data catalogs with proper ML techniques improve the effectiveness of knowledge workers and provide efficient ways of yielding metadata, curating resources and knowledge-sharing methods.

3.4   Commercial-based data lakes

In this section, we explore three major commercial DLs: Azure data lake (ADL) environment, IBM data lake (IBM DL) and Amazon Web Services (AWS) Galaxy data lake (GDL). We explain each of the DLs with respective components.

3.4.1   Azure data lake environment

ADL environment provides an on-demand task service that processes massive data jobs within seconds [38]. Rather than installing virtual machines, deploying servers/clusters and tuning hardware, one can write queries to alter their data and extract potential insights. The analytics service in Azure can tackle highly scalable jobs instantaneously by adjusting the respective settings. The users can pay the amount for their respective jobs that are running in the current situation within a cost-effective strategy. ADL environment provides resources dynamically and allows users to do analytics on Petabytes of data.

- An advantage of ADL is that users can pay only for the used processing power. Also, depending upon the variation of the data deposited (growing/decreasing), the number of computing resources utilized, users need not have to rewrite the code.
- ADL unifies with Visual Studio and users can use the most common tools to run, debug and regulate their code.
- ADL analytics consists of a query language known as U-SQL that enhances the declarative features of SQL along with the efficient power of c#. The U-SQL language employs the same distributed runtime environment that drives Microsoft's internal massive-scale DL.
- ADL analytics enables visualizations of user code that runs at large-scale and one can easily detect efficiency bottlenecks and get the best (optimized) computing costs.

- *Azure blob storage* is highly scalable and secure entity storage for cloud-native workloads, DLs, superior-performance computing and ML. Azure Blob Storage enables users to form DLs for their analytical needs and facilitate storage to construct effective cloud-native and mobile applications.
- ADL analytics provides a cost-effective solution for handling big data workloads. DL analytics works with ADL storage, Azure storage blobs, Azure SQL, Azure warehouse to maintain superior performance, throughput and parallelization.

The limitations of the ADL are as follows [39]. (i) Customers cannot employ both Blob APIs and DL storage APIs to write to the same specimen of a file. Writing to a file using DL storage APIs, the respective blocks of the file are not visible to the Get Block List of Blob API. Users can overwrite a file either by using DL Storage APIs or Blob APIs. (ii) The List Blobs operation without mentioning a delimiter results in both directories and blobs. At present the only supported delimiter is forward slash (/). (iii) The removal of blob snapshots is still not yet assisted. (iv) Currently, there exists a bug that impacts the archive access tier. (v) The life cycle management policy guidelines are not yet assisted in premium BlockBlobStorage records. (vi) Data cannot be transferred from premium tier to lower tiers. (vii) Presently, the operation Delete Blob is not endorsed.

3.4.2   Developing a data lake with IBM (IBM DL)

One of the significant commercial repositories for storing huge volumes of data is IBM DL. In this section, we present various components of IBM DL. The following are the key aspects of IBM DL. (i) IBM DL enables the process of reporting and tracking lineage that are required for various regular customers' needs. (ii) It works as the foundation for developing advanced analytical models, designing risk insights and operating efficient predictive methods. (iii) It comprises superior and effective metadata management strategies, facilitates customers for a better understanding of consuming data, data governance methodology and data management process [40].

3.4.3   Amazon Web Services (AWS) Galaxy data lake (GDL)

The GDL is a component of a big data environment and named internally as Galaxy. The GDL is built on an object storage service known as Amazon's Simple Storage Service (Amazon S3) that provides matchless availability, durability and scalability. The major layers in GDL are *Data source*, *Data ingestion*, *Catalog layer* and *Client layer*.

- The DIL embedded with AWS Glue, which is a fully governed ETL service and provides an easier mechanism for preparing and loading for analytics. Also, the GDL works with AWS Database Migration Service that is used to onboard several datasets into Amazon S3.
- The GDL joins metadata from different services such as Amazon Redshift, Amazon RDS and AWS Glue Data Catalog into a combined catalog layer constructed on top of a key/value document database known as Amazon

DynamoDB. Galaxy employs Amazon ElasticSearch for faster querying on the catalog.

• After the data cataloging, the Client layer provides various services such as Amazon Athena, Amazon Redshift and Amazon SageMaker. Amazon Athena provides interactive querying, ad hoc exploratory querying service using SQL. Amazon Redshift serves for structured querying and reporting. SageMaker is an ML service for various kinds of analytics on massive datasets.

Recently AWS has created a new service known as *AWS lake formation*. The role of AWS lake formation is to harmonize the process of creation of DLs and construct a secure DL within few days rather than in months. The lake formation supports customers to accumulate and catalog data from databases. The object storage moves the data into customer's new Amazon S3 DL, applies the ML algorithms to classify the data. Moreover, lake formation also provides a secure access mechanism to customer's complicated data.

3.5   Open source-based data lakes

In this section, we present two open-source DLs: delta lake and BIGCONNECT data lake (BDL).

3.5.1   Delta lake

Delta lake is an open-source storage layer that provides ACID transactions to Apache Spark and big data workloads [41]. DLs are embedded with several data pipelines to read and write data concurrently. Hence, data engineers are facing a complex process to guarantee data integrity, due to the absence of transactions. Delta lake provides ACID transactions to customer's own DLs. It facilitates serializability and a strong isolation level. Delta lake handles large-scale tables with billions of split-ups and files by leveraging Spark-distributed environment to govern the metadata management. Delta lakes allow developers to ingress and regress to previous versions of data for audits by providing snapshots. A table in delta lake will act as both batch table and as a streaming source and destination. Delta lake has the capability of detecting schema, imposes it and ensures the correctness of data types, shows required columns by preventing corrupted data. Delta lake is completely compatible with Apache Spark, and developers can utilize the delta lake with the available data pipelines.

3.5.2   BIGCONNECT data lake

BIGCONNECT is an open-source DL embedded with intelligent pipelines, extreme analytics for data enrichment, data discovery, data exploration for both structured and unstructured data [42]. BIGCONNECT runs in the cloud, on-premise and is extensively scalable, highly secure that develops solutions to industry necessities from financial to social media analyses, including security issues. The core features of BDL are *Explorer dynamic data model*, *discovery*, *cypher lab* and *Sponge*. The

Explorer tool is meant for handling unstructured data, semantic models, data ingestion, mapping, enrichment, link analysis and spatial analysis, etc. The *dynamic data model* denotes how one can store, correlate and query the total information using the concepts, relations and properties. The feature *discovery* is an end-to-end visual analytics tool to discover, transform and visualize the massive amounts of data. Moreover, *CipherLab* is an absolute workbench, a data exploration platform to test, run, tune and visualize the graph data using Cypher queries. Further, the *Sponge* tool that transforms the endless unstructured data into useful information using a distributed crawler. Hence, BDL is a universal DL that handles both structured and unstructured data at a large scale to meet any requirement.

3.5.3 Best practices for data lakes

In this section, we discuss some of the best practices of DLs [14].

- *Devise and develop a DL that satisfies the needs of both business and technology.* Combine both conventional and most recent big data technologies such as Hadoop 3.x, Spark 2.x and Flink 1.x. Moreover, create self-service functionalities for data scientists, data analysts, business customers, R&D scientists. Monitor the DL and its respective users for business amenability by applying data governance on all enterprise data.
- *Simplify the developed DL with a scalable onboarding process.* The success of DLs depends on the way of handling the onboarding data. Production tools have to be operated at high speed and large scale. Accept and adopt methodologies such as agile data integration (DI), early prototypes that are repeatable for productiveness, consistency and governance. Also, automate the process of metadata management employing metadata injection. Minimize dependency on hand-coded computational programming as it is not reusable.
- *Depend on DI tools for the effective functioning of DL.* DI tools include native Hadoop support (Hadoop 3.x) and support for various big data platforms for data movement. The support of most recent versions of Hadoop 3.x, Spark 2.4, Flink 1.11 and Storm makes the DL process easier and provides service to the users in an effective manner. The DI tools for metadata management such as Apache Avro support for business, technical and operational metadata.
- *Integrate individual DL with enterprise data architectures.* Many of the DLs are integrated with massive enterprise data architectures like ERP, various kinds of analytics stacks, content management, multichannel marketing, data archiving, etc. DLs with Hadoop-integrated environment support 360-degree view of users, a broad range of customer analytics and data exploration.
- *Adopt the best and new data management methodologies for a DL.* While ingesting data, form the metadata or explore the data in DL. Adopt early ingestion and late refining methods of data. Modernize DI tools and technologies for efficient utilization of DL. Also, extend the data management techniques to many more structures of data. Finally, rather than applying analytics on sample data, do analytics on whole data.

- *Enrich best latest practices for business analytics through a DL*. Integrate the self-services such as data ingress, data exploration, data preparation, data visualization and data analysis. Since organizations need to work with beyond OLAP and SQL for querying, more advanced analytics are to be employed rather than using existing older analytics. Moreover, employing multiple types of analytics on the data at the same time provides different types of insights into data. Extract value from human language, text and unstructured data through analytics by using Hadoop-based DLs.

3.6   Case studies

In this section, we explore two case studies: Hitachi's LDL and TDL for banking and explain the key aspects of both the DLs.

- *Hitachi LDL*: 85% of the big data projects fail due to the DLs that are transforming into data swamps. Big data initiatives in most of the industries comprise lots of silos. These silos need a lot of tools to store and find one's required data. The data will be unreliable, unsearchable and unusable without proper curation, catalog, data management, governance from end to end. LDL is a scalable, enterprise solution to minimize the cost, complicatedness of big data and provides a native-cloud integration environment to store massive amounts of data [43]. LDL is five times cost-effective than public cloud stores. Integrating Hadoop between the store and computing process is highly expensive, complex at scale and ineffective to handle all the workloads that are needed for customers. LDL facilitates curation, catalog on cost-efficient, multi-cloud object storage facilities along with customer-operated management and requires limited coding or no coding. LDL is developed on an economic and rich-metadata cloud storage environment. The stages like data curation, cataloging and governance easily reveal, understand and utilize data for various kinds of analytics. The customer-supported (self-service) management employs inbuilt dataflows and automate self-service management and allows collaborations among stakeholders. The architecture of LDL mainly consists of three zones. They are *Raw zone, Curated zone* and *Published* zone. Major functionalities are data ingestion, data preparation and data analyzation. In LDL, at first structured and unstructured data are ingested from data sources to the Raw zone. The data will be profiled, tagged and secured automatically and the data is trusted, usable in the curated zone. Finally, the data is forwarded into the published zone. Customers can apply various types of analytics on the data available in the published zone. Hitachi's LDL helps customers, data scientists and controls big data costs drive data cataloging, curation and data governance moved from a single cloud approach to a hybrid cloud approach.
- *TDL for digital banking*: TDL is the next-generation data hub and management combined with the richest embedded functionalities and the most advanced cloud-native platform with cutting-edge AI technology [44]. Temenos is the

world's topmost banking solutions organization that provides software to financial organizations of any size, across all over the world.

- *TDL* utilizes the *Temenos analytics*, Temenos banking products and facilitates banks to uncover the rapid variations of extremely scalable streaming data and data extraction using Temenos banking products like *Temenos transact* with the power of AI. TDL is incorporated with event streaming systems such as Apache Kafka, Amazon Kinesis that enables seamless integration with bank's enterprise architecture.
- TDL accomplishes extremely scalable data ingestion, ETL actions and also perform real-time ML. TDL allows limitless scalability with no requirement for specific coding or distributed processing and storage environment. TDL attains a superior performance of communication using native APIs from source to destination systems.
- TDL provides extremely optimized, refined and prepared data on a large number of cloud and database platforms. TDL allows various analytics and reports case studies with complete documentation, provides access to data. Moreover, TDL accelerates analytics with time-relevant data allowing trend analysis and forthcoming predictions.
- *Temenos AI* Temenos is the first of its kind to provide *transparency* and *explainability of AI* with machine-driven decision making to the banking industries. The *Temenos solutions* constitute *explainable AI* (XAI) platform, embedded with ML techniques and accessible to all Temenos software either through APIs provided on-premise or via an easy-to-use interface in the cloud. The XAI's platform solves one of the primary issues of the banking using AI applications that the banks usually function as "black boxes" comprising small if any visible insight into transforming decisions. XAI provides cutting-edge innovations to the banking organizations utilizing transparency into the previous decisions. XAI provides illustrations with clear explanations of the procedure of AI-based decision-making in plain language to the customers.
- The feature *XAI* in Temenos solution technology is useful for fraud detection, payment exceptions, cross-selling, tailored pricing, customer management, optimization of collections and current roadmap for extending Robo-advisor, etc.
- The Temenos XAI comprises another significant model for banking known as a *credit scoring model* that minimizes the credit risk that has the capability of increasing pass rates while keeping or minimizing present default risk. TDL also integrated with another significant feature known as *Temenos Infinity* that takes hand-operated writings to the higher level using AI automatic decision-making system.

The XAI platform is completely integrated with the TDL to provide banks a real-time, end-to-end smart data lake, offering the rich quality of data from diverse sources. Hence, banks can make quick, more precise and explainable decisions powered by AI algorithms. The Temenos platform with XAI technology is vital to the Temenos strategy to send both cloud-agnostic and on-premise commodities to banks.

3.6.1   Machine learning in data lakes

The goal of ML is to learn from data of a system instead of having explicit pro-
graming [16,45]. Since the DLs comprise large-scale datasets, it is suggested to
employ the learning algorithms using big data technologies such as Spark MLlib,
Mahout, FlinkML and Orange which are open-source solutions [2]. Spark MLlib
comprises algorithms relevant to supervised and unsupervised learning. Classification
and regression are related to supervised learning, whereas clustering and pattern
mining are related to unsupervised learning. However, Neo4j Bloom is an ML
tool for visualizing graphs. Moreover, Amazon ML, Azure ML, IBM Watson ML
are commercially based ML tools. In the process layer of DLs, data scientists
utilize the learning algorithm to model the data from MLlib, FlinkML or other
ML tools according to the need for various kinds of application problems.

3.6.2   Data lake challenges

- More advanced methods have to be developed that handle the metadata management mechanism effectively to govern machine-served scans, data file
  organization and lineage tracking of each modification of data.
- One significant challenge that organizations are facing problems is to expand
  the benefits of DLs among a broad range of customers while an effective way
  of accessing the data and update the data for efficient business advantages.
- One of the important challenges is to maintain the security of massive volumes
  of data from the end-to-end process of various organizations.
- Allowing diverse datasets with different data types relevant to various wings of
  an organization to move the data into a DL independently by providing
  effective and efficient methods of data security, consistency and data governance, most recent ML tools with big data technologies is a challenging task.

3.7   Conclusion

Big data analytics play a significant role in storing, managing and processing
large-scale datasets. DLs are the most recent technologies to maintain massive
data repositories with several kinds of datasets from heterogeneous data sources.
In this chapter, we have explored various stages that involve storing, managing
and processing massive raw datasets in DLs. Initially, we have explained the
major differences between data warehouses and DLs. Next, we have explained the
architecture of a DL, including several layers, and explored distinct components
of each of the layers. Moreover, three commercial-based and two open-source-
based DLs are demonstrated. Further, we have discussed the role of data scientists, major best practices of DLs in a systematic manner. Furthermore, two case
studies for DLs: LDL and TDL for digital banking are presented. Finally, we have
given some of the challenges that DLs are facing in storing and processing of
massive datasets.

References

[1] Chen M, Mao S, and Liu Y. Big data: A survey. Mobile Networks and Applications. 2014;19(2):171–209.

[2] Rao TR, Mitra P, Bhatt R, *et al.* The big data system, components, tools, and technologies: A survey. Knowledge and Information Systems. 2019:1–81.

[3] Nogueira ID, Romdhane M, and Darmont J. Modeling data lake metadata with a data vault. In: Proceedings of the 22nd International Database Engineering & Applications Symposium; 2018. p. 253–261.

[4] Dixon J. Pentaho, Hadoop, and data lakes; October 2010. https://jamesdix-onwordpresscom/2010/10/14/pentahohadoop-and-data-lakes. [Online; accessed 15-June-2020].

[5] O'Leary DE. Embedding AI and crowdsourcing in the big data lake. IEEE Intelligent Systems. 2014;29(5):70–73.

[6] IBM. IBM data lake: What is a data lake and how can it help you; 2020. https://wwwibmcom/downloads/cas/ON4WK472.

[7] Ravat F and Zhao Y. Metadata management for data lakes. In: European Conference on Advances in Databases and Information Systems. Springer; 2019. p. 37–44.

[8] Mehmood H, Gilman E, Cortes M, *et al.* Implementing big data lake for heterogeneous data sources. In: 2019 IEEE 35th International Conference on Data Engineering Workshops (ICDEW); 2019.

[9] Stein B and Morrison A. The enterprise data lake: Better integration and deeper analytics. PwC Technology Forecast: Rethinking Integration. 2014;1(1–9):18.

[10] Heudecker N and White A. The data lake fallacy: All water and little substance. Gartner Report G. 2014:264950.

[11] Rivera J and van der Meulen R. Gartner says beware of the data lake fallacy. Gartner; 2014, http://www gartner com/newsroom/id/2809117.

[12] IBM DataOps. Five myths about the data lake. https://www.ibm.com/downloads/cas/BOGPM93R; 2020 (last accessed 20-July-2020).

[13] Khine PP and Wang ZS. Data lake: A new ideology in big data era. In: ITM Web of Conferences. vol. 17. EDP Sciences; 2018. p. 03025.

[14] Russom P. Emerging best practices for data lakes. In: TDWI Checklist Report. Available from: https://tdwi.org/research/2016/12/checklist-emer-ging-best-practices-for-data-lakes.aspx?tc=page0 tc=assetpg m=1. 2016.

[15] Jain A and Nalya A. Learning Storm. Birmingham, UK: Packt Publishing; 2014.

[16] Wibowo M, Sulaiman S, and Shamsuddin SM. Machine learning in data lake for combining data silos. In: International Conference on Data Mining and Big Data. Springer; 2017. p. 294–306.

[17] Wilder-James E. Breaking Down Data Silos. *Harvard Business Review*, https://hbr.org/2016/12/breaking-down-data-silos, 2020 (last accessed 01 July 2020).

[18] Lacefield J. 5 Ways to Break Down Data Silos. www.datastax.com/blog/2018/10/5-ways-break-down-data-silos, 2020 (last accessed 01 July 2020).

[19] Giebler C, Gröger C, Hoos E, *et al.* Leveraging the data lake: Current state and challenges. In: International Conference on Big Data Analytics and Knowledge Discovery. Springer; 2019. p. 179–188.

[20] Chessell M, Scheepers F, Nguyen N, *et al.* Governing and Managing Big Data for Analytics and Decision Makers. IBM Redguides for Business Leaders; 2014.

[21] NetApp. Build your data fabric [homepage on the Internet]; July 2020. Available from: https://www.netapp.com/us/data-fabric.aspx.

[22] Eckerson Group. Data Fabric – Hype, Hope, or Here Today? [homepage on the Internet]; July 2020. Available from: https://www.eckerson.com/articles/data-fabric-hype-hope-or-here-today.

[23] NetApp. Build your data fabric [homepage on the Internet]; July 2020. Available from: https://www.netapp.com/us/data-fabric.aspx.

[24] Sawadogo P and Darmont J. On data lake architectures and metadata management. Journal of Intelligent Information Systems. 2020:1–24.

[25] John T and Misra P. Data Lake for Enterprises. Birmingham, UK: Packt Publishing Ltd; 2017.

[26] Dobbelaere P and Esmaili KS. Kafka Versus RabbitMQ; 2017. arXiv preprint arXiv:170900333.

[27] Apache. Apache Sqoop – Overview. https://blogs.apache.org/sqoop/entry/apache sqoop overview, 2020 (last accessed 24 June 2020).

[28] Hoffman S. Apache Flume: Distributed Log Collection for Hadoop. Birmingham, UK: Packt Publishing Ltd; 2013.

[29] AWS. Amazon Kinesis, Easily Collect, Process, and Analyze Video and Data Streams in Real Time. https://aws.amazon.com/kinesis/, 2020 (last accessed 24 June 2020).

[30] Rabkin A and Katz RH. Chukwa: A system for reliable large-scale log collection. In: LISA. vol. 10; 2010. p. 1–15.

[31] Kreps J, Narkhede N, Rao J, *et al.* Kafka: A distributed messaging system for log processing. In: Proceedings of the NetDB; 2011. p. 1–7.

[32] Megdiche I, Ravat F, and Zhao Y. A use case of data lake metadata management. Data Lakes. 2020;2:97–122.

[33] Dean J and Ghemawat S. MapReduce: Simplified data processing on large clusters. Communications of the ACM. 2008;51(1):107–113.

[34] Mathis C. Data lakes. Datenbank-Spektrum. 2017;17(3):289–293.

[35] Varga J, Romero O, Pedersen TB, *et al.* Towards next generation BI systems: The analytical metadata challenge. In: International Conference on Data Warehousing and Knowledge Discovery. Springer; 2014. p. 89–101.

[36] LaPlante A and Sharma B. Architecting Data Lakes: Data Management Architectures for Advanced Business Use Cases. CA, USA: O'Reilly Media Sebastopol; 2016.

[37] Bauer DN, Erice LG, Rooney JG, *et al.* Computerized methods and programs for ingesting data from a relational database into a data lake. Google Patents; 2020. US Patent App. 16/020,829.

[38]   Microsoft Azure. Microsoft Azure data lake analytics. https://azur-emicrosoftcom/en-in/services/data-lake-analytics/, 2020 (last accessed 27 June 2020).

[39]   Microsoft Azure. Known issues with Azure Data Lake Storage. https://docsmicrosoftcom/en-us/azure/storage/blobs/data-lake-storage-known-issues, 2020 (last accessed 15 June 2020).

[40]   IBM. IBM Industry Model support for a data lake architecture. https://www.ibm.com/downloads/cas/DNKPJ80Q, 2020 (last accessed 10 June 2020).

[41]   Delta Lake. Reliable Data Lakes at Scale. https://delta.io/, 2020 (last accessed 23 June 2020).

[42]   BIGCONNECT. BIGCONNECT, Universal data lake, The platform for understanding data. www.bigconnect.io/, 2020 (last accessed 23 June 2020).

[43]   Hitachi. Hitachi Vantara, Lumada Data Services. https://wwwhitachivantaracom/en-us/products/data-management-analytics/lumada-data-services/lumada-data-lakehtml, 2020 (last accessed 8 July 2020).

[44]   Temenos. Temenos Data Lake. https://wwwtemenoscom/products/data-and-analytics/data-lake/, 2020. (last accessed 23 June 2020).

[45]   Qiu J, Wu Q, Ding G, *et al.* A survey of machine learning for big data processing. EURASIP Journal on Advances in Signal Processing. 2016;2016 (1):67.

Chapter 4

Query optimization strategies for big data

*Nagesh Bhattu Sristy[1], Prashanth Kadari[1] and
Harini Yadamreddy[2]*

Query optimization for big data architectures like MapReduce, Spark, and Druid is challenging due to the numerosity of the algorithmic issues to be addressed. Conventional algorithmic design issues like memory, CPU time, IO cost should be analyzed in the context of additional parameters such as communication cost. The issue of data resident skew further complicates the analysis. This chapter studies the communication cost reduction strategies for conventional workloads such as joins, spatial queries, and graph queries.

We review the algorithms for multi-way join using MapReduce. Multi-way Θ-join algorithms address the multi-way join with inequality conditions. As Θ-join output is much higher compared to the output of equi join, multi-way Θ-join further poses difficulties for the analysis. An analysis of multi-way Θ-join is presented on the basis of sizes of input sets, output sets as well as the communication cost. Data resident skew plays a key role in all the scenarios discussed. Addressing the skew in a general sense is discussed. Partitioning strategies that minimize the impact of skew on the skew in loads of computing nodes are also further presented.

Application of join strategies for the spatial data has dragged the interest of researchers, and distribution of spatial join requires special emphasis for dealing with the spatial nature of the dataset. A controlled replicate strategy is reviewed to solve the problem of multi-way spatial join.

Graph-based analytical queries such as triangle counting and subgraph enumeration in the context of distributed processing are presented. Being a primitive needed for many graph queries, triangle counting has been analyzed from the perspective of skew it brings using an elegant distribution scheme. Subgraph enumeration problem is also presented using various partitioning schemes and a brief analysis of their performance.

[1]Department of Computer Science and Engineering, National Institute of Technology Andhra Pradesh, Tadepalligudem, India
[2]Department of Information Technology, Vignan's Institute of Information Technology, Visakhapatnam, India

4.1   Introduction

The surge of tools generating data in large volumes necessitated tech giants like Google, Facebook, Amazon, and LinkedIn to look for data handling engines with capacity to accommodate ever-increasing volumes of data. MapReduce [24] is one of the cornerstone frameworks in the evolution of new-age big data architectures. MapReduce achieves its objective of distributing the computations by decomposing larger tasks into manageable smaller tasks that can be expressed as the two core abstractions of the architecture: map and reduce. The desirable characteristics of fault-tolerance, effective scheduling of multiple workloads, templetized way of distributing the computations make the framework easy for the users to transform the conventional data analytical workloads into MapReduce-based programs. Relational databases that are used for many years as the core technology to handle large volumes of data have seen significant changes with the advent of the MapReduce. Though the framework offers a new playground for conventional query workloads, there are several issues to be considered for efficiently running the queries on MapReduce framework. Conventional database systems use parallelism to handle the larger datasets. The design of database query optimizer is quite complex, as most of the query optimization problems are NP-Hard. Designing the query optimizer for MapReduce framework is further complicated by the increase in the number of parameters to be considered. Conventional database systems optimize for reducing the overall disk I/O. MapReduce framework has to address the I/O cost of distantly located computing nodes and also the communication cost of moving the data across different computing nodes. Distributional skew also plays a key role in the query optimization.

This chapter reviews some of the query optimization strategies adopted in designing the workflows for MapReduce framework. We review the query optimization issues of multi-way join, skew-aware multi-way join, Θ-join, and multi-way Θ-join. We review basic graph query optimization for triangle counting. We also review spatial data processing and optimization of spatial queries for multi-way join.

There are several surveys [1–5] focusing on various aspects of MapReduce workflows. The study in [3] is one of the earlier surveys on MapReduce. It focuses on several issues of MapReduce which are new to the research community at that time. The study in [1] is a more comprehensive survey of analytical workflows on MapReduce. It elaborately studies various frameworks on the big data for different query loads. It also surveys briefly the join strategies on MapReduce. The study in [5] surveys the contributions in the context of Apache Hadoop framework. The study in [4] is another survey that focuses on extensions of MapReduce for various workloads. The study in [2] focuses on some of the recent abstractions on the top of MapReduce such as GridGain[*] and Mars[†] for understanding the scalability issues to large GPU-based and shared-memory architectures. The current book chapter

---

[*]http://www.gridgain.com/
[†]https://www.cse.ust.hk/gpuqp/Mars.html

rather focuses on the algorithmic framework to resolve the issues that arise in distributing the computation. The algorithmic issues considered are general and are applicable for various workflows. None of the earlier surveys cover the algorithmic issues in the necessary level of detail which might help as a guide to various people thinking of distributing arbitrary computations.

4.1.1 MapReduce preliminaries

The MapReduce programming model consists of input and output where each of it is a set of key and value pairs. The programmer should specify the following two functions:

1. map $(key_1, value_1) \rightarrow list(key_2, value_2)$
2. reduce $(key_2, list(value_2)) \rightarrow list(key_3, value_3)$

The authors in [24] have explain the details of the MapReduce paradigm in detail, explaining the significance of each of the phases of map, shuffle-sort, and reduce. Figure 4.1 depicts these phases of a typical MapReduce program. Though MapReduce offers a distributed way of computing, executional efficiency of jobs on the MapReduce platform is largely influenced by the communication cost. Complex workflows involving multiple MapReduce phases are further influenced by distributional skews, as multiple phases of the workflow are strictly sequential.

4.1.2 Organization of the chapter

The content of this survey is divided into three subsections: the first section elaborately discusses different issues arising in the context of multi-way joins. It discusses several state-of-the-art algorithms with an analysis of communication cost for each approach. The algorithms discussed include shares algorithm, SharesSkew, Θ-join, and multi-way Θ-join. The second section of the chapter emphasizes the distributing paradigms of graph queries. The addressed queries include counting triangles and subgraph enumeration. The last portion of the review covers join strategies for spatial data. For a ready reference, Table 4.1 contains the notations used throughout the chapter.

4.2 Multi-way joins using MapReduce

Join operation is a binary operation used to relate two datasets based on common attributes. Multi-way join is an extension of two-way join for multiple relations.

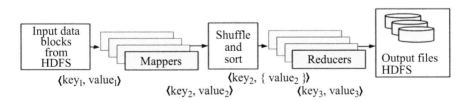

Figure 4.1 MapReduce framework

Table 4.1 Notations

Notations	Descriptions
Multi-way join	
P, Q, R, S	relational tables
A, B, C, D, E	attributes of the relational tables
N_p, N_q, N_r, N_s	sizes of the tables P, Q, R, S
a, b, c, d, e	values of the attributes
s_a, s_b, s_c, s_d, s_e	shares of the attributes A, B, C, D, E
p, q, r, s	tuples of the relations P, Q, R, S
K	number of reducers
$\mathcal{C}$	communication cost
$h(t_a), h(t_b), h(t_c), h(t_e)$	hash values of a, b, c, d
A_i	represents ith attribute
$\bowtie$	join
Graph algorithms	
$IM(H)$	set of isomorphic matchings of pattern graph H
H_i	partial pattern graph matched till ith step
h_i	ith component of pattern graph decomposition
D_p	decomposition of pattern graph
d_{max}	maximum degree of the graph
$G(V_G, E_G)$	graph G with its vertex set V_G and edge set E_G
$\mathcal{N}(u)$	neighbors of vertex u
$\langle u, \mathcal{N}(u) \rangle$	adjacency list of vertex u
G_{ijk}	graph formed by combining vertex disjoint sets V_i, V_j, V_k and edges of the graph connecting any of these vertices
G'_{ijk}	graph formed by combining vertex disjoint sets V_i, V_j, V_k and edges of the graph connecting these vertices lying in different partitions
Multi-way spatial join	
Overlaps (r,s)	returns true if the two rectangles r and s overlap
CrossesCellBoundary (r)	returns true if rectangle r crosses the cell boundary
Split (r)	returns the cells over which rectangle r splits
Mark (r)	marks the rectangle r for replication

The study in [6] illustrates various issues of processing multi-way joins in the context of database systems. Consider a join of relations $R(A, B)$, $Q(B, C)$, $R(C, D)$, and $S(D, E)$ where A, B, C, D, E are attribute sets. The first two plans depicted in Figure 4.2 show the alternatives considered by traditional database query optimizer. The typical query optimizer based on System R uses only a subset of all the space of query plans, namely, the left-deep or right-deep. Bushy plans are ruled out as they involve storing of the intermediate results in temporary relations, which further increases the overall I/O. The computational complexity of using a dynamic programming approach as in System R reduces to $O(n2^{n-1})$ as opposed to naïve $O(n!)$. MapReduce-based query optimizers on the other hand look for other query plans too. The rightmost plan in Figure 4.2 shows the possible method of performing the same multi-way join using MapReduce. Here, all the relations are joined using a single MapReduce job.

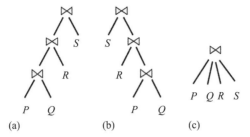

Figure 4.2   Join methods. (a) Left deep join, (b) Right deep join, (c) Simple multi-way join

Afrati and Ullman [7] have shown various optimization issues that arise while optimizing the multi-way joins. Before discussing the algorithmic aspects of the multi-way join, it is formally introduced as follows.

Definition 4.1 Multi-way join *Let A, B, C and D be attributes of interest for the join operation. Let there be relations P(A, B), Q(B, C), and R(C, D) over these attributes. The multi-way join operation between the three relations P, Q, and R is defined as*

$$P \bowtie Q \bowtie R = \Big\{ \langle a, b, c, d \rangle | (a, b) \in P, (b, c) \in Q \wedge (c, d) \in R \Big\}.$$

4.2.1   Sequential join

A naïve way of performing the join is a sequential approach that is depicted in Algorithm 1. Here the first map phase takes as input tuples t of type $p \in P$ or $q \in Q$. If t is of type $p(q)$, it can be expressed as (t_a, t_b) (t_b, t_c) corresponding to attributes $A(B)$ and $B(C)$, respectively. In either case, the emit statement in step 3 sends such tuples to reducer identified by $h(t_b)$. Such mapping ensures that p and q with matching values of attribute B are available in the same reducer for performing the actual join. The code in reducer corresponds to the per node computational logic to actually do the join on partitioned datasets. Except for the fact that the data is transported over network transparently, such a joining approach is quite similar to hash join in conventional dbms. The output of reducer in step 7 is tuples of type $\langle (p, q) \rangle$ where p and q satisfy the joining condition $p_b == q_b$. The second mapper takes as input, the output of the first reducer of type (p, q) or the tuples of the third relation $r \in R$. In either case, such records are sent to reducer based on attribute C. Step 11 indicates the former case, while step 13 indicates the latter one. The second reducer receives either tuples that are either the output of the first phase of the form (p, q) or $r \in R$ based on the partition function $h(q_c)$ or $h(r_c)$. The sets PQ_c and R_c are joined using joining constraint and outputted in step 19 of Algorithm 1.

Algorithm 1 MR-SequentialJoin(P, Q, R)

1: **Map 1**
2: **Input:** $\langle \Phi; t \rangle \, t \in P \cup Q$
3: emit $\langle (h(t_b)); t) \rangle$
4: **Reduce 1:**
5: **Input:** $\langle c; L_c = \{t | t \in P \cup Q\} \rangle$
6: Partition L_c into $P_c = \{p | p \in P \cap L_c\}$ and $Q_c = \{q | q \in Q \cap L_c\}$
7: **for** $(p, q) : p \in P_c \wedge q \in Q_c \wedge p_b == q_b)$ **do** emit $\langle \Phi; (p, q) \rangle$
8: **end for**
9: **Map 2:**
10: **if** Input of type $\langle \Phi; (p, q) \rangle$ ▸ Reduce1.output **then**
11:      emit $\langle h(q_c); (p, q) \rangle$
12: **else**   ▸ Input of type $\langle \Phi; r \in R \rangle$
13:      emit $\langle h(r_c); r \rangle$
14: **end if**
15: **Reduce 2:**
16: **Input:** $\langle c; L_c = \{(p, q) | (p, q) \in Reduce1.output\} \cup \{r | r \in R\} \rangle$
17: Partition L_c into $PQ_c = \{(p, q) | (p, q) \in Reduce1.output \cap L_c\}$ and $R_c = \{r | r \in R \cap L_c\}$
18: **for** $(p, q) \in PQ_c \wedge r \in R_c \wedge (q_c == r_c)$ **do**
19:      emit $\langle \Phi; (p, q, r) \rangle$
20: **end for**

Algorithm 1   MR-sequential join

Algorithm 1 is simple and can be extended to joins of arbitrary with simple extension. Such query plans are treated as naïve in MapReduce due to the fact that they result in large intermediate relations and it is required to transport the intermediate relations over the network that might be costly. If each tuple of one relation joins with k tuples of the other relation on average, the size of intermediate relation in the lth stage which needs to be transported over the network is of size $O(k^l |T|)$, where T is the size of these tables (assume that they are of equal size).

4.2.2   Shares approach

The authors in [7] have illustrated a slightly different approach for performing the three-way join of relations P, Q, and R. The approach uses a single MapReduce phase. The mapper takes as input, tuples of any of the relations P, Q, or R. The key concept of their approach is the arrangement of all the reducers in the form of rectangular grid structure (square for simplicity) shown in Figure 4.3. The number of reducers is σ^2 where σ is the number of cells in a row or column of the grid structure. The MapReduce code of this approach is depicted in Algorithm 2. The map phase deals with records of all the three relations P, Q, R. If a tuple $t \in P$, such t is sent to all the reducers of the grid structure in the row identified by $h(t_b)$. Similarly, if a tuple $t \in R$, such t is sent to all the reducers of the grid structure in

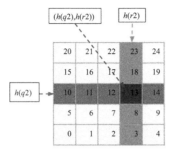

Figure 4.3   Multi-way join grid

the column identified by $h(t_c)$. If a tuple $t \in Q$, such t is sent to unique reducer identified by $(h(t_b), h(t_c))$. That way, the communication cost of such an approach is computed as $2 * \sigma * T + T$. This cost looks similar to that of the cost sequential join $(O(k * T + T))$. The key difference is that the cost of the sequential approach is depending on the data-dependent parameter k, while the approach in Algorithm 2 is dependent on σ that is square root of the number of reducers. If we account for the I/O cost too, the cost of storing the intermediate relation on the Hadoop file system will outweigh the I/O cost single MapReduce approach.

A special case of such a join is when the last relation is $R(C, A)$ and the join has additional constraint of $r_a == p_a$ for $r \in R$ and $p \in P$ in any join tuple (p, q, r) where the original join has two constraints $p_b == q_b$ and $q_c == r_c$. Such a query finds triangular relationships across the three relations. It has found applications large-scale web analytics such as page-rank computation.

When the number of reducers is fixed, the three relational joins can be more formally analyzed for its communication cost. Let the number of tuples in relations P, Q, R be N_p, N_q, N_r, respectively. Let the number of reduces be K. A general join algorithm can use a hypercube instead of the rectangular grid structure shown in Figure 4.3 using the attributes A, B, C for each dimension of the hypercube. The hashing scheme used earlier can be further generalized to the case of hypercube represented by triplets (a,b,c) where each of a, b and c represents a bin of values from the domains A, B and C, respectively. When such a relational join is performed using hypercube-based distribution of computation, one would try to find the shares of attributes A, B, C in locating the cube along the respective dimensions in such a way that the communication cost is minimized. Let the shares of attributes A, B, C be s_a, s_b, s_c, respectively.

Now we describe how the tuples of the relations are distributed over the hypercube. For a tuple $(p_a, p_b) \in P$, we apply hash functions $a = h(p_a)$ and $b = h(p_b)$ to identify the bins along dimensions A and B of the hypercube. The distribution scheme for tuple p involves sending it all the bins along the dimension C of the hypercube as attribute C is not present in P. So, each tuple of relation P is distributed to s_c reducers. Similarly, each tuple q of relation Q is distributed to s_a reducers. Each tuple r of relation R is distributed to s_b reducers. The communication cost is $O = N_p * s_c + N_q * s_a + N_r * s_b$. When we find the solution of this objective w.r.t. s_a, s_b, s_c under the constraint that $s_a * s_b * s_c = K$, we get $s_a = \sqrt[3]{N_p N_r K / N_q^2}$, $s_b = \sqrt[3]{N_p N_q K / N_r^2}$, $s_c = \sqrt[3]{N_q N_r K / N_p^2}$; thus, the minimum communication cost is $\sqrt[3]{N_p N_q N_r K}$. For a detailed discussion of this derivation, one can refer to [7].

The authors in [7] have used dominance rule to further order the importance of attributes in the earlier shares strategy. Consider the relational join being performed among several relations where some of them contain attributes A and/or B. If every relation containing A also contains B then A does not require a share of its own, as it is covered by attribute B. In such a case, A is said to be dominated by B. Assuming such dominance rule in the previous example, the communication cost reduces to $C = N_p * s_c + N_q + N_r * s_b$.

4.2.3 SharesSkew

The shares strategy presented in the previous section assumes that the values of each of the attributes are uniformly distributed. On the contrary, real-world datasets exhibit skewness, which severely affects the performance of join queries. During the distribution of skewed data over hypercube structure described in the shares approach, only some of the reducers will get the majority of the input, while many reducers quickly complete the task allotted to them. The overall performance of the job is dependent on the total turn-around time that includes time taken by the longest reducer.

The authors in [8] have proposed an approach to address the skewness in the context of relational joins. Their approach consists of identifying attribute values having a larger frequency (which are the cause of skew in join workload). Such skewed value identification is done for every attribute. Let the original join be horizontally partitioned into the number of bins.

Let $A_1, A_2, \ldots, A_t$ be attributes of interest for the relational join involving relations $R_1, R_2, \ldots, R_n$ where t is the number of attributes and n is the number of relations, respectively. If each attribute A_i has k_i skewed values, we partition the values of A_i into $k_i + 1$ subsets, represented as

$$VS_{A_i} = \left\{ \{v_1^{A_i}\}, \{v_2^{A_i}\}, \ldots, \{v_{k_i}^{A_i}\}, A_i' \right\}$$

where $\left\{v_j^{A_i}\right\}$ is a singleton set containing jth skewed value of attribute A_i. A_i' represents all the other values of A_i leaving the k_i skewed values. Let us consider the original join horizontally partitioned into the following sub results.

$$
\begin{aligned}
\text{Let } R &= R_1 \bowtie R_2 \bowtie \ldots \bowtie R_n \\
&= \cup_{(u_1, u_2, \ldots, u_t)} \sigma_{(R.A_1 = u_1 \wedge R.A_2 = u_2 \wedge \ldots \wedge R.A_t = u_t)} (R_1 \bowtie R_2 \bowtie \ldots \bowtie R_n)
\end{aligned}
$$

where $(u_1, u_2, \ldots, u_t) \in VS_{A_1} \ X \ VS_{A_2} \ X .. X \ VS_{A_t}$

The number of horizontal partitions $(u_1, u_2, \ldots, u_t)$ on the R.H.S. of previous equation is $\prod_{i=1}^{t} (k_i + 1)$. This partitioning of join result enables us to distribute a skewed join computation into smaller results that are manageable. The shares approach optimizes for minimization of communication cost for a given number of reducers. SharesSkew approach limits the workload on a reducer to a manageable limit and decides the number of reducers for each partitioned join output.

Consider the following multi-way join query:

$$P(A, B) \bowtie Q(B, C, D) \bowtie R(D, E, A)$$

Let there be two larger frequency values for each of the attributes B and D. The values of B and D are divided into three partitions B', B_1, B_2, and D', D_1, D_2, respectively, where B_1, B_2 and D_1, D_2 are larger frequency values, and B', D' are sets of all low-frequency values in their respective domains. Considering the sizes of these relations P, Q, R to be N_p, N_q, N_r, respectively, and shares of attributes A, B, C, D, E in the join key of hypercube structure to be s_a, s_b, s_c, s_d, s_e, respectively, the actual communication cost of this join without considering any dominance rule is as follows:

$$C = N_p * s_c * s_d * s_e + N_q * s_a * s_e + N_r * s_b * s_c$$

The first term represents the cost of communicating N_p tuples of relation P to each of the bins covered by shares s_c, s_d, s_e along C, D, E dimensions (which are absent in P). The relation Q does not have A and E attributes due to which it is sent to all the reducers in a slice of size $s_a * s_e$ of the hypercube. The relation R does not have attributes B and C due to which it is sent to all the reducers in a slice of size $s_b * s_c$ of the hypercube.

As we have three partitions for each of B and D attributes, we get $3 \times 3 = 9$ different horizontal partitions of the join. All the nine horizontal partitions of the join are depicted in Figure 4.4. A distinct path connecting A' and E' represents one horizontal partition of the join. Now we describe the communication cost for each of horizontal partition of the join by taking into consideration of dominance relation between attributes. The dominance rules are summarized as follows:

- If an attribute B appears in all the relations that have attribute A and in addition if B appears in at least one relation that does not have A, then we say that A is *dominated by B*. In such a case A will have a share of 1 in the hash function.
- In addition, attribute B to dominate A, B should not contain any larger frequency values.

(a) Consider the horizontal partition A', B', C', D', E' of the join, since attribute C is dominated by B and D the share of C (s_c) becomes 1 and attribute E

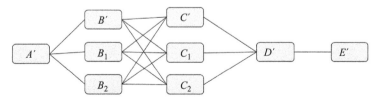

Figure 4.4 Partitioning of join

is dominated by A, D the share of E (s_e) becomes 1. The communication cost expression becomes

$$C = N_p * s_d + N_q * s_a + N_r * s_e$$

(b) The horizontal partition A', B', C', D_1, E' has the larger frequency value D_1. Hence, the share of D becomes $1(s_d = 1)$. Since C and E are dominated by attributes B and A, respectively, the shares of C (s_c) and E (s_e) become 1. The communication cost expression becomes

$$C = N_p + N_q * s_a + N_r * s_b$$

(c) The horizontal partition A', B', C', D_2, E' is having the same set of attribute values as in case b, except for the change in larger frequency value of attribute D (D_2). Such a change does not impact the communication cost expression.

$$C = N_p + N_q * s_a + N_r * s_b$$

(d) The horizontal partition A', B_1, C', D', E' has one larger frequency value B_1 and all others are low-frequency values. The share of B (s_b) becomes 1. The attribute C is dominated by D, attribute E is dominated by A, and D the share of C (s_c) and E (s_e) becomes 1. The communication cost expression for this join is

$$C = N_p * s_d + N_q * s_a + N_r$$

(e) The horizontal partition A', B_1, C', D_1, E' has attributes B_1 and D_1 two larger frequency values. The shares of B (s_b) and D (s_d) become 1. And hence E is dominated by A, its share (s_e) becomes 1. The communication cost expression becomes

$$C = N_p * s_c + N_q * s_a + N_r * s_c$$

(f) The horizontal partition A', B_1, C', D_2, E' has the same set of characteristics as case e, as the difference between them is that the larger frequency value D_1 is replaced by D_2. The communication cost expression is

$$C = N_p * s_c + N_q * s_a + N_r * s_c$$

(g) The horizontal partition A', B_2, C', D', E' has the same characteristics as that of case d, as the difference between them is that B_1 is replaced by B_2. The communication cost for this case is

$$C = N_p * s_d + N_q * s_a + N_r$$

(h) The horizontal partition A', B_2, C', D_1, E' has the same characteristics as that of case e, as the difference between them is that B_1 is replaced by B_2. The communication cost for this case is

$$C = N_p * s_c + N_q * s_a + N_r * s_c$$

(i)   The horizontal partition A', B_2, C', D_2, E' has the same characteristics as in case e, as the difference between them is that B_1 is replaced by B_2 and D_1 is replaced by D_2. The cost expression is as follows:

$$C = N_p * s_c + N_q * s_a + N_r * s_c$$

4.2.4   Θ-Join

The join approaches considered till now have equality as the joining condition. A more general and difficult case is when such equality is replaced by arbitrary inequality constraints known as Θ join.

Definition 4.2 *Multi-way Θ join let A, B, C be attributes of interest for the join operation. Let there be relations P(A, B), Q(B, C). The Θ-join operation between the relations P and Q is defined as* $P \bowtie Q \bowtie R = \{\langle a, b_1, b_2, c \rangle | (a, b_1) \in P, (b_2, c) \in Q \wedge b_1 \Theta b_2\}$.

Unlike the traditional equi join, the number of output tuples is much higher and the distribution of Θ-join requires more keen analysis on the number of output tuples generated by each compute task. With suitable partitioning function, equi join can be made to ensure the uniformity of loads across different partitions of the data. Such partitioning is more complicated in the context of Θ-join, as tuples $p \in P$ which have attribute values $p_b \leq q_b$ for all $q \in Q$ must be available where ever q is present (through appropriate partitioning). Θ-Join should accommodate for the variance in the input sizes.

4.2.4.1   Binary Θ-join

An approach for processing binary Θ-join is suggested in [9]. Let the two relations being joined be P and Q with cardinalities N_p and N_q, respectively. Let the domains of the two attributes involved in the join of B in P and B in Q be listed sequentially as columns of domain grid structure in Figure 4.5. The size of such grid structure is $N_p * N_q$ which is also the size of cross product (the superset of any join). If K is the number of reducers employed for computing the cross product, uniform distribution of the load would put a load of $S = N_p * N_q / K$ on every computing node. The input to any reducer which receives a grid of c cells from Figure 4.5 will be at least $2 * \sqrt{c}$. Treating these as lower bounds for the output size from a reducer and input

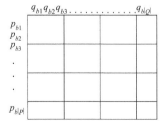

Figure 4.5   Θ-Join

size to a reducer, respectively, a good partitioning of the data grid can be obtained by dividing it into squares of size $\sqrt{S} \times \sqrt{S}$. Such partitioning of the grid will almost all be perfect except for the last row and column which might be lower in height and width, respectively. Let $m = \lfloor N_p/\sqrt{S} \rfloor$ and $n = \lfloor N_q/\sqrt{S} \rfloor$. We can fill the grid region in Figure 4.5 with $m*n$ squares of size $\sqrt{S} \times \sqrt{S}$. Using $\gamma = \min(m, n)$, we can accommodate the last row and column by taking a slightly higher sized squares $(\sqrt{S} + 1/\gamma)X(\sqrt{S} + 1/\gamma)$ which can subsume all the data.

Algorithm 2 Single-MR-Join(P, Q, R)

```
 1: Map
 2: Input: ⟨Φ; t⟩ t ∈ P ∪ Q ∪ R
 3: if t ∈ P then
 4:      Let i = h(t_b)
 5:      for j in range(1,σ) do
 6:          emit ⟨(i, j); t⟩
 7:      end for
 8: else if t ∈ R then
 9:      Let j = h(t_c)
10:      for i in range(1,σ) do
11:          emit ⟨(i, j); t⟩
12:      end for
13: else                                              ▷ t ∈ Q
14:      Let i = h(t_b)
15:      Let j = h(t_c)
16:      emit ⟨(i, j); t⟩
17: end if
18: Reduce Input: ⟨c; L_c = {t|t ∈ P ∪ Q ∪ R}⟩
19: Partition L_c into P_c = {p|p ∈ P ∩ L_c}, Q_c = {q|q ∈ Q ∩ L_c} and R_c = {r|r ∈ R ∩ L_c}
20: for (p, q) : p ∈ P_c ∧ q ∈ Q_c ∧ p_b == q_b) do
21:      for (q, r) : q ∈ Q_c ∧ q_c == r_c) do
22:          emit ⟨Φ; (p, q, r)⟩
23:      end for
24: end for
```

Algorithm 2   Single-MR-join

The overall performance of such joins is often decided by few nodes that run for longer time compared to the majority of other nodes. Bounding the maximum amount of input taken by the reducers and maximum amount of output produced would help in keeping the overall computation to be uniform across all the nodes. Using the previous construction, one can conclude that maximum reducer output is at most four times the ideal value of $\sqrt{S} \times \sqrt{S}$. Similarly the maximum input to a reducer has an upper bound of two times the lower bound $(2 * \sqrt{S})$. For reasonably higher values of m and n, these bounds can be much more tighter and nearer to the optimal.

A careful reader can observe that the grid of type shown in Figure 4.5 often is obtained from histograms rather than through explicit maintenance. The analysis done thus far applies to cross product rather than Θ-join. If the mapping of cross product output to reducers is available through the grid structure, a MapReduce program can be designed to map corresponding domain values of $P(B)$ and $Q(B)$, respectively, to the reducer numbers in the corresponding row and column of the grid structure, respectively. Preparing such mapping requires a separate pass over the dataset to map the respective value to the row-id of the grid structure. Rather a simpler approach of randomly selecting an arbitrary row of the grid and sending the tuple to reducers matching that row is followed in [9]. Such an approach is randomized and satisfies the bound on maximum reducer input and output probabilistically. The algorithm is depicted in Algorithm 3. The mapper takes the tuples of relations P or Q and uses the p_b or q_b to identify the row or column of the grid structure of the data space. Once such identification is done, such tuple t is sent to all the reducers of the corresponding row or column, respectively. The processing at the reducer involves the actual Θ-join on the partitioned inputs.

Algorithm 3 $MR - \Theta\text{-Join}(P, Q)$

1: **Map**
2: **Input:** $\langle \Phi; t \rangle \, t \in P \cup Q$
3: **if** $t \in P$ **then**
4:      Let $i = \text{Random}(1, m)$
5:      **for** j in range$(1, n)$ **do**
6:          emit $\langle (i, j); t \rangle$
7:      **end for**
8: **else**   ▸ $t \in R$
9:      Let $j = \text{Random}(1, n)$
10:     **for** i in range$(1, m)$ **do**
11:         emit $\langle (i, j); t \rangle$
12:     **end for**
13: **end if**
14: **Reduce Input:** $\langle c; L_c = \{t | t \in P \cup Q\} \rangle$
15: Partition L_c into $P_c = \{p | p \in P \cap L_c\}$ and $Q_c = \{q | q \in Q \cap L_c\}$
16: **for** $(p, q) : p \in P_c \wedge q \in Q_c \wedge p_b <= q_b)$ **do**
17:     emit $\langle \Phi; (p, q, r) \rangle$
18: **end for**

Algorithm 3   MR Θ-join

Though the analysis done till this part is meant for cross product, for several cases where the join deals with 50% of the cross product, a max-reducer output is close to the optimal by means of the randomization, whereas max-reducer input is also provable to be sufficiently closer.

4.2.4.2 Multi-way Θ-join

Multi-way Θ-join follows an extension of the approach in [9]. The work in [10] considers arbitrary combination of multi-way Θ-joins and expresses them as the combination of multiple chain joins. Chain joins are solved using a partitioning

approach that carefully considers the variance among the loads of different compute nodes as done in [9]. We will present the multi-way join using a two-way join
involving three relations $P(A, B)$, $Q(B, C)$, and $R(C, D)$. Consider the cross product
of these three relations. The size of such product is $N_p * N_q * N_r$. If K is the
number of reducers each reducer would get $S = N_p * N_q * N_r/K$ for uniform distribution of load across all the reducers.

4.3   Graph queries using MapReduce

We review some of the works that deal with graph-based query processing over
distributed architectures. Prominent work in this domain is the work on counting
triangles, which is a crucial operation used in computing network strength.
Subgraph enumeration is another problem that has a large number of applications
ranging from chemistry, biochemistry, bioinformatics, social network analysis, etc.
We review some of the works on subgraph enumeration in the context of
MapReduce to understand the communication cost reduction strategies.

4.3.1   Counting triangles

Let there be a graph $G(V, E)$ where V is the vertex set and E is the edge set
connecting an arbitrary pair of vertices. The problem of counting triangles tries to
find all the triangles of the graph $\langle u, v, w \rangle$ such that $(u, v), (v, w), (w, u) \in E$. A
naïve approach for counting the triangles is using two-phase MapReduce approach
presented in Algorithm 4. The first stage takes the raw graph expressed as edges
(u, v) and forms for each vertex its neighborhood $\mathcal{N}(u)$ which is like adjacency list
representation of the node's neighbors. Steps 1–7 of Algorithm 4 indicate the same.
In the second MapReduce phase, mapper takes a pair of vertices v, w from $\mathcal{N}(u)$
and forms a key value pair $\langle (v, w), u \rangle$. The mapper also takes the original graph in
the form of edges (u,v) given in step 11 and forms key value pairs of the form
$\langle (u, v), \Phi \rangle$ in step 13 of Algorithm 4. A reducer will either receive records of the
form $\langle (v, w), u \rangle$ or at most one record of the form $\langle (v, w), \Phi \rangle$. When a record
$\langle (v, w), u \rangle$ is seen by a reducer, it indicates that both v and w have an edge with u. In
addition to this, if the same reducer sees another record, $\langle (v, w), \Phi \rangle$, it indicates that
the pair of vertices v, w forms an edge of the graph. The same reducer can now
declare $\langle u, v, w \rangle$ to be a triangle. There can be several possible triangles of the form
$\langle (v, w), u \rangle$ which are decided to be triangles on the basis of the presence of edge
between v and w. Steps 15–20 depict the different steps of the second reducer.

   Algorithm 4 may overcount each triangle six times. To avoid such overcounting, the vertices are all ordered and the edges considered in triangles are
all in increasing order of these indices. Despite all these preliminary precau-
tions, Algorithm 4 may take lot of time for some of the reducers, whereas many
of the reducers may complete quite early. This is due to the fact that few of the
vertices of many real-world graphs have high degrees and Reducer 1 takes long
time if $\mathcal{N}(u)$ is of the order of million as it has to form $O(\mathcal{N}(u)^2)$-ordered pairs.
To avoid such overloading on some of the reducers, authors in [11] have

suggested a way of partitioning the graph in such a way that neighborhood lists of vertices (which are huge) are distributed over multiple reducers. Such partitioning enables the distribution of the computation more uniformly across all the reducers.

If the original graph is $G(V, E)$, the vertex set V is partitioned into R disjoint sets such that $V_1 \cup V_2 \cup \cdots \cup V_R = V$ and $V_i \cap V_j = \phi$ for all i and j. R is chosen such that $\binom{R}{3}$ is the number of reducers. Let us consider the subgraphs of the original graphs defined $G_{ijk}(V_{ijk}, E_{ijk})$ where $V_{ijk} = V_i \cup V_j \cup V_k$ and $E_{ijk} = \{(u, v) | u, v \in V_{ijk}\}$. The number of such subgraphs is $\binom{R}{3}$ each handled at different reducers. Instead of counting the triangles on the bigger graph G, the reducers count the triangles on the smaller graphs G_{ijk}. Such an approach can be implemented as a single MapReduce approach depicted in Algorithm 5.

Algorithm 4 $MR - CountingTriangles(G(V, E))$

1: **Map 1**
2: **Input:** $\langle \Phi; (u, v) \in E \rangle$
3: Emit(<u,v>)
4: **Reduce 1 Input:** $\langle u; N(u) = \{v | (u, v) \in E\} \rangle$
5: **for** Every pair of vertices $v, w \in N(u)$ **do**
6:     emit(<u,(v,w)>)
7: **end for**
8: **Map 2**
9: **Input:** $\langle \Phi; u, (v, w) \rangle, \langle \Phi; (u, v) \in E \rangle$
10: **if** record is of type $\langle \Phi; u, (v, w) \rangle$ **then**
11:     Emit(<(v,w),u>)
12: **else**
13:     Emit($\langle (u, v), \Phi \rangle$)
14: **end if**
15: **Reduce 2 Input:** $\langle (v, w), u \rangle$ or $\langle (v, w), \Phi \rangle$
16: **for** Every pair of vertices $v, w \in N(u)$ **do**
17:     **if** $\langle (v, w), \Phi \rangle$ is also in the input to the reducer **then**
18:         emit($\langle (u, v, w) \rangle$)   ▶ Count Triangle
19:     **end if**
20: **end for**

Algorithm 4   MR triangles

The map phase of Algorithm 5 takes every edge (u, v) from the original graph and identifies the reducers *ijk* which handle the enumeration of triangles of the subgraph G_{ijk}.

When triangles are counted in the respective reducers, we have to observe that the graph partitioning is not nonoverlapping due to which counting of the same triangle can happen in multiple reducers. The different cases that arise in such duplicate enumeration of triangles is illustrated in Figure 4.6. Let us think that the four quadrants identify four different vertex sets $V_1 = \{e, f, g\}$, $V_2 = \{a, b, c\}$, $V_3 = \{d\}$ and $V_4 = \{h\}$. There can be four subgraphs G_{ijk} formed with these vertex sets, namely, G_{123}, G_{124}, G_{134}, and G_{234}. Let us consider the triangles enumerated. Triangle *efg* is completely contained in V_1 and hence counted in each of G_{123}, G_{124},

G_{134}, resulting in overcounting by a factor of 3. In the general case, such triangles (identified as type 1 here after) are overcounted in $\binom{R-1}{2}$ subgraphs in which such vertex set is part of. The triangles for which one end point lies in one vertex set and other two end points lie in a different vertex set are identified as type 2 triangles. In Figure 4.6, the triangles abd, egc, bch, ghc are all examples of type 2 triangles. Let us consider the triangle egc that is counted once in subgraph G_{123} and once in G_{124}. In the general case, type 2 triangles are overcounted by a factor of $\binom{R-2}{1}$. The type 3 triangles have their end points in all different vertex sets. cgh, bdh are examples of type 3 triangles. They are counted exactly once as only one subgraph observes them.

Algorithm 5 $MR - CountingTrianglesUsingPartitioning(G(V, E))$

1: **Map 1**
2: **Input:** $\langle \Phi; (u, v) \in E \rangle$
3: Let $u \in V_m$ and $v \in V_n$
4: **for** All G_{ijk} containing V_m and V_n **do**
5:     Emit($\langle ijk, (u, v) \rangle$)
6: **end for**
7: **Reduce 1 Input:** $\langle ijk; \{(u, v) \in E_{ijk}\} \rangle$
8: **for** each triangle $(u, v, w) \in G_{ijk}$ **do**
9:     **if** (u, v, w) is type 1 triangle **then**
10:         emit($\Phi, \frac{1}{\binom{R-1}{2}}$)
11:     **else if** (u, v, w) is type 2 triangle **then**
12:         emit($\Phi, \frac{1}{R-2}$)
13:     **else**   ▸ Type 3 triangle
14:         emit($\Phi, 1$)
15:     **end if**
16: **end for**

Algorithm 5   MR-triangles-partitioning

The reduce function of Algorithm 5 (steps 7–14) uses three cases for each of type 1, 2, 3 triangles and divides by a factor of respective overcounting of these cases. Step 8 that identifies the triangles one after another is not obvious. Any algorithm useful for handling data in-memory can be used to perform the task of step 8. If N is the number nodes in a subgraph, the complexity of in-memory triangle enumeration has the complexity of $O(m^{3/2})$. The study in [12] suggested an approach to further reduce the complexity of such overcounting. The approach consists of using the $\binom{R}{3}$ subgraphs to count only the type 3 triangles. Type 2 and type 1 triangles are not counted by them. Instead they are counted by $\binom{R}{2}$ other subgraphs $G_{ij}(V_{ij}, E_{ij})$ where $V_{ij} = V_i \cup V_j$ and $E_{ij} = \{(u, v) | u, v \in V_{ij}\}$. The earlier subgraphs G_{ijk} are transformed into $G'_{ijk} = (V_{ijk}, E'_{ijk})$ where $E'_{ijk} = \{(u, v) | u \in V_{i'} \wedge v \in V_{j'} \forall i', j' \in \{i, j, k\}, i'! = j'\}$. Type 1 triangles are not overcounted in $\binom{R-1}{2}$ nodes, but only in $R - 1$ nodes. Type 2 triangles are not overcounted.

4.3.2   Subgraph enumeration

Subgraph enumeration has wide range of applications in application areas like network motif computing [13] for biochemistry, neurobiology and bioinformatics,

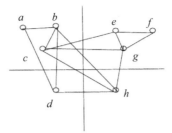

Figure 4.6   Graph partitioning

chemical (synthesis of target structure) [14], and social networks [15]. Given a large real-world graph $G(V_G, E_G)$ and a query graph $H(V_H, E_H)$, the objective of subgraph enumeration is to find all the isomorphic subgraphs of H in G. The letters V and E are used for vertex set and edge set of the given graph. Two graphs $g_1(V_{g_1}, E_{g_1})$ and $g_2(V_{g_2}, E_{g_2})$ are said to be isomorphic if there exists a one–one and onto function $f{:}V_{g_1} \rightarrow V_{g_1}$ such that $(v_1, v_2) \in E(g_1)$ *iff* $(f(v_1), f(v_2)) \in E(g_2)$.

Given a graph $G(V_G, E_G)$ and a pattern graph $H(V_h, E_h)$, the subgraph enumeration approach finds the set $\mathscr{S}_G^H = \{g(V_g, E_g) | V_g \subseteq V_G, E_g \subseteq E_G \wedge \exists f{:}V_g \rightarrow V_h\}$. Though the problem is NP-complete, because of its practical relevance in the wide range of application areas, several research efforts looked into the various aspects of the problem. Some of the works addressed the task of distributing the subgraph enumeration over frameworks such as MapReduce. The general idea in applying MapReduce paradigm for solving the problem of subgraph enumeration is to divide the original query pattern graph using a graph decomposition method and applying a left deep join framework to compose the matches of the query graph based on the decomposition in a stage-wise manner. Partial matched patterns in the data graph are combined using join operation. In this manner, parallelism can be achieved by distributing input data graph as well as query graph among various nodes in the cluster. There are several MapReduce algorithms that differ from each other in the distribution plan. This section explains different methods of distributing query graph. The input data graph G is represented as graph G_u formed using $\langle u, \mathscr{N}(u)\rangle$ (adjacency list of vertex u), $u \in V_G$, and $\mathscr{N}(u)$ is the set of neighboring vertices of u.

4.3.2.1   EdgeJoin

The author in [16] has addressed subgraph enumeration problem using EdgeJoin approach that uses edge-wise processing of pattern graph. The query graph decomposes into set $D_p = \{h_0, h_1, h_2, \ldots, h_p\}$, where $p = |E_H| - 1$. To illustrate the decomposition used in [16], we use a pattern graph given in Figure 4.7(a). The query graph has four vertices and five edges. Using EdgeJoin-based approach, we obtain decomposition given in Figure 4.7(b), where each element h_i is an edge. The decomposition elements are the edges $h_0(v_1, v_2), h_1(v_1, v_3), h_2(v_2, v_3), h_3(v_2, v_4), h_4(v_3, v_4)$.

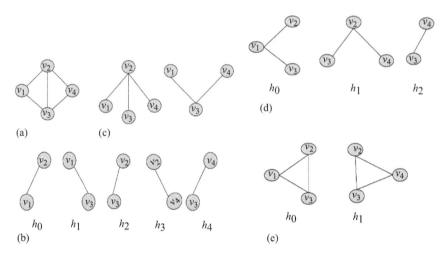

Figure 4.7   (a) Query graph, (b) EdgeJoin decomposition, (c) Star Join decomposition, (d) TwinTwig Join decomposition, (e) SEED decomposition

Algorithm 6 depicts the generic steps used by all the subgraph enumeration methods that solve the problem using partial results in a stage-wise approach. Implementation of EdgeJoin involves $p+1$ rounds of MapReduce as given in Algorithm 6. Each round involves joining the partial matching (H_{i-1}) results with the same graph G to match h_i. The common nodes of H_{i-1} and h_i are used as joining attributes. The partial matching results of each stage (i) is indicated as $IM(H_i)$ representing isomorphic matchings of partial pattern H_i.

The EdgeJoin procedure is depicted in Figure 4.8(a). Let the 0th round of algorithm produce the single-edge matchings. Let the result of such matching be $IM(H_0)$ matching $h_0(v_1, v_2)$ where H_0 represents partial pattern (h_0 itself). The first round consists of joining subgraphs representing edges $h_0(v_1, v_2)$ with edges $h_1(v_1, v_3)$ on v_1 (a self-join) to form the matches as paths of the form $v_2 - v_1 - v_3$ (a partial pattern of the given query graph) indicated in the bottom most step of Figure 4.8(a). The second phase of computation in Figure 4.8(a) (second step from bottom) consists of joining $IM(H_1)$ (matches of pattern $v_2 - v_1 - v_3$) with G to match the edge $h_2(v_2, v_3)$ to form the matches of partial pattern of triangle $H_2(v_1, v_2, v_3)$. Let the result of phase 2 be $IM(H_2)$. The third phase consists of joining $IM(H_2)$ with the G to match next pattern in the decomposition $h_3(v_2, v_4)$ (shown in third step from bottom of Figure 4.8(a)). The result of third phase is all the matches of the partial pattern $H_3(v_1, v_2, v_3, v_4)$. The fourth phase consists of joining output of third phase $IM(H_3)$ with G based on join pattern $h_4(v_3, v_4)$ (shown in fourth step from bottom of Figure 4.8(a)). The result of subgraph enumeration is $IM(H_4)$ where H_4 represents the query pattern.

As observed in other forms of data, sequential approach for solving such a problem results in a large amount of intermediate results which make both communication cost and I/O cost to increase enormously for even small pattern graphs.

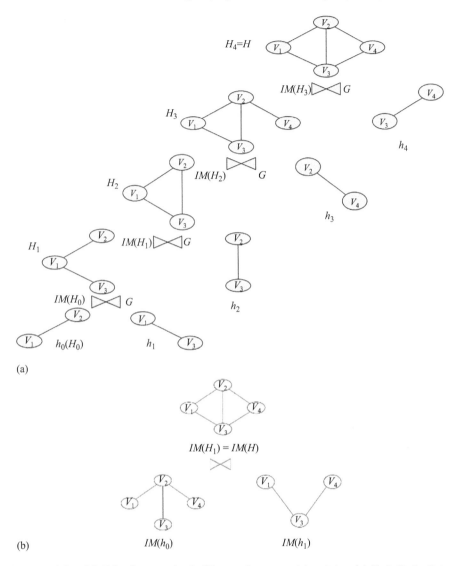

*Figure 4.8   (a) EdgeJoin method, (b) star decomposition join, (c) TwinTwig Join,
(d) SEED Join*

4.3.2.2   Star Join

The authors in [17] have approached the same problem using a star-based decomposition. The decomposed set contains stars which is $D_p = \{h_i | \forall i \ h_i$ is a star$\}$. Figure 4.7(c) shows how the query graph decomposed into stars. The two stars h_0 and h_1 are rooted vertices v_2 and v_3, respectively. We can observe that the number of such elements in the decomposition set D_p is lesser compared to the EdgeJoin

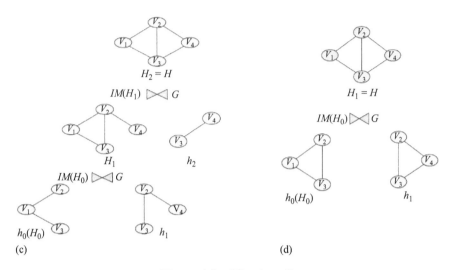

Figure 4.8   (Continued)

approach, which implies that the number of MapReduce rounds will also be lesser with subsequent reduction in intermediate result sizes. Figure 4.8(b) illustrates how the left-deep join tree forms while joining the matching results of G with respect to each decomposed element h_i. This method utilizes the structural information of the graph rather simply decomposing it as edges. For the example query graph in Figure 4.7(a), the first step consists of matching h_0 on graph G to produce the result $IM(H_0)$. The result $IM(H_0)$ is then joined with graph G to match h_1. The second step is indicated in bottom step of Figure 4.8(b). Subgraphs enumerated by this approach are contained in $IM(H_1)$ where the partial pattern H_1 matches the query pattern.

Though star decomposition is effective in improving the performance of subgraph enumeration, data-dependent skew can still pose a problem. If a vertex has a large number of neighbors, stars of even smaller size result in a large number of matches though not all will match the whole pattern graph. If N is the number of neighbors of a vertex (certain vertices can have million neighbors) and k is the number of neighbors of the root of star pattern, then $O(N_{c_k})$ is the number of intermediate matches generated by this approach.

4.3.2.3   TwinTwig Join

The authors in [18] have proposed TwinTwig Join approach that decomposes the query graph into decomposition elements called TwinTwigs. TwinTwig is a graph formed by a node with one or two incident nodes as shown in Figure 4.7(d). As the stars in TwinTwigs are constrained to size 2, the number of partial matches is limited to $O(N_{c_2})$. Figure 4.7(d) shows the decomposition of five edge query graph into two twin-twig of size 2 and an edge. The first twin-twig is rooted at v_1 and the second twin-twig is rooted at v_2. The third twin-twig is the edge (v_3, v_4). Figure 4.8(c) shows the formation of twin-twig-based matches from a given data graph using Algorithm 6. The first step of twin-twig join consists of preparing the matches of pattern $h_0(H_0)$ using one pass of the graph dataset represented in adjacency list form. $IM(H_0)$ (the matches of h_0) are then matched against the original graph G using the common vertex v_2. The pattern H_1 represents the combination of two twin-twigs h_0 and h_1. $h_2(v_3, v_4)$ is simple edge. The third step involves iterating over all the matches of $IM(H_1)$ to join it with G to match h_2 joining along the common vertices v_3 and v_4. The final result of matches of the pattern graph is collected into $IM(H_2)$.

The twin-twig approach for subgraph enumeration tries to find the balance between larger structure enforcement in the patterns and reduction in the number of intermediate results. As the technique employs left-deep join framework, finding the optimal left-deep join-based twin-twig decomposition requires exploration of $O(d_{max} * m * 2^m)$ possibilities, where d_{max} is the maximum degree and m is the number of edges of the pattern graph. Such search is performed using A^* search approach. Though the twin-twig approach has shown its merit for Erdos–Renyi random graphs [19], the power-law-based graphs [20] (which are the most common real-world datasets) are found to be harder cases for the algorithm.

4.3.2.4   SEED Join

The authors in [21] have refined the left-deep-join-based subgraph enumeration to consider cliques and stars as decomposition elements. To accommodate cliques and address the problems associated with stars, authors in [21] have changed the representation of the graph fed as input to the MapReduce framework. The study in [21] uses the local graph around node u, G_u formed using $V_{G_u} = \{u\} \cup \mathcal{N}(u)$ and $E_{G_u} = \{(u, v) | (u, v) \in E_G \wedge u, v \in V_{G_u}\}$ as input to the MapReduce framework. Decomposing the pattern graph to enable join-based enumeration of subgraphs involving cliques and stars requires exploration of bushy query plans as opposed to left-deep plans as done in the previous approaches. The study in [21] used a dynamic programming-based approach to find the optimal bushy decomposition over the remaining possibilities.

The query graph in Figure 4.7(a) can be decomposed into two cliques (triangles) as shown in Figure 4.7(e) The first clique has nodes v_1, v_2, v_3. The second clique has nodes v_2, v_3, v_4. SEED approach uses a first phase to match the clique decomposition element over the input graph. The partial matches are tagged as $IM(H_0)$ given in the lower left corner of Figure 4.8(d) The results of such partial matches $IM(H_0)$ are joined with the data graph G to match the common vertices between H_0 and h_1, namely, v_2 and v_3. The result will contain matches of the query graph as the composition of the two cliques h_0 and h_1 gives the query graph.

The generic algorithm that is used in graph-decomposition-based approaches to enumerate the subgraphs of data graph is given in Algorithm 6. First step is to find the set of decomposed elements $\{h_0, h_1, h_2, \ldots, h_p\}$ based on the methods EdgeJoin, StarJoin, TwinTwig Join, SEED shown in line 1 of Algorithm 6. The MapReduce phase from line 3 to 17 executes $p+1$ times as each iteration gives matches of joining structure formed in the previous round with current decomposed element as shown in Figure 4.8(a)–(d). In the last iteration, it gives $IM(H_p)$ which is all the subgraphs G isomorphic to H. During iteration 0, the mapper takes as input G_u. In the later iterations, it takes $IM(H_{i-1})$ or $IM(h_i)$. $IM(H_{i-1})$ gives matches of G to the graphical substructure H_{i-1} calculated in the previous round. $IM(h_i)$ are matches of G with h_i. The set of vertices common between H_{i-1} and h_i in the current iteration is captured $(v_{a_1}, v_{a_2}, \ldots, v_{a_k})$ in step 4 of Algorithm 6. These vertex indices in the pattern graph are used to locate the corresponding vertices in the actual matchings found at steps 8, 12, and 16 of Algorithm 6. The matchings of H_{i-1} and h_i that have identical mapping $(f(v_{a_1}), f(v_{a_2}), \ldots, f(v_{a_k}))$ will be received by the same reducer. Let $m = (u_{a_1}, u_{a_2}, \ldots, u_{a_k})$ be the combination of vertices identifying the key (reducer). The matchings of type H_{i-1} sharing the same key m are put under one list f_1. The matchings of h_i sharing the same key m are grouped into list f_2. Any combination of elements in f_1 and f_2 will match the pattern H_i, if they satisfy the additional constraint in line 21 (removal of common items in m from them should result in no further intersection). If this condition is satisfied, both the vertices are combined to represent the pattern H_i and outputted for further processing in the next round.

Algorithm 6 MR-SubgraphEnumearion(G, H)

1: Find decomposition $\{h_0, h_1, h_2, \ldots, h_p\}$
2: **for** i=0 to p **do**
3:      $Map_i(key = \phi;$ value is either G_u or $f_1 \in IM(H_{i-1})$ or $f_2 \in IM(h_i)$
4:      $\{v_{a_1}, v_{a_2}, \ldots, v_{a_k}\} = V_{H_{i-1}} \cap V_{h_i}$
5:      **if** value=G_u **then**
6:          IM(H_0) = all matches of H_0 in G
7:          **for** each match $f_1 \in IM_u(H_0)$ **do**
8:              return<$(f_1(v_{a_1}), f_1(v_{a_2}), \ldots, f_1(v_{a_k})), f_1$>
9:          **end for**
10:     **else if** value=$IM(H_{i-1})$ **then**
11:         **for** each match $f_1 \in IM_u(H_{i-1})$ **do**
12:             return<$(f_1(v_{a_1}), f_1(v_{a_2}), \ldots, f_1(v_{a_k})), f_1$>
13:         **end for**
14:     **else if** value=$IM(h_i)$ **then**
15:         **for** each match $f_1 \in IM_u(h_i)$ **do**
16:             return<$(f_2(v_{a_1}), f_2(v_{a_2}), \ldots, f_2(v_{a_k})), f_2$>
17:         **end for**
18:     **end if**
19:     $Reduce_i(key = m : \{u_{a_1}, u_{a_2}, \ldots, u_{a_k}\}, value = f_1 : \{f_{11}, f_{12}, \ldots\}, f_2 : \{f_{21}, f_{22}, \ldots\})$
20:     **for** all $(f_{1i}, f_{2j}) \in (f_1 X f_2) i, j = 1, 2, 3, \ldots$ **do**
21:         **if** $(f_{1i} - m) \cap (f_{2j} - m) = \Phi$ **then**
22:             Return <$\Phi, f_{1i} \cup f_{2j}$>
23:         **end if**
24:     **end for**
25:     IM(H_i) = IM(H_{i-1}) $\bowtie$ IM(h_i))
26: **end for**
27: return(IM(H_p))

Algorithm 6   MR-subgraph enumeration

4.4   Multi-way spatial join

Spatial join is a kind of join dealing with spatial objects and applying join operations such as overlap and range instead of equality and inequality applicable for numerical attributes. We review a method [22] of performing multi-way spatial join over MapReduce. The spatial objects are usually represented as bounding boxes (axes aligned rectangles) to ensure their efficient storage and retrieval. Overlap of rectangles is a joining criterion used for relating two spatial datasets. Consider the spatial dataset consisting of country borders, cities, coastline border, and military regions. An interesting query for this dataset is to retrieve the area covered by the military along the nation's border or the cities that overlap with coastline and military base.

MapReduce framework is explored for running such queries over multiple datasets. Let us assume that P, Q, R, S are spatial datasets. Figure 4.9 shows a series of objects represented as rectangles overlapping with each other. The rectangles p_1, q_1, r_1, s_1 overlap with each other and they represent one tuple of multi-way join among relations $P, Q, R,$ and S. How to perform such join for arbitrary-sized datasets using MapReduce?

Algorithm 7 MRSpatialJoin(P, Q)

1: **Map 1**
2: **Input:** $\langle \Phi; p \rangle\ p \in P \cup Q$
3: Let $C_p =$ split(p)
4: **for** $(c, p) : c \in C_p$ **do**
5:      emit $\langle (c; p) \rangle$
6: **end for**
7: **Reduce 1:**
8: **Input:** $\langle c; L_c = \{r | r \in P \cup Q\} \rangle$
9: Partition L_c into $P_c = \{p | p \in P\}$ and $Q_c = \{q | q \in Q\}$
10: **for** $(p, q) : p \in P_c \land q \in Q_c \land Overlaps(p, q)$ **do**
11:      emit $\langle \Phi; (p, q) \rangle$
12: **end for**

Algorithm 7   MR-spatial-binary

If spatial join has to be performed on MapReduce framework, the entire region of spatial objects is divided into disjoint subregions called cells as depicted in Figure 4.9. The cells are numbered squares from 0 to 24. When spatial objects are processed, they are sent to cells (reducers) on the basis of the position of the object. Consider the case of overlap join that has to be performed between P and Q spatial datasets. We can observe that q_1 overlaps with multiple cells as it lies on the cell boundary. q_1 overlaps with cells 7 and 12 and hence it can overlap with the objects of P lying in either of these cells. Hence, we send such spatial objects to all the cells with which they overlap. The operation used to identify the overlapping cells of a rectangle is called split. $C_q = split(q)$ gives a set of cells with which rectangle q overlaps. A binary join of relations P and Q can be performed by a single MapReduce-based approach as depicted in Algorithm 7. The mapper will perform the splitting of all the spatial objects $p \in P$ and $q \in Q$. Rectangle $p(q)$ is sent to all reducers in the set $C_p(C_q)$ (as given in

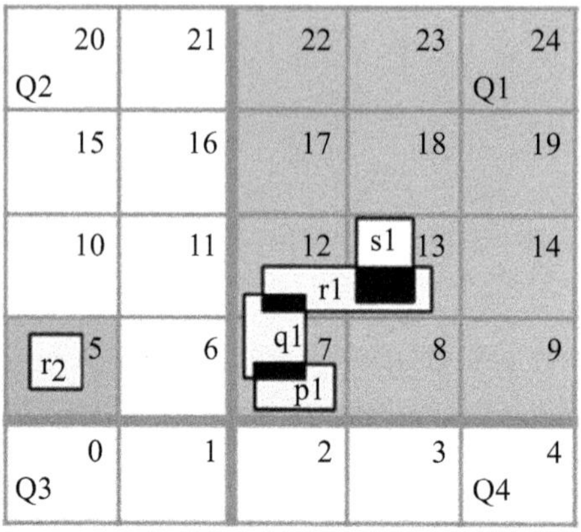

Figure 4.9   Cells

steps 3–6). The reducers that handle the workload of each of the cells 0–24 depicted in Figure 4.9 will perform the binary spatial join on a portion of the datasets P_c and Q_c received in cell c. The code from lines 10–12 represents the per node spatial join. In addition to the steps considered here, there is a duplicate avoidance strategy usually used to ensure that the same output tuple is not generated by two different reducers. Usually, the cell containing the mid-point of the overlapping region is a choice that ensures that each tuple is generated exactly once.

The previous algorithm can be extended for any number of steps successively for performing the multi-way spatial join. Such an approach will carry all the disadvantages of sequential join discussed in the section named Sequential Join. If we want to follow multi-way join approach for spatial data, the primary challenge lies in dealing with the boundary objects. In Figure 4.9 we can see that the join tuple $\langle p_1, q_1, r_1, s_1 \rangle$ can not be formed by any of the reducers (cells) as none of them receive all the rectangles through splitting. Spatial overlap across multiple relations is observed over multiple cells. To cover for such cases, replicate operation is performed. Let $C_{tr}(p)$ be set of cells in the top right quadrant of any rectangle p. $C_{tr}(p_1) = \{c_7, c_8, c_9, c_{12}, c_{13}, c_{14}, c_{17}, c_{18}, c_{19}, c_{22}, c_{23}, c_{24}\}$. Replicate (p) is an operation similar to split and involves sending the rectangle p to all the cells in $C_{tr}(p)$. Though the replicate operation looks naïve sending the rectangle to all over the grid structure, it enables addressing the problem associated with multi-way spatial join (a single reducer is unable to receive all the joining rectangles). Using replicate operation, we can ensure that at least one of the cells in the grid structure receives all the joining rectangles. But several reducers receive it. Naïvely replicating all the rectangles using this approach will overload the network as each replicate operation involves sending the rectangular objects from mappers to several reducers over the network (requiring costly communication overhead).

The authors in [22] presented a way of controlling the replicate operation needed for multi-way spatial join. Controlled-replicate analyses the possible

---

Algorithm 8 MR-Controlled-Replicate(P,Q,R,S)

1: **Map 1: Input:** $\langle \Phi; p \in$ any of the sets $P, Q, R, S \rangle$
2: **for** $(c, p) : c \in split(p)$ **do** emit $\langle (c; p) \rangle$
3: **end for**
4: **Reduce 1: Input:** $\langle c; L_c = \{r | r \in P \cup Q \cup R \cup S\} \rangle$
5: Partition L_c into $P_c = \{r | r \in L_c \wedge r \in P\}$, $Q_c = \{r | r \in L_c and r \in Q\}$
6: $R_c = \{r | r \in L_c \wedge r \in R\}$ and $S_c = \{r | r \in L_c \wedge r \in S\}$
7: **for** $(q, r) : q \in Q_c \wedge r \in R_c \wedge Overlaps(q, r)$ **do**
8:      **if** $!CrossesCellBoundary(q) \wedge !CrossesCellBoundary(r)$ **then**
9:          **for** $p \in P_c \wedge Overlaps(p, q)$ **do**
10:             **for** $s \in S_c \wedge Overlaps(r, s)$ **do** emit$(\langle \Phi; (p, q, r, s) \rangle)$ ▸ Generate part of the output
11:             **end for**
12:         **end for**
13:     **else**
14:         **for** $p \in P_c \wedge Overlaps(p, q)$ **do** Mark(p)
15:         **end for**
16:         **for** $s \in S_c \wedge Overlaps(r, s)$ **do** Mark(s)
17:         **end for**
18:         Mark(q) and Mark(r)
19:     **end if**
20: **end for**
21: **for** $q \in Q_c \wedge CrossesCellBoundary(q)$ **do**
22:     **for** $p \in P_c \wedge Overlaps(p, q)$ **do** Mark(p)
23:     **end for**
24: **end for**
25: **for** $r \in R_c \wedge CrossesCellBoundary(r)$ **do**
26:     **for** $s \in S_c \wedge Overlaps(r, s)$ **do** Mark(s)
27:     **end for**
28: **end for**
29: **for** $p \in P_c \cup S_c \wedge CrossesCellBoundary(p)$ **do** Mark(p)
30: **end for**
31: **for** $p \in P_c \cup Q_c \cup R_c \cup S_c \wedge Marked(p) \wedge Project(p)$ **do** emit$(\langle \Phi; p \rangle)$
32: **end for**
33: **Map 2: Input:** $\langle \Phi; p \in$ any of the sets $P, Q, R, S \rangle$
34: **for** $c \in C_{cr}(p)$ **do** emit$(\langle c; p \rangle)$ ▸ Replicate operation
35: **end for**
36: **Reduce 2: Input:** $\langle c; L_c = \{r | r \in P \cup Q \cup R \cup S\} \rangle$
37: Partition L_c into $P_c = \{r | r \in P\}$, $Q_c = \{r | r \in Q\}$
38: $R_c = \{r | r \in R\}$ and $S_c = \{r | r \in S\}$
39: **for** $(p, q, r, s) : p \in P_c \wedge q \in Q_c \wedge r \in R_c \wedge s \in S_c$
40: $\wedge Overlaps(p, q) \wedge Overlaps(q, r) \wedge Overlaps(r, s)$ **do**
41:     **if** c can compute the output tuple (p, q, r, s) **then**   ▸ Duplicate Avoidance
42:         emit $\langle \Phi; (p, q, r, s) \rangle$
43:     **end if**
44: **end for**

Algorithm 8   MR-controlled replicate (P,Q,R,S)

joining tuples formed by each of the rectangles and replicates only the rectangles for which it is needed. Consider Figure 4.10. There are two cells that are depicted here, c_1 and c_2. Each of them has some overlapping rectangles. Cell c_1 observes the joining tuple $\langle (p_1, q_1, r_2, s_2) \rangle$ which lies completely with in the boundary of the cell. Such tuples can be generated with the information available within the cell. There will several such tuples of this category. Such tuples can be identified by a simple rule. If you take any pair of overlapping (q, r) ($q \in Q$ and $r \in R$), if at least one of

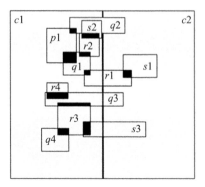

Figure 4.10   All replicate

them overlaps with the cell boundary, then such rectangles need replication. (q_1, r_2) lies completely inside, hence r_2 need not be replicated as it overlaps only with q_1 that is completely inside. But q_1 overlaps with r_1 that overlaps with the boundary, forcing both to be replicated. For the same reason, p_1 is also replicated as it forms a partial tuple p_1, q_1, r_1 which is going out of the boundary of cell c_1.

The MapReduce code for this is depicted in Algorithm 8. The first MapReduce phase performs the analysis of which rectangles of the dataset are to be replicated and which are not to be replicated (steps 5–31). It also generates the output corresponding to join tuples completely lying inside the boundary of the cell (steps 8–12). The second MapReduce phase actually performs the replication (steps 33–35) of all the rectangles marked for replication. For a rectangle to be marked for replication, it should be either crossing the cell boundary (steps 29–30, 31–32) or overlapping with another rectangle through which there is scope of join tuple getting formed (steps 13–19, 21–24, 25–28). The authors in [22] have shown several experiments over real and synthetic data for which controlled replicate strategy fares much better than the sequential and all-replicate strategies. The work in [22] presented these ideas but the lower-level details of the same and detailed algorithm are not provided.

Though controlled replicate approach reduces the number of unnecessary replications, the method of replication has inherent drawback in the distribution of work. The replication happens toward top right corner of the grid structure. Such approach overloads the compute nodes handling the corner of the grid structure resulting in the curse of last reducer. The authors in [23] have proposed an approach to address the skewness in the load distribution. They used a two-stage approach like controlled-replicate. The first phase consists of performing the spatial join of overlapping rectangles if the connecting rectangles are completely inside the bounding box of the cell. The second phase consists of nonspatial partitioning of overlapping rectangles in the line of shares approach [7] to address the skew in loads of reducers. Such an approach has resulted in an order of improvement in the performance of the multi-way join.

Table 4.2 Summary of join algorithms

Problem domain	Approach and publication details	Comments
Equi join	Shares [7] IEEE Transactions on Knowledge and Data Engineering SharesSkew [8] Information Systems ELSEVIER	Multi-way join is done in a single MR-based approach Communication cost is improved over sequential approach Works well for uniformly distributed datasets Performs poorly for skewed dataset Performs well for skewed datasets
Θ-Join	Θ-Join [9] SIGMOD	Optimizes for per reducer workload Analyses the input/output load of nodes for effective distribution of load Applicable to binary Θ-join
	Multi-way Θ-join [10] VLDB-2012	Can handle arbitrary join graphs efficiently Uses Hilbert-curve-based distribution scheme over hypercube of reducers
Counting triangles	WWW-2011 [11] CIKM-2013 [12]	Counts triangles using efficient distribution scheme to handle the skewness in graph node degrees Categorizes the triangles into types to reduce the redundant counting done in previous approach Reduces the mapper output size by $O(mp)$ compared to previous approach (m is the number of edges and ρ is the number of partitions of VertexSet)
Subgraph enumeration	[16] Journal of Parallel and Distributed Computing ELSEVIER VLDB 2012 [17] VLDB 2015 [18] VLDB 2016 [21]	Uses edge-oriented left-deep join approach Large number intermediate results are generated making the computation infeasible even for small query graphs Uses a star-oriented left-deep join approach Nodes of larger neighborhood result in a huge number of matches making it inefficient for even small subgraphs Uses twin-twig-based decomposition in the left-deep join framework Proved instance optimality of twin-twig decomposition Works well for Erdos–Renyi random graphs Power-law random graphs a Uses clique/star decomposition using bushy join trees Empirically proved that the bushy join framework is better compared to left-deep joins in terms of intermediate result sizes

Table 4.2 (*Continued*)

Problem domain	Approach and publication details	Comments
Multi-way Spatial Join	EDBT-2013 [22]	Uses controlled replicate strategy to curb the excessive replicate operations by adding an additional phase of analysis
		Shown phenomenal improvement in the performance of empirical results compared to all-replicate
		Replication scheme is still skewed
	GeoInformatica-Springer [23]	Uses a replication scheme addressing skewness in load distribution
		Uses a redistribution strategy to address the data-dependent skew of real-world datasets
		Works well for larger multi-way chain joins

4.5　Conclusion and future work

This chapter presents several approaches for designing data wrangling workflows using MapReduce. The content presents the algorithmic principles behind each of the approaches discussed and depicts all the details of the algorithms. Each of the algorithms is also analyzed for communication cost of various alternatives. The applications considered are equi join, involving numerical attributes, Θ-join, covering the inequality constraints, graph-based analysis using triangle counting addressing skew in the loads of computing nodes, subgraph enumeration, and multi-way spatial joins. The observations of this study are summarized in Table 4.2.

Though the work on SharesSkew provides some aspects of addressing skew in distributed computation, there are many aspects that are actively looked at by researchers both from theoretical and practical perspectives. Skewness brings different kinds of problems while dealing with different types of data. Some of the open issues, worthy to pursue, are finding lower/upper bounds of result sizes when the queries are computed in distributed mode. Though Shares are SharesSkew run in single-round MapReduce to compute multi-way join, there are cases where such single round approach is not worthy. Formally studying the conditions under which multi-round approach is better than single round is also a research issue to be pursued. It is also an important research challenge to study the influence of skew in a multi-round MapReduce algorithm.

References

[1]　Doulkeridis, C., and NOrvag, K. (2014). A Survey of Large-scale Analytical Query Processing in MapReduce. *The VLDB Journal*, 23(3), 355–380. https://doi.org/10.1007/s00778-013-0319-9.

[2]　Khezr, S. N., and Navimipour, N. J. (2017). MapReduce and Its Applications, Challenges, and Architecture: A Comprehensive Review and Directions for Future Research. *Journal of Grid Computing*, 15(3), 295–321. https://doi.org/10.1007/s10723-017-9408-0.

[3]　Lee, K.-H., Lee, Y.-J., Choi, H., Chung, Y. D., and Moon, B. (2012). Parallel Data Processing With MapReduce: A Survey. *SIGMOD Record*, 40(4), 11–20. https://doi.org/10.1145/2094114.2094118.

[4]　Li, R., Hu, H., Li, H., Wu, Y., and Yang, J. (2016). MapReduce Parallel Programming Model: A State-of-the-Art Survey. *International Journal of Parallel Programming*, 44(4), 832–866. https://doi.org/10.1007/s10766-015-0395-0.

[5]　Polato, I., Ré, R., Goldman, A., and Kon, F. (2014). A Comprehensive View of Hadoop research—A Systematic Literature Review. *Journal of Network and Computer Applications*, 46(C), 1–25. https://doi.org/10.1016/j.jnca.2014.07.022.

[6] Chaudhuri, S. (1998). An overview of query optimization in relational systems. *Proceedings of the Seventeenth ACM SIGACT-SIGMOD-SIGART Symposium on Principles of Database Systems – PODS '98*, 34–43. https://doi.org/10.1145/275487.275492.

[7] Afrati, F. N., and Ullman, J. D. (2011). Optimizing Multiway Joins in a Map-Reduce Environment. *Knowledge Creation Diffusion Utilization*, 23(9), 1282–1298.

[8] Afrati, F., Stasinopoulos, N., Ullman, J. D., and Vassilakopoulos, A. (2018). SharesSkew: An Algorithm to Handle Skew for Joins in MapReduce. *Information Systems*, 77, 129–150.

[9] Okcan, A., and Riedewald, M. (2011). Processing theta-joins using MapReduce. *Proceedings of the 2011 ACM SIGMOD International Conference on Management of Data*, 949–960.

[10] Zhang, X., Chen, L., and Wang, M. (2012). Efficient Multi-Way Theta-Join Processing Using MapReduce. *Proceedings of the VLDB Endowment*, 5(11), 1184–1195. https://doi.org/10.14778/2350229.2350238.

[11] Suri, S., and Vassilvitskii, S. (2011). Counting triangles and the curse of the last reducer. *Proceedings of the 20th International Conference on World Wide Web*, 607–614. https://doi.org/10.1145/1963405.1963491.

[12] Park, H.-M., and Chung, C.-W. (2013). An efficient MapReduce algorithm for counting triangles in a very large graph. *Proceedings of the 22nd ACM International Conference on Information & Knowledge Management*, 539–548. https://doi.org/10.1145/2505515.2505563.

[13] Milo, R., Shen-Orr, S., Itzkovitz, S., Kashtan, N., Chklovskii, D., and Alon, U. (2002). Network Motifs: Simple Building Blocks of Complex Networks. *Science*, 298(5594), 824–827. https://doi.org/10.1126/science.298.5594.824.

[14] Rücker, G., and Rücker, C. (2001). Substructure, Subgraph, and Walk Counts as Measures of the Complexity of Graphs and Molecules. *Journal of Chemical Information and Computer Sciences*, 41(6), 1457–1462. https://doi.org/10.1021/ci0100548.

[15] Kairam, S., Wang, D. J., and Leskovec, J. (2012). The life and death of online groups: Predicting group growth and longevity. *WSDM 2012 – Proceedings of the 5th ACM International Conference on Web Search and Data Mining*, 673–682. https://doi.org/10.1145/2124295.2124374.

[16] Plantenga, T. (2013). Inexact Subgraph Isomorphism in MapReduce. *Journal of Parallel and Distributed Computing*, 73(2), 164–175. https://doi.org/10.1016/j.jpdc.2012.10.005.

[17] Sun, Z., Wang, H., Wang, H., Shao, B., and Li, J. (2012). Efficient Subgraph Matching on Billion Node Graphs. *Proceedings of the VLDB Endowment*, 5(9), 788–799. https://doi.org/10.14778/2311906.2311907.

[18] Lai, L., Qin, L., Lin, X., and Chang, L. (2015). Scalable subgraph enumeration in MapReduce. *Proceedings of the VLDB Endowment* (Vol. 8, Issue 10, pp. 974–985). Association for Computing Machinery. https://doi.org/10.14778/2794367.2794368.

[19] Erdös, P., and Rényi, A. (1960). On the Evolution of Random Graphs. Publication of The Mathematical Institute of the Hungarian Academy of Sciences, 17–61. http://citeseerx.ist.psu.edu/viewdoc/summary?doi=10.1.1. 153.5943.

[20] Chung, F., Lu, L., and Vu, V. (2003). Eigenvalues of Random Power law Graphs. *Annals of Combinatorics*, 7, 21–33.

[21] Lai, L., Qin, L., Lin, X., Zhang, Y., Chang, L., and Yang, S. (2016). Scalable Distributed Subgraph Enumeration. *Proceedings of the VLDB Endowment*, 10(3), 217–228. https://doi.org/10.14778/3021924.3021937.

[22] Gupta, H., Chawda, B., Negi, S., Faruquie, T. A., Subramaniam, L. V., and Mohania, M. (2013). Processing multi-way spatial joins on MapReduce. *Proceedings of the 16th International Conference on Extending Database Technology*, 113–124. https://doi.org/10.1145/2452376.2452390.

[23] Bhattu, S. N., Potluri, A., Kadari, P., and Subramanyam, R. B. V. (2020). Generalized Communication Cost Efficient Multi-Way Spatial Join: Revisiting the Curse of the Last Reducer. *GeoInformatica*, 24, 557–589. https://doi.org/10.1007/s10707-019-00387-6.

[24] Dean, J., and Ghemawat, S. (2008). MapReduce: simplified data processing on large clusters. *Communications of the ACM*, 51(1), 107–113.

Chapter 5

Toward real-time data processing: an advanced approach in big data analytics

Shafqat Ul Ahsaan[1], Harleen Kaur[1] and Sameena Naaz[1]

Nowadays, a huge quantity of data are produced by means of multiple data sources. The existing tools and techniques are not capable of handling such voluminous data produced from a variety of sources. This continuous and varied generation of data requires advanced technologies for processing and storage, which seems to be a big challenge for data scientists. Some research studies are well defined in the area of streaming in big data. Streaming data are the real-time data or data in motion such as stock market data, sensor data, GPS data and twitter data. In stream processing, the data are not stored in databases instead it is processed and analyzed on the fly to get the value as soon as they are generated. There are a number of streaming frameworks proposed till date for big data applications that are used to pile up, evaluate and process the data that are generated and captured continuously. In this chapter, we provide an in-depth summary of various big data streaming approaches like Apache Storm, Apache Hive and Apache Samza. We also presented a comparative study regarding these streaming platforms.

5.1 Introduction

In today's world, nobody can deny the truth that there are a large number of sources from which a huge amount of data are generated continuously at a pace that is out of range for current technologies in order to capture, store and analyze it. Data are being generated from almost everywhere, whether it is a conversation over a mobile phone, any type of e-commerce activity, bank transactions, sensors and medical records of patients and some other sources. However, as far as social media is concerned like Facebook, Twitter, WhatsApp, Instagram and many more types of social media, it added fuel to the fire and makes the situation even worse. The size of data that are being generated from multiple sources over the Internet has touched the scale of 2 exabytes on a single day. A new study revealed that over 4 million queries are being received by Google every minute, e-mails sent by users reach the

[1]Department of Computer Science and Engineering, School of Engineering Sciences and Technology, Jamia Hamdard, New Delhi, India

limit of 200 million messages, 72 h of videos are uploaded by YouTube users, 2 million chunks of content are shared over Facebook and 277,000 Tweets are generated every minute on Twitter, WhatsApp users share 347,222 photos, Instagram users post 216,000 new photos every minute [1,2].

The data, derived by means of social media, form 80 percent of the data globally and report for 90 percent of big data [3]. From the previous discussion, we came to know that data are being generated from almost each and every source. Data scientists, academicians and researchers are in a race, to develop innovative tools and techniques to handle such voluminous data and make it easy to process and analyze these data. However, if there are no tools available to analyze the varied data then it is nothing other than garbage. The problems related to stream processing forced the data analysts to think over different scenarios like (i) how to propose ascendable background, (ii) how to offer data integrity in situations when hardware or software failure occurs, (iii) how to put forward well-organized solutions. Under the conditions given, the setup for the computing of real-time data is primarily designed to manipulate a very large quantity of data and make decisions on the fly. However, we know that big data is an emerging technology and is still in its infancy stage; multiple organizations have begun to put into power different streaming approaches to solve the most important budding big data problems that are much related to smart ecosystems, health-care sector, social media, etc. [4]. For example in smart cities where different types of sensors like weather monitoring devices, GPS, smart cards for public transport and installation of different types of traffic cameras at sensitive regions, e.g., traffic lights, trains, buses and water lines. With the installation of these sensors, voluminous and varied data are collected on a large scale. It is very important to analyze such a massive amount of data to get value from the very large stream of data. Second, social media is another platform that plays a key role in generating data for big data that needs real-time data handling and manipulation to get the results.

Actually, a massive quantity of data are generated without any break, at once from a broad collection of devices that are connected with each other by means of the Internet and websites, for example, photo and video distribution applications (such as Viber, Telegram, Snapchat Flicker, WhatsApp, Instagram and YouTube), networks that are suitable for the needs of a business (LinkedIn, Foursquare and ReverbNation), and social networks (Twitter, Vine, Facebook, Tumblr and Line) [5]. The process of starting to use new frameworks for data streaming that offers repetitive processing and learning potential permits to efficiently execute particular tasks like sentiment analysis, social network analysis and links prediction. Keeping in view the real-world scenarios discussed previously, it is the need of the hour to design a structure for the manipulation of huge dimensions of data to get value from it. Finding the appropriate structure for big stream-oriented applications becomes a promising dilemma. There are quite a lot of systems proposed in the literature. The chapter is distributed into six sections; Section 5.2 sheds light on basics of big data and how it is generated; Section 5.3 elaborates what stream processing is; Section 5.4 highlights a couple of techniques used for stream mining; Section 5.5 discusses Lambda architecture; in Section 5.6, a detailed summary of important frameworks for big data, their structural design and their internal performance is discussed and Section 5.7 provides a comparative study of various streaming methods in a tabulated form as per their key features.

5.2   Real-time data processing topology

5.2.1   Choosing the platform

The real-time data processing has been implemented by means of multiple frameworks like Storm, Hive, Flume and Spark. One major advantage of using such platforms is that these are distributed in nature and thus guarantee high performance, broad range of flexibility, and are fault tolerant in order to handle failures that provide the required level of reliability.

5.2.2   Entry points

The real-time processing system takes data from multiple sources. The core aim of such systems is to perform some analytics from the input data in real time as to keep the model contemporary. Different frameworks have different points for data ingestion: for Storm, the data entry points are called spouts, transformations and actions in Spark and in the case of Flink, the client takes data and transforms it to the Job Manager.

5.2.3   Data processing infrastructure

The data processing layers constitute the core of the real-time data processing systems. The various layers for real-time processing systems are as follows.

5.2.3.1   Formality layer

The formatting layer is used to convert the tuples into unified format. The challenging task for real-time data processing is that the data items that are being generated from multiple resources are in different formats. The formatting layer is responsible for handling data that exist in multiple formats. This stage simples and unifies data processing for the next phase.

5.2.3.2   Filtering layer

After passing through the formatting layer, the data streams are filtered and the data contents are not important and lead to inconsistency, and data redundancy from the processing point of view are removed. In this stage, the size of data streams decreases and reduces the complexity which is significant for the effectiveness and performance of the data processing algorithms.

5.2.3.3   Analytics layer

The core of the analytics layer consists of machine learning algorithms called incremental algorithms that are highly optimized to process streaming data in real time.

5.2.3.4   Storing layer

The application of the storage layer is to preserve the data and processing results into the data storage (Figure 5.1). In the storing layer, the bolts are used for filtration, aggregation and analysis phases of data streaming. The bolts act as connection points to the database, which plays a key role in achieving the reliability of the system.

5.3   Streaming processing

A data stream can be defined as an unbounded sequence of data objects (S, T) where S is a sequence of tuples and T is a sequence of positive real-time intervals.

There are multiple resources that generate data at a constant rate such as machine-to-machine communications, sensor networks, Internet of Things and social media platforms. However, in data streams, the ordered series of objects can be read only once. It is important that the machine used to process data streams should be very powerful and the reading process should utilize the limited computing and storage capabilities. The attributes of real-time data are constant coming of data objects, the messy appearance of data items and potentially uncontrolled size of streams [6]. There are a number of platforms that play a key role in producing data streams such as sensor networks, stock market and social media. Regarding data streams, there are a number of queries that are to be considered such as aggregate queries, join queries and continuous queries.

Aggregate queries: This class of queries includes MIN, MAX, COUNT, SUM and AVG operators [7].

Join queries: Join queries are used to detect whether the data object is present in the two selected regions R1 and R2. For example, if there are two sensors each in regions R1 and R2. Join query returns the object that is detected in both regions R1

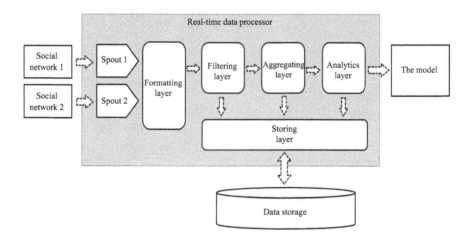

Figure 5.1   Real-time data processing topology

and R2. Join queries are used in monitoring applications where a couple of devices like sensors generate data called measurement data.

Continuous queries: In some cases, there is a need to monitor and detect changes in data continuously to answer queries. This uninterrupted execution of data streams makes it possible to allow applications to continuously monitor data streams and generate alerts, e.g., weather forecasting system.

5.4   Stream mining

The literal meaning of "mining" is to extract useful rules from data that will be very fruitful for taking decisions in the future. Data stream mining is the means to extract knowledge/useful information from continuous and rapid data records. In real-time data mining applications, the emphasis is on how to forecast the class or importance of novel occurrence in the data stream provided some understanding about the class association or values of earlier occurrences in the data stream. There are a variety of machine learning techniques that can be used to find out the prophecy from labeled patterns in an automatic way. Some of the machine learning techniques are summarized as follows.

5.4.1   Clustering

Clustering can be defined as a method of grouping a set of objects on the basis of similarity. If we have *n* groups of objects, while applying to the cluster, it forms a new group of objects that includes all those objects that have some kind of similarity in any sense whether they (a group of objects) have common features, functionalities or some other kind of similarity [8]. It is a type of unsupervised learning. There are mainly two types of clustering: (i) hard clustering and (ii) soft clustering or fuzzy clustering. Hard clustering depicts whether every object is a member of a cluster or not. On the other hand, in fuzzy clustering, every object is a member of each cluster to a definite degree. There are different types of clustering models that can be deployed while having machine learning in practice. Some of the typical clustering models are connectivity model, centroid model, distribution model, density model and neural model.

5.4.2   Classification

Classification falls under the category of supervised machine learning. Basically, in supervised learning, the machine is trained by means of well-labeled data where the output of data used to train the machine is known to the user [9]. After the training phase is over, a new set of data (example) is provided to the machine as input; supervised learning algorithm is applied to analyze the training data and accordingly generates an acceptable result from labeled data [10]. In classification, a predefined classifier is used on the basis of purpose with two data sets—labeled data and unlabeled data. The classifier is trained by means of labeled data, and the unlabeled data can then be classified with the help of a trained classifier.

5.4.3   Frequent

Item set mining: It is a technique that is used to find sets of items that appear frequently in a data set, where a collection of similar items come out together in some precise context. It is used for market basket analysis [11]. The most important point of this method is to trace out homogeneity in the shopping practices of customers of supermarkets, online shops, mail-order companies, etc.

5.4.4   Outlier and anomaly detection

In machine learning, studies carried out by experts who are developing predictive models suggest that two-thirds of the effort are being dedicated to data understanding and preprocessing stages of data mining process. Anomaly and outlier detection techniques are used all through data understanding and preprocessing stages. In data science discipline, anomalies are described as data points that do not satisfy the criteria of an anticipated pattern of the other items in the data set [12]. Anomalies might be ingested in data for a couple of reasons like malevolent activity, e.g., terrorist activity, cyber intrusion and credit card fraud. Anomaly detection is the method of tracing patterns in data which do not fulfill the criteria to expected behavior. Anomaly detection has a wide range of applications like intrusion detection for cybersecurity, fault detection in safety-critical systems, health care and insurance, frauds related to credit card transactions and military surveillance for enemy activities.

As per the definition of data science [13], an outlier is an observation point that is isolated from other observations. An outlier may appear in data as a result of inconsistency in the measurement or it may be an experimental glitch. There is a very less chance of an outlier to be included in a respective data set. Outliers in the data may lead to prediction distortion and influence the accuracy if remain undetected.

5.5   Lambda architecture

Lambda architecture is defined [14] as a data processing structural design to manipulate gigantic volumes of data by taking advantage of stream processing and batch processing. It lies on the top of MapReduce and Storm in order to build stream processing applications as shown in Figure 5.2.

Lambda architecture is based on a data model possessing append-only, inflexible data sources that act as a system of record. The unchangeable sequence of records is captured and ingested in coordination with a batch system and stream processing system. How data are processed in Lambda architecture? Business information logic is put into operation twice, on one occasion in the stream processing system and one time in the batch processing system. At query time, output generated from both the systems is consolidated in order to generate the result [15].

The main objective of Lambda architecture is to build applications that have to execute with low latency. The batch processing system suffers from a major problem that is the time it takes. During the intervening time, data are appearing

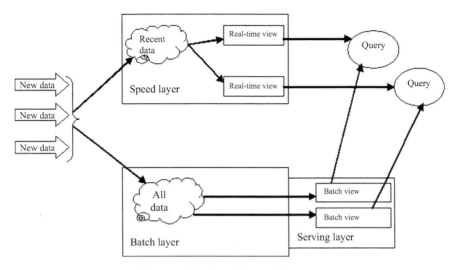

Figure 5.2 Lambda architecture

constantly, and consecutive processes or services keep on working with previous data. The solution to this problem lies in the real-time layer, as it captures a replica of data, processes it swiftly and saves it in a fast store and the store needs to be updated on regular basis.

However, Lambda architecture has disadvantages too. There is a call to compile the similar code multiple times for real-time and batch processing layers that are a cumbersome task. To tackle this problem, there also exists a solution called summingbird framework. Summingbird is a library that allows the developer to write down MapReduce programs that resemble with Scala or Java and implement them on a variety of popular distributed platforms. That means a similar code can be carried out in cooperation of layers in Lambda architecture [16–18].

5.6   Stream processing approach for big data

There are a variety of frameworks that have been introduced to perform real-time stream processing for a huge amount of data. Here, the main focus is on a good number of familiar stream processing frameworks that have proved to be efficient for big data stream processing.

5.6.1   *Apache Spark*

Apache Spark is a low-latency, extremely parallel processing framework for big data analytics. It presents a platform for handling massive amounts of heterogeneous data. Spark laid a background of its existence in 2009 at UC Berkeley [19]. Spark is very easy to use as it can support Python, Java, Scala and R programming languages to write applications. It is possible for Spark to run over a single machine.

The working principle of Spark is based on a data structure known as resilient distributed datasets (RDDs). RDDs basically consist of a read-only multi-set of data objects that are scattered over the whole batch of machines. It is feasible to use Spark for machine learning, but what is required is a cluster manager and a distributed storage system like Hadoop. Spark performs two operations on RDDs: (i) transformations and (ii) actions. Transformation operations are responsible for the formation of new RDDs from the current ones via functions such as join, union, filter and map. On the other hand, action operations carry out the computational results of RDDs [20]. The core elements of Spark are as follows:

- **Spark SQL:** It is responsible for the manipulation of data frames by means of domain-specific languages.
- **Spark Streaming:** Spark Streaming is a Spark library that provides scalable and high throughput in order to process live data streams. In Spark Streaming, data are used in mini-batches for RDD transformations which make it possible to use the similar set of application code that is being created for batch processing and can also be used to carry out stream processing.
- **Spark MLlib:** Spark is perfect for machine learning via Spark MLlib. It is nothing other than a library that makes machine learning tasks very easy to execute for Spark extensively.
- **GraphX:** It is a framework for graph processing which is distributed in nature and it resides on the top of Apache Spark.

In Spark Streaming, the input can be taken from multiple sources like Twitter, Flume, Kafka and with the help of algorithms having high-level functions like join, filter, map, union and reduce, the data are processed efficiently at a large scale as shown in Figure 5.3.

After the processing of data, the output can be stored in file spaces, databases and live dashboards. In a nut-shell, Spark is a good candidate for processing of live data streams as depicted in Figure 5.4, by applying machine learning and graph processing algorithms.

5.6.2   Apache Flink

There are very few data processing frameworks that work in a batch mode as well as in real-time mode. Likewise, Flink is an open-source distributed data processing

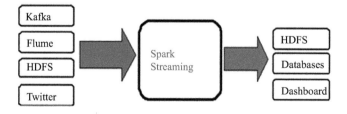

Figure 5.3   Spark Streaming

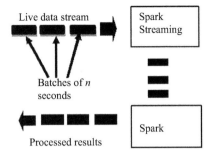

Live data stream

Spark Streaming

Batches of *n* seconds

Spark

Processed results

Figure 5.4   Spark processing

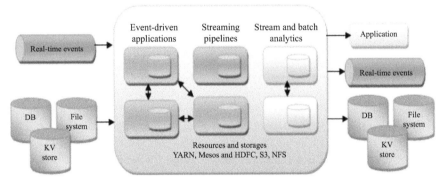

Figure 5.5   Architecture of Flink framework

framework written in Java and Scala that operates in both batches and real-time mode. Moreover, it supports the implementation of iterative algorithms with high-speed performance. It is loaded with a number of features like fault tolerance in the case of system failures and efficient computation on a large scale [21]. The working model of Flink is based on MapReduce as depicted in Figure 5.5. In addition to the function-alities provided by MapReduce, Flink appears to be more powerful as it provides some additional high-level features like filter, aggregation and joins. Flink ingests data that are being collected by multiple tools such as Flume, Kafka and permits repetitive processing and computation on data streams in real time [22]. It also provides a range of APIs on a conceptual level; hence, let the users instigate distributed computation in a crystal clear and straightforward manner. Flink supports the in-memory and scalable implementations and executions on both bounded and unbounded streams of data.

Unbounded data streams: The unbounded data streams have a starting point, but no definite termination point. They deliver the data at the time of its generation and need to be processed continuously without any delay. Because there is no defined ending of the incoming data, it is not feasible to wait for the arrival of entire data stream. Furthermore, in order to get desired results the processing of the data is required to be in some particular order.

Bounded data streams: The bounded data streams have definite starting as well as ending point. The processing of these data streams can be done by taking entire data before the actual implementation. The bounded data stream processing is also called batch processing.

Apache Flink is best suited for the processing of both bounded and unbounded types of data streams. Its ability to precisely control the state and time of the system during runtime makes it suitable for unbounded streams, while its capability to process the data structures and algorithms internally yields exceptional performance. There are two core API's in Flink: one is batch processing and the other is stream processing. The core of Flink comprises a dataflow engine that is distributed in nature. It acts as a common framework to abstract both bounded and unbounded processing. On top of Flink APIs, domain-specific libraries create DataSet and DataStream API programs, FlinkML for machine learning, table for SQL-like operations and Gelly for processing of graphs. The Flink cluster constitutes of three processes: the Job Manager, the client and one Task Manager. The flow of working for Flink is from client to Job Manager. The client accepts the program code, converts the program code into dataflow graph and then puts forward to the Job Manager for further processing. While transforming the program code into dataflow graphs, the data types are also examined among operators (Figure 5.6).

The responsibility of Job Manager is to coordinate the distributed execution of the dataflow. It monitors the state and advancement of every operator and stream, lists new operators and synchronizes recovery and checkpoints. The Job Manager maintains a set of metadata at all checkpoints as such a standby Job Manager can rebuild the checkpoint and recuperate the flow of execution from the point of failure, hence, provides fault-tolerance storage. The processing is actually carried out by the Task Manager. The Task Manager executes one or more operators that generate streams and provide information about their status to the Job Manager.

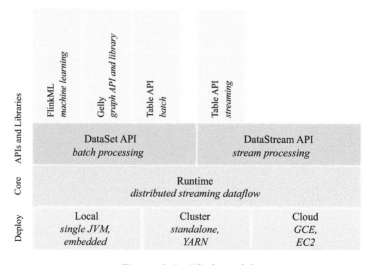

Figure 5.6   Flink model

The Task Manager maintains a buffer for the streams that are coming and retains the network connections to switch over the data streams among operators.

5.6.3   Apache Samza

Apache Samza is considered to be an open-source data processing framework, distributed in nature, and is being developed by LinkedIn to offer solutions to different kinds of streaming problems like data logging, data tracking and data as input for real-time services [23,24]. Since its development, Samza was implemented and used in a variety of projects. It has gained the distributed feature for messaging via Apache Kafka, scheduling and distributed allocation of resources, fault tolerance, security, processor isolation and resource management by means of Hadoop YARN in the cluster as shown in Figure 5.7.

The working of Samza is carried out by three layers. The first layer is dedicated to streaming data and it makes the use of Apache Kafka as a medium in order to make data transfer. The distributed processing background is offered by the second layer on the basis of the YARN resource manager and is responsible to handle CPU and memory usage over a cluster of machines that are served by a single software-as-a-service vendor server [25,26]. The core element of Samza is presented by the third layer and has (third layer) capabilities of processing and offers API for the generation and execution of stream tasks in the cluster. In this layer, users are capable of performing particular processing jobs with the help of implementation of different conceptual classes. These classes are executed by MapReduce to guarantee distributed processing.

5.6.4   Apache Storm

Storm, an open-source, fault-tolerant configuration allows the processing of voluminous and high-velocity structured, semi-structured and unstructured data in real time. As far as Storm is concerned, it proves to be a very effective framework for the analysis of real-time data, sequential and repetitive computation and machine

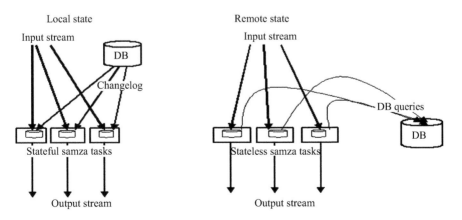

Figure 5.7   Apache Samza

learning. The Storm is based on master–slave architecture, therefore a cluster is chiefly made-up of master and worker or slave nodes, with coordination offered by Zookeeper [27]. The responsibility of the master node is to control the slave nodes and allot everyday jobs to them. If a situation arises where it is spotted that the slave node is out of order, it is a master node that reallocates the job to a different node. The data structure of the Storm is known as tuple and it supports every data type. In order to do the computations in real time in Storm, *topologies* are created. These topologies are demonstrated using directed acyclic graphs (DAG) so as to represent the programs, where the edges of the DAG indicate data transport [28] and the node consists of logic behind the processing. There are two types of nodes in DAG: (i) bolts and (ii) spouts. The spouts or entry points correspond to the data sources in a Storm program. On the other hand, bolts are used to specify the functions that are being executed on the data. The network consisting of bolts and spouts is collectively called topology in which a node might either be a bolt or a spout and the links among them are responsible for the flow and processing of the data. The data streams can flow either from a bolt to another bolt or from a spout to a bolt. For the routing of the tuples within the network, stream grouping is done in one of the following manners:

Shuffle grouping: In this type of grouping, equal numbers of tuples are distributed in a random manner all across the bolts that are executing.

Field grouping: Field grouping is done on the basis of the same values within the fields, and the remaining ones are left externally. The grouped tuples are sent to the executing bolts afterward.

Global grouping: All the available data streams are grouped into a single chunk and forwarded to a single bolt. This type of grouping collects all the input instances of tuples and sends to a single target, usually the one with the lowest ID number.

All grouping: In this type of grouping, a copy of every tuples is sent to all the available instances of the receiver bolts. This grouping is suitable for sending signals to the bolts and is helpful in join operations.

5.6.5 *Apache Flume*

Apache Flume is an open-source, consistent, distributed framework that offers aggregation, collection and shifting of a huge quantity of record data. It owns a plain and supple structural design characterized by streaming data flows. It has a couple of attractive features like powerfulness and fault tolerance with an adjustable consistency mechanism and loads of fail-overs and recuperation system [29]. Flume makes use of basic flexible data representation that helps online logical applications (Figure 5.8).

    Flume event: A Flume event is the fundamental data unit transferred within the Flume. It consists of two parts: the header that is optional and the byte payload in the form array as shown in Figure 5.9.

    Flume agent: A Flume agent is a daemon process that is independent. It accepts the incoming data from the clients or other agents within the Flume and sends it

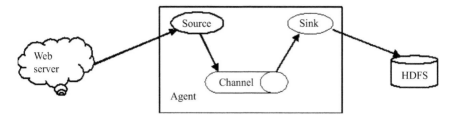

Figure 5.8   Apache Flume

Figure 5.9   Flume event

Figure 5.10   Flume agent

ahead to the next target either the agent or the sink. A Flume agent consists of three main components: source, channel and sink. Figure 5.10 shows its diagrammatic representation.

Source: This component of the Flume agent gathers the data from the data producers and transmits it to the channel (one or more depending upon the requirement).

Channel: A channel gets the data and the events from source temporarily and it keeps it until it is asked by the sink. It basically works as a connecting bridge between the source and sink. It is capable of handling any number of sources and sinks.

Sink: This component is responsible for storing the data into consolidated storages like HDFS and HBase. It takes the data from the channel and sends it to the targeted destination that could be the storage or any other agent.

5.6.6   *Apache Kafka*

Apache Kafka [30] is defined as a fault-tolerant, low-latency, extensible and high-throughput stream processing system developed by LinkedIn, written in Java and Scala. However, Kafka is deployed as a kernel for data stream architecture. Additionally [31], Kafka has the ability to connect to peripheral systems in order to import/export data by means of Kafka Connect and make available a Java stream processing library for Kafka Streams. The stream-centric architecture of LinkedIn is shown in Figure 5.11.

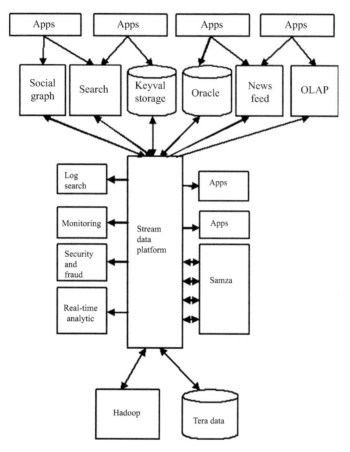

Figure 5.11   Kafka

Kafka permits the building of data streaming pipelines in real time. They support the in-memory architecture and help in making systems for analysis, transformation, aggregation and join of real-time data. It can be used for restoring the states, syncing of nodes and replication of data among the nodes. It supports multiple application areas such as messaging, auditing, log aggregation and click-based tracking.

For the streaming of data in real time, the Apache Kafka is normally implemented in combination with Apache Storm, HBase and Spark. It has the capability to deliver streams of messages irrespective of the application domain. The implementation of Kafka is usually done in the form of clusters on more than one server. These clusters contain the messages that comprise elements like key. It consists of following four APIs:

Producer API: Producer API allows the applications to broadcast the stream of messages or records to topics (either on one or more than one).

Table 5.1 Comparison of stream processing frameworks

Features	Spark	Flink	Samza	Storm	Flume	Kafka
Programming model	Transformation and action	Actions functions	MapReduce jobs	Bolts	Flexible	Kernel-based
Programming languages	Java, Scala Python	Java	Java	Java	Java	Java, Scala
Data format	DStream	DStream	Message	Tuples	Message	Message
Data sources	HDFS DBMS Kafka	HDFS DBMS Kafka	Kafka	Spoots	HDFS	HDFS DBMS
Elasticity	Yes	No	No	Yes	Yes	Yes
Cluster manager	Hadoop YARN	Hadoop YARN	YARN	Zookeeper	Hadoop YARN	Kafka cluster
Machine-learning compatibility	Spark MLib	FlinkML	SAMOA API	SAMOA API	No	No
Messaging	Exactly once	Exactly once	Exactly once	Atleast once	Atleast once	Exactly once
Latency	Few seconds	Sub-seconds	Sub-seconds	Sub-seconds	Sub-seconds	Sub-seconds
Auto parallelization	On demand	Pipelined processing	On demand	Pipelined processing	On demand	Pipelined processing
Stream query	Spark SQL	No	Yes Samza SQL	No	No	KSQL
Data partitioning	Yes	No	Yes	No	No	Yes

Consumer API: Consumer API permits the applications to subscribe to the topics (either on one or more than one). The processing of the record streams is also done by this API.

Streams API: Streams API are responsible for taking the input streams from the topics and converting them into output streams.

Connector API: Connector API produces the executing produces as well as consumers that connect the topics to the prevailing applications.

5.7 Evaluation of data streaming processing approaches

The stream processing frameworks that have been discussed in the last section, and a comparative study on the basis of different features like latency and messaging capacities, programming model, programming language supported, cluster manager, types of data sources and data format are covered in Table 5.1. From the discussions in the previous section regarding multiple frameworks, we came to know that the beauty of Spark lies in micro-batch processing potential, in-memory features chiefly step-by-step and repetitive processing. However, Spark has considered one of the best stream processing approaches as a result of RDDs. It is recognized by its low throughput and fault tolerance. The fault tolerance feature of Spark is guaranteed by its micro-batch processing concept. Flink, on the other hand, resembles Spark in its characteristics and similarities. Flink has the potential to deal with multidimensional big data structures. As far as the processing power of Flink and Spark is concerned, they are loaded with precise APIs and tools for extrapolative study and machine learning.

5.8 Conclusion

The data are generating at a pace never before by billions of devices that are connected with each other via the Internet. In order to process this gigantic amount of data, stream processing has become the key requisite for big data frameworks. The main objective of this chapter is to study the most accepted frameworks for large-scale stream data processing. The various frameworks like Spark, Storm, Flink and Samza were presented and classified according to their main features. We primarily further make a classification of the considered frameworks on the basis of particular features of stream-processing methods. With the passage of time, we will provide a deep analysis of the abovementioned stream processing frameworks in the future.

Acknowledgment

This research work was catalyzed and supported by the National Council for Science and Technology Communications (NCSTC), Department of Science and Technology (DST), Ministry of Science and Technology (Govt. of India), New Delhi, India [grant recipient: Dr. Harleen Kaur and grant No. 5753/IFD/2015-16].

References

[1] Jaseena, K. U., and David, J. M. "Issues, challenges, and solutions: Big data mining." CS & IT-CSCP 4, no. 13, (2014): pp. 131–140.

[2] Lawal, Z. K., Zakari, R. Y., Shuaibu, M., and Bala, A. "A review: Issues and challenges in big data from analytic and storage perspectives." International Journal of Engineering and Computer Science 5, no. 3, (2016): pp. 15947–15961.

[3] Landset, S., Khoshgoftaar, T. M., Richter, A. N., and Hasanin, T. "A survey of open source tools for machine learning with big data in the Hadoop ecosystem." Journal of Big Data 2, no. 1, (2015): p 24.

[4] Gandomi, A., and Haider, M. "Beyond the hype: Big data concepts, methods, and analytics." International Journal of Information Management 35, no. 2, (2015): pp. 137–144.

[5] Gama, J., and Gaber, M. M. (Eds.). Learning From Data Streams: Processing Techniques in Sensor Networks. Springer Science & Business Media, Springer, Berlin, Heidelberg, 2007.

[6] Namiot, D. "On big data stream processing." International Journal of Open Information Technologies 3, no. 8, (2015).

[7] Subramaniam, S., and Gunopulos, D. "A survey of stream processing problems and techniques in sensor networks." In Data Streams, Springer, Boston, MA, 2007, pp. 333–352.

[8] Gorunescu, F., Data Mining: Concepts, Models and Techniques. Vol. 12. Springer Science & Business Media, Springer-Verlag Berlin Heidelberg, 2011.

[9] Wang, F., and Liu, J. "Networked wireless sensor data collection: Issues, challenges, and approaches." IEEE Communications Surveys & Tutorials 13, no. 4, (2010): pp. 673–687.

[10] Manning, C., Raghavan, P., and Schütze, H. "Introduction to information retrieval." Natural Language Engineering 16, no. 1, (2010): pp. 100–103.

[11] Chui, C. K., Kao, B., and Hung, E. "Mining frequent itemsets from uncertain data." In Pacific-Asia Conference on Knowledge Discovery and Data Mining, Springer, Berlin, Heidelberg, 2007, pp. 47–58.

[12] Gogoi, P., Bhattacharyya, D. K., Borah, B., and Kalita, J. K. "A survey of outlier detection methods in network anomaly identification." The Computer Journal 54, no. 4, (2011): pp. 570–588.

[13] Jabez, J., and Muthukumar, B. "Intrusion detection system (IDS): Anomaly detection using outlier detection approach." Procedia Computer Science 48, (2015): pp. 338–346.

[14] Yang, F., Merlino, G., Ray, N., Léauté, X., Gupta, H., and Tschetter, E. "The RADStack: Open source lambda architecture for interactive analytics." In Proceedings of the 50th Hawaii International Conference on System Sciences, (2017): pp. 1703–1712.

[15] Ahsaan, S. U., Kaur, H., and Naaz, S. "An empirical study of big data: Opportunities, challenges and technologies." In New Paradigm in Decision Science and Management, Springer, Singapore, 2020, pp. 49–65.

[16] Pathak, A. R., Pandey, M., and Rautaray, S. "Construing the big data based on taxonomy, analytics and approaches." Iran Journal of Computer Science 1, no. 4, (2018): pp. 237–259.

[17] Boykin, O., Ritchie, S., O'Connell, I., and Lin, J. "Summingbird: A framework for integrating batch and online MapReduce computations." Proceedings of the VLDB Endowment 7, no. 13, (2014): pp. 1441–1451.

[18] Baboota, R., and Kaur, H. "Predictive analysis and modelling football results using machine learning approach for English Premier League." International Journal of Forecasting 35, no. 2, (2019): pp. 741–755.

[19] Inoubli, W., Aridhi, S., Mezni, H., Maddouri, M., and Nguifo, E. "A comparative study on streaming frameworks for big data." In VLDB 2018—44th International Conference on Very Large Data Bases: Workshop LADaS-Latin American Data Science, Aug (2018), pp. 1–8.

[20] Zaharia, M., Chowdhury, M., Franklin, M. J., Shenker, S., and Stoica, I. "Spark: Cluster computing with working sets." HotCloud 10, (2010): p. 95.

[21] Apache Flink. "Scalable Batch and Stream Data Processing. 2016." Apache Flink: Scalable Batch and Stream Data Processing (2016). https://flink. apache.org.

[22] Kaur, H., Alam, M. A., Jameel, R., Mourya, A. K., and Chang, V. "A proposed solution and future direction for blockchain-based heterogeneous Medicare data in cloud environment." Journal of Medical Systems 42, no. 8, (2018): p. 156.

[23] Dean, J., and Ghemawat, S. "MapReduce: Simplified data processing on large clusters." Communications of the ACM 51, no. 1, (2008): pp. 107–113.

[24] Noghabi, S. A., Paramasivam, K., Pan, Y., *et al.* "Samza: Stateful scalable stream processing at LinkedIn." Proceedings of the VLDB Endowment 10, no. 12, (2017): pp. 1634–1645.

[25] Chauhan, R., Kaur, H., Lechman, E., and Marszk, A. "Big data analytics for ICT monitoring and development." In Catalyzing Development through ICT Adoption, Springer, Cham, 2017, pp. 25–36.

[26] Kleppmann, M., and Kreps, J. "Kafka, Samza and the Unix philosophy of distributed data." IEEE Data Engineering Bulletin 38, no. 4, (2015): pp. 4–14.

[27] Van der Veen, J. S., van der Waaij, B., Lazovik, E., Wijbrandi, W., and Meijer, R. J "Dynamically scaling apache storm for the analysis of streaming data." In 2015 IEEE First International Conference on Big Data Computing Service and Applications, IEEE, Mar 30 (2015): pp. 154–161.

[28] Tang, K. "GOFS: A model for solving overload on distributed stream calculating system." In 2018 International Conference on Network, Communication, Computer Engineering (NCCE 2018). Atlantis Press, May 2018.

[29] Makeshwar, P. B., Kalra, A., Rajput, N. S., and Singh, K. P. "Computational scalability with Apache Flume and Mahout for large scale round the clock analysis of sensor network data." In 2015 National Conference on Recent Advances in Electronics & Computer Engineering (RAECE), IEEE, Feb 13 (2015): pp. 306–311.

[30] Kafka, A. "A high-throughput distributed messaging system." 5, no. 1 (2014). kafka.apache.org.

[31] Kreps, J. "Putting Apache Kafka to Use: A Practical Guide to Building a Stream Data Platform (Part 1)." (2015): pp. 741–755. blog.confluent.io.

Chapter 6

A survey on data stream analytics

Sumit Misra[1], Sanjoy Kumar Saha[2] and
Chandan Mazumdar[2]

With the exponential expansion of the interconnected world, we have large volume, variety and velocity of the data flowing through the systems. The dependencies on these systems have crossed the threshold of business value, and now such communications have started to be classified as essential systems. As such, these systems have become vital social infrastructure that needs all of prediction, monitoring, safe guard and immediate decision-making in case of threats. The key enabler is data stream analytics (DSA). In DSA, the key areas of stream processing constitute prediction and forecasting, classification, clustering, mining frequent patterns and finding frequent item sets (FISs), detecting concept drift, building synopsis structures to answer standing and ad hoc queries, sampling and load-shedding in the case of bursts of data and processing data streams emanating from a very large number of interconnected devices typical for Internet-of-Things (IoT). The processing complexity is impacted by the multidimensionality of the stream data objects, building 'forgetting' as a key construct in the processing, leveraging the time-series aspect to aid the processing and so on. In this chapter, we explore some of the aforementioned areas and provide a survey in each of these selected areas. We also provide a survey on the data stream processing systems (DSPSs) and frameworks that are being adopted by the industry at large.

6.1 Introduction

DSA has emerged as an active area of research in the last two decades. The mathematical foundation that dates much early did not have use cases to implement and hence did not take off at that point in time. However, with increased usage of the Internet- and browser-based applications, and significant development in image processing, interesting use cases emerged, which acted as bootstrap for the rise of real-life implementation problems. At this point, new algorithms for DSA were

[1]RS Software (India) Limited, Kolkata, India
[2]Centre for Distributed Computing, Department of Computer Science and Engineering, Jadavpur University, Kolkata, India

proposed; however, the hardware and network resource limitations resulted in falling of the interest, only to rise again as new sets of hardware and fast network implementation became reality. Hence we see a flurry of research activities especially in the latter half of the past decade. At present as IoT, 5G network and Gaming Processors are on the rise we can expect to see heightened interest in this field.

Dealing with massive data is evolved into two branches: big data analytics and DSA. The purpose of analytics is to (a) determine certain data characteristics, (b) provide answers to some of the associated business questions and (c) build a model that approximates the generative systems which generate the data. As per [1], 'the most commonly accepted definition of data mining is the discovery of models for data'. The models are one of the following:

1. **Statistical models**: Represents an underlying data distribution from where the data belonging to the massive data set or data stream is drawn.
2. **Machine learning models**: Models representing the data that is used especially when there is little idea about what is being looked for in the data. For example, it is unclear why some people like certain books but you would like to recommend a few books to a prospective reader.
3. **Computational approach to models**: Computer scientists' perspective of model is either of the following:
    (i) **Summarization**: Representing the data using one of the techniques – (a) *ranking*, where a relative rank is assigned to the data object and (b) *clustering*, where the data object is assigned to one or more data clusters.
    (ii) **Feature extraction**: Extract the most important pattern embedded in the data such as (a) *FISs*, where the data, which is viewed as a set of items, is mined to obtain frequently occurring item sets or (b) *similar items*, where the objective is to find all occurrences of items that have high similarity (overlap of values for the attributes among the items).

    Algorithms and associated data structures provided the processing power which enabled to answer queries by mining massive data sets [1,2]:
4. **Data stream models**: Models that represent the data streams need to support the facts [3] that (a) the data comes continuously, only a *tiny fraction of it can possibly be stored*, if at all, (b) the algorithms can only *scan the data once* and (c) the underlying generative system of the data may *change or drift with time*. Data arrival rates of data streams vary with time. In systems with multiple data streams, the rate of arrival of data objects varies from one stream to another. Data stream models will need to detect the change considering these complex properties of data streams. Ideally, the models should be such that it could be updated incrementally, or at least refreshed altogether based on certain parameters.

In the early days, DSA was treated as micro-batches, and it is only recently that streaming analytics in its true sense has gained momentum.

In this survey, we have selected a few pertinent areas of DSA as detailed under Section 6.2. We have also surveyed a set of popular computational frameworks for data stream processing (DSP) in light of the required features for DSA. The rest of the chapter provides a detailed survey for each of the areas – covering surveys for prediction and forecasting in Section 6.3, outlier detection in Section 6.4, concept drift in Section 6.5, FIS mining in Section 6.6 and finally Section 6.7 provides the computational paradigm and survey of the popular DSP frameworks (DSPFs). The sections have a sub-section on the future direction for each of the areas.

6.2   Scope and approach

For our survey, we have chosen four areas of application of machine learning in DSA; two of which are forecasting (regression) and outlier detection (classification) along with two areas that influence these two – concept drift detection and frequent item-set mining. Moreover, we have taken popular use cases of the application in each area as the motivating examples. For forecasting (regression), we have taken forecasting of stock price, and for outlier detection we have taken detecting credit card fraud as the motivational use case. The surveys for the concept drift detection and frequent item-set mining are generic in nature. We have added a section on survey of the DSPSs with a computational paradigm perspective. In that section, we have identified a set of attributes that determine the implementation aspects of DSPS and used them as measures for the comparison of the popular open-source DSPS: Apache Storm, Apache Spark and Apache Flink.

In our survey, we have studied published papers for last two decades (2000–20). The number of the papers was almost equally spread across the four areas covered in the survey. The important ones have been referred to in the respective sections.

In the early part of the last two decades, we have seen rise of the research in each of these areas which were primarily dealing with large but static or batch-oriented data. In the middle part of the decade, the research interest fell only to rise again at the end of the past decade where application to data streams became prominent. The methods and algorithms developed for batch or static data processing required significant innovation before applying to data streams.

Most of the surveys conducted in prediction (forecasting) and outlier detection were predominantly vertical focused, i.e. it took a topic or a subtopic and covered in detail analysis from computational paradigm. The surveys largely covered batch or static data and provided a broader perspective. In prediction and forecasting, we find surveys specific to areas such as Bayesian predictive methods [4], imbalanced classes [5], density-based forecasting [6], forecasting using many predictors [7]. Similarly for outlier detection, there have been surveys covering a wide range of algorithms but largely focused on static or batch data [8–11] with a few work on data stream [12–14].

Concept drift detection and mining frequent item sets inherently deal with processing of time sequence of data be it data streams. On concept drift detection, seminal work was done by Gama *et al.* [15] and more recently by Barros and Santos [16]. Survey on application of concept drift on different fields was conducted by

Khamassi *et al.* [17]. Mining frequent item sets in data stream has been well researched as these have a large number of applications in various fields of forecasting, classification, outlier detection and clustering [18]. The research on frequent item-set mining started with Apriori algorithm of Agrawal and Srikant [19] and continued with interest since then [20,21]. Recently, it has spawned research in mining high utility patterns as presented in the survey by Fournier-Viger *et al.* [22]. In our survey we have captured a chronology of evolution of these two areas and have concisely presented the same.

6.3   Prediction and forecasting

In data streams, it is important to predict or forecast the value of the attributes of the stream data objects. Data stream represents a time-ordered sequence, also known as time-series data. If the prediction of the value is in-sample, it is usually termed 'prediction' and if it is out-of-sample, it is termed 'forecasting'. The approach to forecasting a set of values out in the future with high accuracy is usually to build a model learned through mining the past data and then apply the past set of actual values to (a) forecast the values in the future and (b) determine the quality of the model itself and make a decision whether to refresh or incrementally update the model. Forecasting also becomes a precursor to detecting changes in the system also known as concept drift (detailed in Section 6.5) that could be a gradual or abrupt or something in between.

Assuming Y as the value of an arbitrary data object attribute and $\hat{Y}$ is the forecasted value, $\hat{Y}(T + N)|Y(T)$ is N-period look ahead based on all actual values observed till time T. The N-period ahead in forecasting is the process of forecasting the value N number of time-steps ahead in time. The $P - lag$ means that P number of values of the stream data object attribute for past P time steps are used for forecasting the value at time T, or $\hat{Y}(T)|\{Y(T - 1), Y(T - 2), \ldots, Y(T - P + 1)\}$. The forecasting error is the difference between the forecast value $\hat{Y}(T)$ and the actual value $Y(T)$. The process of forecasting uses the forecast error as the feedback to fine-tune the forecasting model.

In the literature, there are essentially two approaches of estimating the value of the random variable, which in this case is an attribute of the data stream object. The first approach uses a statistical filter approach, where it uses Kalman filter (KF) and extended Kalman filter (EKF) to predict the value. In the second approach, it uses machine learning techniques like regression-based techniques such as autoregressive integrated moving average (ARIMA) or deep learning (DL) to forecast. In [23], Sun *et al.* applied EKF to update state parameters such as stored water content and soil curve number and applied autoregressive (AR) method to update the model output errors for the output assimilation. The approach resulted in better result using either EKF or AR for short-term prediction (1–4 days), but AR provided better result for longer-term predictions (5–7 days). In [24], EKF is used to recursively predict and update network parameters, which helped in a quick detection of temporal changes in network structures where the static attributes were modelled using generalized linear model. Interestingly, [25] has used EKF to detect change in the edges of the sparse network that is built on interconnectedness and systemic risk levels of financial institutes to predict financial impact. KF is also used [26,27] for forecasting stock prices. Another area where stream processing is using a variant of KF, called Ensemble KF, is for multi-data set assimilation and [28] uses it in investigations of volcanic activity. Working under strenuous conditions increases core temperature of human body, which can only be determined by invasive means. KF has been successfully used to predict the core temperature, and the research findings are presented in a book chapter by Guo *et al.* [29].

Regression-based prediction and forecasting systems have been used for forecasting power requirement [30], electricity pricing [31,32], load distribution in network traffic [33,34], stock price [35], healthcare [36–39] and many other domains. In healthcare, regression has been used to predict acute kidney injury risk [40] as no treatment exists once the injury happens; hence, early identification and prevention is the key. Recently, researchers are using a combination of neural network (NN) and ARIMA-based techniques. In [41], the authors have used a combination of linear regression to model stock prices and then used inspiration from KF to adjust the prediction based on the past error; however, if the deviation is high, the model is rebuilt again. In [42], Ma *et al.* have used NN to model a co-movement pattern of all traffic flows at network scale and then applied ARIMA to post-process residuals of the NN to extract location-specific traffic features. DL is being used for forecasting as well, such as forecasting solar flares 24 h before they occur [43], transportation network congestion [44], short-term forecasting of passenger demand [45], air quality [46], flood forecasting [47] and much more.

From the survey, it is clear that the forecasting and prediction in DSA is a contemporary problem space. The novelties are primarily in the application of the techniques from KF to ARIMA to DL in solving complex domain needs.

6.3.1 Future direction for prediction and forecasting

The ability to forecast or predict with high accuracy is key objective. This depends on the ability to model the generative system as close as possible by observing the manifestation of the system which are data streams emanating from that system. Systems are modelled using statistical techniques and machine learning techniques. The accuracy of the machine learning models depends on availability of labelled data and degree of learning supervision – which are supervised, unsupervised or semi-supervised learning.

With time the underlying system concepts drift and hence the models need to be updated. For application in data streams, the ability of the model to be updated incrementally is extremely important.

The concept drift detection and incremental model update are both active areas of research. Following are some of the future directions of research for prediction and forecasting:

- **Temporal dependence**: In many of the time-series data, there is a strong autoregressive property which could be with finite delay. Finding the delay, which could change with time, and then factoring the same for the prediction, remains one of the research questions.

- **Dealing with high dimension**: The regression and classification both are impacted as the data dimensions increase. Dealing with high dimension and identifying subspaces which exhibit similarity of behaviour remains an area of active interest.
- **Delayed feedback labels**: The models are updated based on feedback labels. There are systems that generate the feedback labels with large delays. Dealing with models with large feedback delays is an interesting area of research.

6.4   Outlier detection

An important problem in DSA is to detect outliers. The deviation could be minor one-off deviation as part of noise or it could be significant from business application perspective. A good book on outlier analysis [48] provides a detailed study on outlier detection.

The steps for outlier detection involve the following:

- **Data selection**: A time-window needs to be defined that will be used to collect the data from the data stream. Here, the simplest method is to select all the data objects in the time-window. However, for very fast streams, the data stream is sampled based on certain criteria. Filters may also be used for selecting the data objects, and data value-based filter can be used along with the time-based sampling. The data set so obtained would be used to build the model.
- **Learning the model**: The techniques used for outlier detection comprise either prediction-based or non-prediction-based methods. For prediction-based outlier detection, the stream of data object needs to be converted to a model. The model could be a statistical model, or an in-memory data structure, or a machine learning model, etc. For prediction-based methods, the model is used to predict the next data object values in the data stream. This predicted value would be compared with the actual data value to flag a possible outlier. For non-prediction-based methods, statistical models are used to model the past data. The probability of the current data object values belonging to the population is statistically computed and based on this outlier is detected.
- **Supervision type**: The model building could be done using (a) unsupervised learning or (b) supervised learning, or (c) semi-supervised learning. In unsupervised learning, the data stream objects are used to identify clusters, and any data stream object that does not belong to any of the clusters is a candidate for outlier. In supervised learning, the data stream is used to create models which are then used to classify the data stream objects in any of the defined classes. If the data stream object does not belong to any of the defined classes it is identified as a candidate outlier. A nave use case is that of binary classifier. In which case the seeking cluster in unsupervised case and the seeking class in

supervised case define the expected class and anything other than that is identified as an outlier. For semi-supervised learning the models are built with partial supervision which assigns an error bound to the results.

- **Distance computation**: Most of the algorithms of outlier detection in data streams are either directly distance based or cluster based, and cluster also needs computation of distances. The notion of Euclidean distance is figuratively used in determining the deviation between the expected data and the actual data. This distance is based on the domain, the dimensions and the data types of the dimensions. For numeric data types the distance could be Euclidean distance or some variations, or correlation between data objects, or distance between probabilistic data distributions. For time-series or discrete sequence, it could be distance based, frequency-based, Hidden Markov Model based, KF based, autoregressive model based, etc. In the case of multidimensional-based data objects, it could be clustering based (K-nearest neighbour (KNN)) or density based. For multi-structure like text, it could be latent semantic analysis based group formation followed by TF-IDF method; cosine-distance could also be used for texts. For graph-like structures, distance could be based on minimal description length principle, Ising model, EM and local outlier factor (LOF) algorithm. Categorical data uses ranking of outliers within subspace as a method.
- **Assertion**: This determines if the distance measured qualifies the observation to be an outlier. For example in statistical models with random variables, if the deviation of the value of the data object is beyond 3σ from the mean μ, it can be termed an outlier. In the case of evolving streams, the mean μ and standard deviation σ keep evolving, which needs to be updated for making a right assertion. These measures are different for different data types.

Outlier detection in data streams uses data characteristics-specific innovative methods for implementing the five steps as mentioned before. For text mining, Ahmad and Dowaji [49] used semantic approach to detect outlier; for complex structured event streams, Kazachuk *et al.* [50] used elliptic clustering in the higher dimensional space of attributes. Lazhar [51] used Welch's *t*-statistics for outlier detection. Density-based outlier detection [52] is conducted using LOF. Categorical data typically has issues in computing 'distance'. Suri *et al.* [53] provided techniques for outlier detection in categorical data. For a deep dive into one domain, we have selected fraud detection in credit card transaction for illustrating the research footprints.

The motivating application of outlier detection is fraud detection in credit card payment domain. Data is available for this domain. Hence, without loss of generality, outlier detection is applied on credit card fraud detection to test the techniques. In credit card fraud detection problem space, the class distribution is heavily skewed and obtains high precision, and recall becomes difficult considering correct fraud detection as the true positive. Kou *et al.* [54] did a detailed survey on supervised and unsupervised techniques in fraud detection. Ghosh and Reilly [55] applied NN and labelled data from financial institute to train the models. Different types of fraud classes such as lost cards, stolen cards, application fraud, counterfeit fraud, mail-order fraud and NRI (non-received issue) fraud labels were used. Brause *et al.* [56] applied association rules mining with NNs to obtain a low false alarm rate. Supervised learning techniques such as artificial neural network (ANN) by Ogwueleka [57] and support vector machine (SVM) by Singh *et al.* [58] were used for fraud detection. Awoyemi *et al.* [59] provided a comparative study of the application of machine learning techniques on fraud detection, including naïve Bayes, *K*NNs and logistic regression combined with data sampling techniques. Randhawa *et al.* [60] applied ensemble of AdaBoost and majority voting which provided a better result. Chebyshev function link ANN (CFANN) was used in fraud detection by Mishra and Dash [61] that had two parts – functional expansion and learning. The chapter performs a comparative study between CFANN, multi-layer perceptron (MLP), and the decision tree algorithms.

Apart from machine learning models, another technique that has been used is to mine rules from the data and use the rules to detect fraud. Seeja and Zareapoor [62] used frequent item-set mining to detect the rules. Further, optimization techniques such as genetic algorithms were used by RamaKalyani and UmaDevi [63], and migrating bird optimization was applied in [64].

Learning intrinsic patterns associated with the fraudulent behaviour were explored by Fu *et al.* [65] using convolution NN. For imbalanced classes such as credit card fraud, the paper also discusses cost-based sampling to overcome the class imbalance. DL technique is used by Pumsirirat and Yan [66] where a combination of autoencoders and restricted Boltzmann machines (RBMs) has been used. The RBM, which is energy-based probabilistic model, is used to learn the distribution of data, and the reconstruction error of autoencoder is leveraged to classify imbalanced classes. A combination of autoencoder and classifiers is used [67] to detect fraud. To prove the generality of the model the result of the method has been studied using multiple classifiers such as MLP, *K*NN and logistic regression.

6.4.1 *Future direction for outlier detection*

Outlier detection continues to be an area of active interest. As the concept drift 6 impacts the models [68], based on the degree of the drift, the models can be incrementally adjusted or might need a complete regeneration. The future research on outlier detection could be the following areas:

- **Processing high-dimensional data**: The premise of the outlier detection inherently lies in finding distances between data stream objects. A high number of dimensions make it difficult to discern based on distances as the hyper-space becomes sparse. Researchers are using methods such as projections, autoencoders, RBM to reduce the parameters of hyper-space and facilitate better distance calculations.

  Detecting outliers embedded in the subspace is another area of research that is emanating from the high-dimensional problem area.

  Detection of rare and novel class in multidimensional data streams is an active area for research as well.

- **Working with categorical data**: Categorical data does not inherently yield to distance measurement, and interestingly enough, many of the data elements in real life take categorical values. This makes a direct application of statistical (other than frequency), or density measure, or principal component analysis based approach, or proximity-based methods inapplicable. One-hot-encoding is a way out, but this further increases the dimensions and hence the hyperspace. Ranking of outliers in subspace is another technique that is used as well. Research needs to be extended to find better proximity measures and formalise the impact of attributes in finding proximity in categorical data. Outlier detection using rough sets is gaining momentum in building approximate clusters, which is used for detecting outliers.
- **Distributed processing**: Outlier detection is typically a single-thread processing as detection is a global process. Improving the processing efficiency by using distributed processing needs complex pre-processing or post-processing or both. However, distributed processing architecture is a powerful tool for big DSP. Moreover, with GPU at our disposal the parallel processing is possible at node levels. Another aspect is distributed processing at the hub and the spoke topology. Research focus is applicable in all these areas as well.

6.5   Concept drift detection

Identification of concept drift is important as it has ramification across the processing of the data stream down the line. Generally, it is assumed that the underlying system that generates the data stream can be represented by a model provided the system generates a stationary pattern. This model represents a concept. The entire study of DSA hinges on this premise that the concept is stationary, be it forecasting, prediction, clustering, classification, frequent item-set mining, outlier detection or any other data stream mining and analytics area. However, in reality the concept changes with time. The change can be gradual, incremental, recurring or seasonal, or even abrupt. If the change is for a very short period it is like an outlier and may be processed as such. Hence, it is important to detect any drift or change in the concept as quickly as possible. The ensuing stream mining and analytics processes which are impacted due to concept drift needs to be adjusted or even re-processed/re-modelled all over again.

In 2016 Webb *et al.* [69] provided a comprehensive framework for quantitative analysis of drift. It is supported by a set of formal definitions of types of concept drift which provides a comprehensive taxonomy of concept drift types. Table 6.1 provides the taxonomy of the drift categories which captures the essence of the diagram in the paper but represented in a tabular fashion.

Traditional machine learning algorithm has two primary components training/learning and forecasting/prediction. Lu *et al.* [74] have defined three components for learning under concept drift, which are as follows:

- **Drift detection**: to ascertain a drift has truly occurred;

Table 6.1   Framework for quantitative analysis of drift [69]

CID	Drift category	TID	Drift type	Drift sub-type	Comments
A	**Drift subject**	1	Class drift		Real concept drift or prior probability shift
		1.1		Sub-concept	Sub-classes are affected, also referred to as intersected drift (drift severity [70])
		1.2		Full concept	All classes are affected, also referred to as severe drift (drift severity [70])
		2	Covariate drift		Virtual concept drift
		3	Novel class		Appearance of a new class [71] [72]
B	**Drift fre-quency**				
B.I	Drift duration	1	Abrupt, sudden		Could be major or minor drift based on thresholds
		1.1		*Blip*[*]	Very low drift duration, however, it is not outlier [73]
		2	Extended		
B.II	Concept duration				
C	**Drift transi-tion**	1	*Gradual*[*]		Not abrupt, but small changes
		2	*Incremental*[*]		Usually monotonic in nature
		2.1		*Probabilistic*[*]	Distribution of classes change with time [70]
D	**Drift recurrence**				
		1	Non-recurring		
		2	Recurring		Drift is periodic in nature
		2.1		Cyclical	When two or more concepts recur in specific order it is cyclical. It could be possible to have a drift predictability [70]
		2.1.1		Fixed duration	
		2.1.2		Varying duration	
		2.2		Non-cyclical	No order of recurrence can be observed
E	**Drift magnitude**				This determines drift adaptation strategy

*The concepts are not mutually exclusive at a peer level, whereas normal indicates that the concepts are mutually exclusive.

- **Drift understanding**: to obtain answers to when the drift has occurred, how it has occurred (abruptly, gradually, etc.), where, i.e. on which the principal component of a multidimensional data it has occurred;
- **Drift adaptation**: to determine the strategies for updating the learning model based on the drift severity as identified using drift understanding properties.

  While reviewing algorithms of concept drift in data streams, it is essential to understand whether the method supports all the components or addresses specific areas only.

  The paper [74] goes to define a general framework for drift detection which has four stages:

- **Stage 1 (data retrieval)**: Extracts a window of data from the stream with sufficient data distribution information to construct a reliable data model.
- **Stage 2 (data modelling)**: Build a model which abstracts the data within the window. Attempt is to capture the key features that are likely to be impacted in the event of a drift. This is an optional step as the main objective of the step is to reduce the data volume so as to meet the storage constraints which in turn is guided by the online processing speed requirements.
- **Stage 3 (test statistics calculation)**: Measure the dissimilarity or distance of the data which has impact in alerting and confirming a concept drift. This is a vital step in concept drift detection and needs to abide by the constraints of the DSP.
- **Stage 4 (hypothesis test)**: Measures the statistical significance of the difference or distance or change observed in Stage 3. It assigns a confidence interval, which expresses the likelihood of the change being due to concept drift rather than noise or an outlier.

For data retrieval, it is typical to use a window for collecting the data stream objects in order to build the data model. The variations in the body of research of concept drift detection in data streams relied on variations in the use of (a) the Data Retrieval windows, both in the type (fixed length, variable length) and count (single, double, more than two), (b) the data models, which varied from statistical models, such as statistical distributions, prediction error rates; to in-memory data structures like trees, lists, graphs and combinations of the same. The test statistics employ different types of distances based on the data domain. The prevalent methods are (a) measuring difference in online error rate, where the classification or feedback or labelling is available immediately, (b) measuring change in data distribution computed as distribution or density distance between past and the present windows of data, like Bhattacharyya distance, Kolmogorov–Smirnov test, etc. and (c) using multiple hypothesis tests which could be executed in parallel or in hierarchical manner.

In the context of drift understanding, all the methods can identify 'when' the drift occurred. However, a few of them effectively determine 'how' the drift has occurred and actually has a variation in strategy based on the same to address drift adaptation. Usually a full model refresh or replacement is used instead of model update. Even a lesser number of the methods determine the 'where' part and use that effectively for model adaptation.

Early works used fixed windows of data stream objects and modelled using Hoeffding-based decision trees – such as very fast decision tree (VFDT) [75–77], concept adapting VFDT (CVFDT) [78]. Modified CVFDT used variable and adaptive window lengths in Hoeffding Window Tree [79], Hoeffding Adaptive Tree [79], Hoeffding Option Tree [80,81] and others [82–85].

In a different strategy, three sets of stream data objects from the recent past were used to build models – one with all positive data instances, another with some positive data instances and the third with all negative instances. The first in this series was FLOating Rough Approximation (FLORA) [86]. FLORA2 [87] used automated adjustment of window size to cater to detecting gradual drifts. FLORA3 [88] used recurring drifts and finally FLORA4 [89] maintained improved criteria for the modification of hypothesis. Thus FLORA family used supervised incremental learning that also had forgetting past information built into it. Klinkenberg and Joachims [90] proposed SVM-based method. Similarly, other methods like Bernoulli trial-based method [91] and adaptive windowing [92], a variable window based methods were proposed.

Another approach used is two windows to compare statistics and decide if drift has occurred. Lazarescu *et al.* [93] used two windows – medium window (MW) and small window (SW) where MW is twice as large as SW. MW held the recent past data and SW held the current data.

Certain systems are capable of giving immediate feedback. Hence, if classification is wrong it returns 0 else it returns 1. This forms a stream of data similar to Bernoulli error stream. Ross *et al.* [94] used error stream statistics to detect concept drift.

In process mining, Bose *et al.* [95] had used change point detection (CPD), which leverages PELT (pruned exact linear time) [96] algorithm. The method deals with two populations at a time from the data sequence and compares the data sets using statistical measures. Aminikhanghahi and Cook [97] provided a survey of time-series CPD techniques. Hypothesis testing (HT) has been suitably used in the area of process mining as well to detect concept drift. Changes in statistics (mean and variance) of a given distribution, as proposed by Martjušev *et al.* [98], have been utilized to detect the changes. Misra *et al.* [99] proposed a mechanism to arrive at the window lengths using discrete Fourier transform of past data, named Fourier Inspired Windows for Concept Drift (FIWCD). Compared to CPD and HT, FIWCD had a better drift understanding and a drift adaptation based on the drift understanding metrics.

Windowing technique considers concept drift as a uniform phenomenon; hence it is not good at detecting local concept drifts but does well to detect global concept drifts. Khamassi *et al.* [17] have discussed and criticized the various windowing techniques. It also discussed that overlapping windows help in the context of imbalanced classes in the stream data especially where the available sample of data for both classes are limited.

6.5.1   Future direction for concept drift detection

The survey establishes that though research has been done on detecting concept drift in data streams; there are a number of areas that need research attention. The same are listed below with some references provided as example where similar or adjacent research findings are available:

- **Determining the dynamic window size for concept drift detection**: Drift detection needs to detect change first and then confirm or reject the hypothesis that a drift has happened. The change means that a comparison needs to be done between past and now, and in both cases one needs to collect a set of data. The determination of the window size remains an area of interest and its impact on determining the parameters such as 'when', 'how' and 'where'. Some of the recent works are [99,100].
- **Having better drift understanding**: Drift understanding is knowing the 'when', 'how' and 'where' of the drift. Research is needed to measure the impact of techniques with respect to the distribution of data on accuracy of these parameters. Pertinent research can be found in recent works [101,102].
- **Dealing with labels that arrive after long interval**: Drift detection is confirmed based on feedback. In certain cases the feedback comes much later. Research is needed to analyse, qualify and quantify the effects and then suggest algorithms to deal with such situations. Hu *et al.* [103] have conducted some research in this aspect.
- **Drift recurrence**: Recurrence of drift has been studied to some extent as discussed by Anderson *et al.* [104,105]. However, in many cases the 'seasonal' drifts change in characteristics between two epochs. For example, average spent pattern increases prior to festival, but with passing years the amount changes due to inflation. Research is needed to study this aspect.
- **Drift detection in rule-based systems for adjusting the rule parameters**: For deterministic systems, rules are used to detect changes, drifts, outliers, etc. However, the parameter values need adjustment with time. Research is needed to study and define quantifiable methods on this.
- **Faster detection through collaboration of drift detection at the edges and at hub**: With data privacy, the central processing may not have access to all the details of the data; however, the processing can be performed at the edges and the result of these can be processed centrally. Some work has been done on this [106,107], although more research is needed in this aspect.

6.6   Mining frequent item sets in data stream

Frequent item-set mining (FIM) was conceived in 1993 by Agrawal and Srikant [19] and has been an active area of interest for researches for past 25+ years. The objective is to look at a large volume of transactional data and identify which items co-occur frequently, assuming that a set of items form a part of the information of the transaction. From a nave perspective, it is a counting problem to find out the frequency of occurrence of all the combinations of the items for an arbitrary number of items. The space and time complexity of this approach is very high $O(2^D)$, where D is the total number of distinct items. The challenges are (a) the universal set of items are very large, (b) for exact results, there needs to be multiple passes made on the database of transactions and (c) the memory requirement for maintaining the intermediate results and final results could be very large. The first FIM algorithm was Apriori [19] and Hegland [108] computed the time complexity is $O(D^2 n)$, where D is the count of distinct items and n is the count of transactions in the data being processed.

The algorithms developed since differ in the following parameters: (a) the search strategy breadth first or depth first, (b) the data structure used internally or externally, (c) generation or identification of next item set that would be searched in the search space, (d) mechanism to count the occurrences of the data sets and qualify it as above or below the support threshold and (e) whether it can handle batch transactions only or can address transaction data stream as well.

In our survey we have confined the scope of frequent item-set mining to data streams. Stream processing typically necessitates using the concept of recency as, for DSP, result of recent frequent item set holds a higher value over past frequent item set.

FIS mining is applicable for data streams with a data stream object that has item sets as its content. Nave approach is to generate all the combinations of the items from the universal set and count them. A shade better is to generate all combinations from the items seen so far and count them. None of these approaches are practical as (a) candidate generation takes large processing time and (b) the candidate combinations, which is $O(k^2)$ where k is the length of the FIS, would result in exponential memory requirement where both of these are not suitable for DSA. In an item set, the order of items has no significance; hence, order-agnostic item-set representation is needed.

First single-pass FIS mining algorithm for data stream was LOSSY COUNTING [109] proposed by Manku and Motwani. Here, fixed-size landmark window of data stream objects is processed and a tuple of (item set, count, error) is maintained in a tree structure. If the item set appears in the arriving data stream objects, the count or frequency is increased; error indicates the number of windows that have passed since the tuple was added to the tree. If the count falls below a support level, the tuple is pruned. The quality is determined by the error which indicates gap in appearance of the item set. This algorithm is false positive oriented, that is it does not allow false negative. Yu *et al.* [110] defined frequent data stream pattern mining which does not allow false positive. The probability of finding FIS is user defined (δ) for a support threshold (θ). The window size is so chosen that it satisfies the Chernoff bound for δ.

As recent FIS gained prominence in requirement, Chang and Lee [111] proposed estDec algorithm that estimated frequent item set by leveraging the Apriori [19] philosophy where no superset of item set can have frequency greater than frequency of its subsets. Subsequent algorithms evolved estDec using damped window [112–114].

Jin and Agrawal [115] used sliding window and applied a two-phase single-pass algorithm named STREAM MINING. In first phase it enhanced Karp–Papadimitriou–Shenker (KPS) [116] algorithm to find the two item sets and then in the second phase applied Apriori property to generate frequent k item sets, where $k > 2$.

Giannella *et al.* [117] used a tiled window to provide a compressed history of the FIS of the data stream. The candidate FISs are identified using the FP-Tree and for a given error factor (ε) with pruning done similar to LOSSY COUNTING [109].

Depending on the expected number of FIS, either maximal frequent item sets (MFI) or closed frequent item sets (CFIs) are chosen to have a concise representation instead of storing all FISs in order to save memory. CFI is such that every super item set of it has less support, and MFI is such that every super item sets of it is not frequent, i.e. below the support threshold.

Ranganath and Murty [118] used CFI without candidate generation. Zaki and Hsiao [119] proposed closed association rule mining which has concise representation using CFI and identification of all CFIs. However, it has a disadvantage of potentially running out of memory as it needed all CFIs to be in memory. While earlier methods are good for item sets with short length, the performance degrades for larger lengths or for lower support thresholds. Wang *et al.* proposed CLOsed item SET+ (CLOSET+) [120] which use depth-first strategy that reduces the search space for long FIS and uses FP-Stream data structure.

Chi *et al.* [121] developed maintaining CFIs by Incremental Updates (MOMENT), the first algorithm to mine CFI from data streams that used Closed Enumerated Tree (CET) and lexicographical ordering to record CFI and item sets and other sets. The CET recorded nodes for infrequent, unpromising, intermediate and closed (CFI), and by tracking, the count of these four types MOMENT maintained the count of the set of CFIs.

Jiang and Gruenwald [122] proposed CFI-Stream which maintained all closed item sets whether frequent or not in an in-memory data structure called DIrect Update (DIU) tree. Each DIU-Tree mode stored closed item sets along with its current support information and links to its immediate parent and child nodes. As there is no pruning applied, for sparse data sets, the DIU-Tree grows very large and hence not suitable.

Since 2008, improvements were made in the tree-storage, update and search [123,124]. Zhang *et al.* proposed BitVector [125] to reduce storage requirement of the in-memory tree structure. Yen *et al.* [126] proposed a new algorithm CloStream. The algorithm incrementally mined closed item sets from a data stream. The CFI information is captured using two tables instead of table and graph data structures of MOMENT. The processing time is improved compared to MOMENT [121], CFI-Stream [122] and NewMOMENT [127].

Another approach was to find top-k CFIs. Xiaojun [128] used weighted support count to find top-k CFIs. Kumar and Satapathy [129] applied variable sliding window based on concept drift detection. The drift is detected based on past FI and current FI. If drift is detected the window is reduced; else it is expanded in length.

Amphawan and Lenca [130] and ur Rehman *et al.* [131] modified the top-*k* algorithm by introducing minimum and maximum length of FIs to prune less probable candidate. Shah *et al.* [132] used big data on single- and multi-node configuration along with item-set lattice structure coded using BitVector to process top-*k* CFIs.

Density of data was used as a determinant of a set of algorithms in FIS. Iwanuma *et al.* [133] used a combination of LOSSY COUNTING [109] and CloStream [126] to build LC-CloStream algorithm where the density of data was used to address the error estimation challenge. Caiyan and Ling [134] proposed a method to dynamically build the tree and compute densities of the FIS weighted using penalized time factor. The FISs with lower densities are removed from the tree to increase overall efficiencies.

LOSSY COUNTING [109] suffers from possible memory overflow. Iwanuma *et al.* proposed SKIPP-LCSS [133] which merged the LOSSY COUNTING (LC) [109] with space saving (SS) [135] which tried to combat the space issue. Lim and Kang [136] proposed time-weighted mining in data streams – finding top-*k* item sets (TWMINSWAP-IS), a time-weighted counting of recent item sets. The method maintains top-*k* item sets and applies randomized down-sampling to item sets if the list tends to exceed a fixed upper limit on memory size. Misra *et al.* [137] proposed a method to maintain a list of candidate item sets obtained through candidate generation from a short window of data stream objects along with the frequencies. The frequencies decayed with time and when the size of the list reaches some threshold, the list is down-sampled using a pruning method which used a threshold derived from Jensen's Inequality [138]. The algorithm performed better than the SKIP-LCSS and TWMINSWAP-IS.

6.6.1   *Future direction for frequent item-set mining*

FIM is an area that has remained relevant for long and remains an area of research interest even after 25+ years. Its application to batch of data has been there since inception and in the last decade the application in data stream has gained prominence. In last few years, focus on mining frequent item set in streams has received attention and we find that several incremental models with higher weightage to recent item set emerge. The future direction of research in frequent item-set mining in data streams could be, but not limited to, the following:

- **Finding frequent sequence of item sets**: In certain analysis, it is interesting to find sequence of items that appear periodically in the data stream. Research is needed on this area as it is not a monotonic behaviour of data. Certain measures have been studied such as standard deviation of periods and the sequence periodic ratio [139–141]. Further study is needed in this field.
- **Applying distributed processing for FIM in data streams**: FIM usually follows detection as a global maximal item-set approach. However, increasingly the processing needs to be distributed due to data privacy. Some study has been done on this as evident from the works [142–144]; however, further study is needed on this.

- **Enhancing performance of FIM in data streams for dense data and long transactions**: Most of the algorithms and interim storage principles assume sparse FISs. However, the space–time complexity is impacted if the FIS pattern present in the data is dense. Recent researches [145,146] have progressed with some results and more study is needed in this area.

- **Applying FIM for complex data objects in data streams**: While dealing with the stream data objects, it is usually assumed that it is of low dimension and has simple data structures. However, in real life, a stream data object could be quite complex especially for medical data, geological data, astronomical data, etc. where dimensions could be image, graph, list, map, sound bits, etc. along with simple data like floating number, integers, categorical data and others. Research is needed on how to deal with such information sets.

- **Finding rare item sets**: On contrary to finding FISs, use cases for finding rare item sets is also important and some work [147,148] has been done. Further research is needed as information content for rare item set is of larger value.

- **Applying FIM in data stream for new domains, like high occupancy item sets**: Innovative application of algorithms for commercial use cases is an important aspect of any research, and FIM is no exception. We find certain applications as detailed in [149]. This needs to be a continuous research effort and is always important to explore.

6.7   Computational paradigm

The standard topology of DSP is typically a directed acyclic graph (DAG). The links are the pathways for the data stream objects to flow and the nodes are the processing units that transform or work with the stream data objects. Architecture for processing of data streams started with the Lambda Architecture (LA) [150,151], a name coined by Nathan Marz. LA is a design pattern for data processing for massive data. It is built as an integrated framework for processing data sourced from either data streams or batches or both. Kiran *et al.* [152] provided the cost effectiveness in use of LA. However, LA needed maintenance of two separate systems and their interfaces. The objective of DSPSs is to process the stream data as raw data in real time and provide real-time or near-real-time responses for decision support systems to be effective. Examples are autonomous vehicle navigation, health monitoring systems of critical care units, fraud detection.

The first set of notable stream processing initiatives was between 2000 and 2010 Aurora [153], Borealis [154], SPADE [155] and StreamIt [156]. The effort matured significantly between 2011 and 2015 with a development of frameworks for DSPS such as STORM and SPARK. STORM was started by Marz in 2011 and was later donated to community as Apache Storm project in 2014. Matei Zaharia incubated SPARK since 2013 and the first release was also in 2014. The webpage [157] lists all the popular Apache streaming projects. The website [158] provides a comparison between the streaming projects in a tabular manner. The popular DSPS frameworks that are currently being widely used are Apache Storm, Apache Spark,

Apache Flink and Apache Samza. Surveys for the DSPS started around 2014 [159] and have been done by a number of researchers since then [160] and very recently [161] as well.

The seminal book [1] chapter on mining data streams has a simplistic schematic architecture diagram which is enhanced in the papers [160,161]. The researchers have first defined a DSPS framework by enlisting the components, providing the required features of the components, and then have gone on to compare the popular DSPS, both open-source and commercial versions, with respect to the framework thus defined.

Drawing inspiration from the previous work we have used a set of DSPS components and provided a commentary comparing the implementation of each in the previously mentioned DSPS frameworks.

The DSPS components are listed as follows:

1. **Data stream ingestion (DSI)**: The purpose of DSI is to provide an interface for the external system to integrate. The integration could use APIs, Sockets, REST APIs, etc. The payload, the data stream object, could be text, JSON, XML, image, etc. and there needs to be a reader to read the format. It is typical to do a transformation from the data stream object to a canonical object that is universally used within the DSPS, which immunes the internals of the DSPS from external payload format changes.

2. **Data transport (DT)**: In some frameworks, this is treated as part of the DSI. However, DT is so varied and specialized nowadays that it merits a focused attention. It is implemented as queue and is used to match the difference in data arrival and data-processing speed. Queuing components that are commonly used are Apache Kafka, RabbitMQ, etc. under open-source license, or it can as well be commercial solutions such as IBM WebSphere MQ (IBM MQ), Microsoft Message Queuing, etc. Unlike normal queues, where the producers and consumers are expected to be live and listening, here, the consumers may be offline by design or by accident. To handle this, the queues use storage-first broker, where the data is persisted before sharing, such as Kafka. The other variation is standard transient-broker based queue which achieves low-latency performance, such as RabbitMQ. DT implements the transport (the links) of the DAG, and the DSP units implement the nodes of DAG. With storage-first broker, it is easy to (a) re-post messages from near past, improving fault tolerance and (b) post the same message to multiple end points, which can provide alternate mechanism for replication.

3. **Data stream processing (DSP)**: DSP forms the heart of the processing. The features of DSP are well listed in [161]. These are as follows:

    (i) **Programming model**: Deals with stream data object transformation and processing. Stream data objects are either processed one at a time in a continuous basis or collected in a window and processed. The window can be time based or count based. The windows in sequence can be landmark window, sliding window, session window, etc. The transformations can be either stateless, like map, filter; or stateful, like aggregate, group-by-aggregate, join, sort. This aspect is implemented under programming model.

(ii) **Data source interaction model**: Data interaction could be either push method, where the DSP daemon continuously listens to collect the data as it arrives from the source, or it could be pull method, where the DSP pulls data from source at finite intervals.

(iii) **Data-partitioning strategy**: Data object is partitioned and processed in parallel for high performance. The partitioning can be horizontal, like range partitioning, or it can be vertical, where data is partitioned on columns and processed.

(iv) **State management**: As the stream data objects flow through the DAG, the transformation and processing can be stateless, where no history information is needed for processing, or it can be stateful, where past values and results of the data processed impact the processing of the subsequent data, such as aggregate of amount withdrawn in a day from a card. Earlier the state management was separate from DSP; however, to improve efficiency, it is now part of the DSP.

(v) **Message processing guarantee**: This ensures message delivery as at-most-once, at-least-once or exactly-once. The guarantee is implemented through processing of acknowledgements. The type of guarantee is decided by the application domain. The fastest and weak guarantee is at-most-once and strong guarantee but higher processing overhead is exactly-once.

(vi) **Fault tolerance and recovery**: The ability to continue to process in the event of a failure is fault tolerance. As the streaming system is unbound in volume, rate, speed, etc. there could be situations of failure due to lack of resources, application fault or even hardware fault. The strategy for fault tolerance in a distributed DSP could be (a) passive – where the state is preserved at checkpoints and system can restart from that point or inputs are preserved and restoration can be done through source replay, or (b) active – by replication.

(vii) **Deployment**: The deployment could be in a cluster or in cloud. The Data Stream Resource Manager takes care of the automation in configuration – for both static and dynamic parts.

(viii) **Support base**: This deals with (a) the availability of an active community support, (b) high-level language supported by the DSP, (c) the advanced input sources format handlers supported, (d) storage interface provided for both in-memory and secondary storage and (e) the analytics library that is indigenously supported.

4. **Data stream resource management (DSRM)**: The implementation of the processing topology that is represented as a DAG, the management and scheduling of the resources and the tasks, the handling of the exceptions and alerts are all handled by the DSRM. It is possible to have a DSRM definition separated from the implementation of the same. The DSRM can overlay on more

than one implementation of DSPS making it portable across DSP technology frameworks. Flow control is an important aspect of DSP. The downstream nodes are prevented from choking by DSRM controlling the flow of data objects served at a rate the node can be processed. To improve the performance, the stateless data stream objects are optionally configured with stickiness such that they are processed through the same cluster or node in order to take advantage of cached information available in that cluster or node. Some of the DSPS orchestrates the resources and tasks internally; however, others leverage external resource management tools such as ZooKeeper, Yet Another Resource Negotiator (YARN), Mesos.

5. **Data stream storage (DSS)**: DSPS leverages high-speed in-memory data stores that are typically used in DSPS are Redis, VoltDB, etc. and for long-term data store it uses file systems such as HDFS, Baidu File System; distributed RDBMS such as PostgreSQL; document storage systems like MongoDB; NoSQL databases like Cassandra. The time-based window concept can be implemented as part of Programming Model or can be implemented using certain properties of in-memory data store. Google MillWheel and Flink provide indigenous support for the time-window as part of the DSPF whereas Storm, Samza, Neptune does not, and Spark provides for batch. When DSP does not provide window feature indigenously, DSS can implement the time-window, for example, sliding window can be implemented by configuring time-to-live property of data objects stored in Redis. DSS plays a vital role in the implementation of Fault Tolerance and Recovery – be it passive mode (checkpoint state storage) or active mode (replication). In certain cases the DSS replicates itself between production data centre (PR-DC) and disaster recovery data centre (DR-DC) in active–active manner or active–passive manner without application intervention. However, for very high throughput systems, it is seen that the replication is done through the application, i.e. the data stream objects are posted to ingestion points of both PR-DC and DR-DC where the same DSPS application is running.

6. **Data stream output (DSO)**: The DSP result is sent to a sink port for it to flow out of the DSPS. However, the DSO deals with all the user interfaces like alerts, messages, dashboards, reports that the DSPS uses to interact with the user according to their roles. The user interfaces are varied. Starting from designing the topology (DAG) of the DSPS to the running of DSP algorithms in sandbox mode or in stealth mode in production, user interfaces impact the quality of the DSPS framework. The visualization differs based on the stream data object types. A survey on visualization is provided by Liu *et al.* [159]. For *text visualization*, there are tools like Word Clouds or Phrase Nets for static texts and TextFlow, EventRiver, SparkClouds for dynamic texts. For *graph visualization* tools like TreeNetViz are used for static graphs (matrix, node-link, etc.) and for dynamic graphs (animation, mental maps, etc.) StoryFlow is available. BirdVis is used for *map*

visualization. Multidimensional Scaling projection tools are used for *multivariate data visualization.*

Table 6.2 provides comparative information from implementation perspective on the open-source data stream frameworks Apache Storm, Apache Spark and Apache Flink.

Table 6.2   Comparison of Apache Storm, Apache Spark and Apache Flink

No.	Attributes	Apache Storm	Apache Spark	Apache Flink
A	Structure			
A.1	Nodes	Bolt	RDD	Operator on a Data-Stream
A.2	Links	Stream	Implicitly defined by operator on RDD	Implicitly defined by operator on Data-Stream
A.3	User created	Yes	No	No
A.4	Message	Tuple	RDD	DataStream
A.5	HL language	Java	Java, Scala	Java, Scala
A.6	Topology name	Topology	Stream Processing Job	Stream Processing Job
B	Ingestion	Spout	Third party integration components for Kafka, HDFS, S3, RDBMS	REST API
C	Transport	Tuples (named list of values)	DataFrames or Data-sets	DataSet
D	Processing			
D.1	Programming model	Native	Micro-batch, Continuous Processing	Native: Bounded Stream, Unbound Stream, Real-time Stream, Recorded Stream
D.2	Data source interaction model	Spout	DataFrames or Data-sets API (available for R, Python, Scala, and Java)	DataStream API
D.3	Data partitioning strategy	Shuffle, Field, Partial Key, All, Global, None, Direct, Local, Custom	Hash, Range	Same, Hash, Random
D.4	State management	Key Value, Redis	Write Ahead, Other State Stores	Key Value Store
D.5	Message processing guarantee	At-least-Once, Exactly-Once through Trident	Exactly-Once, At-least-Once	Exactly-Once
D.6	Fault tolerance and recovery	Checkpoint, Stream Replay	Checkpoint	Checkpoint, Stream Replay
D.7	Deployment	Cluster and Cloud	Cluster and Cloud	Cluster and Cloud

(Continues)

Table 6.2   (Continued)

No.	Attributes	Apache Storm	Apache Spark	Apache Flink
D.8	Support base	Large community, Java as HLL	Large very active community, Java Scala and Python as HLL	Growing active community, Java, Scala and Python as HLL, rich ML library – FlinkML
E	Data stream resource management	YARN, Mesos, Docker and Kubernetes	YARN, Mesos; can also run Spark Standalone cluster	YARN, Mesos, and Kubernetes can also run as a stand-alone cluster
F	Data stream storage	In-memory like Redis; Secondary store like HDFS, Cassandra, Solr, Hbase, Hive, MongoDB, etc.	In-memory like Redis; Secondary store like CSV file, Parquet (columnar), NoSQL, etc.	Provides checkpoints and support replay, supports connectors to Kafka, Kinesis, Elasticsearch, and JDBC database systems
G	Data stream output	Visual tools for Storm Topology; Other tool integration supported	Integration with Zeppelin and other tools	Visual tools for execution plan; Other tool integration supported

6.7.1   Future direction for computational paradigm

DSP being a dynamic field, research opportunities continuously arising in various aspects of the DSPF. Some of the relevant areas are listed as follows:

- **Complex data stream objects**: With the increase in complexity of the stream data objects along with the varied rate of arrival of the data objects, the processing complexity of the ingestion, transport and processing is ever increasing. Research would be needed to optimize the canonical structure to hold the complex information yet make it portable so that interoperability may be achieved.
- **Comprehensive machine learning and stream analytics support**: The libraries that are made available with the latest frameworks lack the completeness of the machine learning and analytics libraries. It would be advantageous to develop a portable construct so that the libraries become pluggable across the frameworks, thus separating the framework from the algorithm implementations.
- **Advanced visualization**: Research would be needed to evaluate if the visualization metadata can be abstracted out and built as a portable layer. Apache Zeppelin is in that direction; however, there are lot more aspects to be covered.
- **Benchmark**: The frameworks are benchmarked based on the area of the focus of the said framework. Research is needed to build benchmark parameters for the components of the DSPF so that based on the requirement, one might select the DSPF by referring to these benchmark figures.

6.8   Conclusion

DSA is an evolving area of contemporary research. Interconnected systems that generate data streams are on the rise. In this chapter, we have conducted a brief survey of four areas of DSA – forecasting, outlier detection, drift detection and mining frequent item sets form data streams.

Monitoring, forecasting and taking action for such systems in the event of threats are necessary. Application domain of DSA includes forecasting power requirement, formulating electricity pricing, managing load distribution in network traffic, forecasting stock prices, monitoring and acting in healthcare areas and much more. It has also been applied in domains such as forecasting solar flares, transportation network congestion, short-term passenger demand, air quality and flood forecasting. There has been a good body of knowledge built over decades; however, with recent availability of high memory and high computing power, it has become possible to step into doing more complex processing. Future research has become possible where the data stream objects are of high dimensions. Accuracy of the forecasting system is contingent of the quality of the model. The quality learning of model is contingent on the feedback system. Real-life systems provide feedback after substantial delay. Hence, strategy is needed to handle such situations.

Outlier detection finds its use in anomaly detection which typically necessitates emergency actions to be rolled out to contain the impact, or it could be an early warning for some changes that are about to emerge. In either case the detection has direct business or even life-changing impacts, hence very crucial. The fundamental aspect is finding the 'distance' of arriving data stream object with the past data and then flagging it as within bounds or as an outlier. The distance computation needs further research investment for high-dimensional data, for categorical data, etc. With data privacy becoming important, distributed processing of data streams is gaining momentum and research is needed in adapting outlier detection for distributed processing.

Detection of concept drift is an active area of research and of high importance as it impacts all other model-based decisions. With DSP being applied to various domains and systems, the changes that happen to the underlying system concepts are unique and the manifestations are varied. Research has been done in this field; however, it is very recently that the drift understanding, which constitutes 'when', 'how' and 'where', is being measured. Earlier the focus was on the quality of detection but now the explainability is added over and above quality. From out survey, it is clear that this remains an active area of research.

FIS mining in data streams is an interesting area that has adjacent ramification such as causal analysis, basket analysis, pattern discovery and much more. This remains a continued area of interest especially with new aspects of distributed processing, finding rare item sets, efficient processing of dense FIS mining and much more.

To enable the DSPSs, we have seen that a number of frameworks have evolved – both in open-source community and in commercial area. It is only recently that a common framework is being conceived to measure, compare and communicate the properties of the DSPS. In this chapter, we have proposed one such tool and used it to compare the computational paradigm of the popular tools in open-source community.

The progresses made are positive in each of the areas; however, there are opportunities for further research in each. Without a loss of generality, we feel that application of findings of one area of DSA research can be applied in adjacent areas successfully.

References

[1]   Leskovec J, Rajaraman A, and Ullman JD. Mining of massive data sets. Cambridge University Press; 2020.

[2]   Han J, Kamber M, and Pei J. Data mining concepts and techniques Third edition. Elsevier Science Ltd; 2011.

[3]   Aggarwal CC. Data streams: Models and algorithms. vol. 31. Springer Science & Business Media; 2007.

[4]   Vehtari A and Ojanen J. A survey of Bayesian predictive methods for model assessment, selection and comparison. Statistics Surveys. 2012;6:142–228.

[5]   Branco P, Torgo L, and Ribeiro R. A survey of predictive modeling under imbalanced distributions. ACM Computing Surveys. 2016;49(2):1–31.

[6]   Tay AS and Wallis KF. Density forecasting: A survey. Journal of Forecasting. 2000;19(4):235–254.

[7]   Stock JH and Watson MW. Forecasting with many predictors. Handbook of Economic Forecasting. 2006;1:515–554.

[8]   Hodge V and Austin J. A survey of outlier detection methodologies. Artificial Intelligence Review. 2004;22(2):85–126.

[9]   Chandola V, Banerjee A, and Kumar V. Outlier detection: A survey. ACM Computing Surveys. 2007;14:15.

[10]   Gogoi P, Bhattacharyya D, Borah B, *et al.* A survey of outlier detection methods in network anomaly identification. The Computer Journal. 2011; 54(4):570–588.

[11]   Wang H, Bah MJ, and Hammad M. Progress in outlier detection techniques: A survey. IEEE Access. 2019;7:107964–108000.

[12]   Pawar AD, Kalavadekar PN, and Tambe SN. A survey on outlier detection techniques for credit card fraud detection. IOSR Journal of Computer Engineering. 2014;16(2):44–48.

[13]   Souiden I, Brahmi Z, and Toumi H. A survey on outlier detection in the context of stream mining: Review of existing approaches and recommendations. In: International Conference on Intelligent Systems Design and Applications. Springer; 2016. p. 372–383.

[14]   Tamboli J and Shukla M. A survey of outlier detection algorithms for data streams. In: 2016 3rd International Conference on Computing for Sustainable Global Development (INDIACom). IEEE; 2016. p. 3535–3540.

[15] Gama J, Žliobaitė I, Bifet A, *et al.* A survey on concept drift adaptation. ACM Computing Surveys (CSUR). 2014;46(4):1–37.

[16] Barros RSM and Santos SGTC. A large-scale comparison of concept drift detectors. Information Sciences. 2018;451:348–370.

[17] Khamassi I, Sayed-Mouchaweh M, Hammami M, *et al.* Discussion and review on evolving data streams and concept drift adapting. Evolving Systems. 2018;9(1):1–23.

[18] Aggarwal CC, Bhuiyan MA, and Al Hasan M. Frequent pattern mining algorithms: A survey. In: Frequent pattern mining. Springer, Cham; 2014. p. 19–64.

[19] Agrawal R and Srikant R. Fast algorithms for mining association rules. In: Proc. 20th Int. Conf. Very Large Data Bases, VLDB. vol. 1215; 1994. p. 487–499.

[20] Luna JM, Fournier-Viger P, and Ventura S. Frequent itemset mining: A 25 years review. Wiley Interdisciplinary Reviews: Data Mining and Knowledge Discovery. 2019;9(6):e1329.

[21] Cafaro M and Pulimeno M. Frequent itemset mining. In: Business and consumer analytics: New ideas. Springer, Cham; 2019. p. 269–304.

[22] Fournier-Viger P, Lin JCW, Truong-Chi T, *et al.* A survey of high utility itemset mining. In: High-utility pattern mining. Springer, Cham; 2019. p. 1–45.

[23] Sun L, Seidou O, and Nistor I. Data assimilation for streamflow forecasting: State–parameter assimilation versus output assimilation. Journal of Hydrologic Engineering. 2017;22(3):04016060.

[24] Gahrooei MR and Paynabar K. Change detection in a dynamic stream of attributed networks. Journal of Quality Technology. 2018;50(4):418–430.

[25] Ebrahimi S. Modeling high dimensional multi-stream data for monitoring and prediction. Doctoral dissertation, Georgia Institute of Technology; 2018.

[26] Xu SY and Berkely CU. Stock price forecasting using information from Yahoo finance and Google trend. In: Proc. of ACM Intl. Conf. on Knowledge; 2012.

[27] Yan X and Guosheng Z. Application of Kalman filter in the prediction of stock price. In: Proc. of Intl. Symposium on Knowledge Acquisition and Modeling (KAM); 2015.

[28] Gregg PM and Pettijohn JC. A multi-data stream assimilation framework for the assessment of volcanic unrest. Journal of Volcanology and Geothermal Research. 2016;309:63–77.

[29] Guo J, Chen Y, Fan WP, *et al.* Kalman filter models for the prediction of individualised thermal work strain. In: Kalman filters-theory for advanced applications. IntechOpen, London; 2018.

[30] Chen Y, Dong G, Han J, *et al.* Multi-dimensional regression analysis of time-series data streams. In: VLDB'02: Proceedings of the 28th International Conference on Very Large Databases. Elsevier; 2002. p. 323–334.

[31] Kivipold T and Valtin J. Regression analysis of time series for forecasting the electricity consumption of small consumers in case of an hourly pricing system. Advances in Automatic Control, Modelling and Simulation. 2013; 34(2):127–132.

[32]   Weron R. Electricity price forecasting: A review of the state-of-the-art with a look into the future. International Journal of Forecasting. 2014; 30(4):1030–1081.

[33]   Cranor C, Gao Y, Jhonson T, *et al.* GigaScope: High performance network monitoring with an SQL interface. In: Proc. of ACM Int. Conf. on Management of Data (SIGMOD 2002); 2002. p. 623–623.

[34]   Gilbert AC, Kotidis Y, Muthukrishnan S, *et al.*. QuickSAND: Quick summary and analysis of network data. DIMACS Technical Report, New Jersey; 2001.

[35]   Zhu Y and Shasha D. StatStream: Statistical monitoring of thousands of data streams in real time. In: Proc. of Int. Conf. on Very Large Data Bases; 2002. p. 358–369.

[36]   Garg MK, Kim D, Turaga DS, *et al.* Multimodal analysis of body sensor network data streams for real-time healthcare. In: Proc. of Intl. Conf. on Multimedia Information Retrieval; 2010. p. 469–478.

[37]   Raghupathi W and Raghupathi U. Big data analytics in healthcare: Promise and potential. Health Information Science and Systems. 2014;2(3):7–12.

[38]   Belle A, Thiagarajan R, Soroushmehr SM, *et al.* Big data analytics in healthcare. BioMed Research International. 2015.

[39]   Kennedy EH, Wiitala WL, Hayward RA, *et al.* Improved cardiovascular risk prediction using nonparametric regression and electronic health record data. Med Care. 2013;51(3):251–258.

[40]   Sutherland SM, Chawla LS, Kane-Gill SL, *et al.* Utilizing electronic health records to predict acute kidney injury risk and outcomes. Canadian Journal of Kidney Health and Disease. 2016.

[41]   Misra S, Saha SK, and Mazumdar C. A dynamic model for short-term prediction of stream attributes. Innovations in Systems and Software Engineering. 2017;13(4):261–269.

[42]   Ma T, Antoniou C, and Toledo T. Hybrid machine learning algorithm and statistical time series model for network-wide traffic forecast. Transportation Research Part C: Emerging Technologies. 2020;111:352–372.

[43]   Hada-Muranushi Y, Muranushi T, Asai A, *et al.* A deep-learning approach for operation of an automated realtime flare forecast. arXiv preprint arXiv:160601587. 2016.

[44]   Ma X, Yu H, Wang Y, *et al.* Large-scale transportation network congestion evolution prediction using deep learning theory. PLoS One. 2015;10(3).

[45]   Ke J, Zheng H, Yang H, *et al.* Short-term forecasting of passenger demand under on-demand ride services: A spatio-temporal deep learning approach. Transportation Research Part C: Emerging Technologies. 2017;85:591–608.

[46]   Freeman BS, Taylor G, Gharabaghi B, *et al.* Forecasting air quality time series using deep learning. Journal of the Air & Waste Management Association. 2018;68(8):866–886.

[47]   Liu F, Xu F, and Yang S. A flood forecasting model based on deep learning algorithm via integrating stacked autoencoders with BP neural network.

In: 2017 IEEE Third International Conference on Multimedia Big Data (BigMM). IEEE; 2017. p. 58–61.

[48] Aggarwal CC. Outlier analysis. In: Data mining. Springer, Cham; 2015. p. 237–263.

[49] Ahmad H and Dowaji S. A semantic approach for outlier detection in big data streams. Webology. 2019;16(1).

[50] Kazachuk M, Petrovskiy M, Mashechkin I, *et al.* Outlier detection in complex structured event streams. Moscow University Computational Mathematics and Cybernetics. 2019;43(3):101–111.

[51] Lazhar F. Fuzzy clustering-based semi-supervised approach for outlier detection in big text data. Progress in Artificial Intelligence. 2019;8(1):123–132.

[52] Mishra S and Chawla M. A comparative study of local outlier factor algorithms for outliers detection in data streams. In: Emerging technologies in data mining and information security. Springer, Singapore; 2019. p. 347–356.

[53] Suri NR and Athithan G. Outlier detection in categorical data. In: Outlier detection: Techniques and applications. Springer, Cham; 2019. p. 69–93.

[54] Kou Y, Lu CT, Sirwongwattana S, *et al.* Survey of fraud detection techniques. In: Proceedings of the 2004 International Conference on Networking, Sensing and Control. vol. 2. Taipei, Taiwan: IEEE; 2004. p. 749–754.

[55] Ghosh S and Reilly DL. Credit card fraud detection with a neural-network. In: Proceedings of the Twenty-Seventh Hawaii International Conference on System Sciences. vol. 3. Wailea, HI, USA: IEEE; 1994. p. 621–630.

[56] Brause R, Langsdorf T, and Hepp M. Neural data mining for credit card fraud detection. In: Proceedings of the 11th International Conference on Tools with Artificial Intelligence. Chicago, IL, USA: IEEE; 1999. p. 103–106.

[57] Ogwueleka FN. Data mining application in credit card fraud detection system. Journal of Engineering Science and Technology. 2011;6(3):311–322.

[58] Singh G, Gupta R, Rastogi A, *et al.* A machine learning approach for detection of fraud based on SVM. International Journal of Scientific Engineering and Technology. 2012;1(3):194–198.

[59] Awoyemi JO, Adetunmbi AO, and Oluwadare SA. Credit card fraud detection using machine learning techniques: A comparative analysis. In: Proceedings of the 2017 International Conference on Computing Networking and Informatics (ICCNI). Lagos, Nigeria: IEEE; 2017. p. 1–9.

[60] Randhawa K, Loo CK, Seera M, *et al.* Credit card fraud detection using AdaBoost and majority voting. IEEE Access. 2018;6:14277–14284.

[61] Mishra MK and Dash R. A comparative study of Chebyshev functional link artificial neural network, multi-layer perceptron and decision tree for credit card fraud detection. In: Proceedings of the 2014 International Conference on Information Technology. Bhubaneshwar, India: IEEE; 2014. p. 228–233.

[62] Seeja K and Zareapoor M. FraudMiner: A novel credit card fraud detection model based on frequent itemset mining. The Scientific World Journal. 2014;2014:1–10.

[63]   RamaKalyani K and UmaDevi D. Fraud detection of credit card payment system by genetic algorithm. International Journal of Scientific & Engineering Research. 2012;3(7):1–6.

[64]   Duman E and Elikucuk I. Solving credit card fraud detection problem by the new metaheuristics migrating birds optimization. In: Proceedings of the 2013 International Work-Conference on Artificial Neural Networks. Tenerife, Spain: Springer; 2013. p. 62–71.

[65]   Fu K, Cheng D, Tu Y, *et al.* Credit card fraud detection using convolutional neural networks. In: Proceedings of the 2016 International Conference on Neural Information Processing. Kyoto, Japan: Springer; 2016. p. 483–490.

[66]   Pumsirirat A and Yan L. Credit card fraud detection using deep learning based on auto-encoder and restricted Boltzmann machine. International Journal of Advanced Computer Science and Applications. 2018;9(1):18–25.

[67]   Misra S, Thakur S, Ghosh M, *et al.* An autoencoder based model for detecting fraudulent credit card transaction. Procedia Computer Science. 2020;167:254–262.

[68]   Tran L, Fan L, and Shahabi C. Outlier detection in non-stationary data streams. In: Proceedings of the 31st International Conference on Scientific and Statistical Database Management; 2019. p. 25–36.

[69]   Webb GI, Hyde R, Cao H, *et al.* Characterizing concept drift. Data Mining and Knowledge Discovery. 2016;30(4):964–994.

[70]   Minku LL, White AP, and Yao X. The impact of diversity on online ensemble learning in the presence of concept drift. IEEE Transactions on Knowledge and Data Engineering. 2009;22(5):730–742.

[71]   Masud M, Gao J, Khan L, *et al.* Classification and novel class detection in concept-drifting data streams under time constraints. IEEE Transactions on Knowledge and Data Engineering. 2010;23(6):859–874.

[72]   Widmer G and Kubat M. Learning in the presence of concept drift and hidden contexts. Machine learning. 1996;23(1):69–101.

[73]   Dongre PB and Malik LG. A review on real time data stream classification and adapting to various concept drift scenarios. In: 2014 IEEE International Advance Computing Conference (IACC). IEEE; 2014. p. 533–537.

[74]   Lu J, Liu A, Dong F, *et al.* Learning under concept drift: A review. IEEE Transactions on Knowledge and Data Engineering. 2018;31(12):2346–2363.

[75]   Domingos P and Hulten G. Mining high-speed data streams. In: Proceedings of the Sixth ACM SIGKDD International Conference on Knowledge Discovery and Data Mining; 2000. p. 71–80.

[76]   Hoeffding W. Probability inequalities for sums of bounded random variables. In: The collected works of Wassily Hoeffding. Springer, New York, NY; 1994. p. 409–426.

[77]   Maron O and Moore AW. Hoeffding races: Accelerating model selection search for classification and function approximation. In: Advances in neural information processing systems. Morgan Kaufmann, San Francisco; 1994. p. 59–66.

[78] Hulten G, Spencer L, and Domingos P. Mining time-changing data streams. In: Proceedings of the Seventh ACM SIGKDD International Conference on Knowledge Discovery and Data Mining; 2001. p. 97–106.

[79] Bifet A and Gavaldà R. Adaptive learning from evolving data streams. In: International Symposium on Intelligent Data Analysis. Springer; 2009. p. 249–260.

[80] Hoeglinger S and Pears R. Use of Hoeffding trees in concept based data stream mining. In: 2007 Third International Conference on Information and Automation for Sustainability. IEEE; 2007. p. 57–62.

[81] Kohavi R and Kunz C. Option decision trees with majority votes. In: ICML. vol. 97; 1997. p. 161–169.

[82] Pfahringer B, Holmes G, and Kirkby R. New options for Hoeffding trees. In: Australasian Joint Conference on Artificial Intelligence. Springer; 2007. p. 90–99.

[83] Alippi C and Roveri M. Just-in-time adaptive classifiers in non-stationary conditions. In: 2007 International Joint Conference on Neural Networks. IEEE; 2007. p. 1014–1019.

[84] Alippi C and Roveri M. Just-in-time adaptive classifiers Part II: Designing the classifier. IEEE Transactions on Neural Networks. 2008;19(12):2053–2064.

[85] Carpenter GA, Grossberg S, Markuzon N, *et al.* Fuzzy ARTMAP: A neural network architecture for incremental supervised learning of analog multi-dimensional maps. IEEE Transactions on Neural Networks. 1992;3(5):698–713.

[86] Kubat M. Floating approximation in time-varying knowledge bases. Pattern Recognition Letters. 1989;10(4):223–227.

[87] Widmer G and Kubat M. Learning flexible concepts from streams of examples: FLORA2. In: Proceedings of the 10th European Conference on Artificial Intelligence. John Wiley & Sons, Inc., New York, NY; 1992. p. 463–467.

[88] Widmer G and Kubat M. Effective learning in dynamic environments by explicit context tracking. In: European Conference on Machine Learning. Springer; 1993. p. 227–243.

[89] Widmer G. Combining robustness and flexibility in learning drifting concepts. In: ECAI. PITMAN; 1994. p. 468–472.

[90] Klinkenberg R and Joachims T. Detecting concept drift with support vector machines. In: ICML; 2000. p. 487–494.

[91] Gama J, Medas P, Castillo G, *et al.* Learning with drift detection. In: Brazilian Symposium on Artificial Intelligence. Springer; 2004. p. 286–295.

[92] Bifet A and Gavalda R. Learning from time-changing data with adaptive windowing. In: Proceedings of the 2007 SIAM International Conference on Data Mining. SIAM; 2007. p. 443–448.

[93] Lazarescu MM, Venkatesh S, and Bui HH. Using multiple windows to track concept drift. Intelligent Data Analysis. 2004;8(1):29–59.

[94]   Ross GJ, Adams NM, Tasoulis DK, *et al.* Exponentially weighted moving average charts for detecting concept drift. Pattern Recognition Letters. 2012;33(2):191–198.

[95]   Bose RJC, Van Der Aalst WM, Žliobaitė I, *et al.* Dealing with concept drifts in process mining. IEEE Transactions on Neural Networks and Learning Systems. 2013;25(1):154–171.

[96]   Killick R, Fearnhead P, and Eckley IA. Optimal detection of change points with a linear computational cost. Journal of the American Statistical Association. 2012;107(500):1590–1598.

[97]   Aminikhanghahi S and Cook DJ. A survey of methods for time series change point detection. Knowledge and Information Systems. 2017;51(2):339–367.

[98]   Martjušev J, Bose R, and Maggi F. Efficient algorithms for discovering concept drift in business processes. Master's thesis, University of Tartu. 2013.

[99]   Misra S, Biswas D, Saha SK, *et al.* Applying Fourier inspired windows for concept drift detection in data stream (accepted). In: CALCON (2020). IEEE Xplore; 2020. p. 000–000.

[100]   Grulich PM, Saitenmacher R, Traub J, *et al.* Scalable detection of concept drifts on data streams with parallel adaptive windowing. In: EDBT; 2018. p. 477–480.

[101]   Lu J, Liu A, Song Y, *et al.* Data-driven decision support under concept drift in streamed big data. Complex & Intelligent Systems. 2020;6(1):157–163.

[102]   Demšar J and Bosnić Z. Detecting concept drift in data streams using model explanation. Expert Systems with Applications. 2018;92:546–559.

[103]   Hu H, Kantardzic M, and Sethi TS. No Free Lunch Theorem for concept drift detection in streaming data classification: A review. Wiley Interdisciplinary Reviews: Data Mining and Knowledge Discovery. 2020;10(2):e1327.

[104]   Anderson R, Koh YS, and Dobbie G. Classifying imbalanced road accident data using recurring concept drift. In: Australasian Conference on Data Mining. Springer; 2019. p. 143–155.

[105]   Anderson R, Koh YS, Dobbie G, *et al.* Recurring concept meta-learning for evolving data streams. Expert Systems with Applications. 2019;138:112832.

[106]   Ding W, Yen GG, Beliakov G, *et al.* IEEE access special section editorial: Data mining and granular computing in big data and knowledge processing. IEEE Access. 2019;7:47682–47686.

[107]   Van Quoc HH, Küng J, Dang TK. A parallel incremental frequent itemsets mining IFIN+: Improvement and extensive evaluation. In: Transactions on Large-Scale Data-and Knowledge-Centered Systems XLI. Springer; 2019. p. 78–106.

[108]   Hegland M. The apriori algorithm–a tutorial. In: Mathematics and computation in imaging science and information processing. World Scientific Publishing, Singapore; 2007. p. 209–262.

[109]   Manku GS and Motwani R. Approximate frequency counts over data streams. In: VLDB'02: Proceedings of the 28th International Conference on Very Large Databases. Elsevier; 2002. p. 346–357.

[110] Yu JX, Chong Z, Lu H, *et al.* False positive or false negative: Mining frequent itemsets from high speed transactional data streams. In: VLDB. vol. 4; 2004. p. 204–215.

[111] Chang JH and Lee WS. Finding recent frequent itemsets adaptively over online data streams. In: Proceedings of the Ninth ACM SIGKDD International Conference on Knowledge Discovery and Data Mining; 2003. p. 487–492.

[112] Gupta A, Bhatnagar V, and Kumar N. Mining closed itemsets in data stream using formal concept analysis. In: International Conference on Data Warehousing and Knowledge Discovery. Springer; 2010. p. 285–296.

[113] Leung CKS and Jiang F. Frequent itemset mining of uncertain data streams using the damped window model. In: Proceedings of the 2011 ACM Symposium on Applied Computing; 2011. p. 950–955.

[114] Tanbeer SK, Ahmed CF, Jeong BS, *et al.* Sliding window-based frequent pattern mining over data streams. Information Sciences. 2009; 179(22):3843–3865.

[115] Jin R and Agrawal G. An algorithm for in-core frequent itemset mining on streaming data. In: Fifth IEEE International Conference on Data Mining (ICDM'05). IEEE; 2005. p. 8–pp.

[116] Karp RM, Shenker S, and Papadimitriou CH. A simple algorithm for finding frequent elements in streams and bags. ACM Transactions on Database Systems (TODS). 2003;28(1):51–55.

[117] Giannella C, Han J, Pei J, *et al.* Mining frequent patterns in data streams at multiple time granularities. Next Generation Data Mining. 2003; 212:191–212.

[118] Ranganath B and Murty MN. Stream-close: Fast mining of closed frequent itemsets in high speed data streams. In: Data Mining Workshops, 2008. ICDMW'08. IEEE International Conference on. IEEE; 2008. p. 516–525.

[119] Zaki MJ and Hsiao CJ. CHARM: An efficient algorithm for closed itemset mining. In: Proceedings of the 2002 SIAM International Conference on Data Mining. SIAM; 2002. p. 457–473.

[120] Wang J, Han J, and Pei J. CLOSET+: Searching for the best strategies for mining frequent closed itemsets. In: Proceedings of the Ninth ACM SIGKDD International Conference on Knowledge Discovery and Data Mining. ACM; 2003. p. 236–245.

[121] Chi Y, Wang H, Yu PS, *et al.* Moment: Maintaining closed frequent itemsets over a stream sliding window. In: Fourth IEEE International Conference on Data Mining (ICDM'04). IEEE; 2004. p. 59–66.

[122] Jiang N and Gruenwald L. CFI-Stream: Mining closed frequent itemsets in data streams. In: Proceedings of the 12th ACM SIGKDD International Conference on Knowledge Discovery and Data Mining; 2006. p. 592–597.

[123] Mao G, Yang X, and Wu X. A new algorithm for mining frequent closed itemsets from data streams. In: Intelligent Control and Automation, 2008. WCICA 2008. 7th World Congress on. IEEE; 2008. p. 154–159.

[124] Li H, Lu Z, and Chen H. Mining approximate closed frequent itemsets over stream. In: Software Engineering, Artificial Intelligence, Networking, and Parallel/Distributed Computing, 2008. SNPD'08. Ninth ACIS International Conference on. IEEE; 2008. p. 405–410.

[125] Zhang G, Lei J, and Wu X. Mining frequent closed itemsets over data stream based on Bitvector and digraph. In: Future Computer and Communication (ICFCC), 2010 2nd International Conference on. vol. 2. IEEE; 2010. p. V2–241.

[126] Yen SJ, Wu CW, Lee YS, *et al.* A fast algorithm for mining frequent closed itemsets over stream sliding window. In: Fuzzy Systems (FUZZ), 2011 IEEE International Conference on. IEEE; 2011. p. 996–1002.

[127] Li HF, Ho CC, and Lee SY. Incremental updates of closed frequent itemsets over continuous data streams. Expert Systems with Applications. 2009;36(2):2451–2458.

[128] Xiaojun C. Mining accurate top-K frequent closed itemset from data stream. In: Computer Science and Electronics Engineering (ICCSEE), 2012 International Conference on. vol. 2. IEEE; 2012. p. 180–184.

[129] Kumar V and Satapathy SR. A novel technique for mining closed frequent itemsets using variable sliding window. In: Advance Computing Conference (IACC), 2014 IEEE International. IEEE; 2014. p. 504–510.

[130] Amphawan K and Lenca P. Mining top-k frequent-regular closed patterns. Expert Systems with Applications. 2015;42(21):7882–7894.

[131] ur Rehman Z, Shahbaz M, Shaheen M, *et al.* FPS-tree algorithm to find top-k closed itemsets in data streams. Arabian Journal for Science and Engineering. 2015;40(12):3507–3521.

[132] Shah RA, Meena MJ, and Ibrahim SS. Efficient mining of top k-closed itemset in real time. In: Proceedings of the 3rd International Symposium on Big Data and Cloud Computing Challenges (ISBCC-16). Springer; 2016. p. 317–324.

[133] Iwanuma K, Yamamoto Y, and Fukuda S. An on-line approximation algorithm for mining frequent closed itemsets based on incremental intersection. In: EDBT; 2016. p. 704–705.

[134] Caiyan D and Ling C. An algorithm for mining frequent closed itemsets with density from data streams. International Journal of Computational Science and Engineering. 2016;12(2–3):146–154.

[135] Metwally A, Agrawal D, and El Abbadi A. Efficient computation of frequent and top-k elements in data streams. In: International Conference on Database Theory. Springer; 2005. p. 398–412.

[136] Lim Y and Kang U. Time-weighted counting for recently frequent pattern mining in data streams. Knowledge and Information Systems. 2017; 53(2):391–422.

[137] Misra S, Thakur S, Ghosh M, *et al.* Mining recent frequent cooccurring items from transaction stream. International Journal of Data Science. 2019;4(4):288–304.

[138]   Chandler D. Introduction to modern statistical mechanics. Oxford University Press; Sep 1987. p. 288. ISBN-10: 0195042778, ISBN-13: 9780195042771.

[139]   Fournier-Viger P, Li Z, Lin JCW, *et al.* Efficient algorithms to identify periodic patterns in multiple sequences. Information Sciences. 2019; 489:205–226.

[140]   Mukherjee S and Rajkumar R. Frequent item set, sequential pattern mining and sequence prediction: Structures and algorithms. In: International Conference on Intelligent Computing and Smart Communication 2019. Springer; 2020. p. 219–234.

[141]   Bustio-Martnez L, Letras-Luna M, Cumplido R, *et al.* Using hashing and lexicographic order for frequent itemsets mining on data streams. Journal of Parallel and Distributed Computing. 2019;125:58–71.

[142]   Gan W, Lin JCW, Fournier-Viger P, *et al.* A survey of parallel sequential pattern mining. ACM Transactions on Knowledge Discovery from Data (TKDD). 2019;13(3):1–34.

[143]   Cano A. A survey on graphic processing unit computing for large-scale data mining. Wiley Interdisciplinary Reviews: Data Mining and Knowledge Discovery. 2018;8(1):e1232.

[144]   Wang T, Li N, and Jha S. Locally differentially private frequent itemset mining. In: 2018 IEEE Symposium on Security and Privacy (SP). IEEE; 2018. p. 127–143.

[145]   Lessanibahri S, Gastaldi L, and Fernández CG. A novel pruning algorithm for mining long and maximum length frequent itemsets. Expert Systems with Applications. 2020;142:113004.

[146]   Chon KW, Hwang SH, and Kim MS. GMiner: A fast GPU-based frequent itemset mining method for large-scale data. Information Sciences. 2018;439:19–38.

[147]   Biswas S and Mondal KC. Dynamic FP tree based rare pattern mining using multiple item supports constraints. In: International Conference on Computational Intelligence, Communications, and Business Analytics. Springer; 2018. p. 291–305.

[148]   Ghonge MM, Rane NP, and Potgantwar AD. A review on infrequent (rare) pattern patterns analysis in data mining. In: 2018 International Conference On Advances in Communication and Computing Technology (ICACCT). IEEE; 2018. p. 388–391.

[149]   Deng ZH. Mining high occupancy itemsets. Future Generation Computer Systems. 2020;102:222–229.

[150]   Hasani Z, Kon-Popovska M, and Velinov G. Lambda architecture for real time big data analytic. ICT Innovations. 2014:133–143.

[151]   Marz N and Warren J. Big data: Principles and best practices of scalable realtime data systems. Manning, Shelter Island, NY; 2015.

[152]   Kiran M, Murphy P, Monga I, *et al.* Lambda architecture for cost-effective batch and speed big data processing. In: 2015 IEEE International Conference on Big Data (Big Data). IEEE; 2015. p. 2785–2792.

[153]   Carney D, Çetintemel U, Cherniack M, *et al.* Monitoring streams a new class of data management applications. In: VLDB'02: Proceedings of the 28th International Conference on Very Large Databases. Elsevier; 2002. p. 215–226.

[154]   Abadi DJ, Ahmad Y, Balazinska M, *et al.* The design of the borealis stream processing engine. In: CIDR. vol. 5; 2005. p. 277–289.

[155]   Gedik B, Andrade H, Wu KL, *et al.* SPADE: The system s declarative stream processing engine. In: Proceedings of the 2008 ACM SIGMOD International Conference on Management of Data; 2008. p. 1123–1134.

[156]   Thies W, Karczmarek M, and Amarasinghe S. StreamIt: A language for streaming applications. In: International Conference on Compiler Construction. Springer; 2002. p. 179–196.

[157]   Woodie A. Understanding your options for stream processing frameworks; 2019. Available from: https://www.datanami.com/2019/05/30/understanding-your-options-for-stream-processing-frameworks/.

[158]   Hellstrom I. What are the differences between Apache Spark, Storm, Flink, Beam, Apex; 2017. Available from: https://www.quora.com/What-are-the-differences-between-Apache-Spark-Storm-Heron-Samza-Flink-Beam-Apex.

[159]   Liu X, Iftikhar N, and Xie X. Survey of real-time processing systems for big data. In: Proceedings of the 18th International Database Engineering & Applications Symposium; 2014. p. 356–361.

[160]   Kamburugamuve S and Fox G. Survey of distributed stream processing. Bloomington: Indiana University. 2016;.

[161]   Isah H, Abughofa T, Mahfuz S, *et al.* A survey of distributed data stream processing frameworks. IEEE Access. 2019;7:154300–154316.

Chapter 7

Architectures of big data analytics: scaling out data mining algorithms using Hadoop–MapReduce and Spark

Sheikh Kamaruddin[1,2] and Vadlamani Ravi[1]

Many statistical and machine learning (ML) techniques have been successfully applied to small-sized datasets during the past one and half decades. However, in today's world, different application domains, viz., healthcare, finance, bioinformatics, telecommunications, and meteorology, generate huge volumes of data on a daily basis. All these massive datasets have to be analyzed for discovering hidden insights. With the advent of big data analytics (BDA) paradigm, the data mining (DM) techniques were modified and scaled out to adapt to the distributed and parallel environment. This chapter reviewed 249 articles appeared between 2009 and 2019, which implemented different DM techniques in a parallel, distributed manner in the Apache Hadoop MapReduce framework or Apache Spark environment for solving various DM tasks. We present some critical analyses of these papers and bring out some interesting insights. We have found that methods like Apriori, support vector machine (SVM), random forest (RF), *K*-means and many variants of the previous along with many other approaches are made into parallel distributed environment and produced scalable and effective insights out of it. This review is concluded with a discussion of some open areas of research with future directions, which can be explored further by the researchers and practitioners alike.

7.1 Introduction

In the current digital era, there is enormous progress in the computational world; in other words, there is a spectacular development of the Internet or online world technologies. These developments in return account for a huge volume of data in structured, semi-structured, and unstructured manner. These massive quantities of data are produced by and about people, things, and their interactions. So today we

[1]Centre of Excellence in Analytics, Institute for Development and Research in Banking Technology, Hyderabad, India
[2]School of Computer and Information Sciences (SCIS), University of Hyderabad, Hyderabad, India

have a gold mine of data from which hidden insights can be drawn. These large voluminous data are generated in various forms like structured, semi-structured, and unstructured data. These data are also produced in a very fast manner from different types of the Internet of Things (IoT) devices and other digitization sources. This kind of data generation has led to the definition of big data defined by Gartner which states, "Big data is high-volume, high-velocity and/or high variety information assets that demand cost-effective, innovative forms of information processing that enable enhanced insight, decision making, and process automation" [1].

The voluminous data can be attributed to business sales records, the collected results of scientific experiments, or real-time sensors used in the IoT. Data may also exist in a wide variety of file types, including structured data, such as SQL database stores; unstructured data, such as document files; or streaming data from sensors. Further, big data may involve multiple, simultaneous data sources, which may not otherwise be integrated resulting in as a source of a variety of data formats. Finally, velocity refers to the speed at which big data must be analyzed. Every BDA project will ingest, correlate, and analyze the data sources and then render an answer or result based on an overarching query.

McKinsey Global Institute specified the potential of big data in five main topics [2]: healthcare, public sector, retail, manufacturing, and personal location data.

The big data computation requires a scalable solution with distributed parallel computation. The scaling is defined as the ability of the system to adapt to increased demands regarding data processing. The big data processing platforms can be categorized into the following two types of scaling:

- Horizontal scaling: Horizontal scaling involves distributing the workload across many machines that may be even commodity hardware. It is also known as "scale out," where multiple independent computing devices are added together to improve the processing capability [3].
- Vertical scaling: Vertical scaling involves installing more processors, more memory, and faster hardware, typically, within a single machine. It is also known as "scale up," and it usually involves a single instance of an operating system [1].

As part of this review chapter, we would like to address the following research questions:

Q1: Can statistical and machine learning algorithms meant for data mining tasks be made scalable for big datasets in Hadoop and Spark frameworks?

Q2: If "yes" what are they, why they are scalable and what sort of insights are obtained through the analytics?

Q3: Can some pointers be suggested using which any researcher can attempt parallelizing hitherto unparallelized ML techniques?

These research questions shall be answered in Section 7.5 after reviewing the papers.

In this chapter, we reviewed the papers concerned with distributed parallel computing environment implemented with horizontal scaling. The review is performed keeping in mind the different DM tasks with the concerned ML techniques. The critical analysis of the papers is furnished pointing the areas for future research work. There are some dedicated big data journals that came into existence in the recent past, viz., *Big Data Research, Journal of Big Data, IEEE Transactions on Big Data, International Journal of Big Data Intelligence, Big Data*. We collected papers from these journals apart from the journal and proceeding articles from well-known publishers.

The rest of the chapter is organized as follows. Section 7.2 presents the literature review; in other words, it lists out the previous review works carried out by the community in the big data area. Section 7.3 discusses the review methodology that has been conducted for the current review work followed by Section 7.4 presenting the review of the articles that were included in the review process. Section 7.5 discusses the insights gained out of the review work. Section 7.6 that is the last part presents the conclusion and future direction followed by the reference.

7.2   Previous related reviews

The current literature presents many review articles dealing with various aspects of big data processing. Some papers discussed hardware platform issues. The scope and challenges in different hardware platforms with different configuration and their performance were analyzed. Singh and Reddy [3] examined different platforms available for performing BDA. They reviewed different hardware platforms available for BDA and estimated the advantages and drawbacks of various platforms on the basis of different metrics such as scalability, data I/O rate, fault tolerance, real-time processing, data size supported, and iterative task support. Saecker and Markl [4] presented a review of hardware architectures used for BDA. The authors considered the horizontal and vertical scaling with the technical aspect for the BDA. Chen *et al.* [5] in the survey work reviewed the related technologies of big data such as cloud computing, IoT, data centers, and Hadoop. The survey work highlighted the four phases of the value chain of big data, i.e., data generation, data acquisition, data storage, and data analysis. The review included the technical challenges and the latest advances for each phase. Liu *et al.* [6] presented an analysis of the open-source technologies that support big data processing in a real-time or near real-time fashion. They analyzed their system architectures and platforms.

There are some review works concerning the software aspects as data models supporting big data, discussing risks and challenges in big data computational environments. In addition, there are studies concerning the analysis of MapReduce computational environment, with its challenges. Sharma *et al.* [7] presented a review paper on leading big data models that are leading contributors to the NoSQL era and claim to address big data challenges in reliable and efficient ways. The survey paper compares the features of different data models serving for big data analysis. Al-Jarrah *et al.* [8] presented a review of the theoretical and experimental data-modeling literature, in large-scale data-intensive fields. The study is related to model efficiency while learning the new algorithmic approaches with the least memory requirements and the processing power to minimize computational cost while maintaining/improving its predictive/classification accuracy and stability. Sagiroglu and Sinanc [9] presented an overview of big data's content, scope, samples, methods, advantages, and challenges and discussed privacy concern on it. Sri and Anusha [10] presented a survey of big data where they analyzed the Hadoop architecture, including HDFS and MapReduce environment and its security issues. Khan *et al.* [11], Ekbia *et al.* [12], Chen and Zhang [13] had reviewed the challenges, techniques, and technologies involved in the big data computational environment. The survey work also included the risks and security issues involved with big data environment. Lee *et al.* [14] presented a review paper on the parallel data processing with MapReduce. They have analyzed various technical aspects of the MapReduce framework. The inherent pros and cons were discussed along with the introduction to the optimization strategies for MapReduce programming. Ward and Barker [15] presented a survey on big data definitions. The review paper has collated various definitions that have gained some degree of attraction and had furnished a clear and concise definition of the term "big data."

The research community has also presented some review work considering individual DM tasks like clustering, data analysis aids like visualization methods and studied in-memory data management system. Shirkhorshidi *et al.* [16], Fahad *et al.* [17] presented a survey of clustering algorithms for big data. The survey work included analysis of the improved clustering algorithms for the big data paradigm. Gorodov and Gubarev [18] presented a review of data visualization methods in application to big data. They reviewed the existing methods for data visualization in application to big data. The survey work included classification of visualization methods in application to big data. Zhang *et al.* [19] presented a review of in-memory data management and processing on big data paradigm. The survey involved a broad range of in-memory data management and processing systems, including both data storage systems and data processing frameworks.

Table 7.1 presents the details of all the previous review papers. The following are the key reasons that necessitated writing the current, unique review work:

1. The existing literature on the review of big data covered the hardware platforms, data models, challenges, risks, and security issues in BDA, data visualization, and a DM task like clustering.
2. It is evident that there is no survey paper existing, which exclusively deals with DM tasks with different ML techniques applicable to parallel distributed programming considering horizontal scaling platform, viz., Apache Hadoop MapReduce, and Apache Spark framework.
3. This review by virtue of its theme provides a plethora of opportunities to budding researchers in parallelizing various DM tasks applied to any domain. This will allow researchers and practitioners to not only employ the extant scaled versions of the popular ML techniques for DM tasks in diverse domains but also suggest pointers to develop scaled versions of hitherto unparallelized algorithms.

Table 7.1 Previous review papers

Reference	Journal/ conference	Journal/proceeding name	Publisher	Scope of review
[3]	Journal	Journal of Big data	Springer	Hardware platforms
[4]	Conference	European Business Intelligence Summer School (eBISS), 2012	Springer	Hardware architectures
[5]	Journal	Mobile Networks and Applications	Springer	Challenges, and the latest advances in data generation, data acquisition, data storage, and data analysis
[6]	Conference	International Database Engineering & Applications Symposium, 2014	ACM	Technologies that support big data processing in a real-time or near real-time fashion
[7]	Journal	Data Science Journal	Ubiquity Press	Data models
[8]	Journal	Big Data Research	Elsevier	Theoretical and experimental data-modeling literature for model efficiency while learning with least memory requirements
[9]	Conference	International Conference on Collaboration Technologies and Systems	IEEE	Scope, methods, advantages, challenges, and privacy concern of big data
[10]	Journal	Indonesian Journal of Electrical Engineering and Informatics	Institute of Advanced Engineering and Science (IAES)	HDFS and MapReduce environment and its security issues
[11]	Journal	The Scientific World Journal	Hindawi	Challenges, techniques, and technologies involved in the big data computational environment. Risks and security issues
[12]	Journal	Journal of the Association for Information Science and Technology	Wiley	
[13]	Journal	Information Sciences	Elsevier	Various technical aspects of the MapReduce framework
[14]	Journal	ACM SIGMOD Record	ACM	Definition of big data
[15]	Journal	CoRR	–	Clustering algorithms for big data
[16]	Conference	–	Springer	
[17]	Journal	IEEE Transactions on emerging topics in computing	IEEE	
[18]	Journal	Journal of Electrical and Computer Engineering	Hindawi	Data visualization methods in application to big data
[19]	Journal	IEEE Transactions on Knowledge and Data Engineering	IEEE	In-memory data management and processing on big data paradigm

Therefore, the present review will be a significant contribution to the BDA research from the view point of parallelizing analytical techniques.

7.3   Review methodology

The review covers all the articles in the different DM tasks that discuss about different ML techniques that are carried out in the parallel distributed computational environment of Apache Hadoop/Spark. Thus, the scope of the review can be considered as the intersection of these three (Figure 7.1). The current review work has followed four main steps (Figure 7.2) to bring the review work to its final form. The steps are review definition, search of articles, filtration of articles for review, and analysis of the review process.

Step 1: Review definition

Step 1.1: Scope of review. The present literature survey covers the research articles related to the DM tasks employing different ML techniques in big data paradigm. The review chapter has focused only on the research articles related to parallel distributed processing with horizontal scaling. Thus, research articles related to Hadoop MapReduce and Spark are only considered for the review process.

Step 1.2: Goal of the review process. The review chapter aims to provide analytical insights from the past papers with indications to the research gaps and suggesting directions for future work.

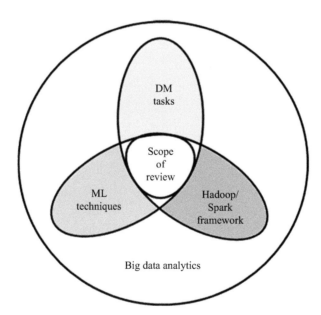

Figure 7.1   Scope of review

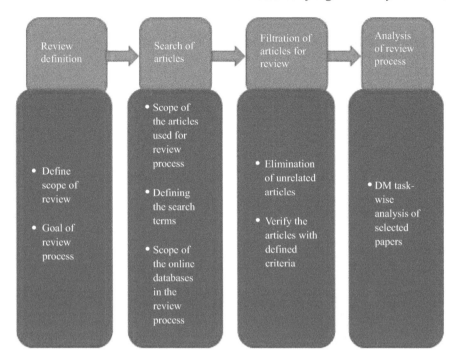

Figure 7.2   Review process methodology

Step 2: Search for articles

Step 2.1: Scope of the articles used for the review process. The articles are about DM tasks, viz., association rule mining (ARM), regression, classification, clustering, outlier detection (OD), recommendation along with the associated ML techniques form the focus of the present review. Further, we restrict our attention to only horizontal scaling, i.e., parallel distributed processing with a cluster of nodes. Hence, the review process considered only the Hadoop- and Spark-based papers (Figure 7.1).

It did not include parallelization using field-programmable gate array (FPGA), Message Passing Interface, or general-purpose graphics processing unit (GPGPU). The research works related to social media analytics and visualization were not included in the purview of the current review. This review did not focus on application domains such as healthcare, finance, bioinformatics, and telecommunication sectors. We have excluded the articles from paid journals. The edited volumes were excluded from the scope of the review.

Step 2.2: Defining the search terms. We refined our search using various words like "MapReduce," "Apache Spark," along with words representing DM tasks such as, "clustering," "classification," "ARM," "K-means," "SVM."

Step 2.3: Scope of the online databases in the review process. Primarily, we gathered research papers from the scientific articles databases such as ACM Digital Library, Taylor & Francis, ScienceDirect, Wiley, Google Scholar, Springer, and IEEE Xplore. We collected around 700 articles that were published during 2009–19.

Step 3: Filtration of articles for review

Step 3.1: Elimination of unrelated articles. The scope of the articles was defined, and the articles were filtered with the specified criteria.

The collection and filtration process resulted in 249 papers to review for this survey that were published during 2009–19 in various conferences and journals.

Step 3.2: Verification of the articles with defined criteria. The articles were validated to have used real-world or synthetic datasets for the experiment with some results, compared with some ML techniques (Figure 7.3).

Step 4: Analysis of the review process

Step 4.1: DM-task-wise analysis of selected papers with future research direction. DM task wise, the articles were reviewed and categorized with Hadoop-and Spark-based articles, in chronological order. The critical analysis of the articles in each section of DM task led to identifying research gaps and addressed for future

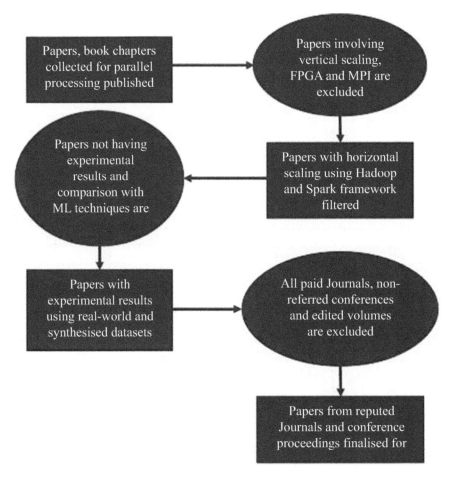

Figure 7.3   Filtering procedure for the selection of articles to review

research work. The bird's-eye view of the analysis of the reviewed articles with some suggestions for future research work concluded the review chapter along with the conclusion section.

7.4   Review of articles in the present work

The review process involves articles related to distributed parallel computing environment of Hadoop and Spark with different DM tasks with ML techniques (Figure 7.1). Various DM tasks with the ML techniques used for distributed parallel processing covered in the review process are depicted in Figure 7.4.

7.4.1   Association rule mining/pattern mining

7.4.1.1   Hadoop MapReduce-based journal papers

Karim *et al.* [20] proposed an approach for mining maximal contiguous frequent patterns (FPs) in large DNA sequence data. The concerned works included *Human Genome* (HomoSapiens GRCh37.64 DNA Chromosome Part 1), and *Bacteria DNA sequence* datasets downloaded from the National Center of Biotechnology Information Gene Expression Omnibus (NCBI GEO) repository. The experimental results presented the efficacy of the approach.

Karim *et al.* [21] proposed a distributed model for mining of useful patterns in large datasets. The proposed method was applied to the real-world datasets, viz., *Connect-4*, *Mushroom*, and *Agaricus*, that were downloaded from UCI repository [22]. Experimental results exhibited that the proposed technique was efficient and scalable.

Bhuiyan and Al Hasan [23] proposed a frequent subgraph mining algorithm called FSM-H implemented on iterative MapReduce framework. The experimental work was carried out with the following datasets: (i) six real-world graph datasets that were obtained from an online source [24] that contain graphs extracted from the PubChem website [25], (ii) a graph dataset from DBLP Computer Science Bibliography data, considering publications in the year range 1992–2003 [26], and (iii) four synthetic datasets using a tool called GraphGen [27]. The experimental results showed that the performance of FSM-H was significantly better than that proposed by Hill *et al.* [28].

Xun *et al.* [29] proposed an approach FiDoop-HD, an extension of FiDoop, for parallel mining of frequent itemsets. To evaluate the performance of the proposed method, a synthetic dataset *D1000W* was generated using the IBM quest market-basket synthetic data generator, and a real dataset *Celestial Spectral* Dataset was used. The experimental results showed that the proposed approach was sensitive to both data distribution and dimensions.

Salah *et al.* [30] suggested parallel mining of maximally informative *k*-itemsets (miki) based on joint entropy, called Parallel Highly Informative *k*-ItemSet (PHIKS). The authors used three real-world datasets: the *complete 2013 Amazon Reviews* dataset [31], *the 2014 English Wikipedia* dataset [32], and *a sample of ClueWeb English* dataset [33]. The proposed approach, PHIKS, outperformed an alternative parallel approach.

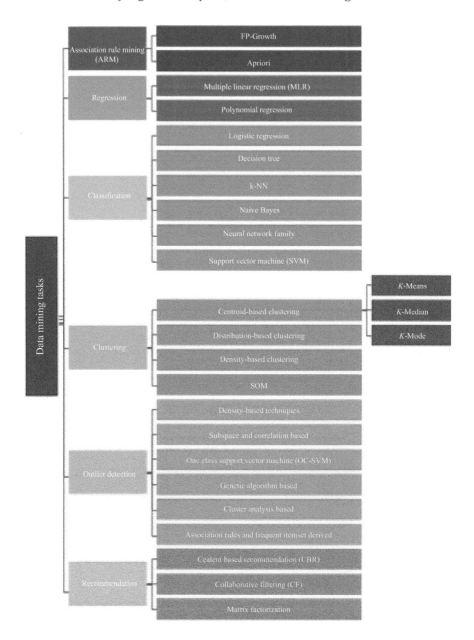

Figure 7.4   Data mining tasks and machine learning techniques parallelized for BDA

Breier and Branišová [34] have proposed a dynamic rule creation based on anomaly detection method for recognizing security breaches in log files. The datasets used were *1998 DARPA Intrusion Detection Evaluation Set* [35] and *Snort logs* [36] created by analyzing the DARPA dataset. The proposed approach found to perform better than FP-Growth and Apriori methods.

Yan *et al.* [37] employed a parallel mining algorithm for the constrained FP, called PACFP. The experimental work involved the *SDSS star spectrum* datasets provided by the National Observatory of China. Experimental results claimed availability, scalability, and expandability of the algorithm.

Leroy *et al.* [38] introduced item-centric mining, a new semantics for frequent itemset mining (FIM) over long-tailed datasets. The proposed algorithm, TopPI, was compared with parallel FP (PFP)-Growth. The research study involved analysis of two real-world datasets, viz., *Supermarket and LastFM*. The experimental results showed the effectiveness of the proposed algorithm over standard itemset mining and global top-*k* algorithms.

Sohrabi and Taheri [39] proposed a Hadoop-based parallel implementation of PrePost+ algorithm (HBPrePost+) for FIM. The experimental work was carried out with four datasets: *Pumsb, Connect, Chess*, and *Mushroom* from Frequent Itemset Mining Implementations (FIMI) repository [40]. The experimental results showed that HBPrePost+ algorithm outperformed one of the best existing parallel methods of FIM (PARMA) in terms of execution time.

Liu *et al.* [41] proposed a Heuristic MapReduce-based ARM approach through maximal FIM, HMAM. The experiments were conducted with synthetic datasets generated by the IBM data generator and real datasets *Kosarak, Retail, Accidents* collected from FIMI repository [40]. The proposed HMAM was compared with state-of-the-art maximal FIM algorithms. The experimental results proved that the proposed approach had less execution time with efficient memory utilization and scalability.

Singh *et al.* [42] proposed improved MapReduce-based Apriori algorithms, Variable Size-based Fixed Passes Combined-counting, and Elapsed-Time-based Dynamic Passes Combined-counting. They have also proposed optimized versions of them. The experimental results showed that the optimized versions are more efficient in terms of execution time. The previous experimental work was carried out with the synthetic dataset c20d10k generated by IBM Generator and real datasets, viz., *Chess* and *Mushroom* from FIMI repository [40].

7.4.1.2   Spark-based journal papers

Zhang *et al.* [43] proposed a distributed FIM algorithm. The proposed algorithm presented a reduction in the number of candidate itemsets which was achieved through a matrix-based pruning approach. The datasets used in the research work are *T10I4D100K* and *T40l10D100K* [40]. The experimental result was compared with PFP-Growth and found to outperform PFP in execution time for both the datasets.

Chen and An [44] proposed a parallel high utility itemset (PHUI)-Miner algorithm, which is the parallel version of high utility itemset (HUI)-Miner algorithm.

The experimental study was conducted on different datasets, viz., *Kosarak*, *Accidents*, *Chess* [45], *Twitter* [46], *T5000L10I1P10PL6*, *tafeng* [47], and *globe*, where *T5000L10I1P10PL6* was a synthetic dataset generated using the IBM Quest Data Generator [48], and the rest are real-world datasets. The experimental results showed that the PHUI-Miner had superior performance to its serial counterpart HUI-Miner.

Karim *et al.* [49] proposed an algorithm called maximal FP for finding FPs implemented with Apache Spark. The experiments were carried out with synthetic datasets generated by the IBM Quest [50]; a real dataset *Mushroom* from UCI ML data repository [22]; a real *Retail dataset* [51]; and a *Retail market basket data* from an anonymous Belgian retail store. The experimental results showed that the proposed method outperformed other state-of-the-art maximal FP algorithms.

Martín *et al.* [52] have proposed a generic parallel framework MRQAR for quantitative ARM in Spark framework. The experimental work was carried out with *SUSY*, *Higgs* datasets from UCI repository [22]; *Epsilon* from LIBSVM [53] and ECBDL'14 competition. The proposed framework is to be implemented when any standard algorithm to find quantitative association rule is not able to execute in big data paradigm.

7.4.1.3   Hadoop MapReduce-based conference papers

Hill *et al.* [28] proposed an approach to frequent subgraph mining in biological datasets utilizing iterative MapReduce framework. The experimental study was carried out with (i) synthetic dataset generated using a graph generator [54] and (ii) the real datasets extracted from the PubChem website [25]. The experimental results showed the proposed algorithm outperformed other methods.

Farzanyar and Cercone [55] proposed an approach for an efficient FIM algorithm, called Improved MapReduce Apriori (IMRApriori) algorithm. The experimental study utilized IBM synthetic datasets T10.I5.D1000K [48] and real dataset BMS-POS [56]. The proposed approach had superior execution time in comparison with the MRApriori algorithm.

Farzanyar and Cercone [57] proposed a method of mining of frequent itemsets. The authors have demonstrated a comparative analysis of their proposed algorithm with IMRApriori algorithm [55]. The authors have used synthetic *IBM dataset* for their experiments. The results demonstrated a reduction in communication overhead and execution time.

Mao and Guo [58] proposed an improved association rules mining algorithm, AprioriPMR, which involved power set. The experimental study utilized the *breast cancer* datasets from WEKA. The results presented the superior performance of the proposed algorithm to parallel Apriori algorithm regarding processing time and scalability.

Natarajan and Sehar [59] proposed an algorithm, named ARM based on Hadoop, to extract FPs from large databases. The experimental work carried out with synthetic dataset generated using IBM's Quest synthetic data generator [48]. The proposed algorithm had improved scalability and efficiency compared to BTP-tree.

Rong *et al.* [60] implemented a parallel version of Apriori and FP-Growth algorithms in large-scale data for association rules mining. The study involved the real datasets from FIMI repository [40]. The results showed that the proposed method had high efficiency and good speedup, scalability, and reliability compared to its serial counterpart.

Moens *et al.* [61] analyzed FIM for significant-sized data. The experimental study involved four different datasets: *Abstracts provided by De Bie* [62], *T10I4D100K, Mushroom*, and *Pumsb*, from FIMI repository [40]. The experimental results showed the scalability of the proposed approach.

Chen *et al.* [63] proposed an approach for parallel mining FPs for large-scale data. The experimental study involved synthetic datasets generated by IBM synthetic data generator [50]. The experimental results showed that the proposed approach is efficient and scalable.

Leung and Jiang [64] proposed a data science solution called BigAnt to mine uncertain large-scale data for FPs. The study utilized various datasets, e.g., *Accidents, Connect-4*, and *Mushroom* from the UCI ML repository [22] and the FIMI repository [40] and also the *IBM synthetic* datasets, which were generated using the IBM Quest Dataset Generator [48]. The experimental result was compared with UF-growth algorithm [65] and found that the proposed method had superior execution time with scalability and speedup.

Yu *et al.* [66] designed an efficient algorithm Frequent Patterns Mining (FPM) algorithm based on MapReduce framework (FAMR) by modifying the traditional Apriori algorithm. The experiments were carried out with data generated from the IBM data generator [50]. The experimental results showed that FAMR could reduce the number of candidate itemsets and achieved an excellent reduction in execution time.

Yu *et al.* [67] proposed a new planted (l, d) motif discovery algorithm named MCES, which identified motifs by mining and combining emerging substrings. The experimental work was carried out with simulated data as well as real data from *mESC* (mouse embryonic stem cell) data. Experimental results showed that MCES could identify (l, d) motifs efficiently and effectively.

Zhou and Huang [68] implemented an improved parallel Apriori algorithm in which both count and candidate generation steps were employed. The experimental study utilized the synthetic data generated by an open-source tool package, ARtool [69]. The results showed that the proposed method had a superior performance regarding execution time.

Fumarola and Malerba [70] proposed a parallel algorithm for approximate FIM using MapReduce called MrAdam. The experimental work was carried out with the datasets *Mushroom, Pumsb*, and *Accident*. The experimental results presented the scalability and the superior performance of the proposed algorithm over other FP mining algorithms.

Bhuiyan and Al Hasan [71] proposed a frequent subgraph mining algorithm called FSM-H. The study involved four real-world graph datasets that were collected from the PubChem website [25]. Also, four synthetic datasets were created from a tool called GraphGen [27]. The experimental results showed that the proposed approach was efficient regarding execution time in comparison with existing methods.

Liu *et al.* [72] proposed an FIM algorithm. The proposed approach used improved Apriori algorithm that used the length of each transaction to determine the size of the maximum merge candidate itemsets. The experimental study utilized synthetic dataset. The results presented the efficacy of the proposed approach.

Cao *et al.* [73] proposed an approach for mining of repetitive sequences across a collection of genomes implemented with MapReduce framework called MRSMRS. The dataset used in the experiment contained the base pairs from the genome of six species: human, mouse, rat, dog, chicken, and macaque. The experimental results showed that the proposed approach had superior speedup with linear scalability and less execution time.

Liu and Li [74] proposed an approach for PFP discovery in a non-iterative manner. The experimental work utilized the file *SogouQ* provided by the Sogou Lab. The experimental results showed that the proposed approach had better performance in terms of execution time with comparison to algorithms bagging the idea of traditional Apriori.

Chang *et al.* [75] proposed the Parallel Block FP-Growth (PBFP-Growth) algorithm by combining the Apriori and FP-Growth algorithms. The experimental results proved that the performance of the PBFP-Growth algorithm was better than that of both the Apriori and the FP-Growth algorithms.

Sun *et al.* [76] proposed a new algorithm Vertical-Apriori MapReduce (VAMR) by combining vertical frequent mining method, MapReduce mechanism, and Apriori for mining frequency itemset from the large dataset in a single node. The experimental work involved datasets from FIMI repository [40] and synthesized datasets with a different number of records and a different number of attributes. The performance of the proposed algorithm was measured against OPUS miner and Apriori MapReduce algorithm and found to be better than both.

Ferrucci *et al.* [77] proposed a framework for developing parallel genetic algorithms (GAs). The approach was employed for feature subset selection problem. The *Chicago Crime* dataset from the UCI ML repository [22] was used for experimental work. The results showed that the proposed framework was superior to its serial counterpart with respect to execution period and had comparable accuracy.

Jiang *et al.* [78] proposed a method for mining "following" patterns in big social network mining called MR-PFP with MapReduce framework. The experimental work was carried out with two real-life social network datasets from *Stanford Network Analysis Project* (SNAP) (i) *ego-Facebook* dataset and (ii) *ego-Twitter* dataset [79]. The experiment compared the proposed algorithm MR-PFP with its sequential counterpart, and the result showed a good speedup of the proposed algorithm.

Salah *et al.* [80] proposed an algorithm for parallel mining of miki based on joint entropy called PHIKS algorithm. The experimental study utilized two real-world datasets: *2014 English Wikipedia* dataset articles, sample of *ClueWeb English* dataset. The experimental results showed that the proposed algorithm PHIKS demonstrated significant efficiency in terms of runtime and scalability.

Liu *et al.* [81] proposed an algorithm for the detection of significant patterns called Pampas. The experimental study was carried out with three datasets *EMS-POS*, *Connect-4*, and *Mushroom* collected from FIMI repository [40]. The results showed that the proposed Pampas was efficient, scalable on dataset size and cluster size.

Apiletti *et al.* [82] proposed parallel FPM for high-dimensional data, called PaMPa-HD. The experimental study involved the real dataset Kent Ridge Breast Cancer [83] and two synthetic datasets [84]. The study results showed the efficiency and scalability of PaMPa-HD which outperformed state-of-the-art algorithms.

Baralis *et al.* [85] proposed a Parallel Weighted Itemset (PaWI) Mining algorithm. The experimental study involved a real-world dataset having a collection of 34 million of Amazon reviews. The experimental results showed that PaWI had less execution time with scalability.

Leung *et al.* [86] presented a model for FP analysis. The development of the model utilizes (i) IBM synthetic datasets [50], (ii) the online *Retail* dataset from UCI ML repository [22], and (iii) *ego-Facebook* and *ego-Twitter* datasets from SNAP [79] for its evaluation. The performance of the proposed algorithm outperformed several state-of-the-art algorithms.

Gonen and Gudes [87] proposed an algorithm for mining closed frequent itemsets. The study involved a real dataset *webdocs* from the FIMI repository [40]. The synthetic dataset was generated using the IBM data generator [50]. The experimental results showed that the proposed algorithm had superior execution time and communication cost.

Thakare *et al.* [88] proposed an improved PrePost algorithm. The experimental work utilized synthetic dataset constructed with the spawner data generator tool. *T15I106D100K*, *T15I106D1000K*, and *T15I106D2000K* were used as experimental data. The results showed that with an increase of dataset size, the proposed algorithm performed better.

Chang *et al.* [89] proposed an approach for parallel ARM, called Improved Parallel Association Rule Based on Combination. The experimental study involved synthetic dataset. The experimental results showed that the proposed algorithm outperformed other algorithms substantially in terms of execution time.

Sheshikala *et al.* [90] proposed a parallel approach for finding colocation pattern. The proposed method determines the spatial neighbor relationship to identify colocation instances and colocation rules. The experiment involved synthetic datasets. The experimental results showed that the proposed approach was computationally more efficient.

7.4.1.4   Spark-based conference papers

Gui *et al.* [91] proposed a distributed matrix-based pruning algorithm for FIM. The research work involved synthetic dataset *T10I4D100K*, which is generated by IBM's data generator [50]. The proposed method was compared with MapReduce-based Apriori algorithm and found to have less execution time with scalability.

Deng and Lou [92] proposed an FP-Growth algorithm. The experimental study involved datasets from UCI ML repository and FIM dataset repository, viz., *Mushroom* [22] and *Accidents* [40], respectively. The experimental results showed that the proposed approach had superior efficiency in comparison to other state-of-the-art algorithms.

Rathee *et al.* [93] proposed an algorithm Reduced-Apriori (R-Apriori), which is an efficient Apriori-based algorithm. The experimental study utilized five datasets: (i) *T10I4D100K*, a synthetic dataset generated by IBM's data generator; (ii) *Retail* dataset; (iii) *Kosarak* dataset that contains the click-stream data of a Hungarian on-line news portal; (iv) *BMSWebView2*, used for the KDD Cup 2000 competition; and (v) *T25I10D10K*, a synthetic dataset generated by a random transaction database generator. The experimental results showed that the proposed R-Apriori outperformed other state-of-the-art algorithms.

Utama and Distiawan [94] proposed a method for the mining of frequent *n*-grams, called Spark-gram. The study included *Wikipedia articles collection* dataset collected from Wikipedia dump repository. The experimental results showed that Spark-gram outperformed its Hadoop MapReduce equivalent when more frequent *n*-grams were considered.

Joy and Sherly [95] proposed a method for the prediction of chances of heart attack using parallel FIM. The experimental study involved dataset containing information about heart disease collected from UCI repository [22]. The results showed the proposed approach to be efficient.

The review of articles related to ARM in Hadoop and Spark framework revealed the following research insights:

- *In all the reviewed articles, we can observe that FIM had been more than any other ARM method. The FIM is inherently data independent, i.e., the algorithm can be implemented in different chunks of data in a parallel manner.*
- *Frequent subgraph mining has been less explored in distributed parallel computing environment leading to a fertile ground for research work.*
- *The evolutionary computation has not been used to its full potential in BDA using distributed framework for FPM, which the researchers can explore.*
- *FP-Growth and FP-tree are less explored areas in comparison to Apriori method in Hadoop or Spark environment.*
- *HUI-Miner presents an open space for research in the distributed parallel framework.*

7.4.2   Regression/prediction/forecasting

7.4.2.1   Hadoop MapReduce-based journal papers

He *et al.* [96] proposed an efficient parallel ELM (PELM) for regression. The experimental work involved the *stock* dataset from UCI [22]. The results showed that the proposed algorithm, PELM, had a good speedup, scale-up, and size up performance.

Luts [97] employed semi-parametric regression analysis of large-scale data. The proposed method included *US domestic flight* data to analyze air traffic delays in real time. The proposed method was used in the US domestic airline data in real time which was published on a website [98].

Naimur Rahman *et al.* [99] utilized backpropagation neural network (BPNN) for electricity generation forecasting system. The experimental study involved the US power consumption data which is 20 years of historical data. The experimental results showed that the proposed system could predict the required power generation close to 99 percent of the actual usage.

7.4.2.2 Spark-based journal papers

Chen *et al.* [100] proposed a Patient Treatment Time Prediction algorithm and a Hospital Queuing-Recommendation system. The experimental work carried out with datasets covering 3-years data collected from an actual hospital application. Experimental results showed that the proposed algorithm achieved high accuracy and performance.

Rodríguez-Fdez *et al.* [101] proposed a scalable fuzzy rule learning through evolution for regression (S-FRULER) that is a distributed version of FRULER (a genetic fuzzy system) that learns for regression problems. The study included ten regression datasets from the KEEL project repository [102]: *Delta Ailerons, Delta Elevators, California Housing, MV Artificial Domain, House-16H, Elevators, Computer Activity, Pole Telecommunications, Pumadyn,* and *Ailerons* and a dataset from bioinformatics problem also used. Experimental results showed that S-FRULER scaled well with comparable precision.

Galicia *et al.* [103] proposed a method for predicting time series data in a big data paradigm, i.e., time series with high frequency measurement. It is used to predict a time horizon whereby the generation of prediction models were carried out with linear models like regression and with nonlinear methods based on decision trees (DTs). The experiments were carried out with real-time series data related to the *consumption of electric energy* in Spain. The proposed method presented a reasonable high accuracy.

Talavera-Llames *et al.* [104] proposed an approach for big data forecasting based on *k*-weighted nearest neighbors algorithm. The experiment was conducted with *energy demand time series data* in the Spanish electricity market. The proposed algorithm was compared with deep learning, DT, gradient-boosted tree, RF, and linear regression and found to be outperforming them.

7.4.2.3 Hadoop MapReduce-based conference papers

Yin *et al.* [105] proposed a scalable regression tree learning on Hadoop MapReduce framework using *OpenPlanet*, an open-source counterpart of a proprietary regression tree algorithm PLANET. The experimental study involved 2 years of power consumption data from 24 buildings in the University of Southern California campus. The previous data were extrapolated to larger synthetic datasets utilized in the study. The experimental results showed that the proposed method was efficient and scalable.

Tejasviram *et al.* [106] proposed a hybrid model combining the Auto-Associative Extreme Learning Machine (AAELM) with multiple linear regression

(MLR) for performing regression on scalable data. The experimental work was carried out with (i) *Gas sensor array under dynamic gas mixtures* and (ii) *Airlineflight* datasets collected from UCI repository [22]. The hybrid model was compared with MLR, and the results proved that the proposed model outperformed the MLR in the context of MSE and MAPE.

Rehab and Boufares [107] proposed a parallel MLR. The experimental study used one synthetic dataset and one real-world dataset, i.e., *Airline on-time* dataset. The experimental results showed that the proposed MLR was efficient and scalable with respect to the size of the data and number of nodes in the cluster.

Chavda and Dhobi [108] proposed a method for the prediction of web users browsing behavior using SVM. The experimental study involved *http log* from NASA server. The results showed the proposed approach to be efficient and scalable.

Xu *et al.* [109] proposed a user behavior prediction model for smart home employing BPNN. The experimental study used the smart home dataset generated from intelligent residential districts of a certain distinct in Shanghai, China. The proposed algorithm had a significant improvement in the convergence speed, accuracy, efficiency, and scalability.

7.4.2.4 Spark-based conference papers

Vluymans *et al.* [110] proposed a method for weighted *k*-nearest neighbor (*k*-NN) regression along with a distributed prototype selection method based on fuzzy rough set theory. The experimental work carried out with two health-care datasets: the Washington State Inpatient Database [111] and the Medical Expenditure Panel Survey [112]. The experimental results demonstrated that the proposed prototype selection method improved the performance of *k*-NN.

Oneto *et al.* [113] proposed a method for predicting train delays based on the extreme learning machine (ELM). The study was carried out with the real historical data provided by Rete Ferroviaria Italiana, the Italian infrastructure manager that controls all the traffic of the Italian railway network. The results showed that proposed approach had improved delay prediction.

After reviewing the articles related to the regression in a distributed parallel computational environment, the following research gaps are discovered:

- *It is not explored to its full extent.*
- *There has been very less research work carried out in the field of regression task using the distributed parallel framework which is the goldmine for budding researchers.*
- *During the review process, we found that few articles had utilized artificial neural network (ANN) in the form of BPNN. The other forms of neural network (NN) like general regression neural network (GRNN), radial basis function network (RBFN), wavelet neural network (WNN), and quantile regression neural network (QRNN) are not considered at all.*
- *Evolutionary computation and Fuzzy methods for regression present a great opportunity for researchers to explore it in the distributed parallel framework.*

- *Nonlinear regression has not been explored in the distributed parallel environment leading it to be a fertile area for research.*
- *Support vector regression has not been explored to its extent. It has not been explored in Spark environment at all.*
- *Quantile regression, Ridge regression, Lasso regression, Cox regression, and Poisson regression are not explored at all.*
- *Kernel methods are not explored at all.*
- *Multivariate adaptive regression splines, TreeNet, extreme gradient boosting are not explored at all.*

7.4.3 Classification

7.4.3.1 Hadoop MapReduce-based journal papers

He *et al.* [114] implemented an approach comprising a parallelized version of extreme SVM (ESVM), (PESVM) and an incremental learning algorithm for ESVM (IESVM), which can incorporate online learning to update the existing model. The proposed approach implemented parallelization of IESVM, called PIESVM. The experimental works utilized the *Australian* dataset from the public UCI repository [22]. The large-scale datasets were synthesized by duplicating the data. The experimental results showed that the proposed algorithms PESVM and PIESVM were efficient and scalable.

Janaki Meena *et al.* [115] proposed a parallel version of an ant colony optimization (ACO) algorithm to select features for text categorization. The experimental study involved two datasets formed with documents from the *20NewsGroup* benchmark that consists of documents from Usenet news articles classified into 20 topics. The experimental results exhibited the improved performance of the classifier with the features selected by the proposed method.

Caruana *et al.* [116] presented a parallel SVM algorithm for scalable spam filter training. The experimental work was carried out with the *SpamBase* dataset from UCI repository [22]. The experimental results exhibited an improved accuracy of the proposed approach.

You *et al.* [117] proposed a parallel SVM model for predicting protein–protein interactions (PPI). The experimental work utilized the PPI dataset downloaded from the *Human Protein References Database* [118]. Experimental results exhibited that the proposed method had an excellent speedup performance, scalability with dataset size with comparable performance to its serial counterpart.

Singh *et al.* [119] proposed a framework for peer-to-peer botnet detection using RF-based DT model. The experiment was carried out with the CAIDA UCSD dataset [120]. The experimental results showed that the proposed method produced better accuracy than many other classifiers.

Chen *et al.* [121] proposed an efficient classification method using parallel and scalable compressed model for network intrusion detection (ID). The experimental study involved two publicly available datasets of ID, KDD99, and CMDC2012. The experimental results demonstrated that the proposed approach had a faster execution speed.

Kumar and Kumar Rath [122] implemented proximal SVM (mrPSVM) classifier to classify the microarray data with selected relevant features. The dataset for classification was collected from Kent Ridge Bio-medical Data Set Repository [123] and NCBI GEO [124]. The datasets were *LEukemia, MULTMYEL, ovarian cancer*, and *breast cancer*. The results showed that the mrPSVM was efficient with less execution time in comparison with its sequential counterpart.

Han *et al.* [125] proposed a distributed ELM (DELM), an optimization of ELM for large matrix operations over large datasets along with weighted ensemble classifier based on DELM (WE-DELM), for efficiently classifying uncertain streaming data. The experimental study involved real-world dataset *KDDcup99* [126], and the popular static datasets *Iris* and *SpamBase* [22]. The experimental results showed that the proposed algorithms had better efficiency, accuracy, and speedup.

Barkhordari and Niamanesh [127] proposed a scalable and distributable method to solve patient similarity (ScaDiPaSi) problems. The study utilized real *patient electronic health records* from laboratories and hospitals. The experimental results showed better execution time and accuracy.

López *et al.* [128] proposed a cost-sensitive linguistic fuzzy rule-based classification system (FRBCS) for imbalanced large-scale data. The performance of the proposed approach was evaluated with three datasets from the UCI dataset repository [22], the *KDD Cup 1999* dataset, the *Record Linkage Comparison Patterns* (RLCPs) dataset, and the Poker Hand dataset. The experimental results showed that the proposed approach had a competitive accuracy and execution time.

Xin *et al.* [129] proposed an Adaptive Distributed Extreme Learning Machine (A-ELM*). It overcomes the weakness of ELM* in learning large dataset. The experiment was carried out with the synthetic dataset. A-ELM* was compared with ELM* while increasing dimensionality, the number of records in the dataset, and found to outperform the latter.

Xia *et al.* [130] presented a MapReduce-based nearest neighborhood approach for traffic flow prediction using correlation analysis. The authors have utilized real-world *trajectory* dataset [131] that comprises large-scale GPS trajectories generated by 12,000 taxis and developed a parallel *k*-NN optimization classifier to predict the traffic flow in real-time basis.

Bechini *et al.* [132] proposed a distributed association rule-based classification. The experimental study employed seven big datasets extracted from the UCI repository [22] and LIBSVM repository [53]. The results presented the superiority of the proposed method over DT and were comparable with RF in terms of accuracy.

Kumar *et al.* [133] proposed various statistical methods such as ANOVA, Kruskal–Wallis, and Friedman tests for feature selection and then employed *k*-NN (mrKNN) classifier to classify microarray leukemia data. The three datasets for classification are obtained from the NCBI GEO repository [124], datasets with accession number *GSE13159, GSE13204*, and *GSE15061*. The experimental results exhibited the superiority in performance.

Chen *et al.* [134] proposed an ELM in a distributed framework of MapReduce (MR-ELM) to enable large-scale ELM training. The experimental study involved 9 classification benchmarks and 12 regression benchmarks, both of which come from 2 ML repositories, UCI [22] and FCUP [135]. The experimental results showed the scalability of the proposed algorithm when compared with original ELM and with other parallel versions of ELM.

Huang *et al.* [136] suggested a parallel ensemble of online sequential ELM (PEOS-ELM) algorithm based on MapReduce. The experimental work involved evaluation of PEOS-ELM algorithm with the real and synthetic datasets. The real-world datasets used were *MNIST* [53], *DNA* [53], and *KDDCup99* [126]. The synthetic datasets were generated by extending on the basis of *Flower* by duplicating the original data in a round-robin way. The result demonstrated that PEOS-ELM could learn large-scale data accurately and efficiently in comparison with EOS-ELM and POS-ELM algorithm. The proposed algorithm had excellent scalability and speedup ratio.

Zhai *et al.* [137] employed a voting-based instance selection from large datasets with MapReduce and random weight networks. The proposed algorithm is called MapReduce, and Voting-based instance selection (MRVIS). The experimental study was conducted with eight datasets, including two synthetic datasets and six UCI datasets: *Banana, Cloud, Gaussian, Shuttle, Artificial, Cod_rna, Poker*, and *SUSY*. The proposed algorithm, MRVIS, was compared with three state-of-the-art approaches: CNN, ENN, and RNN. The experimental results showed that the proposed algorithm was effective and efficient.

Huang *et al.* [138] proposed a parallel method for batched online sequential ELM (BPOS-ELM) training using MapReduce. The proposed method BPOS-ELM was evaluated with real data and synthetic data. There were three real-world datasets: *MNIST, DNA* [53], and *KDDCup99* [126] that were used to evaluate training and testing accuracy. Two synthetic datasets were used for training speed evaluation and scalability evaluation: datasets generated based on *Flower* [139] and *CIFAR-10*, respectively. The experimental results exhibited a comparable accuracy with higher execution speed.

Li *et al.* [140] proposed a parallel feature selection method for text classification implemented on iterative MapReduce with Twister. The experimental work involved web page documents in Chinese from Internet and abstracts of papers from CNKI, an electronic journal database of China. The experimental results presented the proposed approach to be efficient and scalable.

Zhai *et al.* [141] implemented the classification of large imbalanced datasets on the basis of MapReduce and ensemble of ELM classifiers. The experimental work involved one synthetic dataset and six datasets collected from UCI ML repository: *Yeast, Abalone, Shuttle, Skin_segment, MiniBooNE*, and *Cod_rna*. The experimental results showed that the performance of the proposed algorithm statistically outperformed the three state-of-the-art approaches: SMOTE-Vote, SMOTEBoost, and SMOTE-Bagging. The proposed algorithm also had a good speedup and scale-up performance.

Jedrzejowicz *et al.* [142] proposed a parallel distributed framework for imbalanced data classification employing MapReduce computation environment. The proposed framework involves implementation of the splitting-based data balancing method (SplitBal) [143] and the dissimilarity-based imbalance data classification [144]. The performance of the proposed framework was tested over the benchmark datasets obtained from KEEL [102] and UCI ML repository [22]. The experimental results showed that the proposed framework is scalable.

Elkano *et al.* [145] proposed an FRBCS for big data classification system with MapReduce framework. The experiment was conducted with 20 binary datasets obtained from 8 different multi-class datasets available at the UCI repository [22]. The experimental results show that the proposed distributed algorithm outperformed its local counterpart in terms of execution time and classification performance.

Thakur and Deshpande [146] proposed a parallel approach for sentiment classification using MapReduce framework. They implemented kernel optimized-SVM classifier to analyze *train review* [147] and *movie review* [148] datasets. The performance of the classifier was compared with SentiWordNet, Naïve Bayes, Linear SVM, and NN. The performance metrics involved accuracy, sensitivity, and specificity. The experimental results proved that the proposed method outperformed the classifiers compared with.

7.4.3.2   Spark-based journal papers

Maillo *et al.* [149] implemented *k*-NN classification based on Apache Spark. The study included three datasets: *PokerHand*, *SUSY*, and *Higgs* collected from the UCI ML repository and one dataset from the *ECBDL'14* competition. The proposed approach *k*-NN-IS achieved the same accuracy as *k*-NN and the execution time was reduced by almost ten times with respect to MR-*k*-NN based on Hadoop.

Arias *et al.* [150] implemented Bayesian network (BN) classifiers for studying their adaptability to MapReduce and Apache Spark frameworks. The experimental work was carried out with *splice* [22], *Epsilon* [53], and *ECBDL'14* datasets along with some synthetic datasets for the test of scalability of the proposed approach. The experimental results showed that the proposed approach was scalable and efficient.

Liu *et al.* [151] proposed a parallel backpropagation neural network (PBPNN) implemented in three distributed computing environments, i.e., Hadoop, HaLoop, and Spark. The experimental work involved *Iris* dataset. The experimental results demonstrated that the proposed PBPNN algorithm outperformed stand-alone BPNN in terms of accuracy and stability.

Chen *et al.* [152] proposed a parallel random forest (PRF) algorithm. The experimental study was carried out by two groups of datasets with large scale and high dimensionality: (i) URL Reputation, YouTube Video Games, Bag of Words and Gas sensor arrays datasets from the UCI ML repository and (ii) Patient, Outpatient, Medicine and Cancer datasets from an actual medical project. The classification accuracy of PRF was evaluated by comparison with RF, dynamic random forest, and Apache Spark MLlib parallelized RF. Experimental results indicated the superiority of PRF over the other algorithms in terms of classification accuracy, performance, and scalability.

Shi *et al.* [153] presented an integrated data preprocessing framework implemented with Spark computational environment for fault diagnosis of power grid equipment. The classification was achieved with logistic regression and SVM. The experiment was carried out with *data collected from State Grid of China*. The proposed method yielded higher classification accuracy than the traditional ones with scalability.

Lin *et al.* [154] proposed an ensemble RF algorithm implemented with Spark. The experiments were conducted with the *insurance business data from China Life Insurance Company*. The experimental results proved that the proposed methodology outperformed SVM and logistic regression in both performance and accuracy.

Nair *et al.* [155] presented a real-time remote health status prediction system. The ML model was deployed on streaming big data through user tweets with Apache Spark environment. The experiments were carried out with *Heart disease dataset* from UCI ML repository [22]. The DT was employed for the prediction of health status as whether heart disease is present or absent.

Gonzalez-Lopez *et al.* [156] proposed a distributed multi-label *k*-NN (ML-*k*-NN) implemented with Apache Spark. The proposed work involved comparison of three strategies, i.e., (i) iteratively broadcasting instances, (ii) using a distributed tree-based index structure, and (iii) building hash tables to group instances. The experimental study involved 22 benchmark datasets, and the experimental results indicate that the tree-based index strategy outperforms the other approaches.

7.4.3.3 Hadoop MapReduce-based conference papers

Magnusson and Kvernvik [157] proposed a subscriber classification within telecom networks. The experimental study involved real traffic data from a telecom operator and synthetic dataset from a randomly generated graph, and another one generated on the basis of the Erdõs–Rényi algorithm [158]. The results showed the performance of the proposed method.

Khuc *et al.* [159] proposed a large-scale distributed system for real-time Twitter sentiment analysis. The experimental study involved *Twitter* dataset. The experimental result showed that the proposed lexicon-and-learning-based classifier obtained higher accuracy than the lexicon-based classifier which only relied on searching for sentiment words/phrases. The proposed approach was scalable with the number of machines and size of data.

Wang *et al.* [160] proposed a hybrid method combining DT and SVM for stock futures prediction. The work carried out with real-world data of one of the stock companies in China. The experimental results exhibited the superior performance of the hybrid architecture in comparison with Bootstrap-SVM, Bootstrap-DT, and BPNN.

Han *et al.* [161] proposed SMRF algorithm, an improved scalable RF algorithm. This study used ten UCI publicly available datasets: *Chess, Corral, DNA, Ionosphere, Iris, Letter, Satimage, Segment, Shuttle,* and *Splice* to compare SMRF algorithm accuracy level with traditional RF algorithm. The experimental results demonstrated that the proposed algorithm had excellent scalability and comparable accuracy with traditional RF algorithm.

Chen *et al.* [162] proposed an ELM ensemble classifier based on MapReduce framework called ELM-MapReduce for large-scale land cover classification. The experimental study used remote sensing image of Takhu Lake Region in East China, captured by LANDSAT-5 satellite. The experimental results showed that ELM-MapReduce presented higher accuracy than single ELM when trained with large datasets. The proposed approach showed high efficiency and scalability.

Liu *et al.* [163] proposed an approach to ML for large-scale dataset with meta-learning. The experiments utilized 11 real-world and 2 synthetic datasets. The real datasets were *Yeast, wineRed, wineWhite, pendigits, SpamBase, musk, telescope, kdd, isolet, org,* and *census* [22]. The two synthetic datasets, *S1* and *S2*, were generated by applying the RDG1 data generator in WEKA DM tool [164]. The experimental results showed that the proposed PML could reduce computational complexity with less error rate.

Lubell-Doughtie and Sondag [165] proposed an approach for distributed classification using the alternating direction method of multipliers algorithm. The experimental work was carried out with historical data consisting of approximately 25 million records of website visit attributes with 440 features per record. The performance of the proposed approach was measured with a change in loss function per iteration. It was found that the loss decreased or in other words, the accuracy consistently improved as more iterations passed.

Al-Madi and Ludwig [166] proposed scalable genetic programming for data classification called MRGP, implemented with MapReduce framework. The experimental study involved six datasets: *Ionosphere, Vertebral Column* (Vertebral-2C and Vertebral-3C), *Blood Transfusion Service Center, Balance Scale, Cardiotocography.* The research results showed that the proposed approach had higher accuracy with speedup and scalability properties.

Kiran *et al.* [167] proposed a method for parallel SVM algorithm. The experimental work involved comparison of sequential SVM and parallel SVM on MapReduce framework. The observed results showed that the proposed approach had the superior efficiency in terms of execution time with the increase in the number of nodes.

Kolias *et al.* [168] implemented a classification rule induction algorithm. The algorithm produces an ordered list of classification rules from massive categorical data. The datasets from UCI ML repository [22] are used for comparing the accuracy of the algorithm and quality of proposed approach and four synthesized datasets are used for verification of the algorithm for scaled-up datasets. The algorithm does not work on the numerical dataset.

Wang *et al.* [169] have presented an instance-weighted variant SVM with a parallel meta-learning algorithm using 11 datasets from UCI data repository [22] and a real-world dataset *Maritime.* The experimental results proved that the proposed method could improve the prediction performance of the classification.

Park and Ha [170] proposed an approach for data classification over imbalanced data for traffic accident prediction. The experimental study utilized traffic data collected from the Korea Highway Corporation. The results showed that the proposed approach was efficient with good accuracy.

López *et al.* [171] proposed a method for linguistic FRBCSs for large-scale data achieved with MapReduce framework, called Chi-FRBCS-BigData. The algorithm had been developed in two versions: Chi-FRBCSBigData-Max and Chi-FRBCS-BigData-Ave. The study involved six datasets from the UCI ML repository. The two versions of the proposed algorithm produced different classification results. The experimental results presented that Chi-FRBCS-BigData-Ave generated more accuracy with higher execution time, whereas Chi-FRBCSBigData-Max produced faster but less accurate result.

Kolias *et al.* [172] proposed a method RuleMR for generating classification rules out of large-scale data. The experimental work involved datasets from UCI repository [22] for measuring the accuracy, viz., *breast, car eval, Connect-4, weather, Mushroom, nursery, vote,* and *tic.* Four synthetic datasets were used for measuring execution time. The experimental results showed that the proposed method had scalability with respect to the size of the dataset and a comparable accuracy with state-of-the-art algorithms.

Kakade *et al.* [173] proposed a spam filtering technique implemented with SVM along with sequential minimal optimization (SMO). The experimental study was carried out with SpamBase dataset available on UCI repository [22]. The experimental results showed that the proposed algorithm with SMO was efficient and had a superior speedup to linear as well as the Gaussian kernel.

Anchalia and Roy [174] proposed the *k*-NN algorithm. The experimental work involved comparison of MapReduce *k*-NN with sequential *k*-NN. The work included synthetic dataset for the study. The experimental results showed that the proposed method MapReduce *k*-NN outperformed the sequential *k*-NN with datasets of large-scale data.

Ke *et al.* [175] proposed a method for distributed SVM for binary and multi-class classifications. The proposed method involves parallel decomposition solver on two datasets *MNIST* and *Cover-Type.* The experimental results projected substantial growth in speedup.

Maillo *et al.* [176] employed *k*-NN classification. The experimental study was carried out over the *PokerHand* dataset, collected from the UCI repository [20]. The experimental results exhibited the reduction of computational time achieved by the proposed algorithm in comparison to its sequential version.

Chatzigeorgakidis *et al.* [177] proposed a new *k*-NN-based algorithm. The proposed Flink zkNN (F-zkNN) algorithm was extended over a Hadoop-based implementation of the *k*-NN (H-zkNN). The experimental work involved data from water usage time-series data, collected on a city scale by smart water meters in Switzerland and Spain. The algorithm was evaluated with respect to forecasting and prediction precision.

Wang *et al.* [178] proposed an ordinal RF algorithm based on the variable consistency dominance-based rough set approach (VC_DRSA). The experimental work utilized two synthetic datasets. The experimental results confirmed that the proposed algorithm was effective and efficient.

Cui and Zhao [179] proposed a method for gender classification. Three classification algorithms were involved: (i) SVM, (ii) k-NN, and (iii) Adaboost to implement gender parallelize machine learning (GPML). The experimental work was carried out with images from the *CAS-PEAL* dataset. The proposed algorithm was compared with parallelized Adaboost. The experimental results showed that GPML had higher recognition rates.

Yuan *et al.* [180] proposed a GA optimized DT algorithm (MR-GAOT) implemented in MapReduce environment. The parallelized MR-GAOT was compared with traditional DT algorithm, and the results showed higher classification accuracy and shorter execution time.

Wakayama *et al.* [181] proposed a distributed RF. The experiments were carried out with *Letter Recognition* dataset from UCI ML repository. The results indicated that the proposed approach had a good classification performance along with lower computational costs compared to the naïve implementation of RFs.

Triguero *et al.* [182] proposed an evolutionary under-sampling method for imbalanced big data classification. The experimental study involved *KDD Cup 1999* dataset from UCI ML repository. The experimental results showed the scalability of the proposed method.

Zdravevski *et al.* [183] proposed an approach for feature ranking based on information gain for large data classification problems. The ranking of features led to feature selection for which the *FedCSIS AAIA'14* DM competition dataset [184] was used for the study. The proposed approach had excellent scalability.

Kumar *et al.* [185] proposed a method for feature selection and classification of microarray data. The experimental study utilized large datasets from NCBI GEO [124], viz., *Leukemia, Ovarian Cancer, Breast Cancer, MULTMYEL,* and *LEukemia*. The experimental results showed that the proposed approach was efficient and scalable.

Bhukya and Gyani [186] proposed a fuzzy associative classification algorithm. The experimental study involved RLCP dataset from UCI ML repository [22]. The study showed that the proposed approach had a superior accuracy and efficiency with a comparison to its sequential counterpart.

Arias *et al.* [187] proposed a k-dependence Bayesian classifier. The proposed approach was evaluated with three datasets: *Splice, ECBLD14,* and *Epsilon*. The experimental work showed the proposed method to be efficient.

Sukanya *et al.* [188] implemented SVMs in linear and parallel distributed frameworks. The experimental study utilized three datasets: *Spam, Wine,* and *Heart*. The experimental results showed MapReduce-based SVM performed superiorly regarding execution time and accuracy with scalability on dataset size.

Yang *et al.* [189] proposed a method for parallelized Rocchio relevance feedback algorithm implemented with the MapReduce framework called MR-Rocchio algorithm. The experimental study involved the earthquake information source text for Beijing. The experimental results showed that the performance of the MR-Rocchio algorithm was significantly improved in comparison with the traditional Rocchio algorithm, better than the *k*-NN algorithm and only slightly inferior to the SVM algorithm.

7.4.3.4   Spark-based conference papers

Peng *et al.* [190] implemented and evaluated parallel LogR models in big data paradigm. The experimental study involved a synthetic dataset, *2D*, and four real-world datasets: *20NewsGroup*, *Gisette*, *ECUESpam*, and *URL-Reputation*. The experimental work involved analysis of three optimization approaches implemented with two computing platforms, Hadoop and Spark framework, to train the LogR model on large-scale, high-dimensional datasets for classification. The results showed that Spark outperformed Hadoop for LogR model implementation.

Tao *et al.* [191] proposed a budgeted mini-batch parallel gradient descent algorithm (BMBPGD) for large-scale kernel SVM training. The experimental work involved three datasets, *a9a*, *w8a*, and *covtype* from UCI/Adult, JP98a, and UCI/Covertype, respectively. The work included a comparison of the proposed method with SVMWithSGD and LibSVM. The accuracy of BMBPGD was higher than SVMWithSGD when selected with the appropriate parameters and number of iterations.

Lin *et al.* [192] implemented LogR and linear SVMs in large-scale data. The study involved datasets from *LIBSVM* dataset page along with *Yahoo-Japan* and *Yahoo-Korea* datasets. The implemented method was efficient and scalable.

Wang *et al.* [193] proposed Weighted Label Propagation Algorithm with Probability Threshold (P-WLPA) algorithm. The experimental study utilized *iris* dataset from UCI repository [22] and a synthetic dataset generated by Gaussian function in MATLAB®. The work involved comparison of serial and parallel P-WLPA. The results showed the feasibility and efficiency of the proposed parallel P-WLPA algorithm.

Roy [194] proposed a method for online feature selection and learning from high-dimensional streaming data using an ensemble of Kohonen neurons. The experimental work was carried out with five datasets: (i) *Leukemia*, (ii) *Central Nervous System*, (iii) *Colon Tumor*, (iv) *Lymphoma*, and (v) *small round blue-cell tumors*. The work involved comparison of the proposed algorithm with the state-of-the-art algorithm for average test error, standard deviation, and an average number of selected features. The Kohonen ensemble had superior performance in almost all cases.

Ramírez-Gallego *et al.* [195] proposed a distributed implementation of the entropy minimization discretizer. The datasets employed in the experiment are (i) *ECBDL'14* which was used at the ML competition of the Evolutionary Computation for Big Data and Big Learning held in 2014, and (ii) *Epsilon*, which was artificially created for the Pascal Large Scale Learning Challenge in 2008. The experimental results demonstrated the improvement in both classification accuracy and execution time for the proposed algorithm.

Bhagat and Patil [196] proposed an enhanced SMOTE algorithm for the classification of imbalanced data using RF. The experimental study involved datasets from UCI ML repository [22]. The datasets were *Landsat*, *Lymphography*, *Zoo*, *Segment*,

Iris, *Car*, *Vehicle*, and *Waveform*. The proposed approach was implemented on Hadoop MapReduce framework and Apache Spark platform. The results showed that the proposed method carried out with Spark outperformed other methods.

Chandorkar *et al.* [197] proposed fixed-size least squares SVM (FS-LSSVM) for large-scale data classification. The model was evaluated with datasets available in UCI repository [22], viz., *Magic Gamma Telescope, Adult, Forest Cover Type*, and *Higgs SUSY* datasets. The experimental results showed that the proposed approach FS-LSSVM had a substantial speedup over the existing FS-LSSVM implementations.

Venturini *et al.* [198] proposed a distributed bagged associative classifier, based on ensemble techniques with voting to provide a unique classification outcome. The experiment was carried out with three datasets, Yeast, nursery, and census, from the UCI repository [22] and a synthetic dataset, generated from IBM data generator [48]. The experimental results showed that bagging achieved an accuracy above or at par with the sampling-only approach.

Semberecki and Maciejewski [199] implemented classification of text documents. The classifier was verified with documents belonging to three categories: Art, History, and Law. ML algorithms such as naïve Bayes classifier, DT, and RFs were utilized for building the classification model. The experimental results showed that the naïve Bayes algorithm had the best accuracy.

Nodarakis *et al.* [200] proposed a method for sentiment analysis on Twitter. The proposed method was evaluated using two Twitter datasets (one for hashtags and one for emoticons) collected through the Twitter Search API. The experimental results showed that the proposed approach was efficient, robust, and scalable.

Ray *et al.* [201] proposed a scalable information gain variant for rapid quantification of the microarray. The proposed method employed a mutual information feature selection method based on spark framework (sf-MIFS) to determine the relevant features. After feature selection process, the logistic regression (sf-LoR) and naïve Bayes (sf-NB) using Spark were implemented to classify the microarray datasets. The dataset utilized for the study was *LEukemia* dataset collected from NCBI GEO [123]. The experimental results showed that sf-MIFS provided better accuracy with sf-NB as compared to sf-LoR.

Tayde and Nagamma Patil [202] proposed an approach for genome data classification. The genome-sequence-encoding schema involved the n-gram method. The features were extracted using n-gram with the help of pattern-matching techniques, viz., k-distance approximate and multiple reference character algorithm pattern matching. The SVM classifier was used to classify the genome data. The experimental work carried out with the genome data of the cat and rat species downloaded from UCSC. The Spark-based approach was found to be efficient in terms of execution time.

Kamaruddin and Ravi [203] proposed a hybrid architecture involving auto-associative neural network (AANN) and particle swarm optimization (PSO) called PSOAANN for credit card fraud detection using one-class classification. The experimental study utilized ccFraud dataset [204]. The experimental results showed that the proposed approach had superior accuracy.

Talavera-Llames *et al.* [205] proposed nearest-neighbor-based algorithm for long time series data forecasting. The experimental work involved datasets related to electrical energy consumption from a Spanish public university. The experimental work showed satisfactory results regarding both mean relative error (MRE) and execution time.

Blessy Trencia Lincy and Nagarajan [206] implemented parallel distributed SVM along with data augmentation for semi-supervised classification. The experimental work analyzed the ECBDL'14, Epsilon, and the SUSY datasets. The proposed methodology was compared with Spark-LR_SGD, Spark-RF, Spark-LSVM, and Spark-DT algorithms. The experimental results showed that the proposed methodology has better performance with respect to execution time and accuracy.

We identified the following research insights during the review of articles related to classification:

- *It has been observed that SVM, ELM, k-NN, DT, and RF are the most implemented in a parallel and distributed manner. Maintaining the same distribution of the samples in all data partitions, we can implement SVM, k-NN, and similar algorithms to run in a parallel manner. The algorithms like DT, RF are inherently parallel as they partition the sample space independently and so can be implemented in a parallel manner.*

- *Logistic regression and fuzzy rule-based classifier are the least explored in distributed parallel architecture leading to an open research space for the researchers.*

- *Only a few papers were found using evolutionary computational method for classification in Hadoop and Spark environment leading to a fertile ground to explore.*

- *The most explored ML technique is SVM with its variants for classification in the distributed parallel environment.*

- *Any architecture of NN is conspicuous by its absence.*

- *The algorithms like very fast DT, classification and regression trees, and chi-square automatic interaction detection are not explored at all.*

- *Extreme gradient boosting is not explored at all.*

- *Kernel methods and class association rule mining (CARM) are not explored at all.*

7.4.4 Clustering

7.4.4.1 Hadoop MapReduce-based journal papers

Sun *et al.* [207] proposed a clustering method using parallel information bottleneck theory clustering method along with centroid-based clustering method to determine the clusters. The experimental study was carried out with *16S rRNA* dataset [208]. Interpolation multidimensional scaling was used for feature dimension reduction for visualization of clustering results in 2D and 3D. The experimental results showed the proposed method to be scalable.

Xu *et al.* [209] proposed a clustering approach *k*-means++. This proposed approach had a significant reduction in communication and I/O costs. The study involved one real dataset *Oxford Buildings* Dataset and a synthetic dataset. The experimental results indicated that the proposed MapReduce *k*-means++ method was much more efficient and scalable.

Cui *et al.* [210] proposed *K*-means algorithm in MapReduce environment to eliminate the iteration dependence and obtain high performance. The experimental study involved a synthetic dataset, *Gauss Distribution Set* and two real datasets, *Bag of Words* and *House* collected from UCI ML repository. The experimental results showed that the proposed algorithm was efficient and superior to parallel *K*-means, *K*-means‖, and stand-alone *K*-means++ algorithms.

Ludwig [211] proposed a parallel approach for fuzzy *c*-means clustering algorithm implemented with MapReduce framework (MR-FCM). The experimental study involved *Covertype* dataset [22]. The proposed algorithm was compared with clustering toolkit (CLUTO), approximate kernel possibilistic *c*-means (akPCM), and approximate kernel fuzzy *c*-means (akFCM). The experimental evaluation demonstrated that comparable purity results could be achieved with excellent scalability.

Yang *et al.* [212] proposed a semi-supervised multi-ant colonies consensus clustering algorithm. The experimental study involved datasets *Iris*, *Wine*, *Balance-scale*, *Sonar*, *Covertype*, *Shuttle*, *MiniBooNE* from the UCI ML repository [22] along with *USCensus1990*, and the image database [213]. Experimental results demonstrated the effectiveness of the proposed method.

Bi *et al.* [214] proposed semantic-driven subtractive clustering method based on SCM and fuzzy *c*-means (FCM), to alleviate the risk of customer churn. Business support system and operations support system data of *China Telecom* were used for customer churn management.

Liu *et al.* [215] proposed a method for similarity join using similarity join tree and extended Fiduccia–Mattheyses algorithms. The work involved two real datasets: dataset containing time-series recordings from UCI ML repository [22] and articles extracted from Wikipedia in the English domain [216]. Experimental results depicted that the proposed approach was more efficient and scalable compared to state-of-the-art algorithms.

Zhang *et al.* [217] proposed a distributed density peaks clustering algorithm with locality-sensitive hashing (LSH-DDP). The experimental study involved nine datasets of different dimensions [22,218]. Experimental results on local cluster and cloud showed that LSH-DDP achieved a factor of 1.7–70× speedup over the naïve Basic-DDP and 2× speedup over the state-of-the-art efficient distributed density peaks clustering algorithm.

Alewiwi *et al.* [219] proposed a document similarity approach with a filtering method of cosine similarity measure. The experimental study utilized the *Enron* [218] and *Reuters* datasets [220]. The observed results demonstrated that the proposed method had superior efficiency.

Fang *et al.* [221] proposed scalable algorithms for nearest neighbor joins on big trajectory data. The experimental study used two spatial–temporal data simulators: *GSTD* and *Brinkhoff* to generate synthetic datasets. Two synthetic datasets DS1 and DS2 were generated from *GSTD* [222], and another dataset DS3 was constructed from *Brinkhoff* [223]. One real dataset *Beijing taxi* [224] was also included in the study. The experimental results showed that the proposed algorithm was efficient and scalable.

Wu *et al.* [225] proposed a SIMPLifying and Ensembling (SIMPLE) framework for parallel community detection. The work involved six network datasets out of which five were of friendship networks derived from different social networking sites, viz., *Oklahoma, UNC, Twitter, Gowalla,* and *LiveJournal*; and *Skitter* is an Internet topology graph. The experimental results showed that SIMPLE could identify high-quality community structures on various networks demonstrated by the Q-function.

Shahrivari and Jalili [226] proposed a single-pass and linear time solution for *K*-means algorithm called *MRK-means*. The experimental study utilized a set of synthesized datasets and four real-world datasets: USCensus, KDD04, Poker, Skin, and Birch collected from UCI ML repository [22]. The experimental results showed that the proposed approach, *MRK-means*, had faster execution times, and higher quality of clustering compared to state-of-the-art algorithms with linear scalability.

Banharnsakun [227] proposed a MapReduce-based artificial bee colony (ABC) called MR-ABC for data clustering. The author has used four synthesized datasets from UCI ML repository [22]; they are *Iris, CMC, Wine,* and *Vowel* by duplicating the records. The experimental results presented that the proposed algorithm had a superior value in comparison with parallel *K*-means (P*K*-means) and *K*-PSO algorithms with respect to *F*-measure.

Capó *et al.* [228] proposed an efficient approximation to the *K*-means algorithm for large data. The experimental results exhibited that the proposed method outperformed other methods like the *K*-means++ and the minibatch *K*-means, regarding the relation between the number of distance computations and the quality of the approximation.

7.4.4.2 Spark-based journal papers

Lu *et al.* [229] proposed an improved *K*-means clustering algorithm with a tabu search strategy, to enable it to handle big data applications. The experimental work involved Iris, Wine, Yeast, and Seeds datasets collected from UCI ML repository [22]. The experimental results disclose that the proposed method had superior solution to the *K*-means algorithm of Spark MLlib.

7.4.4.3 Hadoop MapReduce-based conference papers

Zhao *et al.* [230] proposed a parallel *K*-means clustering. The experimental study utilized synthetic dataset. The experimental results demonstrated the scalability and efficiency of the proposed algorithm.

Ene *et al.* [231] proposed clustering algorithms, viz., *K*-center and *K*-median implemented with MapReduce framework. The study involved a random set of points in R^3 as the dataset. The experimental results showed that the proposed algorithms had comparable accuracy with better execution time in comparison with other tested algorithms.

Zongzhen *et al.* [232] presented a fuzzy clustering approach for document categorization. In experiment, five different classes, *Diabetes*, *Happiness*, *Yoga*, *Ebook*, and *Security*, were selected and 100 articles of each class chosen for training and testing the model. The experimental results were containing the *F*1 measure that exhibited the performance of clustering.

Liao *et al.* [233] proposed an improved parallel *K*-means clustering algorithm. The proposed algorithm presented a superior performance in both processing speed and accuracy than traditional parallel *K*-means algorithm.

Esteves *et al.* [234] proposed a competitive *K*-means algorithm. The experiments were carried out with four datasets: (i) *Hypercube*, a synthetic dataset created by using the hypercube function in the R package *mlbench*; (ii) *Google*, a dataset of failures collected from a Google computer cluster; (iii) *Electrical*; and (iv) *KDD99*, gathered from the UCI ML repository [22]. The experiments involved comparison of the proposed algorithm with serial *K*-means++ and streaming *K*-means. The results showed that the proposed algorithm had increased accuracy and decreased variance with scalability related to the dimension of the dataset.

Kumar *et al.* [235] proposed an approach for the parallel *K*-means algorithm. The experimental result showed that the proposed method had a superior efficiency with scalability.

Lin *et al.* [236] proposed a *K*-means clustering algorithm with optimized initial centers based on data dimensional density. The experimental results demonstrated the stability of the algorithm with a cost of execution time.

Zhang and Wang [237] proposed an enhanced agglomerative fuzzy *K*-means clustering algorithm. Experimental works were carried out on a synthetic dataset, the *WINE* dataset from UCI repository and a randomly generated large dataset. The observed results presented that the proposed algorithm had superior accuracy and scalability.

Bousbaci and Kamel [238] proposed a hybrid architecture with *K*-means and PSO. The experimental work was carried out with two synthetic numerical multi-dimensional datasets [239]. The experimental results presented that the proposed approach had improved execution time and cluster quality.

Garg and Trivedi [240] proposed fuzzy *K*-means clustering. The study involved datasets from UCI ML repository, viz., *Iris*, *Synthetic control*, and *KDD cup 1999* datasets. The experimental results depicted the excellent execution time.

Anchalia [241] proposed an improved method to implement the *K*-means clustering technique. The experiment involved generated synthetic data. The experimental results showed that the proposed method outperformed the regular implementation.

Zhu *et al.* [242] proposed an improved algorithm for the optimal search of medoids to cluster big data using *K*-medoids clustering. The results showed that the proposed algorithm had high efficiency and effectiveness in comparison to its serial counterpart.

Choi and So [243] proposed a method for the *K*-means algorithm with FPGA-accelerated computer cluster. The experimental study used *individual household electric power consumption* dataset collected from UCI ML repository [20]. The experimental results showed that the proposed FPGA *K*-means implementation had superior performance compared to the baseline software implementation.

Garcia and Naldi [244] proposed a method for parallel *K*-means clustering. The experimental work involved five datasets randomly generated with over-lapping mixtures of Gaussian distributions by the MixSim R Package [245]. The results presented that the proposed method outperformed other implementations of *K*-means in terms of execution time.

Daoudi *et al.* [246] proposed a method for parallel differential evolution (DE) clustering algorithm. The experimental study involved 18 publicly available gene expression datasets. The experimental results showed that the proposed approach was efficient and produces comparable results with existing algorithms.

Al-Madi *et al.* [247] proposed an algorithm for clustering large-scale data using parallel glowworm swarm optimization (GSO) implemented with MapReduce, called MRCGSO. The experimental study utilized four real-world datasets: *magic, poker hand, cover type* collected from UCI repository [22], and *Electricity* collected from MOA [248]. Apart from real-world datasets, four synthetic datasets were generated using the data generator [249]. The experimental results demonstrated that the proposed algorithm had good accuracy with scalability and with a linear speedup while maintaining cluster quality.

Jiang and Zhang [250] proposed a parallel *K*-medoids clustering algorithm implemented with Hadoop MR framework, called H*K*-medoids. The experimental study involved *Iris* dataset from UCI repository [22]. The experimental results showed that the proposed H*K*-medoids algorithm had scalability with cluster node count. The results showed that the proposed algorithm had a linear speedup for large-scale data with good clustering result.

Yuan *et al.* [251] proposed a distributed link prediction algorithm based on clustering on social networks. The research work involved five classical datasets on the social network: *USAir, PB, Yeast, Power*, and *Router*. The experimental results proved that the performance in execution time of the parallel algorithm was far superior to its serial counterpart.

Shettar and Purohit [252] proposed an enhanced *K*-means algorithm. The experimental work carried out with two types of datasets. One was randomly generated numbers, and another dataset was collected from the DEBS-2014 grand challenge [253]. The experimental results presented that the proposed method had better accuracy than the traditional counterparts.

Yu and Ding [254] proposed an improved FCM algorithm with the help of canopy algorithm, called canopy-FCM. The research work was carried out with Church dataset. The experimental results presented that the proposed canopy-FCM algorithm in MapReduce had lesser execution time in comparison with FCM algorithm in MapReduce.

Boukhdhir *et al.* [255] proposed an advanced *K*-means algorithm with the removal of outliers and selection of initial centroids, called IM-*K*-means algorithm.

The dataset used in experimental studies was a real dataset collected from the Tunisian stock exchange daily trading in fiscal years 2012, 2013, and 2014. The experimental results presented the superior performance of IM-K-means regarding execution time in comparison with traditional K-means, PK-means, and fast K-means.

Lachiheb *et al.* [256] proposed an improved K-means algorithm, called SMRK-means. The algorithm was applied in the context of stock exchange large datasets clustering to identify risky investment based on stocks variation. The experimental work carried out with (i) a real dataset collected from the Tunisian stock exchange daily trading in fiscal years 2012, 2013, and 2014 and (ii) a synthetic dataset with random values. Experimental results showed that the proposed method reduces the execution time while keeping 80 percent of the clustering accuracy. The proposed algorithm was compared with traditional K-means, PK-means, and Fast$K$-means.

Mao *et al.* [257] proposed an optimal distributed K-means clustering algorithm. The proposed optimal distributed K-means clustering was improvised with (i) partially random center selection algorithm, to select the initial points. (ii) Implementing HaLoop, to support the iterative calculation model of ML while saving the intermediate results generated during each iteration to the cache for improving the efficiency of access task. The experiments utilized data from the *household electricity consumption* datasets provided by UCI. The experimental results showed that the proposed algorithm with HaLoop performed better in terms of execution time than its Hadoop counterpart.

Saranya and Sumalatha [258] proposed a dynamic neighborhood selection (DNS) clustering algorithm that processed a vast amount of data with varying densities. The experimental work involved *person health care* dataset. The results demonstrated, the proposed DNS-MR algorithm was superior in efficiency and had less execution time in comparison to DBCURE-MR.

Ketu *et al.* [259] proposed an approach for large-scale text data clustering using distributed K-means algorithm combined with corpus selection technique for a significant reduction of overall computational time. The experimental study utilized four large text datasets: *Wikilanguage* [260], *Wikilinks* [260], *Enron* [218], and *Wikipedia* dataset [261]. The performance of the proposed algorithm was compared with traditional K-means and parallel K-means. The experimental results showed that the corpus selection technique was significantly effective in reduction of overall processing time.

Karimov and Ozbayoglu [262] developed a hybrid model, $H(EC)^2S$, hybrid evolutionary clustering with empty clustering solution, for clustering of big data. The experimental study involved two datasets, i.e., *public* and *ATM logs*. The results showed that the proposed approach outperformed other models with a significant clustering quality gain.

Karimov *et al.* [263] proposed a method for K-means clustering algorithm with centroid calculation heuristics. The work involved a comparative study of serial and parallel implementations of the proposed algorithm and tested and analyzed with two different datasets, *Individual household electric power consumption, US census* data (1990) [22] with a various number of clusters. The experimental results showed that the proposed method outperformed other compared methods.

Garg *et al.* [264] proposed a modified fuzzy *K*-means clustering implemented with MapReduce. The experimental study involved *Iris*, *Synthetic control*, and *KDD cup 1999* datasets publicly available on UCI ML repository [22]. The experimental result showed that the proposed approach was efficient in terms of execution time as compared to its counterpart.

Ling and Yunfeng [265] proposed a distributed *K*-means clustering algorithm based on set pair analysis, called SPAB-DKMC algorithm. The experimental study used the extended *iris* and *wine* datasets available on UCI ML repository [22]. The experimental work involved comparison of the proposed SPAB-DKMC, CSB-DKMC, and DKMC algorithms in terms of execution time. The results showed that the proposed algorithm was more efficient than other compared algorithms.

Tao *et al.* [266], proposed the parallel *K*-modes algorithm. *K*-modes is a conventional categorical clustering algorithm. The experimental study used *US Census Data* (1990) dataset. The experimental results showed that parallel *K*-modes achieved good speedup ratio with large-scale categorical data.

Phan *et al.* [267] proposed an approach for range-based clustering supporting similarity search in big data. The experimental study involved Gutenberg datasets. The experimental results showed that the proposed method was superior to state-of-the-art algorithms.

Chunne *et al.* [268] proposed a method for real-time clustering of tweets using adaptive PSO technique. The parallel PSO (PPSO) was compared with *K*-means algorithm. The experimental results showed that the *F*-measure was increasing with increase in the number of particles.

Chen *et al.* [269] proposed two distributed clustering algorithms, i.e., distributed density-based clustering (DDC) and distributed grid-based clustering (DGC) algorithms with a reduction in communication and merging overheads. The experimental study was carried out with synthetic dataset generated from a data generator [270]. The experimental results showed that the proposed algorithms DDC and DGC were able to reduce the execution time and achieve scalability.

Wu *et al.* [271] proposed an approach for improved *K*-means algorithm. The experimental study involved *Reuters news* set. The experimental results showed that the proposed approach had superior efficiency in comparison with its serial counterpart and scalability with the increase of cluster nodes and data size.

Gao *et al.* [272] implemented *K*-means clustering for fixed traffic bottleneck detection. The proposed method was evaluated with the data collected from Jilin urban regional road net. The experimental results showed that the proposed method had scalability and was superior with respect to execution time in comparison with state-of-the-art traffic bottleneck identification method.

de Oliveira and Naldi [273] proposed a scalable evolutionary *K*-means clustering method called scalable fast evolutionary algorithm for clustering (SF-EAC). The experimental work was carried out with randomly generated three synthetic datasets with overlapping mixtures of Gaussian distributions by the MixSim R Package [245]. In addition to that one real-world dataset from *Medline database*

(PubMed) was created with a subset of the articles present in it. The experimental results showed that the proposed SF-EAC approach obtained comparable quality with MRMK-means with lesser execution time.

Moertini and Venica [274] employed an enhanced parallel K-means implemented with MapReduce framework for clustering large dataset. The experimental study was carried out with *household energy consumption* dataset obtained from UCI ML repository [22]. The results showed that the proposed method had linear scalability.

Akthar *et al.* [275] proposed a method for K-means clustering algorithm. The *20 Newsgroups* dataset collected from UCI ML repository [22] was considered for the evaluation of the proposed algorithm. The experimental results showed that the proposed approach had a superior performance in terms of precision, recall, and F-measure with less execution time in comparison with the simple K-means algorithm.

Zhong and Liu [276] suggested the application of K-means clustering algorithm for clustering spatial data. The user data of *Sina Weibo* was used for the study. The experimental result showed the efficiency of the proposed approach.

Budhraja *et al.* [277] proposed a fuzzy clustering-based classification for large-scale TCP dump dataset implemented with Hadoop framework. The study included *KDD'99* dataset [126]. The experimental results showed that the proposed FCM algorithm had superior accuracy to the K-means algorithm.

7.4.4.4   Spark-based conference papers

Sarazin *et al.* [278] proposed self-organizing map (SOM) clustering. The experimental work involved datasets from UCI repository [22]. The experimental results showed that the proposed approach had scalability and efficiency in terms of execution time in comparison with its serial counterpart.

Tsapanos *et al.* [279] proposed an approach for distributed implementation of the nearest neighbor and ϵ-ball variations of kernel K-means which was implemented with Apache Spark. The experimental work utilized the *MNIST handwritten digits* database and *BF0502* dataset, containing descriptors of the faces. The proposed approach provided improved results over baseline kernel K-means and approximated kernel K-means in a time-efficient manner.

Govindarajan *et al.* [280] proposed a method for PPSO clustering. The experimental results showed that the proposed algorithm outperformed sequential clustering algorithms and existing parallel algorithms regarding execution time, speedup, inter- and intra-cluster distance measures.

Ketu and Agarwal [281] proposed an approach for distributed K-means clustering for large-scale data analytics. The study included four benchmark datasets: *Wikilanguage* [260], *Wikilinks* [260], *Enron* [218], and *Wikipedia* dataset [261]. The experimental results showed that the proposed distributed K-means is $10\times$ faster than the Hadoop MapReduce implementation.

Zhu *et al.* [282] proposed an approach for distributed SAR image change detection. The proposed method employed that kernel FCM clustering algorithm with Spark called Spark-based KFCM (S-KFCM) was used to group the changed and unchanged area in the difference map. The experimental work involved comparison of S-KFCM and Hadoop-based KFCM (H-KFCM). The SAR images were gathered as the data for the experimental study. The experimental results showed that the S-KFCM was efficient in terms of execution time on H-KFCM.

Peng *et al.* [283] designed a parallel nonlinear clustering algorithm DenPeak. The experimental task involved nine synthetic datasets that represent the typical nonlinearly separable datasets. The experimental results depicted the performance regarding the number of points, the dimension of data, and the number of nodes present in the Spark cluster.

Han *et al.* [284] proposed a parallel DBSCAN clustering algorithm. The experimental setup utilized synthetic dataset generated using the IBM synthetic data generator [48]. The experimental results presented the scalability and efficiency of the proposed algorithm.

Jędrzejowicz *et al.* [285] proposed a classification algorithm based on kernel-based FCM clustering. The proposed algorithm was tested on several datasets from UCI ML repository [22]. The experimental results showed that the proposed approach had better performance in execution time with good accuracy.

Tsapanos *et al.* [286] proposed a kernel *K*-means clustering algorithm with a distributed implementation called trimmed kernel *K*-means that employed subsampling. The experimental study involved *YouTube Faces* dataset. The experimental results indicated that the proposed method run much faster than the original trimmed kernel *K*-means.

Bharill *et al.* [287] proposed fuzzy-based clustering algorithms to handle big data. The proposed algorithm was a partitional clustering algorithm called Scalable Random Sampling with iterative optimization FCM algorithm (SRSIO-FCM). The experimental work involved comparison of proposed algorithm SRSIO-FCM with a scalable version of a clustering algorithm such as literal FCM (LFCM) called SLFCM. The performance of the SRSIO-FCM and SLFCM algorithms was compared with four datasets collected from UCI repository [22], *Minst8m*, *Replicated-USPS*, *Monarch-Skin*, and *SUSY* datasets. The experimental results showed that SRSIO-FCM had superior performance to SLFCM in terms of various measures such as *F*-measure, adjusted rand index, an objective function value, runtime, and scalability.

Gouineau *et al.* [288] implemented an algorithm called PatchWork, a scalable density-grid clustering algorithm. The proposed algorithm was evaluated with four synthetic datasets: *Jain*, *Spiral*, *Aggregation*, and *Compound*. The PatchWork was also tested with a real-world dataset, *SFPD (San Francisco Police Department) Incidents*. The experimental results showed that the proposed algorithm was considerably faster in comparison with the *K*-means implemented with Spark.

After reviewing articles in clustering with distributed parallel computing architecture, the following insights were discovered:

- *The predominant algorithm that has been parallelized is the K-means. It can be implemented on different chunks of data independently and finally merging the results which will be the approximation of the optimal result but with lesser execution time.*

- *K-Means, FCM are highly explored in the distributed parallel environment.*
- *Density-based clustering algorithms are least explored in Hadoop and Spark framework leading to a fertile ground for the new researchers.*
- *Evolutionary methods for clustering are explored to a great extent with ACO, ABC, DE, GSO, PSO, fireworks algorithm, and cuckoo search. These algorithms with modifications and the other algorithms of evolutionary methods can be explored.*
- *SOM is the least exploited technique.*

7.4.5 Outlier detection/intrusion detection system

7.4.5.1 Hadoop MapReduce-based journal paper

Zhu *et al.* [289] proposed an algorithm combining cell-based OD and single-layer perceptron. The experimental data were two-dimensional datasets generated randomly by MATLAB 7.0. The experimental results exhibited that the parallelized cell-based OD algorithm produced better accuracy than its serialized counterpart.

Soltani Halvaiee and Akbari [290] proposed a model for credit card fraud detection using artificial immune system (AIS), known as AIS-based fraud detection model. The experiments worked on transactions collected from a Brazilian bank. The improvization made on the base algorithm AIS demonstrated an improvement of accuracy, reduction in cost, and reduction in system response time in the experimental results.

Natesan *et al.* [291] proposed a Parallel Binary Bat Algorithm for efficient feature selection and classification for network ID in Hadoop platform (HPBBA). The proposed method was evaluated with the *KDDCup99* dataset [126]. The results showed that the proposed method was superior to sequential computing approach.

El-Alfy and Alshammari [292] proposed an approach on the basis of rough sets for scalable attribute subset selection to detect intrusion using the parallel GA. The work utilized four cybersecurity datasets: *SpamBase*, *NSL-KDD*, *Kyoto*, and *CDMC2012*. The experimental results showed that the proposed approach reduced the execution time without degrading the solution quality regarding the reduct size.

Rathore *et al.* [293] proposed a real-time intrusion detection system (IDS) for high-speed big data environments. The study used three publicly available datasets: *DARPA* [35], *KDDCUP99* [126], and *NSL-KDD* [294]. The proposed system employed five different ML classifiers: J48, REPTree, RF tree, conjunctive rule, SVM, and naïve Bayes. The experimental results showed that among all these classifiers, REPTree and J48 are the best classifiers regarding accuracy as well as efficiency.

7.4.5.2 Spark-based journal papers

Carcillo *et al.* [295] presented a SCAlable Real-time Fraud Finder that is an amalgamation of big data tools, viz., Kafka, Spark, and Cassandra with an ML approach for credit card fraud detection. The experimental work involved more than 8 million of *e-commerce transactions* from almost 2 million cardholders. The experimental results showed that the proposed approach is scalable.

7.4.5.3 Hadoop MapReduce-based conference paper

Tanupabrungsun and Achalakul [296] introduced a feature reduction method with GA/*k*-NN for anomaly detection in manufacturing. The experimental study involved six standard datasets from UCI ML repository [22], *Connectionist, WBDC, Ionosphere, Hill Valley, Musk*, and *Wine*. The results showed that the proposed algorithm had a comparable accuracy with its sequential counterpart with excellent scalability.

Aljarah and Ludwig [297] proposed a method for IDS based on a PPSO clustering algorithm, called IDS-MRCPSO. The experimental study involved *KDD99* ID dataset for evaluation of the proposed approach. The results showed that the IDS-MRCPSO was efficient and scalable with dataset size. Also, it had close to linear speedup.

Xiang *et al.* [298] proposed an approach for ID employing ELM with MapReduce framework, called MR_ELM. The experimental study involved KDDcup99 dataset. The experimental result showed that the proposed MR_ELM had an excellent efficiency with respect to execution time, speedup, and sizeup in comparison with the local ELM.

Sharma *et al.* [299] proposed a classification approach for ID. The experimental study used NSL-KDD dataset [294] that was derived from the KDDcup99 dataset by refining it for missing and duplicate values. The experimental results showed that the proposed classifiers in MapReduce environment had more accuracy, specificity, precision, $F1$ scores than its corresponding WEKA implementations.

7.4.5.4 Spark-based conference papers

Gupta and Kulariya [300] proposed a method whereby a fast and efficient ID in the massive network traffic is implemented. The experiment involved two real-time network traffic datasets: *DARPA KDD'99* [126] and *NSL-KDD* [294]. The implemented feature selection algorithms involved correlation-based feature selection and Chi-square feature selection, and classification algorithms included LogR, SVM, RF, gradient boosted DTs, and naïve Bayes. The experimental results were compared and contrasted.

Kumari *et al.* [301] implemented *K*-means clustering for anomaly detection in network traffic utilizing MapReduce programming environment in Apache Spark platform. The experimental work was carried out with the *KDD cup 1999* dataset. The result showed the detection of anomalies in the dataset by implementing threshold to the distance of a data point from the nearest centroid of a cluster.

The following research insights are obtained after reviewing the articles related to OD in Hadoop and Spark frameworks:

- *The OD or ID has been implemented with classification and clustering approaches that are popular in parallel implementation. But, it has not been explored to its full scale.*
- *The DM task, OD is one of the less explored areas in the distributed parallel computational environment, leading it to be a fertile ground for the budding researcher to explore.*

- ANN has not been utilized in OD. Hence, the rich features of ANN can be exploited for OD.
- Evolutionary methods have not been explored to its full extent for OD. Hence, the researchers can exploit it to its full potential.

7.4.6 Recommendation

7.4.6.1 Hadoop MapReduce-based journal paper

Veloso *et al.* [302] presented the parallelization of profiling and recommendation algorithms using crowdsourcing tourism crowdsourced data repositories and streams. The research work implemented collaborative recommendation filter employing singular value decomposition with stochastic gradient descent (SVD-SGD). The work analyzed the *Yelp* dataset [303]. The experimental results showed that the proposed method was effective and scalable.

7.4.6.2 Hadoop MapReduce-based conference papers

Schelter *et al.* [304] proposed a scalable similarity-based neighborhood method. The proposed approach employed pairwise item comparison and top-*n* recommendation. The experimental study was carried out with *Movielens* [305] and *Flixster* datasets [306]. The experimental results showed that the proposed approach had linear scalability with the number of users and a linear speedup with the addition of new computational nodes.

Ghuli *et al.* [307] developed a collaborative filtering (CF) recommendation engine. They presented a comparison between item-based and user-based CF with the help of *MovieLens* dataset [305], where the item-based CF showed better scalability than user-based CF algorithm.

Shang *et al.* [308] proposed a scalable CF recommendation algorithm. The study involved a real-world dataset, *MovieLens* [305], and a synthetic dataset to analyze the performance of the proposed algorithm. The experimental results demonstrated that the proposed implementation had scalability concerning numbers of users and items, ensuring recommendation accuracy.

Pozo and Chiky [309] proposed a method of a distributed SGD (DSGD) for recommender systems based on MapReduce computational environment. The performance of the proposed algorithm was evaluated with the implementation of *MovieLens* dataset [305]. The experimental results showed the better performance of the proposed method in respect of accuracy and scalability.

Lu *et al.* [310] implemented a distributed item-based CF algorithm on Hadoop MapReduce framework. The experimental study utilized the *MovieLens* dataset [305]. The algorithm was evaluated with root mean square error (RMSE) and mean absolute error (MAE). The proposed method improved the accuracy of the algorithm.

Subramaniyaswamy *et al.* [311] proposed an approach for unstructured data analysis on large-scale data. The study used the *Twitter* dataset. The unstructured data were converted to the structured format, and the proposed approach implemented CF and sentiment analysis on the data. The proposed method showed scalability with respect to the size of data.

Shen and Jiamthapthaksin [312] proposed an improved algorithm DIMSUM+ which is the improvized version of DIMSUM algorithm, an all-pair similarity algorithm. The experimental work involved (i) the *MovieLens* 1M dataset provided by GroupLens project [305] and (ii) the *Yahoo! Music* dataset provided by Yahoo! Webscope Program [313]. The experimental results showed that the proposed algorithm DIMSUM+ outperformed DIMSUM regarding accuracy and execution time.

7.4.6.3 Spark-based conference papers

Panigrahi *et al.* [314] implemented a hybrid algorithm involving dimensionality reduction techniques like alternating least square and clustering techniques like *K*-means for User-Oriented Collaborative Filtering method. The algorithm utilized benchmark dataset of *MovieLens* [305]. The experimental results proved the efficacy of the proposed algorithm.

After reviewing the articles related to recommender system in the distributed parallel environment, the following research insights are found:

- *The recommendation system has been implemented with user-based and item-based recommendations. These approaches are susceptible to parallel implementation.*
- *There has been very less research work carried out by the research community in recommendation system utilizing distributed parallel computation. A lot of exploration can be achieved in this rich area.*
- *A few research articles were published related to user-based and item-based CF, thus, resulting into a most explorable area.*
- *Many similarity indices can be explored with different classification or clustering techniques to produce a better result.*

7.4.7 Others

The articles reviewed under this category cover some articles utilizing ML techniques such as BN, Rough set approximations, PSO, SGD, latent Dirichlet allocation (LDA), GA, and ABC.

7.4.7.1 Hadoop MapReduce-based journal papers

Zhang *et al.* [315] suggested a parallel approach for computing rough set approximations. The research work implemented three parallel algorithms involving real dataset *KDDCup-99* from the UCI ML data repository, and three synthetic datasets generated with the help of the WEKA data generator [164]. The performance of the proposed parallel algorithms was evaluated with speedup, scale-up, and sizeup performance metrics and found to be superior to its serial counterpart.

Chen *et al.* [316] employed a feature selection method based on differential privacy and Gini index. The experimental study included validation of the proposed algorithm with the utilization of five benchmark datasets from UCI repository [22], *Car Evaluation*, *Mushrooms*, *Connect-4*, *Covertype*, *PokerHand*; and one synthetic dataset *S1*. The results indicated that the proposed algorithm was time efficient than its centralized counterpart.

Qian *et al.* [317] proposed a parallel feature reduction algorithm. The experiments involved generic parallel algorithms for attribute reduction based on positive region, boundary region, discernibility matrix, and information entropy in data and task parallel as PAAR-PR, PAAR-BR, PAAR-DM, and PAAR-IE, respectively. The experimental study was carried out with two real datasets, i.e., *Mushroom* and *Gisette* from the UCI ML repository [22] and four synthetic datasets (DS3-6). Experimental results showed that the proposed parallel algorithms were efficient and scalable.

Yue *et al.* [318] proposed a parallel and incremental approach for learning of BN from large-scale, distributed, and dynamically changing data by enhancing the scoring and search algorithm. The research work utilized datasets involving (i) *Chest-clinic network* (also called Asia network), a belief network for a hypothetical medical domain about whether a patient has tuberculosis, lung cancer, or bronchitis, related to their X-ray, dyspnea, visit-to-Asia, and smoking status; and (ii) *HepaerII network*, a belief network for diagnosis of liver disorders. The experimental results depict the proposed methods to be scalable and efficient.

Zhang *et al.* [319] proposed i^2MapReduce, an incremental processing extension to MapReduce. Four iterative mining algorithms were implemented: (i) PageRank (one-to-one correlation) with *ClueWeb* dataset [33], (ii) single source shortest path (one-to-one correlation) with *ClueWeb2* dataset [33], (iii) *K*-means (all-to-one correlation) with *BigCross* dataset [320], and (iv) GIM-V (many-to-one correlation) with *WikiTalk* dataset [321] and also a one-step mining algorithm, Apriori, was also implemented with *Twitter* dataset. Experimental results demonstrated significant performance enhancements of i^2MapReduce compared to both plain and iterative MapReduce.

Yue *et al.* [322] presented a method for measuring the similarity among the users utilizing BN called user BN (UBN). The authors used *DBLP* datasets consisting bibliographic information about computer science journals and proceedings in the database, network, and ML. They also tested the effectiveness of the UBN-based user similarities utilizing the *Sina Weibo* dataset. The similarities among the social users do not depend only on the social, behavioral interactions but also on the contents involved in the interaction.

Wang *et al.* [323] proposed cooperative PSO (MRCPSO) that implements CPSO-S, a version of CPSO. The experimental work involved 11 scalable optimization problems introduced in CEC13. The experimental results showed that the proposed algorithm MRCPSO outperformed the original CPSO-S significantly on both time and the quality of the solution.

7.4.7.2 Spark-based journal papers

Qi *et al.* [324] proposed a two-phase parallelization algorithm, called a parallel genetic algorithm based on Spark (PGAS), involving fitness evaluation and genetic operation parallelization for pairwise test suite generation. The experimental work was carried out with 14 pairwise synthetic benchmarks and five real-world benchmarks presented by Jia *et al.* [325] and Garvin *et al.* [326]. The test results showed that PGAS outperformed sequential GA in both the sizes of generated test suites and execution time in almost all benchmarks.

Eiras-Franco *et al.* [327] implemented the parallel version of four traditional feature selection algorithms, i.e., InfoGain, RELIEF-F, CFS, and SVM-RFE. The study included seven high-dimensional datasets: *Higgs*, *Epsilon*, *KDD99*, *Isolet*, *USPS*, *Poker*, and *KDDB*. Experimental results demonstrated that the proposed approach had the speedup and efficiency in comparison with sequential approach.

Ramírez-Gallego *et al.* [328] proposed a parallelized version of the minimum-redundancy–maximum-relevance method, called fast-mRMR for dimensionality reduction. The experimental work involved a comparison of CPU-based, GPU-based, and parallel distributed execution performance. The study included real datasets for a sequential version of fast-mRMR vs. mRMR, viz., *Lung*, *NCI*, *Colon*, *Leukemia*, and *Lymphoma*. Performance comparison of CPU- and GPU-based architecture was executed with the help of a synthetic dataset. The distributed parallel computational environment was studied with *ECBDL'14*, *Epsilon*, and *KDDB* datasets. The experimental results showed that fast-mRMR outperformed the original mRMR.

7.4.7.3 Hadoop MapReduce-based conference papers

Gemulla *et al.* [329] proposed an approach for large-scale matrix factorization with DSGD. They analyzed the *Netflix competition* dataset. They compared DSGD with its sequential counterpart. The results showed that the proposed approach is efficient, scalable, and fast.

Zhang and Sun [330] proposed a method for microblog mining using distributed MicroBlog-Latent Dirichlet Allocation (MB-LDA). The experimental study involved a microblog dataset originally from the *Twitter* dataset for comparative analysis of MB-LDA and distributed MB-LDA. The observed results presented that the proposed MB-LDA outperformed the baseline of LDA.

Thompson *et al.* [331] proposed a fast, scalable selection algorithm. The study involved synthetic dataset generated using the *TeraGen* program included in the Hadoop distribution. The results showed, proposed method outperformed several other alternatives.

Hu *et al.* [332] proposed a MapReduce-enabled simulated annealing GA. The proposed approach was the amalgam of the conventional GA and the SA algorithms. The hybridization in the proposed algorithm led to maintain a higher probability of getting the optimal global solution than traditional GAs. The research work involved traveling salesman problem dataset [333]. The experimental results indicated that the convergence speed of the proposed algorithm significantly outperformed its traditional genetic rivals.

He *et al.* [334] employed a parallel feature selection using a positive approximation, called PSFPA. The experiment used *Shuttle* and *Handwritten* datasets, which were collected from UCI ML repository [22]. The results demonstrated that the proposed algorithm was efficient to process large-scale and high-dimension dataset.

Hilda and Rajalaxmi [335] proposed an approach for feature selection using GA for supervised learning through the k-NN classifier. The experimental study used five datasets: *Wisconsin Breast Cancer*, *Pima Indian Diabetes*, *Heart-Statlog*,

Hepatitis, and *Cleveland Heart Disease*. The experimental results indicated that the parallel GA produced high accuracy than other methods.

Kourid and Batouche [336] proposed an approach for feature selection, using K-means clustering and signal-to-noise ratio combined with optimization technique as binary PSO. The experimental work was carried out with two datasets of *cancer RNA-seq gene expression* data (gastric cancer, ESCA (esophageal carcinoma)). The scalability of the proposed method was validated with a synthetic dataset by duplicating genes of each dataset. The experimental results concluded that the proposed method performed well in comparison to centralized approaches in terms of accuracy and the number of biomarkers selected.

Alshammari and El-Alfy [337] proposed an approach for minimum reduct using parallel GA. The study utilized four ID datasets that are publicly available, viz., *SpamBase*, *NSL-KDD*, *Kyoto*, and *CDMC2012*. The experimental result showed that the proposed approach reduced the execution time with a comparable solution on reduct size.

Yu *et al.* [338] proposed a distributed keyword search (DKS) approach implemented with MapReduce in a parallel way. The proposed method modeled the keyword database as a data graph. A tree covering a part of keywords in a subgraph that can grow into a Steiner tree is called a candidate Steiner tree (CS-tree). Then the data graph was partitioned into multiple subgraphs from which the CS-tree was searched using map operation and later combined in reduce phase to construct the Steiner tree. The top-k keywords could be found by merging Steiner trees generated by reducers.

7.4.7.4   Spark-based conference paper

Li *et al.* [339] presented the implementation of parallel multi-objective ABC (MOABC) algorithm. The study utilized Hypervolume, Epsilon, GD, IGD, and Spread datasets to evaluate the results. The experimental results showed that MOABC performed better and could solve multi-objective optimization problems efficiently.

Hu and Tan [340] proposed an algorithm for feature selection to classify malware based on n-gram partitioning. The experimental study involved malicious files from the VX Heaven virus collection [341]. The results showed the efficiency and superiority of the proposed algorithm.

7.5   Discussion

The review work addressed the two research questions posed in the beginning of Section 7.1. Research question Q1 is answered affirmatively because we could find 249 studies where a majority of statistical and ML family of techniques that are relevant to DM tasks could be scaled up in a distributed and parallel manner under the Hadoop and Spark frameworks. The reason could be that all of them involved several vector–matrix, matrix–matrix, and matrix–vector multiplications, which are easily amenable for parallelization and distributed processing.

Research question Q2 is answered as follows: The techniques left out are either not amenable to parallelization or not yet attempted because of the lack of popularity and/or wide applicability. Examples could be LASSO [342], ridge regression [343], linear discriminant analysis [344], quadratic discriminant analysis [345], canonical correlation analysis [346], factor analysis [347], correspondence analysis [348], conjoint analysis [349], and hierarchical clustering [350].

Various publication resources of this review and distribution of these are presented in Table 7.2. The review noticed that the highest number of papers was from IEEE followed by Elsevier and Springer. Figure 7.5 depicts an eagle eye view of the distribution of articles publisher-wise that has been considered in the current review work. This depicts that the IEEE has the maximum number of publications followed by Elsevier, Springer, and so on. Figure 7.6 depicts the count of articles from individual conference proceedings. It emphasizes that the highest number of articles is from IEEE followed by ACM and Springer. Similarly, Figure 7.7 depicts the count of articles from individual journals that have been surveyed. According to the count, the highest number of journals is published on Information Sciences, Knowledge-Based Systems, and Neurocomputing, followed by IEEE Transactions on Knowledge and Data Engineering and so on.

The year-wise distribution of the reviewed papers with the categorization of Hadoop-MapReduce-based and Apache-Spark-based is depicted in Figure 7.8. The highest number of articles (i.e., 59) appeared in 2015, followed by 2014 and 2016 in Hadoop MapReduce framework category. Similarly, in the case of Apache-Spark-based papers, the highest number of articles (i.e., 24) appeared in 2016 followed by 2015.

Figure 7.9 depicts the distribution of the papers according to various DM tasks. It reveals that there is an almost equal share of classification and clustering articles in horizontal scaling platform using Hadoop MapReduce and Apache Spark followed by ARM/pattern mining and so on.

Figure 7.10 depicts one step further in detail giving the paper distribution, again categorized on computational framework, i.e., Hadoop MapReduce and Apache Spark with journal and conference distribution. It demonstrated that a maximum number of publications have occurred in clustering followed by

Table 7.2   Publication-wise reviewed papers

Source	No. of journal papers	No. of conference papers	Total no. of papers
ACM	–	17	17
Elsevier	43	7	50
IEEE	14	126	140
Springer	25	10	35
Taylor & Francis	4	–	4
Wiley	1	–	1
Others	–	2	2
Total	87	162	249

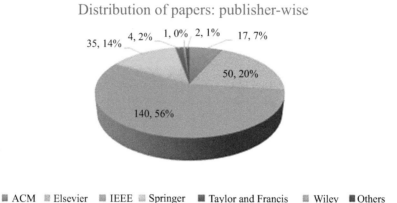

Distribution of papers: publisher-wise

35, 14% 4, 2% 1, 0% 2, 1% 17, 7%

50, 20%

140, 56%

■ ACM ▪ Elsevier ▪ IEEE ▪ Springer ■ Taylor and Francis ▪ Wiley ■ Others

Figure 7.5   Publisher-wise distribution of papers

Conference proceedings-wise distribution of articles

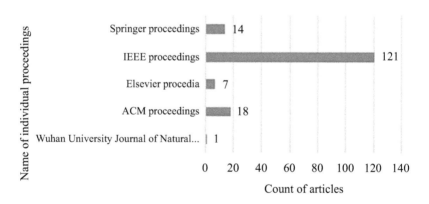

Figure 7.6   Conference proceedings-wise distribution of articles

classification and ARM task in Hadoop-based conference papers, whereas classification task is followed by clustering in the case of Hadoop-based journal articles. Similarly, the publications in the category of classification are followed by clustering and ARM in the case of Spark-based conference articles. Moreover, it depicts that the total count of Hadoop-based articles in each DM task category presents that clustering is the most explored task followed by classification, ARM, and so on. Similarly, the total count of Apache-Spark-based articles present classification is followed by clustering, ARM, and so on.

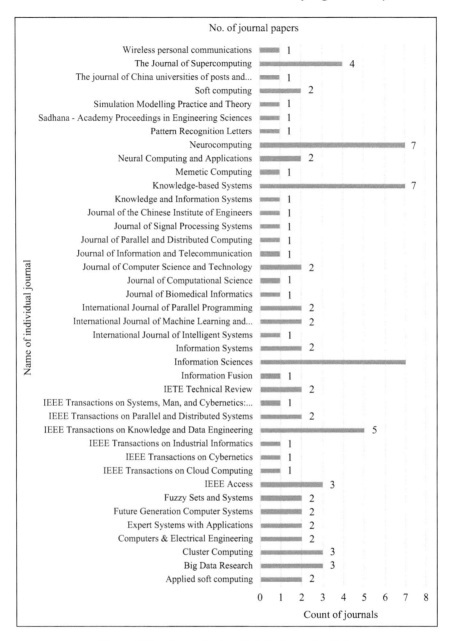

Figure 7.7   Journal-wise distribution of articles

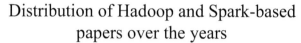

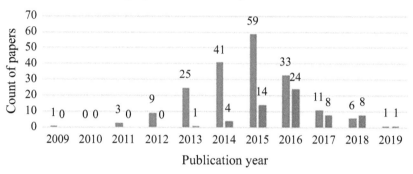

Figure 7.8   Year-wise Hadoop- and Spark-based publication count

Figure 7.11 depicts the distribution of the papers according to different ML techniques involved in various DM tasks further categorized with Hadoop and Spark articles. It presents the distribution of papers in different ML techniques used for ARM/FPM, regression, classification, and clustering. It indicates that some research has been carried out in Apriori and FP-Growth and FP-tree for ARM or FPM. The Apriori technique is the most widely used for ARM. BPNN and ELM have been explored for regression, but overall the regression task has been less explored in Hadoop and Spark platforms. The SVM, *k*-NN, and RF are the most used techniques for classification out of which the SVM is the most widely used technique for classification in both Hadoop and Spark platforms. Similarly, the *K*-means algorithm is rigorously studied by the research community followed by fuzzy clustering. We can observe that the centroid-based clustering technique has fascinated many researchers for its study.

We can figure out that the Apriori for ARM; SVM, *k*-NN for classification; and *K*-means for clustering are widely used in the MapReduce paradigm. It is due to the inherent nature of the algorithm and the fact that the model can be developed with partial data in a parallel and distributed manner.

The "others" mentioned in the ARM category represents all those articles not utilizing Apriori, FP-Growth, or FP-tree approach. They have used other approaches, viz., parallel GA, GA with *k*-NN, HUI-Miner. The "others" mentioned in the regression category represents all articles utilizing SVM, RF, SGD for ELM, etc. The "others" mentioned in the classification category represents all articles utilizing ACO, genetic programming, AANN with PSO, social network analysis (SNA) algorithms, etc. The "others" in clustering category represents all articles utilizing LDA, DE, SOM, ABC algorithms, etc.

DM task wise paper share

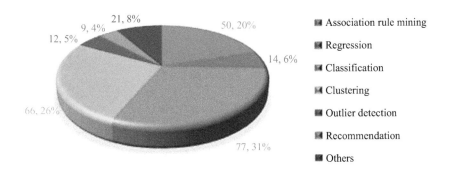

Figure 7.9   Data mining task-wise paper share in the review work

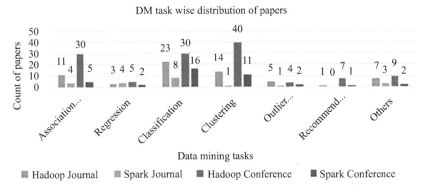

Figure 7.10   Distribution of papers: data mining task wise

Figure 7.12 depicts summarized information of the datasets analyzed in the papers reviewed. It demonstrates that 68 percent of the papers reviewed have used only real-world datasets, 10 percent of the papers have used only synthetic datasets, whereas 16 percent of the papers have used both real and synthetic datasets. This analysis indicates the trend of the researchers for having a preference of real-world dataset over a synthetic one. Figure 7.13 depicts the distribution of different types of the datasets used over Hadoop MR and Spark articles.

These are the different descriptive insights we can draw from the review work. The survey work led us to some research gaps that are presented in the following section in the future direction part.

Apart from the earlier, the review discovers the following insights:

- *The advanced method of the ARM such as PHUI-Miner yielded better results compared to its sequential counterpart. PHIKS, and complete parallel Apriori yielded better results compared to other parallel methods.*

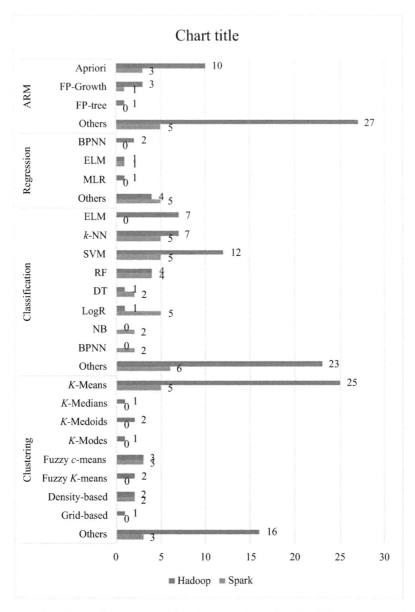

Figure 7.11   ML-technique-wise distribution of articles for different DM tasks categorized with Hadoop and Spark

- *The modified approaches such as PELM, parallel AAELM yielded better results for regression task with respect to their sequential counterpart.*
- *The improved methods, viz., PIESVM, adaptive distributed extreme leaning machine (A-ELM*), and PRF produced better results while solving the*

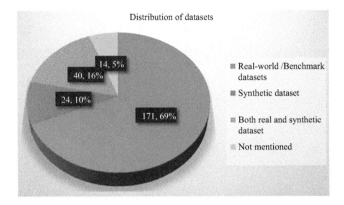

Figure 7.12   Distribution of papers: dataset wise

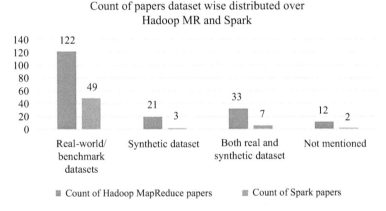

Figure 7.13   Count of papers distributed dataset wise in Hadoop MR and Spark

classification task in comparison with its serial version. The improved method WE-DELM yielded a better result in comparison with PELM.

- *The ANN with its different form along with evolutionary optimization techniques can be employed for regression and classification due to the inherent nature of ANN to be parallelized. The parallelization of ANN is achievable as it involves vector–matrix, matrix–vector, or matrix–matrix multiplication.*
- *The modified method of FCM, called MRFCM, produced a better result than its sequential counterpart. The improved parallel K-means and IM-K-means approach yielded a better result in comparison to the parallel version of K-means.*
- *Many papers are found to experiment with the real-world dataset(s). The synthetic dataset was used for the test of scalability of the algorithms. The synthetic datasets were generated through some data generators or replicating the samples of small real-world datasets.*

- *Neither the large-scale real-world datasets nor the benchmark datasets for evaluating DM tasks in big data paradigm are available in public domain. Therefore, many researchers replicated the existing benchmark dataset many times so as to get an artificial flavor of big data. This jugglery leads to the inaccurate modeling of a DM task and ultimately rendering the model not so useful.*
- *There are only a few works that have been carried out employing ML techniques with evolutionary optimization techniques.*

7.6   Conclusion and future directions

The review work included 249 papers from 2009 to 2019. This chapter presents a comprehensive review of DM tasks with a distributed parallel computing environment with horizontal scaling. The different DM tasks on which we categorize the review papers are ARM/pattern mining, regression/prediction, classification, clustering, OD/ID, and recommendation. We could see that Hadoop MapReduce was the preferred choice over Apache Spark as seen by the number of publications reviewed. One reason for this is the latter is relatively new (Tables 7.3 and 7.4).

The study concludes with some of the key future directions:

- *There remains a lot of work to be carried out in regression/prediction in both Hadoop MapReduce and Apache Spark environment.*
- *The kernel density estimation has not been parallelized.*
- *The rough set approximation is scantily scaled out.*
- *A very few papers were found related to various NN architectures. The different NN architecture such as GRNN, QRNN, PNN, WNN, RBFN, group method of data handling, functional-link neural network, single multiplicative neural network, sigma-pi-sigma neural network, multilayer morphological neural network are not explored at all, thus, resulting it into a fertile ground to explore.*
- *Though a lot of work is reported in clustering, classification, and ARM, they are carried out with Hadoop MapReduce framework. Therefore, there is also a great scope for conducting the research in Apache Spark environment, i.e., with the in-memory computational framework too in order to reap the benefits of the Spark environment.*
- *The least explored OD/ID, and recommendation presents an open area to conduct more research work.*
- *The unbalanced datasets and high-dimensional datasets pose significant challenges in big data paradigm too. These areas need full exploration.*
- *Streaming data analytics, SNA, and social media analysis also pose challenges. There are very few papers on real-time or quasi-real-time streaming analyses. These are open areas for future work.*
- *Scalable Advanced Massive Online Analysis has not been explored at all for streaming data analytics.*

Table 7.3 DM-task-wise categorization of articles describing ML techniques used in it

DM task	Article reference	Year	Machine learning techniques	Performance measure
Association rule mining (ARM)/ pattern mining	*Hadoop-based articles*			
	[20]	2012	FP mining	*Not mentioned*
	[21]	2013	FP-Growth	Interestingness measure, all-confidence, $\alpha(X)=\text{Sup}(X)/\text{Max\_item\_sup}(X)$
	[23]	2015	Frequent subgraph mining	*Not mentioned*
	[29]	2016	Frequent itemset mining	*Not mentioned*
	[30]	2017	Apriori	*Not mentioned*
	[34]	2017	Dynamic rule creation	True-positive rate $(\text{TPR})=\text{TP}/(\text{TP}+\text{FN})$ False-positive rate $(\text{FPR})=\text{FP}/(\text{FP}+\text{TN})$
	[37]	2017	FP-Growth	*Not mentioned*
	[38]	2017	Frequent itemset mining	*Not mentioned*
	[39]	2018	Frequent itemset mining	*Execution time*
	[41]	2018	Maximal frequent itemsets mining	*Execution time*
	[42]	2018	Apriori	Execution time
	[28]	2012	Frequent subgraph mining	*Not mentioned*
	[55]	2013	Apriori	*Not mentioned*
	[57]	2013	Apriori	*Not mentioned*
	[58]	2013	Apriori	*Not mentioned*
	[59]	2013	FP-Tree	*Not mentioned*
	[60]	2013	Apriori+FP-Growth	*Not mentioned*
	[61]	2013	Apriori+Eclat	*Not mentioned*
	[63]	2013	Frequent pattern mining based on bitmap computation	*Not mentioned*
	[64]	2014	FP-Growth	*Not mentioned*
	[66]	2014	Apriori	*Not mentioned*
	[67]	2014	String mining algorithm using suffix array (SA) and the longest common prefix array (LCP)	*Not mentioned*
	[68]	2014	Apriori	*Not mentioned*
	[70]	2014	Frequent itemset mining	*Not mentioned*
	[71]	2014	Candidate-generation-and-test for frequent subgraph mining	*Not mentioned*
	[72]	2014	Apriori	*Not mentioned*
	[73]	2014	Repetitive sequence mining	*Not mentioned*
	[74]	2014	Frequent pattern mining	*Not mentioned*
	[75]	2015	Apriori+FP-Growth	*Not mentioned*
	[76]	2015	Apriori	*Not mentioned*
	[77]	2015	Parallel GA	*Not mentioned*

(Continues)

Table 7.3   *(Continued)*

DM task	Article reference	Year	Machine learning techniques	Performance measure
	[78]	2015	Follower pattern mining	*Not mentioned*
	[80]	2015	PHIKS	*Not mentioned*
	[81]	2015	Vertical mining with breadth-first search	*Not mentioned*
	[82]	2015	Carpenter algorithm+depth first search for closed itemset	*Not mentioned*
	[85]	2015	Weighted itemset mining	*Not mentioned*
	[86]	2016	Apriori	*Not mentioned*
	[87]	2016	Mining closed frequent itemsets	*Not mentioned*
	[88]	2016	PrePost algorithm	*Not mentioned*
	[89]	2016	Apriori+FP-Growth	*Not mentioned*
	[90]	2016	Grid-based partitioning for spatial neighborhood	*Not mentioned*
	Spark-based article			
	[43]	2015	Apriori	Execution time
	[44]	2016	High utility itemset mining	Execution time
	[49]	2018	Maximal frequent pattern mining	*Not mentioned*
	[52]	2018	Quantitative association rule mining	*Not mentioned*
	[91]	2015	Apriori	*Not mentioned*
	[92]	2015	FP-Growth	*Not mentioned*
	[93]	2015	Apriori	*Not mentioned*
	[94]	2015	Suffix method	*Not mentioned*
	[95]	2016	Faster-IAPI	*Not mentioned*
Regression/ prediction	*Hadoop-based articles*			
	[96]	2013	Extreme learning machine (ELM)	Speedup, scale-up, sizeup
	[97]	2015	Semiparametric regression	*Not mentioned*
	[99]	2016	BPNN	MAPE
	[105]	2012	Regression tree	*Not mentioned*
	[106]	2015	Auto-associative ELM (AAELM) and multiple linear regression (MLR)	MSE, MAPE, t-test
	[107]	2015	MLR	*Not mentioned*
	[108]	2015	SVM	*Not mentioned*
	[109]	2016	BPNN	Execution time, accuracy
	Spark-based articles			
	[100]	2016	Random forest (RF)	*Not mentioned*
	[101]	2016	Fuzzy rule learning through GA	*Not mentioned*
	[103]	2018	Linear regression and regression tree	Mean Relative Error (MRE)
	[104]	2018	k-Weighted nearest neighbor	*Not mentioned*

(Continues)

Table 7.3   (*Continued*)

DM task	Article reference	Year	Machine learning techniques	Performance measure
	[110]	2015	Weighted *k*-NN regression+prototype selection method based on fuzzy rough set theory (FRPS)	RMSE
	[113]	2016	Stochastic gradient descent (SGD) for extreme learning machines (ELM)	*Not mentioned*
Classification	*Hadoop-based articles*			
	[114]	2011	SVM	*Not mentioned*
	[115]	2012	ACO	Precision, recall, accuracy
	[116]	2013	SVM	Speedup, efficiency, accuracy
	[117]	2014	SVM	Accuracy (ACC), sensitivity (SN), precision (PE), and Matthews correlation coefficient (MCC) $ACC=(TP+TN)/(TP+FP+TN+FN)$ $SN=TP/(TP+FN)$ $PE=TP/(TP+FP)$ $MCC=(TP*TN-FP*FN)/(((TP+FN)*(TN+FP)*(TP+FP)*(TN+FN))^{0.5}$
	[119]	2014	RF	True-positive rate (TPR), false-positive rate (FPR), precision, recall, Pearson product-moment coefficient
	[121]	2014	Horizontal and vertical compression	*Not mentioned*
	[122]	2015	SVM	*Not mentioned*
	[125]	2015	ELM	*Not mentioned*
	[127]	2015		Execution time, accuracy, precision
	[128]	2015	Fuzzy rule-based classification	*Not mentioned*
	[129]	2016	ELM	*Not mentioned*
	[130]	2016	*k*-NN	MAPE, RMSE, mean absolute error (MAE), maximum error (ME)
	[132]	2016	FP-Growth	*Not mentioned*
	[133]	2016	*k*-NN	Confusion matrix, recall, precision, accuracy
	[134]	2016	ELM	Speedup, sizeup
	[136]	2016	ELM	*Not mentioned*
	[137]	2016	Voting-based instance selection+random weight networks	*Not mentioned*
	[138]	2016	ELM	Speedup

(Continues)

Table 7.3   (Continued)

DM task	Article reference	Year	Machine learning techniques	Performance measure
	[140]	2016	SVM	*Not mentioned*
	[141]	2016	ELM	Speedup, scale-up, precision, recall, *F*-measure and *G*-mean
	[142]	2018	Dissimilarity-based imbalance data classification	*Not mentioned*
	[145]	2018	Fuzzy rule-based classification	Execution time
	[146]	2019	Kernel-optimized SVM	Accuracy, execution time
	[157]	2012	Social network analysis (SNA) algorithms	Centrality measures
	[159]	2012	Sentiment classifier	Accuracy
	[160]	2013	DT+SVM	Precision, recall, *F*1
	[161]	2013	RF	Accuracy
	[162]	2013	ELM	Speedup, sizeup
	[163]	2013	Meta-learning	Accuracy, speedup
	[165]	2013	Logistic regression (LogR)	*Not mentioned*
	[166]	2013	Genetic programming	Accuracy, speedup
	[167]	2013	SVM	*Not mentioned*
	[168]	2014	Classification rule induction	Speedup, scale-up, sizeup
	[169]	2014	SVM	Speedup
	[170]	2014	*K*-Means+LogR	Accuracy, TPR, FPR
	[171]	2014	Fuzzy rule-based classification	Accuracy
	[172]	2014	Classification rule	Accuracy
	[173]	2014	SVM	*Not mentioned*
	[174]	2014	*k*-NN	*Not mentioned*
	[175]	2015	SVM	*Not mentioned*
	[176]	2015	*k*-NN	*Not mentioned*
	[177]	2015	*k*-NN	*Not mentioned*
	[178]	2015	RF	*Not mentioned*
	[179]	2015	SVM, *k*-NN, Adaboost	Speedup
	[180]	2015	GA-optimized DT	*Not mentioned*
	[181]	2015	RF	*Not mentioned*
	[182]	2015	Evolutionary undersampling (EUS)	AUC, *G*-mean
	[183]	2015	Feature ranking	Information gain
	[185]	2015	*k*-NN	*Not mentioned*
	[186]	2015	Fuzzy associative classification	*Not mentioned*
	[187]	2015	Bayesian classifier	*Not mentioned*
	[188]	2015	SVM	Accuracy, execution time
	[189]	2016	TF-IDF+cosine similarity+Rocchio algorithm	Recall, precision, *F*1, speedup
Spark-based articles				
	[149]	2016	*k*-NN	Accuracy, execution time, speedup

(Continues)

Table 7.3   *(Continued)*

DM task	Article reference	Year	Machine learning techniques	Performance measure
	[150]	2016	Bayesian classifier	*Not mentioned*
	[151]	2016	BPNN	Accuracy
	[152]	2017	RF	Accuracy, execution time, speedup
	[153]	2017	LogR, SVM	Accuracy
	[154]	2017	RF	Accuracy, execution time
	[155]	2018	DT	*Not mentioned*
	[156]	2018	Tree-based index	*Not mentioned*
	[190]	2013	LogR	Accuracy, execution time
	[191]	2014	SVM	Accuracy, execution time
	[192]	2014	LogR, linear SVM	Execution time
	[193]	2014	k-NN	Execution time
	[194]	2015	Kohonen neuron	Average error rate, standard deviation (SD)
	[195]	2015	NB+entropy minimization discretizer	Accuracy, execution time
	[196]	2015	SMOTE+RF	Sensitivity, specificity, precision, G-mean, F-measure, execution time
	[197]	2015	Least squares support vector machines	Accuracy
	[198]	2016	Associative classifier	Accuracy
	[199]	2016	Naïve Bayes (NB), DT, RF	Accuracy, sensitivity, specificity
	[200]	2016	k-NN	Accuracy
	[201]	2016	LogR, NB	Accuracy, execution time
	[202]	2016	SVM	Accuracy
	[203]	2016	AANN+PSO	MSE, classification rate
	[205]	2016	k-NN	Mean relative error (MRE)
	[206]	2019	SVM	Accuracy, execution time
Clustering	*Hadoop-based articles*			
	[207]	2014	Centroid-based clustering	*Not mentioned*
	[209]	2014	K-Means++	*Not mentioned*
	[210]	2014	K-Means	Davies–Bouldin index
	[211]	2015	Fuzzy c-means	Cluster purity
	[212]	2015	Ant colony clustering	F-measure, Davies–Bouldin index, Dunn index, speed-up, scale-up, sizeup
	[214]	2016	Semantic-driven subtractive clustering	Execution time
	[215]	2016	Similarity join tree	*Not mentioned*
	[217]	2016	Density peaks clustering	*Not mentioned*
	[219]	2016	Top-k similarity using cosine similarity	Accuracy, execution time
	[221]	2016	k-NN	*Not mentioned*
	[225]	2016	K-Means	*Not mentioned*
	[226]	2016	K-Means	Speedup

(Continues)

Table 7.3   (Continued)

DM task	Article reference	Year	Machine learning techniques	Performance measure
	[227]	2016	Artificial bee colony (ABC)	F-measure, execution time, speedup
	[228]	2016	K-Means	*Not mentioned*
	[230]	2009	K-Means	Speedup, scale-up, sizeup
	[231]	2011	K-Center, K-median	Execution time
	[232]	2013	Text document clustering	Purity, Rand index, F-measure
	[233]	2013	K-Means	Execution time
	[234]	2013	K-Means	Accuracy, execution time
	[235]	2013	K-Means	Execution time
	[236]	2014	K-Means	Accuracy, execution time
	[237]	2014	Fuzzy K-means	*Not mentioned*
	[238]	2014	K-Means	Execution time
	[240]	2014	Fuzzy K-means	Accuracy, execution time
	[241]	2014	K-Means	*Not mentioned*
	[242]	2014	K-Medoids	Silhouette coefficient
	[243]	2014	K-Means	Execution time
	[244]	2014	K-Means	Silhouette coefficient
	[246]	2014	Differential evolution clustering	Purity
	[247]	2014	Glowworm swarm optimization (GSO) clustering	Purity, speedup, scale-up
	[250]	2014	K-Medoids	Speedup
	[251]	2015	Clustering based on similarity of nodes	*Not mentioned*
	[252]	2015	K-Means	Silhouette coefficient
	[254]	2015	Fuzzy c-means	Precision, recall, execution time
	[255]	2015	K-Means	Execution time
	[256]	2015	K-Means	Accuracy, execution time
	[257]	2015	K-Means	Accuracy
	[258]	2015	Dynamic neighborhood selection (DNS)	Execution time, speedup
	[259]	2015	K-Means	Connectivity, Dunn index and Silhouette measure, execution time
	[262]	2015	Evolutionary clustering with fireworks and cuckoo-search-based evolutionary algorithms	Execution time
	[263]	2015	K-Means	Execution time
	[264]	2015	Fuzzy K-means	Execution time
	[265]	2015	K-Means	Execution time
	[266]	2015	K-Modes	Execution time
	[267]	2015	Range-based clustering	Execution time
	[268]	2015	PSO	Precision, recall, F-measure, execution time
	[269]	2015	Density-based, grid-based clustering	Execution time

(Continues)

Table 7.3 (*Continued*)

DM task	Article reference	Year	Machine learning techniques	Performance measure
	[271]	2015	K-Means	Execution time
	[272]	2015	K-Means	Execution time
	[273]	2015	K-Means	Execution time
	[274]	2016	K-Means	Execution time
	[275]	2016	K-Means	Precision, recall, F-measure, execution time
	[276]	2016	K-Means	Execution time, speedup
	[277]	2016	Fuzzy c-means	Execution time
	Spark-based articles			
	[229]	2018	K-Means	*Not mentioned*
	[278]	2014	SOM clustering	Accuracy, Rand index, execution time
	[279]	2015	K-Means	Execution time, accuracy
	[280]	2015	PSO	Processing time, acceleration, intra-cluster distance, and inter-cluster distance
	[281]	2015	K-Means	Execution time
	[282]	2015	Fuzzy c-means	Execution time
	[283]	2016	DenPeak	Execution time
	[284]	2016	DBSCAN	Execution time
	[285]	2016	Fuzzy c-means	Execution time
	[286]	2016	K-Means	Execution time
	[287]	2016	Fuzzy c-means	F-measure, adjusted Rand index, execution time
	[288]	2016	Density-grid clustering	*Not mentioned*
Outlier Detection/ Intrusion Detection System	*Hadoop-based articles*			
	[289]	2014	Cell-based outlier detection	Execution time
	[290]	2014	Artificial immune systems	FPR, accuracy, recall
	[291]	2016	Binary bat algorithm	Speedup, scale-up, sizeup, detection rate, FPR
	[292]	2016	Rough set+genetic algorithm (GA)	Execution time
	[293]	2016	NB, SVM, conjunctive rule, RF tree, REPTree, and J48 (C4.5 Java implementation)	Accuracy
	[296]	2013	GA+k-NN	Accuracy, execution time
	[297]	2013	PSO clustering	TPR, speedup, execution time
	[298]	2014	ELM	TPR, FPR, speedup, sizeup
	[299]	2016	NB+k-NN	Accuracy, sensitivity, specificity, false-positive rate, precision, $F1$ measure
	Spark-based articles			
	[295]	2018	Random forest	*Not mentioned*
	[300]	2016	LogR, SVM, RF, gradient boosted DT, and NB	Accuracy, sensitivity, specificity, execution time
	[301]	2016	K-Means	*Not mentioned*

(Continues)

Table 7.3   (*Continued*)

DM task	Article reference	Year	Machine learning techniques	Performance measure
Recommendation system	*Hadoop-based articles*			
	[302]	2018	SVD	RMSE, target recall
	[304]	2012	Top-*n* recommendation	Prediction quality, speedup
	[307]	2014	Item-based and user-based collaborative filtering (CF)	Execution time, speedup
	[308]	2014	User-based CF	Accuracy, execution time
	[309]	2015	Stochastic gradient descent	Accuracy using RMSE
	[310]	2015	Item-based CF	RMSE, MAE
	[311]	2015	User-based CF	Execution time
	[312]	2016	Cosine similarity, *k*-NN, CF	MAE
	Spark-based articles			
	[314]	2016	User-based CF	RMSE, execution time
Others	*Hadoop-based articles*			
	[315]	2012	Rough set approximations	Speedup, scale-up, sizeup
	[316]	2013	Privacy preserving feature selection	*Not mentioned*
	[317]	2014	Feature reduction	*Not mentioned*
	[318]	2015	Bayesian Network	Execution time, speedup
	[319]	2015	Incremental MapReduce	Execution time
	[322]	2016	Bayesian network	Recall, execution time
	[323]	2016	PSO	Execution time
	[329]	2011	SGD	*Not mentioned*
	[330]	2012	Latent Dirichlet allocation	Execution time, speedup
	[331]	2013	Selection algorithms	Execution time
	[332]	2014	Genetic algorithm and simulated annealing	Execution time
	[334]	2014	Positive approximation	*Not mentioned*
	[335]	2015	GA+*k*-NN	Accuracy=(TP+TN)/ (TP+FP+TN+FN)
	[336]	2015	*K*-Means+SVM	Sensitivity, specificity, accuracy
	[337]	2015	GA	Execution time
	[338]	2016	Steiner tree	*Not mentioned*
	Spark-based articles			
	[324]	2016	GA	Execution time, speedup
	[327]	2016	Feature selection using information gain, RELIEF-F, correlation-based feature selection (CFS), support vector machine recursive feature elimination (SVM-RFE)	*Not mentioned*
	[328]	2016	Minimum-redundancy– maximum-relevance (mRMR)	*Not mentioned*
	[339]	2016	Artificial bee colony	*Not mentioned*
	[340]	2016	*n*-Gram feature selection	Information gain

Table 7.4 Distribution of papers: dataset wise

Type of dataset	Hadoop MapReduce papers		Spark papers		Total count
	References	Count	References	Count	
Real-world/ benchmark datasets	[20,30,34,37,38,39,58,60,61,66,67,70,73,74,77,78,80,81,85,96, 97,105,106,108,109,114,115,116,117,119,121,122,125,127, 128,130,132,133,134, 140–142, 145, 146, 159–162, 166, 169–171, 173, 175–177, 179, 181–183, 185–189,207,211, 212,214,215,217,219,225,232,234,240,243,246,250,251, 254–258,262–267,271,272, 274–277,290–293,296–299,302, 304,307,309–312,318,319,322,329,330,332,334–337]	122	[43,52,92,94,95,100,101,103, 104,110,113,149–156,191, 192,194–197,199–202,203, 205,206,229,259,278,279, 281,282,285–287,295,300, 301,314,327,328,339,340]	49	171
Synthetic dataset	[57,59,63,68,72,88–90,129,174,178,227,228,230,231,238,241, 244,269,289,331]	21	[91,283,284]	3	24
Both real and synthetic dataset	[21,23,28,29,41,42,55,64,71,76,82,86,87,107,136–138,157,163, 168,172,209,210,221,226,237,247,252,273,308,315–317]	33	[49,93,190,193,198,288,324]	7	40
Not mentioned	[75,99,165,167,180,233,235,236,242,268,323,338]	12	[44,280]	2	14

- *Soft computing hybrid models and their applications were explored, but not as much as the field deserves.*
- *Evolutionary algorithms, in their stand-alone mode, were not explored for solving the DM tasks. These are again some open areas for future research.*
- *A few papers were found on fuzzy logic-based techniques covering fuzzy classification and fuzzy clustering. Their combination with optimization techniques can be an area to explore further.*
- *SOM is scantily employed, thus rendering an open space for exploration.*
- *Deep learning is now a growing research area that can handle complex non-linear data with high dimensionality. It can be applied to solve DM tasks. Deep learning architectures are computationally expensive due to the presence of multiple hidden layers, where there is a scope or parallelization. They can be explored with in-memory computing utilizing Apache Spark.*
- *The relevance vector machine, independent component analysis, SVD, latent semantic indexing, one-class SVM (OC-SVM), CARM techniques are not explored at all, thus, resulting into an open space for exploration.*
- *There are hardly any research papers on mining of spatial and temporal data, as they pose numerous challenges due to their high dimensionality which has to be explored with respect to different DM tasks.*
- *It is also found that a few articles were published on GPGPU-based vertical parallelization using MapReduce and Apache Spark. Therefore, this provides a fertile ground for budding and future researchers.*
- *To the best of our knowledge, we came across only a few research papers hybridizing horizontal parallelization with vertical parallelization, i.e., a cluster of GPGPU-based machines. Therefore, the cluster of GPGPU is an area to explore.*
- *Surprisingly, big data visualization using MapReduce or Apache Spark is conspicuously rarely researched topic.*
- *In our current review work, we could include only a few articles based on large-scale optimization algorithms implemented using Hadoop MapReduce or Apache Spark frameworks. Hence, there is a vast scope for the researchers to explore this exciting area.*
- *The absence of papers in banking, insurance, and finance sectors is conspicuous as far as the application domain of BDA is concerned.*

References

[1] What Is Big Data? – Gartner IT Glossary – Big Data [Internet]. [cited 2017 Jul 24]. Available from: https://research.gartner.com/definitionwhatisbig-data?resId=3002918%7B%5C#%7DsrcId=18163325102.

[2] Manyika J, Chui M, Brown B, *et al.* A. Big data: The next frontier for innovation, competition, and productivity. Mobile Networks and Applications. 2011;19(2):171–209.

[3]   Singh D and Reddy CK. A survey on platforms for big data analytics. Journal of Big Data. 2014;2(1):8.

[4]   Saecker M and Markl V. Big Data Analytics on Modern Hardware Architectures: A Technology Survey. In: Marie-Aude A and Esteban Z, editors. Business Intelligence. Brussels, Belgium: Springer, Berlin, Heidelberg; 2012. p. 125–49. (Lecture Notes in Business Information Processing; vol. 138).

[5]   Chen M, Mao S, and Liu Y. Big data: A survey. Mobile Networks and Applications. 2014;19(2):171–209.

[6]   Liu X, Iftikhar N, and Xie X. Survey of real-time processing systems for big data. In: Proceedings of the 18th International Database Engineering & Applications Symposium on – IDEAS '14. Porto, Portugal: ACM Press; 2014. p. 356–61.

[7]   Sharma S, Tim US, Wong J, Gadia S, and Sharma S. A brief review on leading big data models. Data Science Journal. 2014;13(0):138–57.

[8]   Al-Jarrah OY, Yoo PD, Muhaidat S, Karagiannidis GK, and Taha K. Efficient machine learning for big data: A review. Big Data Research. 2015;2(3):87–93.

[9]   Sagiroglu S and Sinanc D. Big data: A review. In: 2013 International Conference on Collaboration Technologies and Systems (CTS). IEEE; 2013. p. 42–7.

[10]   Aruna Sri PSG and Anusha M. Big data-survey. Indonesian Journal of Electrical Engineering and Informatics (IJEEI). 2016;4(1):74–80.

[11]   Khan N, Yaqoob I, Hashem IAT, *et al.* Big data: Survey, technologies, opportunities, and challenges. The Scientific World Journal. 2014;2014:18.

[12]   Ekbia H, Mattioli M, Kouper I, *et al.* Big data, bigger dilemmas: A critical review. Journal of the Association for Information Science and Technology. 2015;66(8):1523–45.

[13]   Philip Chen CL and Zhang C-Y. Data-intensive applications, challenges, techniques and technologies: A survey on Big Data. Information Sciences. 2014;275:314–47.

[14]   Lee K-H, Lee Y-J, Choi H, Chung YD, and Moon B. Parallel data processing with MapReduce: A survey. ACM SIGMOD Record. 2012;40(4):11–20.

[15]   Ward JS and Barker A. Undefined By Data: A Survey of Big Data Definitions. arXiv preprint arXiv:13095821. 2013.

[16]   Shirkhorshidi AS, Aghabozorgi S, Wah TY, and Herawan T. Big Data Clustering: A Review. In: Beniamino M, Sanjay M, Ana MACR, *et al.*, editors. Computational Science and Its Applications – ICCSA 2014. Guimarães, Portugal: Springer, Cham; 2014. p. 707–20. (Lecture Notes in Computer Science; vol. 8583).

[17]   Fahad A, Alshatri N, Tari Z, *et al.* A survey of clustering algorithms for big data: Taxonomy and empirical analysis. IEEE Transactions on Emerging Topics in Computing. 2014;2(3):267–79.

[18]   Gorodov EY and Gubarev VV. Analytical review of data visualization methods in application to big data. Journal of Electrical and Computer Engineering. 2013;2013:1–7.

[19]   Zhang H, Chen G, Ooi BC, Tan K-L, and Zhang M. In-memory big data management and processing: A survey. IEEE Transactions on Knowledge and Data Engineering. 2015;27(7):1920–48.

[20]   Karim MR, Hossain MA, Rashid MM, Jeong B-S, and Choi H-J. A MapReduce framework for mining maximal contiguous frequent patterns in large DNA sequence datasets. IETE Technical Review. 2012;29(2):162–8.

[21]   Karim MR, Ahmed CF, Jeong B-S, and Choi H-J. An efficient distributed programming model for mining useful patterns in big datasets. IETE Technical Review. 2013;30(1):53–63.

[22]   Dua D, Graff C. {UCI} Machine Learning Repository. 2017.

[23]   Bhuiyan MA and Al Hasan M. An iterative MapReduce based frequent subgraph mining algorithm. IEEE Transactions on Knowledge and Data Engineering. 2015;27(3):608–20.

[24]   UCSB Computer Science [Internet]. [cited 2017 Jul 24]. Available from: http://www.cs.ucsb.edu/xyan/dataset.htm.

[25]   The PubChem Project [Internet]. [cited 2017 Jul 24]. Available from: https://pubchem.ncbi.nlm.nih.gov/.

[26]   Universität Trier: Informatikwissenschaften [Internet]. [cited 2017 Jul 24]. Available from: http://www.informatik.uni-trier.de/~ley/db/.

[27]   Cheng J, Ke Y, Ng W, and Lu A. FG-index: Towards verification-free query processing on graph databases. In: Proceedings of the 2007 ACM SIGMOD International Conference on Management of Data – SIGMOD '07. Beijing, China: ACM Press; 2007. p. 857–72.

[28]   Hill S, Srichandan B, and Sunderraman R. An iterative MapReduce approach to frequent subgraph mining in biological datasets. In: Proceedings of the ACM Conference on Bioinformatics, Computational Biology and Biomedicine – BCB '12. New York, NY, USA: ACM Press; 2012. p. 661.

[29]   Xun Y, Zhang J, and Qin X. FiDoop: Parallel mining of frequent itemsets using MapReduce. IEEE Transactions on Systems, Man, and Cybernetics: Systems. 2016;46(3):313–25.

[30]   Salah S, Akbarinia R, and Masseglia F. A highly scalable parallel algorithm for maximally informative k-itemset mining. Knowledge and Information Systems. 2017;50(1):1–26.

[31]   SNAP: Web Data: Amazon Reviews [Internet]. [cited 2017 Jul 23]. Available from: http://snap.stanford.edu/data/web-Amazon-links.html.

[32]   English Wikipedia Articles [Internet]. [cited 2017 Jul 23]. Available from: https://dumps.wikimedia.org/enwiki/latest/.

[33]   The ClueWeb09 Dataset [Internet]. [cited 2017 Jul 23]. Available from: http://www.lemurproject.org/clueweb09.php/.

[34]   Breier J and Branišová J. A dynamic rule creation based anomaly detection method for identifying security breaches in log records. Wireless Personal Communications. 2017;94(3):497–511.

[35]   MIT Lincoln Laboratory: DARPA Intrusion Detection Evaluation [Internet]. [cited 2017 Jul 23]. Available from: http://www.ll.mit.edu/ideval/data/.

[36]   Snort – Network Intrusion Detection & Prevention System [Internet]. [cited 2017 Jul 23]. Available from: https://www.snort.org/.

[37]   Yan X, Zhang J, Xun Y, and Qin X. A parallel algorithm for mining constrained frequent patterns using MapReduce. Soft Computing. 2017;21(9):2237–49.

[38]   Leroy V, Kirchgessner M, Termier A, and Amer-Yahia S. TopPI: An efficient algorithm for item-centric mining. Information Systems. 2017;64:104–18.

[39]   Sohrabi MK and Taheri N. A haoop-based parallel mining of frequent itemsets using N-Lists. Journal of the Chinese Institute of Engineers. 2018;41(3):229–38.

[40]   Frequent Itemset Mining Dataset Repository [Internet]. [cited 2017 Jul 22]. Available from: http://fimi.ua.ac.be/data.

[41]   Liu Z, Hu L, Wu C, Ding Y, Wen Q, and Zhao J. A novel process-based association rule approach through maximal frequent itemsets for big data processing. Future Generation Computer Systems. 2018;81:414–24.

[42]   Singh S, Garg R, and Mishra PK. Performance optimization of MapReduce-based Apriori algorithm on Hadoop cluster. Computers & Electrical Engineering. 2018;67:348–64.

[43]   Zhang F, Liu M, Gui F, Shen W, Shami A, and Ma Y. A distributed frequent itemset mining algorithm using spark for big data analytics. Cluster Computing. 2015;18(4):1493–501.

[44]   Chen Y and An A. Approximate parallel high utility itemset mining. Big Data Research. 2016;6:26–42.

[45]   SPMF: A Java Open-Source Data Mining Library [Internet]. [cited 2017 Jul 24]. Available from: http://www.philippe-fournier-viger.com/spmf/index.php?link=datasets.php.

[46]   Kwak H, Lee C, Park H, and Moon S. What is Twitter, a social network or a news media? In: Proceedings of the 19th International Conference on World Wide Web – WWW '10. New York, NY, USA: ACM Press; 2010. p. 591.

[47]   Grocery Shopping Datasets – RecSysWiki [Internet]. [cited 2017 Jul 24]. Available from: http://recsyswiki.com/wiki/Grocery_shopping_datasets.

[48]   Agrawal R and Srikant R. Fast algorithms for mining association rules. In: Proc 20th Int Conf Very Large Data Bases, VLDB. 1994. p. 487–99.

[49]   Karim MR, Cochez M, Beyan OD, Ahmed CF, and Decker S. Mining maximal frequent patterns in transactional databases and dynamic data streams: A spark-based approach. Information Sciences. 2018;432:278–300.

[50]   IBM Quest Synthetic Data Generator [Internet]. [cited 2018 Aug 27]. Available from: https://sourceforge.net/projects/ibmquestdatagen/.

[51]   Brijs T, Swinnen G, Vanhoof K, and Wets G. Using association rules for product assortment decisions. In: Proceedings of the Fifth ACM SIGKDD International Conference on Knowledge Discovery and Data Mining – KDD '99. New York, NY, USA: ACM Press; 1999. p. 254–60.

[52]   Martín D, Martínez-Ballesteros M, García-Gil D, Alcalá-Fdez J, Herrera F, and Riquelme-Santos JC. MRQAR: A generic MapReduce framework to

discover quantitative association rules in big data problems. Knowledge-Based Systems. 2018;153:176–92.

[53]   LIBSVM Data: Classification, Regression, and Multi-label [Internet]. [cited 2017 Jul 24]. Available from: https://www.csie.ntu.edu.tw/~cjlin/libsvm-tools/datasets/.

[54]   GraphGen – A Synthetic Graph Generator [Internet]. [cited 2017 Jul 24]. Available from: http://www.cse.ust.hk/graphgen/.

[55]   Farzanyar Z and Cercone N. Efficient mining of frequent itemsets in social network data based on MapReduce framework. In: Proceedings of the 2013 IEEE/ACM International Conference on Advances in Social Networks Analysis and Mining – ASONAM '13. Niagara, Ontario, Canada: ACM Press; 2013. p. 1183–8.

[56]   Zheng Z, Kohavi R, and Mason L. Real world performance of association rule algorithms. In: Proceedings of the Seventh ACM SIGKDD International Conference on Knowledge Discovery and Data Mining – KDD '01. San Francisco, CA: ACM Press; 2001. p. 401–6.

[57]   Farzanyar Z and Cercone N. Accelerating frequent itemsets mining on the cloud: A MapReduce-based approach. In: 2013 IEEE 13th International Conference on Data Mining Workshops. IEEE; 2013. p. 592–8.

[58]   Mao W and Guo W. An improved association rules mining algorithm based on power set and Hadoop. In: 2013 International Conference on Information Science and Cloud Computing Companion. IEEE; 2013. p. 236–41.

[59]   Natarajan S and Sehar S. A novel algorithm for distributed data mining in HDFS. In: Advanced Computing (ICoAC), 2013 Fifth International Conference on. IEEE; 2013. p. 93–9.

[60]   Rong Z, Xia D, and Zhang Z. Complex statistical analysis of big data: Implementation and application of Apriori and FP-Growth algorithm based on MapReduce. In: 2013 IEEE 4th International Conference on Software Engineering and Service Science. Beijing, China: IEEE; 2013. p. 968–72.

[61]   Moens S, Aksehirli E, and Goethals B. Frequent itemset mining for big data. In: 2013 IEEE International Conference on Big Data. Silicon Valley, CA, USA: IEEE; 2013. p. 111–8.

[62]   De Bie T. An information theoretic framework for data mining. In: Proceedings of the 17th ACM SIGKDD International Conference on Knowledge Discovery and Data Mining – KDD '11. San Diego, CA, USA: ACM Press; 2011. p. 564–72.

[63]   Chen H, Lin TY, Zhang Z, and Zhong J. Parallel mining frequent patterns over big transactional data in extended MapReduce. In: 2013 IEEE International Conference on Granular Computing (GrC). Beijing, China: IEEE; 2013. p. 43–8.

[64]   Leung CK-S and Jiang F. A data science solution for mining interesting patterns from uncertain big data. In: 2014 IEEE Fourth International Conference on Big Data and Cloud Computing. IEEE; 2014. p. 235–42.

[65]   Leung CK-S, Mateo MAF, and Brajczuk DA. A Tree-Based Approach for Frequent Pattern Mining From Uncertain Data. In: Washio T, Suzuki E, Ting

KM, and Inokuchi A, editors. Advances in Knowledge Discovery and Data Mining. Berlin, Heidelberg: Springer, Berlin, Heidelberg; 2008. p. 653–61. (Lecture Notes in Computer Science; vol. 5012).

[66] Yu R-M, Lee M-G, Huang Y-S, and Chen S-X. An efficient frequent patterns mining algorithm based on MapReduce framework. In: International Conference on Software Intelligence Technologies and Applications & International Conference on Frontiers of Internet of Things 2014. Hsinchu, Taiwan: Institution of Engineering and Technology; 2014. p. 1–5.

[67] Yu Q, Huo H, Chen X, Guo H, Vitter JS, and Huan J. An efficient motif finding algorithm for large DNA data sets. In: 2014 IEEE International Conference on Bioinformatics and Biomedicine (BIBM). IEEE; 2014. p. 397–402.

[68] Zhou X and Huang Y. An improved parallel association rules algorithm based on MapReduce framework for big data. In: 2014 11th International Conference on Fuzzy Systems and Knowledge Discovery (FSKD). IEEE; 2014. p. 284–8.

[69] ARtool Project [Internet]. [cited 2017 Jul 24]. Available from: http://www. cs.umb.edu/~laur/ARtool/index.html.

[70] Fumarola F and Malerba D. A parallel algorithm for approximate frequent itemset mining using MapReduce. In: 2014 International Conference on High Performance Computing & Simulation (HPCS). Bologna, Italy: IEEE; 2014. p. 335–42.

[71] Bhuiyan MA and Al Hasan M. FSM-H: Frequent subgraph mining algorithm in Hadoop. In: 2014 IEEE International Congress on Big Data. Anchorage, AK, USA: IEEE; 2014. p. 9–16.

[72] Liu S-H, Liu S-J, Chen S-X, and Yu K-M. IOMRA – A high efficiency frequent itemset mining algorithm based on the MapReduce computation model. In: 2014 IEEE 17th International Conference on Computational Science and Engineering. Chengdu, China: IEEE; 2014. p. 1290–5.

[73] Cao H, Phinney M, Petersohn D, Merideth B, and Shyu C-R. MRSMRS: Mining repetitive sequences in a MapReduce setting. In: 2014 IEEE International Conference on Bioinformatics and Biomedicine (BIBM). Belfast, UK: IEEE; 2014. p. 463–70.

[74] Liu C and Li Y. Non-iteration parallel algorithm for frequent pattern discovery. In: 2014 13th International Symposium on Distributed Computing and Applications to Business, Engineering and Science. Xian Ning, China: IEEE; 2014. p. 127–32.

[75] Chang H-Y, Tzang Y-J, Lin J-C, Hong Z-H, Chi T-Y, and Huang C-Y. A hybrid algorithm for frequent pattern mining using MapReduce framework. In: 2015 First International Conference on Computational Intelligence Theory, Systems and Applications (CCITSA). IEEE; 2015. p. 19–22.

[76] Sun D, Lee VC, Burstein F, and Haghighi PD. An efficient vertical-Apriori MapReduce algorithm for frequent item-set mining. In: 2015 IEEE 10th Conference on Industrial Electronics and Applications (ICIEA). IEEE; 2015. p. 108–12.

[77]   Ferrucci F, Salza P, Kechadi M-T, and Sarro F. A parallel genetic algorithms framework based on Hadoop MapReduce. In: Proceedings of the 30th Annual ACM Symposium on Applied Computing – SAC '15. New York, NY, USA: ACM Press; 2015. p. 1664–7.

[78]   Jiang F, Kawagoe K, and Leung CK. Big social network mining for "following" patterns. In: Proceedings of the Eighth International C* Conference on Computer Science & Software Engineering – C3S2E '15. Yokohama, Japan: ACM Press; 2015. p. 28–37.

[79]   Stanford Large Network Dataset Collection [Internet]. [cited 2017 Jul 24]. Available from: http://snap.stanford.edu/data/.

[80]   Salah S, Akbarinia R, and Masseglia F. Fast parallel mining of maximally informative k-itemsets in big data. In: 2015 IEEE International Conference on Data Mining. Atlantic City, NJ, USA: IEEE; 2015. p. 359–68.

[81]   Liu J, Wu Y, Xu S, Zhou Q, and Xu M. MapReduce-based efficient algorithm for finding large patterns. In: 2015 Seventh International Conference on Advanced Computational Intelligence (ICACI). Wuyi, China: IEEE; 2015. p. 164–9.

[82]   Apiletti D, Baralis E, Cerquitelli T, Garza P, Michiardi P, and Pulvirenti F. PaMPa-HD: A parallel MapReduce-based frequent pattern miner for high-dimensional data. In: 2015 IEEE International Conference on Data Mining Workshop (ICDMW). Atlantic City, NJ, USA: IEEE; 2015. p. 839–46.

[83]   Kent Ridge Breast Cancer Dataset [Internet]. [cited 2017 Jul 24]. Available from: http://mldata.org/repository/data/viewslug/breastcancer-kent-ridge-2.

[84]   Index of /PaMPa-HD [Internet]. [cited 2017 Jul 24]. Available from: http://dbdmg.polito.it/PaMPa-HD/.

[85]   Baralis E, Cagliero L, Garza P, and Grimaudo L. PaWI: Parallel weighted itemset mining by means of MapReduce. In: 2015 IEEE International Congress on Big Data. New York, NY, USA: IEEE; 2015. p. 25–32.

[86]   Leung CK, Jiang F, Zhang H, and Pazdor AGM. A data science model for big data analytics of frequent patterns. In: 2016 IEEE 14th Intl Conf on Dependable, Autonomic and Secure Computing, 14th Intl Conf on Pervasive Intelligence and Computing, 2nd Intl Conf on Big Data Intelligence and Computing and Cyber Science and Technology Congress (DASC/PiCom/DataCom/CyberSciTech). IEEE; 2016. p. 866–73.

[87]   Gonen Y and Gudes E. An improved MapReduce algorithm for mining closed frequent itemsets. In: 2016 IEEE International Conference on Software Science, Technology and Engineering (SWSTE). IEEE; 2016. p. 77–83.

[88]   Thakare S, Rathi S, and Sedamkar RR. An Improved PrePost algorithm for frequent pattern mining with Hadoop on cloud. Procedia Computer Science. 2016;79:207–14.

[89]   Chang H-Y, Hong Z-H, Lin T-L, Chang W-K, and Lin Y-Y. IPARBC: An improved parallel association rule based on MapReduce framework. In: 2016 International Conference on Networking and Network Applications (NaNA). Hakodate, Japan: IEEE; 2016. p. 370–4.

[90] Sheshikala M, Rao DR, and Prakash RV. Parallel approach for finding co-location pattern – A MapReduce framework. Procedia Computer Science. 2016;89:341–8.

[91] Gui F, Ma Y, Zhang F, *et al.* A distributed frequent itemset mining algorithm based on Spark. In: 2015 IEEE 19th International Conference on Computer Supported Cooperative Work in Design (CSCWD). IEEE; 2015. p. 271–5.

[92] Deng L and Lou Y. Improvement and research of FP-Growth algorithm based on distributed Spark. In: 2015 International Conference on Cloud Computing and Big Data (CCBD). Shanghai, China: IEEE; 2015. p. 105–8.

[93] Rathee S, Kaul M, and Kashyap A. R-Apriori: An efficient Apriori based algorithm on Spark. In: Proceedings of the 8th Workshop on PhD Workshop in Information and Knowledge Management. Melbourne, Australia: ACM; 2015. p. 27–34.

[94] Utama PA and Distiawan B. Spark-gram: Mining frequent N-grams using parallel processing in Spark. In: 2015 International Conference on Advanced Computer Science and Information Systems (ICACSIS). Depok, Indonesia: IEEE; 2015. p. 129–36.

[95] Joy R and Sherly KK. Parallel frequent itemset mining with spark RDD framework for disease prediction. In: 2016 International Conference on Circuit, Power and Computing Technologies (ICCPCT). Nagercoil, India: IEEE; 2016. p. 1–5.

[96] He Q, Shang T, Zhuang F, and Shi Z. Parallel extreme learning machine for regression based on MapReduce. Neurocomputing. 2013;102:52–8.

[97] Luts J. Real-time semiparametric regression for distributed data sets. IEEE Transactions on Knowledge and Data Engineering. 2015;27(2):545–57.

[98] Real-time Semiparametric Regression [Internet]. [cited 2017 Jul 24]. Available from: http://realtime-semiparametric-regression.net/.

[99] Naimur Rahman M, Esmailpour A, and Zhao J. Machine learning with big data an efficient electricity generation forecasting system. Big Data Research. 2016;5:9–15.

[100] Chen J, Li K, Tang Z, and Bilal K. A parallel patient treatment time prediction algorithm and its applications in hospital queuing-recommendation in a big data environment. IEEE Access. 2016;4:1767–83.

[101] Rodríguez-Fdez I, Mucientes M, and Bugarín A. S-FRULER: Scalable fuzzy rule learning through evolution for regression. Knowledge-Based Systems. 2016;110:255–66.

[102] Alcalá-Fdez J, Fernández A, Luengo J, *et al.* KEEL data-mining software tool: Data set repository, integration of algorithms and experimental analysis framework. Journal of Multiple-Valued Logic & Soft Computing. 2011;17:255–87.

[103] Galicia A, Torres JF, Martínez-Álvarez F, and Troncoso A. A novel spark-based multi-step forecasting algorithm for big data time series. Information Sciences. 2018.

[104] Talavera-Llames R, Pérez-Chacón R, Troncoso A, and Martínez-Álvarez F. Big data time series forecasting based on nearest neighbours distributed computing with Spark. Knowledge-Based Systems. 2018.

[105] Yin W, Simmhan Y, and Prasanna VK. Scalable regression tree learning on Hadoop using OpenPlanet. In: Proceedings of Third International Workshop on MapReduce and Its Applications Date – MapReduce '12. Delft, The Netherlands: ACM Press; 2012. p. 57.

[106] Tejasviram V, Solanki H, Ravi V, and Kamaruddin S. Auto associative extreme learning machine based non-linear principal component regression for big data applications. In: 2015 Tenth International Conference on Digital Information Management (ICDIM). Jeju, South Korea: IEEE; 2015. p. 223–8.

[107] Rehab MA and Boufares F. Scalable massively parallel learning of multiple linear regression algorithm with MapReduce. In: 2015 IEEE Trustcom/ BigDataSE/ISPA. Helsinki, Finland: IEEE; 2015. p. 41–7.

[108] Chavda PK and Dhobi JS. Web users browsing behavior prediction by implementing support vector machines in MapReduce using cloud based Hadoop. In: 2015 5th Nirma University International Conference on Engineering (NUiCONE). Ahmedabad, India: IEEE; 2015. p. 1–6.

[109] Xu G, Liu M, Li F, Zhang F, and Shen W. User behavior prediction model for smart home using parallelized neural network algorithm. In: 2016 IEEE 20th International Conference on Computer Supported Cooperative Work in Design (CSCWD). Nanchang, China: IEEE; 2016. p. 221–6.

[110] Vluymans S, Asfoor H, Saeys Y, *et al.* Distributed fuzzy rough prototype selection for Big Data regression. In: 2015 Annual Conference of the North American Fuzzy Information Processing Society (NAFIPS) held jointly with 2015 5th World Conference on Soft Computing (WConSC). Redmond, WA, USA: IEEE; 2015. p. 1–6.

[111] HCUP-US SID Overview [Internet]. [cited 2017 Jul 24]. Available from: https://www.hcup-us.ahrq.gov/sidoverview.jsp.

[112] Medical Expenditure Panel Survey [Internet]. [cited 2017 Jul 24]. Available from: https://meps.ahrq.gov/mepsweb/.

[113] Oneto L, Fumeo E, Clerico G, *et al.* Delay Prediction System for Large-Scale Railway Networks Based on Big Data Analytics. In: Angelov P, Manolopoulos Y, Iliadis L, Roy A, and Vellasco M, editors. Advances in Big Data. Springer, Cham; 2017. p. 139–50. (Advances in Intelligent Systems and Computing; vol. 529).

[114] He Q, Du C, Wang Q, Zhuang F, and Shi Z. A parallel incremental extreme SVM classifier. Neurocomputing. 2011;74(16):2532–40.

[115] Janaki Meena M, Chandran KR, Karthik A, and Vijay Samuel A. An enhanced ACO algorithm to select features for text categorization and its parallelization. Expert Systems with Applications. 2012;39(5):5861–71.

[116] Caruana G, Li M, and Liu Y. An ontology enhanced parallel SVM for scalable spam filter training. Neurocomputing. 2013;108:45–57.

[117] You ZH, Yu JZ, Zhu L, Li S, and Wen ZK. A MapReduce based parallel SVM for large-scale predicting protein-protein interactions. Neurocomputing. 2014;145:37–43.

[118] Pan X-Y, Zhang Y-N, and Shen H-B. Large-scale prediction of human protein−protein interactions from amino acid sequence based on latent topic features. Journal of Proteome Research. 2010;9(10):4992–5001.

[119] Singh K, Guntuku SC, Thakur A, and Hota C. Big data analytics framework for peer-to-peer botnet detection using random forests. Information Sciences. 2014;278:488–97.

[120] CAIDA Data – Overview of Datasets, Monitors, and Reports [Internet]. [cited 2017 Jul 24]. Available from: http://www.caida.org/data/overview/.

[121] Chen T, Zhang X, Jin S, and Kim O. Efficient classification using parallel and scalable compressed model and its application on intrusion detection. Expert Systems with Applications. 2014;41(13):5972–83.

[122] Kumar M and Kumar Rath S. Classification of microarray using MapReduce based proximal support vector machine classifier. Knowledge-Based Systems. 2015;89:584–602.

[123] Golub TR, Slonim DK, Tamayo P, *et al.* Molecular classification of cancer: Class discovery and class prediction by gene expression monitoring. Science. 1999;286:5439.

[124] GEO DataSets – NCBI [Internet]. [cited 2017 Jul 24]. Available from: https://www.ncbi.nlm.nih.gov/gds/.

[125] Han DH, Zhang X, and Wang GR. Classifying uncertain and evolving data streams with distributed extreme learning machine. Journal of Computer Science and Technology. 2015;30(4):874–87.

[126] KDD Cup 1999 Data [Internet]. [cited 2017 Jul 24]. Available from: http://kdd.ics.uci.edu/databases/kddcup99/kddcup99.html.

[127] Barkhordari M and Niamanesh M. ScaDiPaSi: An effective scalable and distributable MapReduce-based method to find patient similarity on huge healthcare networks. Big Data Research. 2015;2(1):19–27.

[128] López V, del Río S, Benítez JM, and Herrera F. Cost-sensitive linguistic fuzzy rule based classification systems under the MapReduce framework for imbalanced big data. Fuzzy Sets and Systems. 2015;258:5–38.

[129] Xin J, Wang Z, Qu L, Yu G, and Kang Y. A-ELM*: Adaptive distributed extreme learning machine with MapReduce. Neurocomputing. 2016;174:368–74.

[130] Xia D, Li H, Wang B, Li Y, and Zhang Z. A MapReduce-based nearest neighbor approach for big-data-driven traffic flow prediction. IEEE Access. 2016;4:2920–34.

[131] Data Platform _ Large Data Trading Platform [Internet]. [cited 2017 Jul 24]. Available from: http://www.datatang.com/.

[132] Bechini A, Marcelloni F, and Segatori A. A MapReduce solution for associative classification of big data. Information Sciences. 2016;332:33–55.

[133]   Kumar M, Rath NK, and Rath SK. Analysis of microarray leukemia data using an efficient MapReduce-based K-nearest-neighbor classifier. Journal of Biomedical Informatics. 2016;60:395–409.

[134]   Chen J, Chen H, Wan X, and Zheng G. MR-ELM: A MapReduce-based framework for large-scale ELM training in big data era. Neural Computing and Applications. 2016;27(1):101–10.

[135]   FCUP [Internet]. [cited 2017 Jul 24]. Available from: http://www.dcc.fc.up.pt/*ltorgo/Regression/DataSets.html.

[136]   Huang S, Wang B, Qiu J, Yao J, Wang G, and Yu G. Parallel ensemble of online sequential extreme learning machine based on MapReduce. Neurocomputing. 2016;174:352–67.

[137]   Zhai J, Wang X, and Pang X. Voting-based instance selection from large data sets with MapReduce and random weight networks. Information Sciences. 2016;367–368:1066–77.

[138]   Huang S, Wang B, Chen Y, Wang G, and Yu G. An efficient parallel method for batched OS-ELM training using MapReduce. Memetic Computing. 2017;9(3):1–15.

[139]   Automatic Flower Classification Based on Large Data Sets [Internet]. [cited 2017 Jul 24]. Available from: http://www.datatang.com/data/13152.

[140]   Li Z, Lu W, Sun Z, and Xing W. A parallel feature selection method study for text classification. Neural Computing and Applications. 2017;28(S1):513–24.

[141]   Zhai J, Zhang S, and Wang C. The classification of imbalanced large data sets based on MapReduce and ensemble of ELM classifiers. International Journal of Machine Learning and Cybernetics. 2017;8(3):1009–17.

[142]   Jedrzejowicz J, Kostrzewski R, Neumann J, and Zakrzewska M. Imbalanced data classification using MapReduce and relief. Journal of Information and Telecommunication. 2018;2(2):217–30.

[143]   Sun Z, Song Q, Zhu X, Sun H, Xu B, and Zhou Y. A novel ensemble method for classifying imbalanced data. Pattern Recognition. 2015;48 (5):1623–37.

[144]   Zhang X, Song Q, Wang G, Zhang K, He L, and Jia X. A dissimilarity-based imbalance data classification algorithm. Applied Intelligence. 2015;42(3):544–65.

[145]   Elkano M, Galar M, Sanz J, and Bustince H. CHI-BD: A fuzzy rule-based classification system for Big Data classification problems. Fuzzy Sets and Systems. 2018;348:75–101.

[146]   Thakur RK and Deshpande MV. Kernel optimized-support vector machine and MapReduce framework for sentiment classification of train reviews. Sadhana – Academy Proceedings in Engineering Sciences. 2019;44(6).

[147]   Rajdhani Express Review, Reviews – 41 to 60 – MouthShut.com [Internet]. [cited 2019 Oct 22]. Available from: https://www.mouthshut.com/product-reviews/Rajdhani-Express-reviews-925004322-page-3.

[148]   Movie Review Data [Internet]. [cited 2019 Oct 22]. Available from: http://www.cs.cornell.edu/people/pabo/movie-review-data/.

[149]   Maillo J, Ramírez S, Triguero I, and Herrera F. kNN-IS: An Iterative Spark-based design of the k-Nearest Neighbors classifier for big data. Knowledge-Based Systems. 2017;117:3–15.

[150]   Arias J, Gamez JA, and Puerta JM. Learning distributed discrete Bayesian Network Classifiers under MapReduce with Apache Spark. Knowledge-Based Systems. 2017;117:16–26.

[151]   Liu Y, Xu L, and Li M. The parallelization of back propagation neural network in MapReduce and Spark. International Journal of Parallel Programming. 2017;45(4):760–79.

[152]   Chen J, Li K, Tang Z, *et al.* A parallel random forest algorithm for big data in a spark cloud computing environment. IEEE Transactions on Parallel and Distributed Systems. 2017;28(4):919–33.

[153]   Shi W, Zhu Y, Huang T, *et al.* An integrated data preprocessing framework based on Apache Spark for fault diagnosis of power grid equipment. Journal of Signal Processing Systems. 2017;86(2–3):221–36.

[154]   Lin W, Wu Z, Lin L, Wen A, and Li J. An ensemble random forest algorithm for insurance big data analysis. IEEE Access. 2017;5:16568–75.

[155]   Nair LR, Shetty SD, and Shetty SD. Applying spark based machine learning model on streaming big data for health status prediction. Computers & Electrical Engineering. 2018;65:393–9.

[156]   Gonzalez-Lopez J, Ventura S, and Cano A. Distributed nearest neighbor classification for large-scale multi-label data on spark. Future Generation Computer Systems. 2018;87:66–82.

[157]   Magnusson J and Kvernvik T. Subscriber classification within telecom networks utilizing big data technologies and machine learning. In: Proceedings of the 1st International Workshop on Big Data, Streams and Heterogeneous Source Mining Algorithms, Systems, Programming Models and Applications – BigMine '12. Beijing, China: ACM Press; 2012. p. 77–84.

[158]   Erdős P and Rényi A. On the evolution of random graphs. Publication of the Mathematical Institute of the Hungarian Academy of Sciences. 1960;5 (1):17–60.

[159]   Khuc VN, Shivade C, Ramnath R, and Ramanathan J. Towards building large-scale distributed systems for Twitter sentiment analysis. In: Proceedings of the 27th Annual ACM Symposium on Applied Computing – SAC '12. Trento, Italy: ACM Press; 2012. p. 459–64.

[160]   Wang D, Liu X, and Wang M. A DT-SVM strategy for stock futures prediction with big data. In: 2013 IEEE 16th International Conference on Computational Science and Engineering. IEEE; 2013. p. 1005–12.

[161]   Han J, Liu Y, and Sun X. A scalable random forest algorithm based on MapReduce. In: 2013 IEEE 4th International Conference on Software Engineering and Service Science. IEEE; 2013. p. 849–52.

[162]   Chen J, Zheng G, and Chen H. ELM-MapReduce: MapReduce accelerated extreme learning machine for big spatial data analysis. In: 2013 10th IEEE International Conference on Control and Automation (ICCA). Hangzhou, China: IEEE; 2013. p. 400–5.

[163]   Liu X, Wang X, Matwin S, and Japkowicz N. Meta-learning for large scale machine learning with MapReduce. In: 2013 IEEE International Conference on Big Data. Silicon Valley, CA, USA: IEEE; 2013. p. 105–10.

[164]   Hall M, Frank E, Holmes G, Pfahringer B, Reutemann P, and Witten IH. The WEKA data mining software. ACM SIGKDD Explorations Newsletter. 2009;11(1):10–8.

[165]   Lubell-Doughtie P and Sondag J. Practical distributed classification using the alternating direction method of multipliers algorithm. In: 2013 IEEE International Conference on Big Data. Silicon Valley; CA; USA: IEEE; 2013. p. 773–6.

[166]   Al-Madi N and Ludwig SA. Scaling Genetic Programming for data classification using MapReduce methodology. In: 2013 World Congress on Nature and Biologically Inspired Computing. Fargo, ND, USA: IEEE; 2013. p. 132–9.

[167]   Kiran M, Kumar A, and Prathap BR. Verification and validation of parallel support vector machine algorithm based on MapReduce Program model on Hadoop cluster. In: 2013 International Conference on Advanced Computing and Communication Systems. Coimbatore, India: IEEE; 2013. p. 1–6.

[168]   Kolias V, Anagnostopoulos I, and Kayafas E. A covering classification rule induction approach for big datasets. In: Proceedings – 2014 International Symposium on Big Data Computing, BDC 2014. 2015. p. 45–53.

[169]   Wang X, Liu X, and Matwin S. A distributed instance-weighted SVM algorithm on large-scale imbalanced datasets. In: 2014 IEEE International Conference on Big Data (Big Data). IEEE; 2014. p. 45–51.

[170]   Park SH and Ha YG. Large imbalance data classification based on MapReduce for traffic accident prediction. In: 2014 Eighth International Conference on Innovative Mobile and Internet Services in Ubiquitous Computing. Birmingham, UK: IEEE; 2014. p. 45–9.

[171]   López V, del Rio S, Benitez JM, and Herrera F. On the use of MapReduce to build linguistic fuzzy rule based classification systems for big data. In: 2014 IEEE International Conference on Fuzzy Systems (FUZZ-IEEE). Beijing, China: IEEE; 2014. p. 1905–12.

[172]   Kolias V, Kolias C, Anagnostopoulos I, and Kayafas E. RuleMR: Classification rule discovery with MapReduce. In: 2014 IEEE International Conference on Big Data (Big Data). Washington, DC, USA: IEEE; 2014. p. 20–8.

[173]   Kakade AG, Kharat PK, Gupta AK, and Batra T. Spam filtering techniques and MapReduce with SVM: A study. In: 2014 Asia-Pacific Conference on Computer Aided System Engineering (APCASE). South Kuta, Indonesia: IEEE; 2014. p. 59–64.

[174]   Anchalia PP and Roy K. The k-nearest neighbor algorithm using MapReduce paradigm. In: 2014 5th International Conference on Intelligent Systems, Modelling and Simulation. Langkawi, Malaysia: IEEE; 2014. p. 513–8.

[175] Ke X, Jin H, Xie X, and Cao J. A distributed SVM method based on the iterative MapReduce. In: Proceedings of the 2015 IEEE 9th International Conference on Semantic Computing (IEEE ICSC 2015). IEEE; 2015. p. 116–9.

[176] Maillo J, Triguero I, and Herrera F. A MapReduce-based k-nearest neighbor approach for big data classification. In: 2015 IEEE Trustcom/BigDataSE/ISPA. IEEE; 2015. p. 167–72.

[177] Chatzigeorgakidis G, Karagiorgou S, Athanasiou S, and Skiadopoulos S. A MapReduce based k-NN joins probabilistic classifier. In: 2015 IEEE International Conference on Big Data (Big Data). IEEE; 2015. p. 952–7.

[178] Wang S, Zhai J, Zhang S, and Zhu H. An ordinal random forest and its parallel implementation with MapReduce. In: 2015 IEEE International Conference on Systems, Man, and Cybernetics. IEEE; 2015. p. 2170–3.

[179] Cui T and Zhao H. A novel gender classification method based on MapReduce. In: 2015 6th IEEE International Conference on Software Engineering and Service Science (ICSESS). IEEE; 2015. p. 742–5.

[180] Yuan F, Lian F, Xu X, and Ji Z. Decision tree algorithm optimization research based on MapReduce. In: 2015 6th IEEE International Conference on Software Engineering and Service Science (ICSESS). Beijing, China: IEEE; 2015. p. 1010–3.

[181] Wakayama R, Murata R, Kimura A, Yamashita T, Yamauchi Y, and Fujiyoshi H. Distributed forests for MapReduce-based machine learning. In: 2015 3rd IAPR Asian Conference on Pattern Recognition (ACPR). Kuala Lumpur, Malaysia: IEEE; 2015. p. 276–80.

[182] Triguero I, Galar M, Vluymans S, *et al.* Evolutionary undersampling for imbalanced big data classification. In: 2015 IEEE Congress on Evolutionary Computation (CEC). Sendai, Japan: IEEE; 2015. p. 715–22.

[183] Zdravevski E, Lameski P, Kulakov A, Jakimovski B, Filiposka S, and Trajanov D. Feature ranking based on information gain for large classification problems with MapReduce. In: 2015 IEEE Trustcom/BigDataSE/ISPA. Helsinki, Finland: IEEE; 2015. p. 186–91.

[184] Competition: AAIA '14 Data Mining Competition: Key Risk Factors for Polish State Fire Service [Internet]. [cited 2017 Jul 24]. Available from: https://knowledgepit.fedcsis.org/contest/view.php?id=83.

[185] Kumar M, Rath NK, Swain A, and Rath SK. Feature selection and classification of microarray data using MapReduce based ANOVA and K-nearest neighbor. Procedia Computer Science. 2015;54:301–10.

[186] Bhukya R and Gyani J. Fuzzy associative classification algorithm based on MapReduce framework. In: 2015 International Conference on Applied and Theoretical Computing and Communication Technology (iCATccT). Davangere, India: IEEE; 2015. p. 357–60.

[187] Arias J, Gamez JA, and Puerta JM. Scalable learning of k-dependence Bayesian classifiers under MapReduce. In: 2015 IEEE Trustcom/BigDataSE/ISPA. Helsinki, Finland: IEEE; 2015. p. 25–32.

[188] Sukanya MV, Sathyadevan S, and Sreeveni UBU. Benchmarking Support Vector Machines Implementation Using Multiple Techniques. In: El-Sayed ME-A, Sabu MT, Hideyuki T, Selwyn P, and Thomas H, editors. Advances in Intelligent Informatics. Springer, Cham; 2015. p. 227–38. (Advances in Intelligent Systems and Computing; vol. 320).

[189] Yang W, Fu Y, and Zhang D. An improved parallel algorithm for text categorization. In: 2016 International Symposium on Computer, Consumer and Control (IS3C). IEEE; 2016. p. 451–4.

[190] Peng H, Liang D, and Choi C. Evaluating parallel logistic regression models. In: 2013 IEEE International Conference on Big Data. Silicon Valley, CA, USA: IEEE; 2013. p. 119–26.

[191] Tao H, Wu B, and Lin X. Budgeted mini-batch parallel gradient descent for support vector machines on Spark. In: 2014 20th IEEE International Conference on Parallel and Distributed Systems (ICPADS). Hsinchu, Taiwan: IEEE; 2014. p. 945–50.

[192] Lin C-Y, Tsai C-H, Lee C-P, and Lin C-J. Large-scale logistic regression and linear support vector machines using spark. In: 2014 IEEE International Conference on Big Data (Big Data). Washington, DC, USA: IEEE; 2014. p. 519–28.

[193] Wang S, Wu P, Liu T, and Kong WM. P-WLPA algorithm research on parallel framework Spark. In: 2014 IEEE 7th Joint International Information Technology and Artificial Intelligence Conference. Chongqing, China: IEEE; 2014. p. 437–41.

[194] Roy A. Automated online feature selection and learning from high-dimensional streaming data using an ensemble of Kohonen neurons. In: 2015 International Joint Conference on Neural Networks (IJCNN). IEEE; 2015. p. 1–8.

[195] Ramírez-Gallego S, Garcia S, Mourino-Talin H, and Martinez-Rego D. Distributed entropy minimization discretizer for big data analysis under Apache Spark. In: 2015 IEEE Trustcom/BigDataSE/ISPA. Helsinki, Finland: IEEE; 2015. p. 33–40.

[196] Bhagat RC and Patil SS. Enhanced SMOTE algorithm for classification of imbalanced big-data using Random Forest. In: 2015 IEEE International Advance Computing Conference (IACC). Bangalore, India: IEEE; 2015. p. 403–8.

[197] Chandorkar M, Mall R, Lauwers O, Suykens JAK, and De Moor B. Fixed-size least squares support vector machines: Scala implementation for large scale classification. In: 2015 IEEE Symposium Series on Computational Intelligence. Cape Town, South Africa: IEEE; 2015. p. 522–8.

[198] Venturini L, Garza P, and Apiletti D. BAC: A Bagged Associative Classifier for Big Data Frameworks. In: Mirjana I, Bernhard T, Barbara C, *et al.*, editors. New Trends in Databases and Information Systems. Springer, Cham; 2016. p. 137–46. (Communications in Computer and Information Science; vol. 637).

[199] Semberecki P and Maciejewski H. Distributed Classification of Text Documents on Apache Spark Platform. In: Rutkowski L, Korytkowski M, Scherer R, Tadeusiewicz R, Zadeh L, and Zurada J, editors. Artificial Intelligence and Soft Computing. Springer, Cham; 2016. p. 621–30. (Lecture Notes in Computer Science; vol. 9692).

[200] Nodarakis N, Sioutas S, Tsakalidis A, and Tzimas G. Large scale sentiment analysis on Twitter with Spark. In: Workshop Proceedings of the EDBT/ICDT 2016 Joint Conference. Bordeaux, France; 2016. p. 1–8.

[201] Ray RB, Kumar M, Tirkey A, and Rath SK. Scalable information gain variant on spark cluster for rapid quantification of microarray. Procedia Computer Science. 2016;93:292–8.

[202] Tayde SS and Nagamma Patil N. A Novel Approach for Genome Data Classification Using Hadoop and Spark Framework. In: Shetty NR, Hamsavath PN, and Nalini N, editors. Emerging Research in Computing, Information, Communication and Applications. Singapore: Springer, Singapore; 2016. p. 333–43.

[203] Kamaruddin S and Ravi V. Credit card fraud detection using big data analytics: Use of PSOAANN based one-class classification. In: Proceedings of the International Conference on Informatics and Analytics – ICIA-16. Pondicherry, India: ACM Press; 2016. p. 1–8.

[204] ccFraud Dataset [Internet]. [cited 2018 Jul 31]. Available from: https://packages.revolutionanalytics.com/datasets/.

[205] Talavera-Llames RL, Pérez-Chacón R, Martinez-Ballesteros M, Troncoso A, and Martinez-Álvarez F. A nearest neighbours-based algorithm for big time series data forecasting. In: International Conference on Hybrid Artificial Intelligence Systems. 2016. p. 174–85.

[206] Blessy Trencia Lincy SS, and Nagarajan SK. A Distributed Support Vector Machine Using Apache Spark for Semi-Supervised Classification With Data Augmentation. In: Wang J, Reddy G, Prasad V, and Reddy V, editors. Advances in Intelligent Systems and Computing. Springer, Singapore; 2019. p. 395–405.

[207] Sun Z, Fox G, Gu W, and Li Z. A parallel clustering method combined information bottleneck theory and centroid-based clustering. The Journal of Supercomputing. 2014;69(1):452–67.

[208] Million Sequence Clustering [Internet]. [cited 2017 Jul 24]. Available from: http://salsahpc.indiana.edu/millionseq/mina/16SrRNA_index.html.

[209] Xu Y, Qu W, Li Z, Min G, Li K, and Liu Z. Efficient k-means++ approximation with MapReduce. IEEE Transactions on Parallel and Distributed Systems. 2014;25(12):3135–44.

[210] Cui X, Zhu P, Yang X, Li K, and Ji C. Optimized big data K-means clustering using MapReduce. The Journal of Supercomputing. 2014;70(3):1249–59.

[211] Ludwig SA. MapReduce-based fuzzy c-means clustering algorithm: Implementation and scalability. International Journal of Machine Learning and Cybernetics. 2015;6(6):923–34.

[212]   Yang Y, Teng F, Li T, Wang H, Wang H, and Zhang Q. Parallel semi-supervised multi-Ant colonies clustering ensemble based on MapReduce methodology. IEEE Transactions on Cloud Computing. 2015;6(3):857–67.

[213]   Image Database [Internet]. [cited 2017 Jul 24]. Available from: http://research.microsoft.com/enus/projects/msrammdata/.

[214]   Bi W, Cai M, Liu M, and Li G. A big data clustering algorithm for mitigating the risk of customer churn. IEEE Transactions on Industrial Informatics. 2016;12(3):1270–81.

[215]   Liu W, Shen Y, and Wang P. An efficient MapReduce algorithm for similarity join in metric spaces. The Journal of Supercomputing. 2016;72 (3):1179–200.

[216]   Wikipedia, the Free Encyclopedia [Internet]. [cited 2017 Jul 24]. Available from: https://en.wikipedia.org/wiki/Main_Page.

[217]   Zhang Y, Chen S, and Yu G. Efficient distributed density peaks for clustering large data sets in MapReduce. IEEE Transactions on Knowledge and Data Engineering. 2016;28(12):3218–30.

[218]   Enron Email Dataset [Internet]. [cited 2017 Jul 24]. Available from: http://www.cs.cmu.edu/~./enron/.

[219]   Alewiwi M, Orencik C, and Savaş E. Efficient top-k similarity document search utilizing distributed file systems and cosine similarity. Cluster Computing. 2016;19(1):109–26.

[220]   Lewis DD, Yang Y, Rose TG, and Li F. RCV1: A new benchmark collection for text categorization research. Journal of Machine Learning Research. 2004;5:361–97.

[221]   Fang Y, Cheng R, Tang W, Maniu S, and Yang X. Scalable algorithms for nearest-neighbor joins on big trajectory data. IEEE Transactions on Knowledge and Data Engineering. 2016;28(3):785–800.

[222]   Theodoridis Y, Silva JRO, and Nascimento MA. On the Generation of Spatiotemporal Datasets. In: Ralf HG, Dimitris P, and Fred L, editors. Advances in Spatial Databases. Springer, Berlin, Heidelberg; 1999. p. 147–64. (Lecture Notes in Computer Science; vol. 1651).

[223]   Brinkhoff T. A framework for generating network-based moving objects. GeoInformatica. 2002;6(2):153–80.

[224]   Yuan J, Zheng Y, Zhang C, *et al.* T-drive: Driving directions based on taxi trajectories. In: Proceedings of the 18th SIGSPATIAL International Conference on Advances in Geographic Information Systems – GIS '10. San Jose, CA, USA: ACM Press; 2010. p. 99–108.

[225]   Wu Z, Gao G, Bu Z, and Cao J. SIMPLE: A simplifying-ensembling framework for parallel community detection from large networks. Cluster Computing. 2016;19(1):211–21.

[226]   Shahrivari S and Jalili S. Single-pass and linear-time k-means clustering based on MapReduce. Information Systems. 2016;60:1–12.

[227]   Banharnsakun A. A MapReduce-based artificial bee colony for large-scale data clustering. Pattern Recognition Letters. 2017;93:78–84.

[228] Capó M, Pérez A, and Lozano JA. An efficient approximation to the K-means clustering for massive data. Knowledge-Based Systems. 2017;117:56–69.

[229] Lu Y, Cao B, Rego C, and Glover F. A Tabu search based clustering algorithm and its parallel implementation on Spark. Applied Soft Computing. 2018;63:97–109.

[230] Zhao W, Ma H, and He Q. Parallel K-Means Clustering Based on MapReduce. In: Jaatun MG, Zhao G, and Rong C, editors. Cloud Computing. Beijing, China: Springer, Berlin, Heidelberg; 2009. p. 674–9. (Lecture Notes in Computer Science; vol. 5931).

[231] Ene A, Im S, and Moseley B. Fast clustering using MapReduce. In: Proceedings of the 17th ACM SIGKDD International Conference on Knowledge Discovery and Data Mining – KDD '11. San Diego, CA, USA: ACM Press; 2011. p. 681–9.

[232] Zongzhen H, Weina Z, Liyue, Xiaojuan D, and Fan Y. A fuzzy approach to clustering of text documents based on MapReduce. In: 2013 International Conference on Computational and Information Sciences. IEEE; 2013. p. 666–9.

[233] Liao Q, Yang F, and Zhao J. An improved parallel K-means clustering algorithm with MapReduce. In: 2013 15th IEEE International Conference on Communication Technology. IEEE; 2013. p. 764–8.

[234] Esteves RM, Hacker T, and Rong C. Competitive K-means: A new accurate and distributed K-means algorithm for large datasets. In: Proceedings of the International Conference on Cloud Computing Technology and Science, CloudCom. Bristol, UK: IEEE; 2013. p. 17–24.

[235] Kumar A, Kiran M, and Prathap BR. Verification and validation of MapReduce program model for parallel K-means algorithm on Hadoop cluster. In: 2013 Fourth International Conference on Computing, Communications and Networking Technologies (ICCCNT). Tiruchengode, India: IEEE; 2013. p. 1–8.

[236] Lin K, Li X, Zhang Z, and Chen J. A K-means clustering with optimized initial center based on Hadoop platform. In: 2014 9th International Conference on Computer Science & Education. IEEE; 2014. p. 263–6.

[237] Zhang R and Wang Y. An enhanced agglomerative fuzzy k-means clustering method with MapReduce implementation on Hadoop platform. In: 2014 IEEE International Conference on Progress in Informatics and Computing. IEEE; 2014. p. 509–13.

[238] Bousbaci A and Kamel N. A parallel sampling-PSO-multi-core-K-means algorithm using MapReduce. In: 2014 14th International Conference on Hybrid Intelligent Systems. IEEE; 2014. p. 129–34.

[239] Clustering Benchmark Datasets [Internet]. [cited 2017 Jul 24]. Available from: http://cs.joensuu.fi/sipu/datasets/.

[240] Garg D and Trivedi K. Fuzzy K-mean clustering in MapReduce on cloud based Hadoop. In: 2014 IEEE International Conference on Advanced

Communications, Control and Computing Technologies. Ramanathapuram, India: IEEE; 2014. p. 1607–10.

[241] Anchalia PP. Improved MapReduce k-means clustering algorithm with combiner. In: 2014 UKSim-AMSS 16th International Conference on Computer Modelling and Simulation. Cambridge, UK: IEEE; 2014. p. 386–91.

[242] Zhu Y, Wang F, Shan X, and Lv X. K-Medoids clustering based on MapReduce and optimal search of medoids. In: 2014 9th International Conference on Computer Science & Education. Vancouver, BC, Canada: IEEE; 2014. p. 573–7.

[243] Choi Y-M and So HK-H. Map-reduce processing of k-means algorithm with FPGA-accelerated computer cluster. In: 2014 IEEE 25th International Conference on Application-Specific Systems, Architectures and Processors. Zurich, Switzerland: IEEE; 2014. p. 9–16.

[244] Garcia KD and Naldi MC. Multiple parallel MapReduce k-means clustering with validation and selection. In: 2014 Brazilian Conference on Intelligent Systems. Sao Paulo, Brazil: IEEE; 2014. p. 432–7.

[245] Melnykov V, Chen W-C, and Maitra R. MixSim : An R Package for simulating data to study performance of clustering algorithms. Journal of Statistical Software. 2012;51(12):1–25.

[246] Daoudi M, Hamena S, Benmounah Z, and Batouche M. Parallel differential evolution clustering algorithm based on MapReduce. In: 2014 6th International Conference of Soft Computing and Pattern Recognition (SoCPaR). Tunis, Tunisia: IEEE; 2014. p. 337–41.

[247] Al-Madi N, Aljarah I, and Ludwig SA. Parallel glowworm swarm optimization clustering algorithm based on MapReduce. In: 2014 IEEE Symposium on Swarm Intelligence. Orlando, FL, USA: IEEE; 2014. p. 1–8.

[248] Datasets – MOA Massive Online Analysis [Internet]. [cited 2017 Jul 24]. Available from: https://moa.cms.waikato.ac.nz/datasets/.

[249] Orlandic R, Lai Y, and Yee WG. Clustering high-dimensional data using an efficient and effective data space reduction. In: Proceedings of the 14th ACM International Conference on Information and Knowledge Management – CIKM '05. Bremen, Germany: ACM Press; 2005. p. 201–8.

[250] Jiang Y and Zhang J. Parallel K-medoids clustering algorithm based on Hadoop. In: 2014 IEEE 5th International Conference on Software Engineering and Service Science. Beijing, China: IEEE; 2014. p. 649–52.

[251] Yuan H, Ma Y, Zhang F, Liu M, and Shen W. A distributed link prediction algorithm based on clustering in dynamic social networks. In: 2015 IEEE International Conference on Systems, Man, and Cybernetics. IEEE; 2015. p. 1341–5.

[252] Shettar R and Purohit BV. A MapReduce framework to implement enhanced K-means algorithm. In: 2015 International Conference on Applied and Theoretical Computing and Communication Technology (iCATccT). IEEE; 2015. p. 361–3.

[253] DEBS-Grand Challenge, 8th ACM International conference on Distributed Event-Based systems [Internet]. 2014 [cited 2017 Jul 24]. Available from: http://www.cse.iitb.ac.in/debs2014/?page_id=42.

[254] Yu Q and Ding Z. An improved fuzzy C-means algorithm based on MapReduce. In: 2015 8th International Conference on Biomedical Engineering and Informatics (BMEI). IEEE; 2015. p. 634–8.

[255] Boukhdhir A, Lachiheb O, and Gouider MS. An improved MapReduce design of kmeans for clustering very large datasets. In: 2015 IEEE/ACS 12th International Conference of Computer Systems and Applications (AICCSA). IEEE; 2015. p. 1–6.

[256] Lachiheb O, Gouider MS, and Ben Said L. An improved MapReduce design of Kmeans with iteration reducing for clustering stock exchange very large datasets. In: 2015 11th International Conference on Semantics, Knowledge and Grids (SKG). IEEE; 2015. p. 252–5.

[257] Mao Y, Xu Z, Li X, and Ping P. An optimal distributed K-means clustering algorithm based on cloudstack. In: 2015 IEEE International Conference on Information and Automation. IEEE; 2015. p. 3149–56.

[258] Saranya V and Sumalatha MR. Dynamic neighborhood selection (DNS) clustering using MapReduce. In: 2015 3rd International Conference on Signal Processing, Communication and Networking (ICSCN). Chennai, India: IEEE; 2015. p. 1–5.

[259] Ketu S, Prasad BR, and Agarwal S. Effect of corpus size selection on performance of Map-Reduce based distributed K-means for big textual data clustering. In: Proceedings of the Sixth International Conference on Computer and Communication Technology 2015. Allahabad, India: ACM; 2015. p. 256–60.

[260] DBpedia [Internet]. [cited 2017 Jul 24]. Available from: http://wiki.dbpedia.org/Datasets.

[261] DBpedia : 2014 Downloads [Internet]. [cited 2017 Jul 24]. Available from: http://oldwiki.dbpedia.org/Downloads2014.

[262] Karimov J and Ozbayoglu M. High quality clustering of big data and solving empty-clustering problem with an evolutionary hybrid algorithm. In: 2015 IEEE International Conference on Big Data (Big Data). Santa Clara, CA, USA: IEEE; 2015. p. 1473–8.

[263] Karimov J, Ozbayoglu M, and Dogdu E. k-Means performance improvements with centroid calculation heuristics both for serial and parallel environments. In: 2015 IEEE International Congress on Big Data. New York, NY, USA: IEEE; 2015. p. 444–51.

[264] Garg D, Gohil P, and Trivedi K. Modified fuzzy K-mean clustering using MapReduce in Hadoop and cloud. In: 2015 IEEE International Conference on Electrical, Computer and Communication Technologies (ICECCT). Coimbatore, India: IEEE; 2015. p. 1–5.

[265] Ling S and Yunfeng Q. Optimization of the distributed K-means clustering algorithm based on set pair analysis. In: 2015 8th International Congress on

Image and Signal Processing (CISP). Shenyang, China: IEEE; 2015. p. 1593–8.

[266]   Tao G, Xiangwu D, and Yefeng L. Parallel k-modes algorithm based on MapReduce. In: 2015 Third International Conference on Digital Information, Networking, and Wireless Communications (DINWC). Moscow, Russia: IEEE; 2015. p. 176–9.

[267]   Phan TN, Jager M, Nadschlager S, and Kung J. Range-based clustering supporting similarity search in big data. In: 2015 26th International Workshop on Database and Expert Systems Applications (DEXA). Valencia, Spain: IEEE; 2015. p. 120–4.

[268]   Chunne AP, Chandrasekhar U, and Malhotra C. Real time clustering of tweets using adaptive PSO technique and MapReduce. In: 2015 Global Conference on Communication Technologies (GCCT). Thuckalay, India: IEEE; 2015. p. 452–7.

[269]   Chen C-C, Chen T-Y, Huang J-W, and Chen M-S. Reducing communication and merging overheads for distributed clustering algorithms on the cloud. In: 2015 International Conference on Cloud Computing and Big Data (CCBD). Shanghai, China: IEEE; 2015. p. 41–8.

[270]   Zhang T, Ramakrishnan R, and Livny M. BIRCH: A new data clustering algorithm and its applications. Data Mining and Knowledge Discovery. 1997;1(2):141–82.

[271]   Wu K, Zeng W, Wu T, and An Y. Research and improve on K-means algorithm based on Hadoop. In: 2015 6th IEEE International Conference on Software Engineering and Service Science (ICSESS). Beijing, China: IEEE; 2015. p. 334–7.

[272]   Gao W, Li X, and Li D. Research on fixed traffic bottleneck of K-means clustering based on Hadoop. In: 2015 4th International Conference on Computer Science and Network Technology (ICCSNT). Harbin, China: IEEE; 2015. p. 351–4.

[273]   de Oliveira GV and Naldi MC. Scalable fast evolutionary k-means clustering. In: 2015 Brazilian Conference on Intelligent Systems (BRACIS). Natal, Brazil: IEEE; 2015. p. 74–9.

[274]   Moertini VS and Venica L. Enhancing parallel k-means using map reduce for discovering knowledge from big data. In: 2016 IEEE International Conference on Cloud Computing and Big Data Analysis (ICCCBDA). Chengdu, China: IEEE; 2016. p. 81–7.

[275]   Akthar N, Ahamad MV, and Ahmad S. MapReduce model of improved K-means clustering algorithm using Hadoop MapReduce. In: 2016 Second International Conference on Computational Intelligence & Communication Technology (CICT). Ghaziabad, India: IEEE; 2016. p. 192–8.

[276]   Yurong Zhong and Dan Liu. The application of K-means clustering algorithm based on Hadoop. In: 2016 IEEE International Conference on Cloud Computing and Big Data Analysis (ICCCBDA). Chengdu, China: IEEE; 2016. p. 88–92.

[277] Budhraja T, Goyal B, Kilaru A, and Sikarwar V. Fuzzy Clustering-Based Efficient Classification Model for Large TCP Dump Dataset Using Hadoop Framework. In: Suresh Chandra S, Amit J, Nilesh M, and Nisarg P, editors. Proceedings of International Conference on ICT for Sustainable Development. Springer, Singapore; 2016. p. 427–37. (Advances in Intelligent Systems and Computing; vol. 408).

[278] Sarazin T, Azzag H, and Lebbah M. SOM clustering using Spark-MapReduce. In: 2014 IEEE International Parallel & Distributed Processing Symposium Workshops. Phoenix, AZ, USA: IEEE; 2014. p. 1727–34.

[279] Tsapanos N, Tefas A, and Nikolaidis N, and Pitas I. Distributed, MapReduce-based nearest neighbor and E-ball kernel k-means. In: 2015 IEEE Symposium Series on Computational Intelligence. Cape Town, South Africa: IEEE; 2015. p. 509–15.

[280] Govindarajan K, Boulanger D, Kumar VS, and Kinshuk. Parallel particle swarm optimization (PPSO) clustering for learning analytics. In: 2015 IEEE International Conference on Big Data (Big Data). Santa Clara, CA, USA: IEEE; 2015. p. 1461–5.

[281] Ketu S and Agarwal S. Performance enhancement of distributed K-means clustering for big data analytics through in-memory computation. In: 2015 Eighth International Conference on Contemporary Computing (IC3). Noida, India: IEEE; 2015. p. 318–24.

[282] Zhu H, Guo Y, Niu M, Yang G, and Jiao L. Distributed SAR image change detection based on Spark. In: 2015 IEEE International Geoscience and Remote Sensing Symposium (IGARSS). Milan, Italy: IEEE; 2015. p. 4149–52.

[283] Peng X-Y, Yang Y-B, Wang C-D, Huang D, and Lai J-H. An efficient parallel nonlinear clustering algorithm using MapReduce. In: 2016 IEEE International Parallel and Distributed Processing Symposium Workshops (IPDPSW). Chicago, IL, USA: IEEE; 2016. p. 1473–6.

[284] Han D, Agrawal A, Liao W-K, and Choudhary A. A novel scalable DBSCAN algorithm with Spark. In: 2016 IEEE International Parallel and Distributed Processing Symposium Workshops (IPDPSW). IEEE; 2016. p. 1393–402.

[285] Jędrzejowicz J, Jędrzejowicz P, and Wierzbowska I. Apache Spark Implementation of the Distance-Based Kernel-Based Fuzzy C-Means Clustering Classifier. In: Czarnowski I, Caballero A, Howlett R, and Jain L, editors. Intelligent Decision Technologies 2016. Springer, Cham; 2016. p. 317–24. (Smart Innovation, Systems and Technologies; vol. 56).

[286] Tsapanos N, Tefas A, Nikolaidis N, and Pitas I. Efficient MapReduce kernel k-means for big data clustering. In: Proceedings of the 9th Hellenic Conference on Artificial Intelligence – SETN '16. Thessaloniki, Greece: ACM Press; 2016. p. 1–5.

[287] Bharill N, Tiwari A, and Malviya A. Fuzzy based clustering algorithms to handle big data with implementation on Apache Spark. In: 2016 IEEE

Second International Conference on Big Data Computing Service and Applications (BigDataService). Oxford, UK: IEEE; 2016. p. 95–104.

[288]   Gouineau F, Landry T, and Triplet T. PatchWork, a scalable density-grid clustering algorithm. In: Proceedings of the 31st Annual ACM Symposium on Applied Computing – SAC '16. Pisa, Italy: ACM Press; 2016. p. 824–31.

[289]   Zhu S, Li J, Huang J, Luo S, and Peng W. A MapReduced-based and cell-based outlier detection algorithm. Wuhan University Journal of Natural Sciences. 2014;19(3):199–205.

[290]   Soltani Halvaiee N, and Akbari MK. A novel model for credit card fraud detection using artificial immune systems. Applied Soft Computing Journal. 2014;24:40–9.

[291]   Natesan P, Rajalaxmi RR, Gowrison G, and Balasubramanie P. Hadoop based parallel binary bat algorithm for network intrusion detection. International Journal of Parallel Programming. 2016:1–20.

[292]   El-Alfy E-SM and Alshammari MA. Towards scalable rough set based attribute subset selection for intrusion detection using parallel genetic algorithm in MapReduce. Simulation Modelling Practice and Theory. 2016;64:18–29.

[293]   Rathore MM, Ahmad A, and Paul A. Real time intrusion detection system for ultra-high-speed big data environments. The Journal of Supercomputing. 2016;72(9):3489–510.

[294]   NSL-KDD dataset [Internet]. [cited 2017 Jul 24]. Available from: http://www.unb.ca/cic/research/datasets/nsl.html.

[295]   Carcillo F, Dal Pozzolo A, Le Borgne Y-A, Caelen O, Mazzer Y, and Bontempi G. SCARFF: A scalable framework for streaming credit card fraud detection with spark. Information Fusion. 2018;41:182–94.

[296]   Tanupabrungsun S and Achalakul T. Feature reduction for anomaly detection in manufacturing with MapReduce GA/kNN. In: 2013 International Conference on Parallel and Distributed Systems. Seoul, South Korea: IEEE; 2013. p. 639–44.

[297]   Aljarah I and Ludwig SA. MapReduce intrusion detection system based on a particle swarm optimization clustering algorithm. In: 2013 IEEE Congress on Evolutionary Computation. Cancun, Mexico: IEEE; 2013. p. 955–62.

[298]   Xiang J, Westerlund M, Sovilj D, and Pulkkis G. Using extreme learning machine for intrusion detection in a big data environment. In: Proceedings of the 2014 Workshop on Artificial Intelligent and Security Workshop – AISec '14. Scottsdale, AZ, USA: ACM Press; 2014. p. 73–82.

[299]   Sharma R, Sharma P, Mishra P, and Pilli ES. Towards MapReduce based classification approaches for intrusion detection. In: 2016 6th International Conference – Cloud System and Big Data Engineering (Confluence). Noida, India: IEEE; 2016. p. 361–7.

[300]   Gupta GP and Kulariya M. A framework for fast and efficient cyber security network intrusion detection using Apache Spark. Procedia Computer Science. 2016;93:824–31.

[301]   Kumari R, Sheetanshu, Singh MK, Jha R, and Singh NK. Anomaly detection in network traffic using K-mean clustering. In: 2016 3rd International

Conference on Recent Advances in Information Technology (RAIT). IEEE; 2016. p. 387–93.

[302]   Veloso B, Leal F, González-Vélez H, Malheiro B, and Burguillo JC. Scalable data analytics using crowdsourced repositories and streams. Journal of Parallel and Distributed Computing. 2018;122:1–10.

[303]   Yelp Dataset [Internet]. [cited 2018 Aug 31]. Available from: https://www. yelp.com/dataset.

[304]   Schelter S, Boden C, and Markl V. Scalable similarity-based neighborhood methods with MapReduce. In: Proceedings of the Sixth ACM Conference on Recommender Systems – RecSys '12. Dublin, Ireland: ACM Press; 2012. p. 163–70.

[305]   MovieLens | GroupLens [Internet]. [cited 2017 Jul 24]. Available from: https://grouplens.org/datasets/movielens/.

[306]   Flixster dataset [Internet]. [cited 2017 Jul 24]. Available from: http://www. cs.sfu.ca/~sja25/personal/datasets.

[307]   Ghuli P, Ghosh A, and Shettar R. A collaborative filtering recommendation engine in a distributed environment. In: 2014 International Conference on Contemporary Computing and Informatics (IC3I). IEEE; 2014. p. 568–74.

[308]   Shang Y, Li Z, Qu W, Xu Y, Song Z, and Zhou X. Scalable collaborative filtering recommendation algorithm with MapReduce. In: 2014 IEEE 12th International Conference on Dependable, Autonomic and Secure Computing. Dalian, China: IEEE; 2014. p. 103–8.

[309]   Pozo M and Chiky R. An implementation of a distributed stochastic gradient descent for recommender systems based on Map-Reduce. In: 2015 International Workshop on Computational Intelligence for Multimedia Understanding (IWCIM). IEEE; 2015. p. 1–5.

[310]   Lu F, Hong L, and Changfeng L. The improvement and implementation of distributed item-based collaborative filtering algorithm on Hadoop. In: 2015 34th Chinese Control Conference (CCC). Hangzhou, China: IEEE; 2015. p. 9078–83.

[311]   Subramaniyaswamy V, Vijayakumar V, Logesh R, and Indragandhi V. Unstructured data analysis on big data using map reduce. Procedia Computer Science. 2015;50:456–65.

[312]   Shen F and Jiamthapthaksin R. Dimension independent cosine similarity for collaborative filtering using MapReduce. In: 2016 8th International Conference on Knowledge and Smart Technology (KST). Chiang Mai, Thailand: IEEE; 2016. p. 72–6.

[313]   Webscope | Yahoo Labs [Internet]. [cited 2017 Jul 24]. Available from: https://webscope.sandbox.yahoo.com/.

[314]   Panigrahi S, Lenka RK, and Stitipragyan A. A hybrid distributed collaborative filtering recommender engine using Apache Spark. Procedia Computer Science. 2016;83:1000–6.

[315]   Zhang J, Li T, Ruan D, Gao Z, and Zhao C. A parallel method for computing rough set approximations. Information Sciences. 2012;194:209–23.

[316]   Chen K, Wan WQ, and Li Y. Differentially private feature selection under Map Reduce framework. Journal of China Universities of Posts and Telecommunications. 2013;20(5):85–90.

[317]   Qian J, Miao D, Zhang Z, and Yue X. Parallel attribute reduction algorithms using MapReduce. Information Sciences. 2014;279:671–90.

[318]   Yue K, Fang Q, Wang X, Li J, and Liu W. A parallel and incremental approach for data-intensive learning of Bayesian networks. IEEE Transactions on Cybernetics. 2015;45(12):2890–904.

[319]   Zhang Y, Chen S, Wang Q, and Yu G. i^2MapReduce: Incremental MapReduce for mining evolving big data. IEEE Transactions on Knowledge and Data Engineering. 2015;27(7):1906–19.

[320]   BigCross dataset [Internet]. [cited 2017 Jul 24]. Available from: http://www.cs. uni-paderborn.de/en/fachgebiete/agbloemer/research/clustering/streamkmpp.

[321]   SNAP: Network Datasets: Wikipedia Talk Network [Internet]. [cited 2017 Jul 24]. Available from: http://snap.stanford.edu/data/wiki-Talk.html.

[322]   Yue K, Wu H, Fu X, Xu J, Yin Z, and Liu W. A data-intensive approach for discovering user similarities in social behavioral interactions based on the Bayesian network. Neurocomputing. 2017;219:364–75.

[323]   Wang Y, Li Y, Chen Z, and Xue Y. Cooperative particle swarm optimization using MapReduce. Soft Computing. 2017;21(22):6593–603.

[324]   Qi RZ, Wang ZJ, and Li SY. A parallel genetic algorithm based on spark for pairwise test suite generation. Journal of Computer Science and Technology. 2016;31(2):417–27.

[325]   Jia Y, Cohen MB, Harman M, and Petke J. Learning combinatorial interaction test generation strategies using hyperheuristic search. In: 2015 IEEE/ACM 37th IEEE International Conference on Software Engineering. Florence, Italy: IEEE; 2015. p. 540–50.

[326]   Garvin BJ, Cohen MB, and Dwyer MB. Evaluating improvements to a meta-heuristic search for constrained interaction testing. Empirical Software Engineering. 2011;16(1):61–102.

[327]   Eiras-Franco C, Bolón-Canedo V, Ramos S, González-Domínguez J, Alonso-Betanzos A, and Touriño J. Multithreaded and Spark parallelization of feature selection filters. Journal of Computational Science. 2016;17:609–19.

[328]   Ramírez-Gallego S, Lastra I, Martínez-Rego D, *et al.* Fast-mRMR: Fast minimum redundancy maximum relevance algorithm for high-dimensional big data. International Journal of Intelligent Systems. 2017;32(2):134–52.

[329]   Gemulla R, Nijkamp E, Haas PJ, and Sismanis Y. Large-scale matrix factorization with distributed stochastic gradient descent. In: Proceedings of the 17th ACM SIGKDD International Conference on Knowledge Discovery and Data Mining – KDD '11. San Diego, CA, USA: ACM Press; 2011. p. 69–77.

[330]   Zhang C and Sun J. Large scale microblog mining using distributed MB-LDA. In: Proceedings of the 21st International Conference Companion on

World Wide Web – WWW '12 Companion. Lyon, France: ACM Press; 2012. p. 1035–42.

[331] Thompson LP, Xu W, and Miranker DP. Fast scalable selection algorithms for large scale data. In: 2013 IEEE International Conference on Big Data. Silicon Valley, CA, USA: IEEE; 2013. p. 412–20.

[332] Hu L, Liu J, Liang C, and Ni F. A MapReduce enabled simulated annealing genetic algorithm. In: 2014 International Conference on Identification, Information and Knowledge in the Internet of Things. IEEE; 2014. p. 252–5.

[333] Traveling Salesman Problem [Internet]. [cited 2017 Jul 24]. Available from: http://www.math.uwaterloo.ca/tsp/index.html.

[334] He Q, Cheng X, Zhuang F, and Shi Z. Parallel feature selection using positive approximation based on MapReduce. In: 2014 11th International Conference on Fuzzy Systems and Knowledge Discovery (FSKD). Xiamen, China: IEEE; 2014. p. 397–402.

[335] Hilda GT and Rajalaxmi RR. Effective feature selection for supervised learning using genetic algorithm. In: 2015 2nd International Conference on Electronics and Communication Systems (ICECS). Coimbatore, India: IEEE; 2015. p. 909–14.

[336] Kourid A and Batouche M. A novel approach for feature selection based on MapReduce for biomarker discovery. In: International Conference on Computer Vision and Image Analysis Applications. IEEE; 2015. p. 1–11.

[337] Alshammari MA and El-Alfy E-SM. MapReduce implementation for minimum reduct using parallel genetic algorithm. In: 2015 6th International Conference on Information and Communication Systems (ICICS). Amman, Jordan: IEEE; 2015. p. 13–8.

[338] Yu Z, Yu X, Chen Y, and Ma K. Distributed top-k keyword search over very large databases with MapReduce. In: 2016 IEEE International Congress on Big Data (BigData Congress). San Francisco, CA, USA: IEEE; 2016. p. 349–52.

[339] Li C, Wen T, Dong H, Wu Q, and Zhang Z. Implementation of parallel multi-objective artificial bee colony algorithm based on spark platform. In: 2016 11th International Conference on Computer Science & Education (ICCSE). Nagoya, Japan: IEEE; 2016. p. 592–7.

[340] Hu W and Tan Y. Partitioning Based N-Gram Feature Selection for Malware Classification. In: Ying T and Yuhui S, editors. Data Mining and Big Data. Bali, Indonesia: Springer, Cham; 2016. p. 187–95. (Lecture Notes in Computer Science; vol. 9714).

[341] VX-Heaven: Virus Collection [Internet]. [cited 2017 Jul 24]. Available from: https://vxheaven.org/vl.php.

[342] Tibshirani R. Regression shrinkage and selection via the lasso. Journal of the Royal Statistical Society Series B (Methodological). 1996;58(1):267–88.

[343] Horel EA. Application of ridge analysis to regression problems. Chemical Engineering Progress. 1962;58:54–9.

[344]   Fisher RA. The use of multiple measurements in taxonomic problems. Annals of Eugenics. 1936;7(2):179–88.

[345]   McLachlan G. Discriminant analysis and statistical pattern recognition. Vol. 544. John Wiley & Sons, Inc., Hoboken, New Jersey; 2004.

[346]   Knapp TR. Canonical correlation analysis: A general parametric significance-testing system. Psychological Bulletin. 1978;85(2):410–6.

[347]   Cattell RB. Factor analysis: An introduction and manual for the psychologist and social scientist. American Psychological Association, Washington, DC; 1952.

[348]   Hirschfeld HO and Wishart J. A connection between correlation and contingency. Mathematical Proceedings of the Cambridge Philosophical Society. 1935;31(04):520–4.

[349]   Green PE and Srinivasan V. Conjoint analysis in consumer research: Issues and outlook. Journal of Consumer Research. 1978;5(2):103–23.

[350]   Ward Jr. JH. Hierarchical grouping to optimize an objective function. Journal of the American Statistical Association. 1963;58(301):236–44.

Chapter 8

A review of fog and edge computing with big data analytics

Ch. Rajyalakshmi[1], K. Ram Mohan Rao[2] and Rajeswara Rao Ramisetty[3]

The amount of data created by various sensors, which can all be managed through the Internet of Things (IoT), is expanding tremendously these days as a result of nonstop and unconditional operational situations. In every fraction of second, lots of IoT devices are generating an avalanche of information that is disruptive for predictable data processing and analytics functionality, and all generated data through various devices can be handled by the cloud environment because volume and velocity of the data are very high. Through cloud data acquisition and computing, it is very crucial for the real-time applications, and these consequences can be overcome with fog and edge computing. The promise and potential of the fog and edge computing environment drives a huge social impact on big data analytics. Fog computing is a powerful computing structure that overcomes all disruptions, with powerful computing functionality of cloud environment, based on a deployment of intermediate nodes that are called fog nodes, which reduce all the problems. Big data analytics by a fog computing structure is one of the major emerging phases which require extensive research to generate more proficient knowledge and smart decisions. This analysis summarises the major two fog challenges: (i) power consumption, (ii) environment network connection methods, which also suffer with a lack of mobility support and geo-distribution as well as cyber threats. This chapter main focuses on how various computing paradigms applied with fog and edge computing environment for realising recently emerging IoT applications and cyber security threats, especially a review on fog and edge computing environment usage for recent trends, their background, characteristics, architectures and open challenges. It analyses the business models of fog and edge computing environment and provides the information regarding the various issues, challenges and opportunities in the fog and edge computing environment.

[1]Computer Science and Engineering, B V Raju Institute of Technology, Narsapur, India
[2]National Remote Sensing Center, Indian Space Research Organization, Hyderabad, India
[3]Computer Science and Engineering, Jawaharlal Nehru Technological University Kakinada-University College of Engineering Vizianagaram, Vizianagaram, India

8.1   Introduction

In this review, we present and explore the cloud computing offloading strategies with fog and edge computing that has been accepted in recent years. It reflects a noticeable improvement in the information collection, transmission as well as the management of data in the field for computer consumers. This review is one among the several to analyse the big data and its offloading strategies in detail in the following sections.

8.1.1   What is big data?

Big data is a collection of data with an enormous size and is defined as a term used to describe a large collection of data that increases exponentially over time. For example, data gained by social media sites are Facebook, WhatsApp, Twitter, YouTube, etc. It is possible to have the big data in three different forms: structured big data, unstructured big data and semi-structured big data [1]. Figure 8.1 shows big data analysis is a complex process of analysing a large volume of data or big data, including structured, unstructured and semi-structured data from various sources and its sizes from terabytes to zettabytes. This big data is collected from various sources, such as videos, digital images, sensors, social networks and sales transaction records. Specialised software tools and applications are utilised to perform the big data analytics for analysing a large volume of data.

Recent advances in big data analysis permit the researchers to forecast where terrorists plan to attack, decode human DNA in minutes, which aids you most likely to respond to Facebook and evaluate which gene is most likely to create the particular disease, etc. Many benefits related to the analytics of big data are better sales insight, keep up the customer trend, implement new strategies that are cost effective.

All data that can be stored retrieved and interpreted as a defined format is considered a 'structured' data. For example, an 'employee' table in a database is an example of structured data. In alternative, each and every data of undefined type or

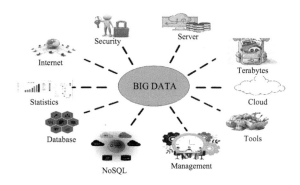

Figure 8.1   Big data

structure is labelled unstructured data. Examples of unstructured data are the information generated from 'Google Search'. A semi-structured data may include both the structured and unstructured data types. One can have a semi-structured data in the form as organised, but it is still not defined in particular. A semi-structured data example is a personal data contained in an XML file [2].

8.1.2   Importance of big data in cloud computing

The cloud will provide big data with a greater scalability. Big data structured and unstructured needs higher computational power, memory and much more. The cloud not only has an interface that is readily available but also the opportunity to really easily scale up this network so you can manage large fluctuations in demand or use [3].

8.1.3   Merits and demerits

The following are some of the merits of big data in cloud computing:

- control observation,
- no capital expenses,
- faster scalability,
- lower computational costs.

The following are some of the demerits of large data in cloud computing:

- less security controls,
- less data protection controls,
- network dependency and latency issues,
- slower backup and restoration of big data in cloud.

8.2   Introduction to cloud computing with IoT applications

Cloud computing is described as a framework for allowing universal, efficient, on-demand access to the network to a common pool of selectable computing resources which can be easily accessed and delivered with marginal control effort or inter-ference between service providers. The installation frameworks of cloud computing are most often known as public cloud, where services are accessed throughout the Internet to users [5].

A financially viable corporation usually owns the public clouds. On the other hand, a private cloud service is usually handled by a private organisation to meet its customers' specific purposes. The private cloud provides a safe atmosphere as well as greater control rate. The hybrid clouds are therefore a combination of public and private clouds. That choice is made available for people since it allows most of the drawbacks of each design to be resolved [6]. A public network, on the other hand, is a cloud service provided by a number of organisations which have the same need to a group of users. To allow customers to choose the platform that suits them, cloud computing services are available on three varying levels, namely the SaaS (software as a service) model, the PaaS (platform as a service) model and finally, the IaaS (infrastructure as a service) model. Therefore, cloud computing has the nearly unlimited storage with computational ability and is at least to some extent an even more proven technology to fix the problem of most of the IoT [7]. The IoT has become a pragmatic approach in which the distinctions between traditional and technological realms have been slowly removed by constant updating each peripheral device into some kind of digital and flexible substitute designed to provide smart facilities in this era. These devices well into the IoT have their very own identities like smart devices, sensors [8]. These are merged together to develop the computer network and then become objects that are actively involved. The IoT, like the Internet, seem to have the capability to change the world and offer a range of possibilities and technologies. Nevertheless, it faces several obstacles that might negatively affect its progress [9]. The IoT concept is mainly focused on an intellectual and self-configuring modules (things) embedded in a complex and worldwide Internet services which actually refer to that of the modern world that has minimal storage and computing power and has major issues of consistency, efficiency and data protection [10].

Therefore, it is required that a futuristic IT model in which cloud and IoT are two contrasting systems fused together will challenge both the existing and the emerging systems and are termed modern framework of cloud–IoT [11]. Figure 8.2 shows both IoT and cloud computing are already rapidly evolving technologies and have unique features of their own. Usually, the IoT is characterised by ubiquitous devices with restricted processing and storage capacities, and these devices face performance, reliability, confidentiality and security issues [12]. Cloud computing, on the other hand, includes a worldwide network with infinite storage capacity and computational power, and it also provides a flexible, robust environment that enables web service integration from different data sources [13]. Hence, the cloud computing solely managed to solve almost all of the IoT issues today. The cloud-based IoT technology is a network that facilitates a cost-effective use of software, data and technology. Although IoT and cloud computing vary from one another, their capabilities are almost similar, and this is the primary reason why many researchers have suggested their alignment with the IoT software strategy of the cloud [14].

By integrating IoT and cloud, we have the possibility to develop the use of the technology available in cloud environments and can be used for apps and data using the IoT technologies because of this combination. Figure 8.3 demonstrates the integration between IoT and cloud technology [15].

Furthermore, the big data can also interact with one another together with the IoT and cloud computing. In fact, the advancement of big data and cloud computing innovations can not only solve problems but also facilitate the large use of the IoT technology [16]. Cloud computing plays a significant role in the processing and handling of that data with the availability of a huge amount of data. This is not just about big data growth but also about extending data analysis frameworks like Hadoop

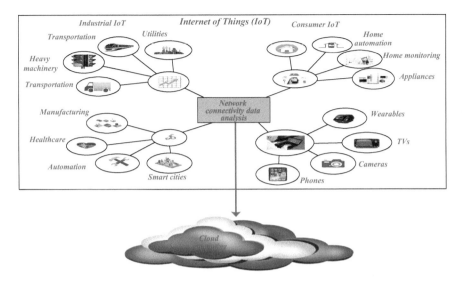

Figure 8.2   Combined IoT and cloud mode

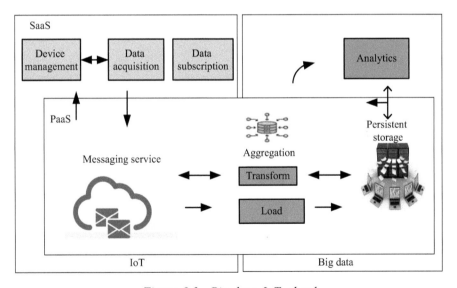

Figure 8.3   Big data–IoT–cloud

and so, in which new opportunities are being created in cloud computing [17]. Therefore, service companies such as AWS, Google and Microsoft have already been providing their own big data systems in a cost-effective way that can be adjusted to individuals and businesses. This, in effect, then leads to a new analytics as a service model and also provides a simpler and more flexible way to combine and evaluate different types of structured semi-structured and unstructured data [18].

Figure 8.3 shows the interrelationship between the three technologies which are exclusive of each other. The growing work space of IoT and big data plays a major role in cloud, in which IoT is the source of data and big data as an emerging technology is the data's analytical tool. A huge amount of producing IoT data will fuel the big data applications [19].

Reducing the difficulty of IoT information blending, it is also one of the requirements for optimising its advantages. If the IoT systems and data exist in storage facilities, the idea behind it is that we will not get the peak performance out of it [20]. Therefore, the best way to gain better insights and make decisions is to combine information (data) from different sources. From all the aspects mentioned earlier, the need for a collaboration of big data–IoT–cloud has been crystal clear and as a conclusion, IoT, big data and cloud computing convergence can provide new possibilities and software across all fields. This will also hand the experts interested in working on the different technology an excellent career range [21].

8.2.1   Cloud computing importance

Cloud computing may well be the twenty-first era's latest charismatic innovation as it also saw the quickest acceptance of any other software in the sector into the main-stream. Such growth was driven by a growing number of computers and mobile devices which can connect to the Internet. Figure 8.4 shows the cloud computing is beneficial for a set of organisations and even for an individual and allows us to execute software applications without downloading them on our computers; it allows us to store and view our digital content via the Internet in addition it allows us to create and review applications without needing servers and so on [22].

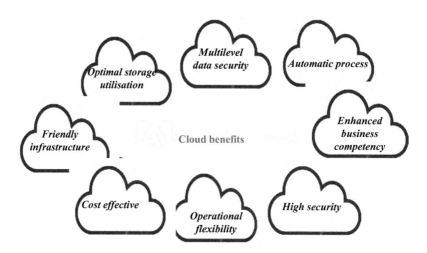

Figure 8.4   Importance of cloud

Actually, despite the numerous individual as well as technological issues we encounter today, we need cloud computing. These issues arise from the procurement and management of valuable operating systems tools that we use in our day-to-day activities to standardise these resources in the most efficient way to our benefit and the good of the whole community. Cloud computing provides numerous advantages in addressing these problems that have exceeded our objectives and offered further than we could have previously imagined, and one of them is offloading cloud process. This can be utilised on the software platform of low-performance hardware such as IoT devices to optimise the consumption of resources capacity and will assign tasks of high difficulty to high performance.

8.2.2   Cloud offloading strategies

Basically the cloud computing is deployed as a service infrastructure. Computational offloading mainly conveys the resource-intensive computational tasks to a separate processor, including external platform or hardware accelerator. Ability of external platform computational offloading over the network offers the computing power and overwhelms the hardware restriction of a device like limited storage, computational power and energy. In the recent years, mobile cloud computing is the trending paradigm in computing community. Mobile devices have some restrictions for delivering all types of services to the users, such as battery lifetime, energy consumption and processing power. These limitations can be overwhelmed by considering the diverse offloading strategies in the cloud computing.

8.2.3   Applications of IoT

Among the various application of IoT, some of them where described in short in this section (Figure 8.5):

1. **Smart home:** One of the top ranked applications of IoT is smart homes, and around 60,000 people search through Internet for 'SMART HOMES'. The smart home registry of the IoT Analytics Company comprises 256 companies and start-ups, and they are active in this field.
2. **Wearable's:** Apple's new smart watch, Sony Smart B Trainer, the Myo gesture control or Look-see bracelet all come under this wearable category. 'JAWBONE' is the one of the known wearable makers of all IoT companies.
3. **Smart city:** Smart city offers a wide range of applications, ranging from traffic congestion to wastewater treatment, water treatment, urban protection as well as disaster response. Its success is driven by the circumstance that many smart city ideas are promising these days to relieve the true discomforts of people in big cities. Smart city IoT systems address congestion and pollution problems.
4. **Smart grids:** Smart grids are a remarkable one and the future smart grid aims to use data about energy supplies and customers' activities in an intelligent way to boost power's performance, stability and economy.

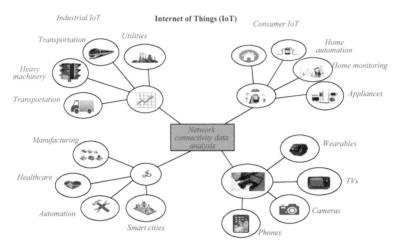

Figure 8.5   Application of IoT

5. **Industrial Internet:** The industrial Internet has become one of the peculiar applications of the IoT and has much to do with it. Compared to other non-consumer-oriented IoT concepts, the industrial Internet gets a massive drive of people on Twitter.

6. **Connected car:** We have not seen much hype across the Internet connected cars yet in the development cycles in the automotive industry. But we are approaching that point, it seems. Some big car companies focus on connected car projects and even some bold newcomers. Unless this nation's BMWs even Fords do not quickly introduce this next-generation Internet-connected vehicle, other well-known companies such as Google, Microsoft and Apple will develop the networks for connected cars. By this approach, we can stay safe and updated about the route and can contact with another in the same route.

7. **Connected health:** The connected health is another remarkable application of IoT, which has a higher potential in medical services, various companies as well as a common individual, but still now it has not been achieved its peak level.

8. **Smart retail:** Connectivity-based marketing tends to take over as a branch of smart shopping. However, the rating of success indicates that it is also a part of a market. An article of LinkedIn is nothing when related to 430 smart homes.

9. **Smart supply chain:** Supply chain with the ability of tracking goods on road or to gather the information about the exchange or supplier is being emerging nowadays. Although it is perfectly reasonable along with the IoT, the concept can get a new effort but it seems that its impact remains constrained till now.

10. **Smart farming:** The method of farmer's work could be revolutionised by the remoteness of farming operations and the large number of animals that could be tracked on the IoT. However, this proposal has so far not come to the

attention of a large scale. Nonetheless, one of the technologies on the IoT should not be overlooked but soon the intelligent agriculture will become the major area of operation in the primary agricultural sector.

8.2.4   Merits and demerits of IoT application with cloud

Some of the merits of the IoT applications with cloud are as follows:

1. **Security:** One can monitor and control our homes through the use of mobile phones.
2. **Stay connected:** All the members of the family can always stay connected with the network.
3. **Efficient usage of electricity and energy:** The home appliances which can communicate with the user can do their maintenance by themselves and will utilise the electricity in an efficient manner.
4. **Pocket personal assistance:** This application of IoT will remind you all your schedules and will alarm you on time.
5. **Road safety:** The embedded system in a car can identify the occurrence of vehicle crashes and accidents on the way of travelling.
6. **Better healthcare and management:** A machine doctor like system can monitor and diagnosis the disease and suggest the method of treatment based on evidences without any knowledge of a doctor.
7. **Cost-efficient business operations:** Various business activities such as managing customers, tracking, marketing, security and sales operations are performed efficiently by the tracking system.

Some of the demerits of the IoT are as follows:

1. **Privacy issues:** By staying connected with our friends and relatives through social media and sharing them about our all life events are not safe, which pave a greater way to hackers to misuse our information.
2. **Supper-reliance on technology and electronic gadgets:** Nowadays people relay on Internet for everything, even for calculations. This makes them potentially dump and even lose our valuable information by hackers.
3. **Becoming indolent:** Citizens seem to be more used to a browse-based jobs that make everyone inactive with their routine for every kind of outdoor activity, applied research, etc.
4. **Unemployment:** Due to these IoT applications, there will be a lot of unemployment problems for unskilled labours in various sectors, because these devices substitute the manpower.

8.3   Importance of fog computing

Some of the important fog computing technologies are as follows:

- Fog computing can offer better security at the low level of cost.

- It has a reduced bandwidth, because of processing the fog nodes before transferring it to cloud.
- For security and privacy concern, the fog will process the data quickly by means of sensing sensors and store the data confidentially in cloud or else in local servers.
- The fog application can be installed anywhere, based on the client requirement, and it has high mobility and can be used for monitoring the environment and disaster conditions.
- Fog computing will diminish the risk of latency and can handle the data in better manner with less bandwidth.

8.3.1   Overview of fog

The researchers from the CISO system have proposed the fog computing in the year 2012 based on handling out the logic of the application and data at the edge. If a concept of fog computing is an inbuilt IoT application then it will work on the basis of the IoT concept. It can offer us a higher level of storage, networking and computation services, etc. based on a virtualised and non-virtualised computing standard. That is, it mainly concentrates on distributing the facilitating service with low latency. This is evident that the use of inactive computing resources close to clients would significantly improve system reliability if the storage size is not that big.

Figure 8.6 displays a fog computing basic model. Every computer that has capability for processing, networking and storage will serve as a tool for fog. The fog will be connected to a huge number of heterogeneous nodes which include sensors as well as the actuators. When necessary, computing is done in fog devices as well as storage facilities which are also in use for a time, at least in certain fog

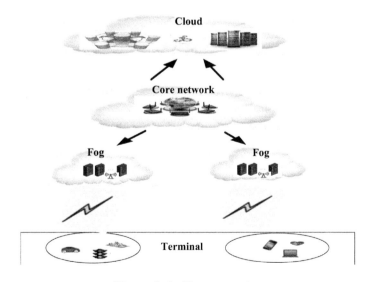

Figure 8.6   Fog computing

devices. Time-sensitive computing is performed in the fog without the intervention of external parties and is mostly performed by the fog processing devices. In a cloudlet-like sandboxed environment, the fog computing framework facilitates running new services or basic network functions and applications. Nonetheless, the subject remains a research challenge as the question remains how the fog can provide such services. Fog computing is basically a cloud extension but similar to the things that work with IoT software. As shown in Figure 8.6, fog computing serves as a cloud-to-end intermediary device taking data, storage and networking resources closer to the end users themselves. Such devices have been termed fog nodes and can be used wherever there is a network connection, for example, switches, routers, embedded servers and video surveillance cameras.

8.3.2 Definition for fog

Fog computing has been defined in different ways by the various research; some of them are described here in this section.

Bonomi *et al.* [25] have stated that fog computing is an extremely virtualised platform that provides services for processing, storing and networking between IoT devices and conventional cloud computing data centres, usually but not necessarily at the edge of the network.

- Cisco System [26] has described the fog computing as a heterogeneous system where various centralised as well as the decentralised devices communicate and cooperate with the network to perform the processing of the data and storage without any interference of the outsiders.
- IBM [27] has termed fog computing the concept for putting such systems and services at the edge of the Internet, rather than setting up networks for cloud storage and use.
- Naha *et al.* [29] have stated fog computing as a geographically dispersed computational system with a resource pool consisting of one or even more omnipresent linked heterogeneous systems at the edge of the network and not solely effortlessly backed up by cloud services to have scalable computing, processing and connectivity in isolated settings to a wide range of customers in the vicinity.

8.3.3 Description of fog architecture

The fog computing can be used in various IoT applications and plays a crucial role in industrial networking sectors. Figure 8.7 shows the basic architecture of fog, which consists of fog nodes, clouds/servers, routers, gateways and endpoints. The cloud/server will be at the top of the architecture, and IoT will be at the lower bottom. The symbols C, N, S represent the computation, networking and the storage capabilities of the server and the fog nodes are utilised to implement the distributed IoT applications.

The endpoint things may be of routers, proxy servers, set-top boxes, switches or some other computing devices. The server in this fog computing system is in

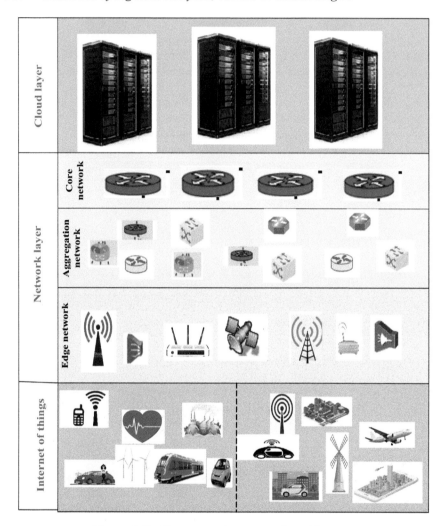

Figure 8.7   Fog computing network architecture

charge of the conversion charge in between the computing environment and the heterogeneous devices. These servers also have the responsibility to handle the fog devices and the gateways and these GW can provide the conversion between the cloud, fog and the IoT layers.

Figure 8.8 shows the layered architecture of fog with six layers named as physical and virtualisation, monitoring, preprocessing, temporary storage, security and transport layers.

Physical and virtualisation layer: The bottom most first layer of the architecture consists of different types of nodes, namely physical nodes, virtual nodes and virtual sensor networks and all controlled and upheld based on the demand of service

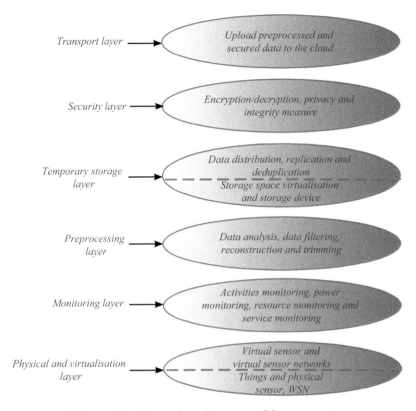

Figure 8.8   Layered architecture of fog computing

and types. The sensors are redistributed in order to monitor the environs and transfer the gathered information for filtering and preprocessing through the gateway to the upper layer.

Monitoring layer: Then the second bottom most layer is the monitoring layer, which monitors the utilisation of resources, network elements and the availability of sensors and fog nodes. All the activities and the performance of the computing network based on various applications will be monitored here in this layer. The energy consumption of the nodes can also be monitored because of various levels of consumption based on the device requirement in an effective manner.

Preprocessing layer: In this layer data management, filtering and trimming is carried out in order to extract the valid information. Then the processed data can be stored in the temporary storage until the preprocessed data is transmitted to the cloud layer through the gateway.

Security layer: In this layer, encryption and decryption of the data is carried out in order to keep away the data from tampering.

Transport layer: This is the last layer of the fog computing layered architecture. In this layer, the monitored, preprocessed and secured data will be uploaded in the cloud through the gateway.

Gateway: The IoT device appliances are connected to the cloud through the gateway, and it stores their later user services, which is also known as smart gateway.

8.3.4   Research direction in fog

Nowadays fog computing is one of the emerging approaches, which has been under the consideration of various research scholars. Based on the analysis of significance, drawbacks, applications and the architecture of fog computing, we conclude that some of the challenges like security and privacy are still being an open issue and hot topic for future direction and will propel the road of achieving attention of huge business sectors with advancement in the near future.

8.4   Significance of edge computing

Edge can be represented as the computing network or resources path in between the data source, centres and cloud, where the data source will be with the sensor or smart device but the edge will be of a smartphone in the case of cloud mobile applications. Some of the significances of edge computing are as follows:

The main significance of edge computing is that the computation is carried out at the nearer location of the data source.

- In addition, the edge computing will take part in both the data consumption and production of data while processing.
- Demanding resources and data, edge devices can execute cloud computing activities.
- An edge node will perform data storage, computer offloading, processing and caching.
- The edge system can also provide clients with applications and support on behalf of the network.
- The edge systems are well designed to meet the standards of security and reliability.

8.4.1   What is edge computing

Edge computing is defined as the computing technology that acts at the edge of the network between the data source and the cloud data centres. For example, the boundary between home and cloud seems to be a smart home gateway and it focuses predominantly on the end of things [31].

8.4.2   Benefits of edge computing

Some of the benefits of edge computing are described in the following section:

- Here, there is no need to transfer the data to the cloud, because the processing of data will be quite near to the data collection source.

- Needs low network and server load.
- This computing can process the data with minimal response time and can be applicable to various IoT applications.
- This computing can incorporate various AI (artificial intelligence) and ML (machine learning) for various sectors.

8.4.3 How edge computing used in IoT applications

The edge computing can be used in IoT application based on the following five aspects:

1. **Increased data security:** While IoT systems are a prime target towards hacking attacks then the edge computing will support you protect the networks and enhance data privacy across the board. Due to the fact that the information is decentralised and dispersed among the devices in which it is generated, it is difficult to remove the entire network or destroy all the data with a single attack.
2. **Better app performance:** The data that travels between the device and the data centre will take some amount of time; but by storing and processing data near to its entire source it consequently reduces the lag time readily and improves the overall performance of the app. As a result, in real time, one can analyse the data, without any delay.
3. **Reduced operational costs:** There is no need of an excess of cloud storage if we store and handle most of the data 'on the top'. However, one can only sort out the unnecessary information and archive the relevant data. As a consequence, the prices of your services will inevitably fall.
4. **Improved business efficiency and reliability:** In addition, lower data loads and less cloud storage contribute to more effective operations. In addition, linkage problems are not going to be incredibly troublesome as they are meant for other cloud-based IoT products. This is based on the fact that without any Internet connection, your devices will operate independently.
5. **Unlimited scalability:** Just as with cloud, edge computing helps one to level the IoT network as required, without relating to the resources (or costs) available. Edge computing is quite glowing when it comes to time-sensitive activities; as a result of the benefits mentioned previously, it has an unlimited scalability.

Some of the merits of edge computing are as follows:

- Edge computing will respond quickly and provide a quality of service.
- Comprises reliable nonstop connection.
- Has less bandwidth and loses less data.
- Lower bandwidth will considerably reduce the cost of devices and applications.

Some of the demerits of edge computing are as follows:

- The edge computing will process and analyse only a subset of data by removing raw data and incomplete insights by itself.

- Here, hackers can access the important data due to its increase in attack paths.
- It requires a greater number of local hardware.

8.4.4   Future of edge computing

By bringing the data and resources closer, edge computing can experience improved throughput, performance and real-time involvement. This draws the attention of many users and the research scholars towards the edge computing, and in future by making the IoT as the prime drive of the edge will further enhance the performance and efficiency of the system applications.

8.5   Architecture review with cloud and fog and edge computing with IoT applications

Figure 8.8, layered architecture of fog computing, depicts the fog layer between the cloud and the Internet of Things, which aids the traditional cloud computing model in connecting to the appropriate networks.

Here, through getting the system and database services right to the edge of the network, significant amounts of tasks will now be handled close to the IoT devices rather than sending data to the cloud all the way. This will result in reduced contact times, causing certain latency-sensitive products that would otherwise have been inefficient to be adopted. The fog layer is made up of several independent fogs with a micro-data centre and different storage and processing capabilities. The fog layer would allow storage, preprocessing, data fusion and other critical services to off-load the cloud and provide IoT users with better QoS. Whenever a node in the IoT layer assigns a task to be handled or stored in the fog to cloud case, the node initially approaches the fog with which it is associated, instead of immediately sending the task to the cloud. Then the fog decides whether to do the job itself or forward it for processing to the cloud.

In the edge layer the edge nodes are installed with the algorithms and inter-connected with the devices which connect sensors and actuators. In order to have integration with the nearest network's communication interfaces are connected. In the figure 8.9 shows the processing of the fog nodes is done through the IoT gateway, server by communication and storage. The function of the edge node can be done with the help of fog layer if necessary, by means of installing some units.

8.5.1   How IoT applications meeting the challenges at edge

The major challenge of IoT applications at the edge will be of its big data and the number of IoT devices at the end. This might sometimes raise the problem of scalability and one even does not know whether the IoT application will mitigate this issue or not. At this condition, the edge computing will separate the scalability domain into various local and outside networks in an efficient way to tackle the big data and the number of IoT devices at the edge [34].

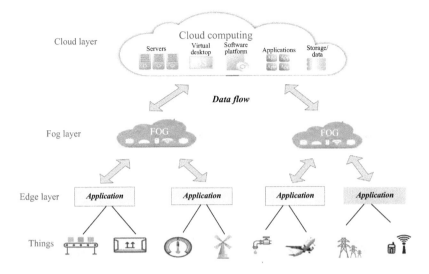

Figure 8.9   The functionalities of edge and fog layers

8.5.2   Review on cyber threats, latency time and power consumption challenges

Fog and edge computing allows computing resources at the edge networks and it locally provides big data analytics instead of transporting them to the cloud to improve power consumption, latency time, and security threats by deploying edge computing based IoT. Utilisation of fog computing applications tackles various security issues like virtualisation, network monitoring and attack detection and data protection. On contrary, for efficient big data analytics and cyber threats, systematic IoT–fog–cloud architecture is deployed to clarify the association between the three layers of IoT, fog and cloud.

8.5.2.1   Challenges of cyber security

Since the cloud and IoT are linked with the fog devices, IoT networks could be exploited using different cyber threats. Because of this, the devices are placed at dangerous locations that are not precisely monitored and preserved. Diverse security problems are mitigated by deploying this fog–IoT–cloud architecture as mentioned in the following:

- authentication and authorisation,
- advanced persistent threats,
- suspicious fog nodes,
- fog data management,
- privacy issues.

IoT infrastructure comprises sensors, and equipment are all around the network, as well as edge network. Several IoT devices fulfil requirements for latency, security and power consumption on the network, whereas the cloud computing does not satisfy such requirements. By deploying the edge computing in IoT network, it can eradicate these problems.

8.5.3 *Applications and future scope of research*

Nowadays, cloud computing offloading strategies are used in various applications, like resource allocations, traffic engineering, network management, and security and Internet traffic classifications. The future scope of cloud computing offloading strategies with fog and edge computing can be determined by implementing scalable and adaptive intrusion detection at the fog layer to attain the low-latency requirement. Moreover, our research extends to deploy diverse privacy techniques to preserve the sensitive information of the users.

8.6 Conclusion

In the recent trends, the fog and edge computing technologies have become important in the computing environment to enable new technologies like IoT. Based on innovating technologies, all the devices are going to be operated in the online mode. In the upcoming years, cloud, fog and edge computing technologies handle and analyse computing performance of the various models. In this chapter, we have discussed how the fog and edge computing architecture would be helpful for IoT-based applications. According to security point of view, the major challenges of cyber security issues can be reviewed.

References

[1]   N. Raden, "Big Data Analytics Architecture", Hired Brains Inc, 2012.
[2]   V. Christos, V. Hervatis, and N. Zary, "Introduction to Big Data in Education and Its Contribution to the Quality Improvement Processes," Big Data on Real-World Applications, vol. 113, 2016.
[3]   Big Data in the Cloud: Why Cloud Computing is the Answer to Your Big Data Initiatives by Mike Chan. 2018. http://www.thorntech.com/2018/09/big-data-in-the-cloud/.
[4]   A. Agrawal and S. Tripathi, "Integration of Internet of Things and Cloud Computing," SSRN Electronic Journal, 2018. doi:10.2139/ssrn.3166084.
[5]   R. Buyya, C. Shin, S. Venugopal, J. Broberg, and I. Brandic, "Cloud Computing and Emerging IT Platforms: Vision, Hype, and Reality for Delivering Computing as the 5th Utility," Future Generation Computing Systems, 2009, pp. 599–616.
[6]   M. Armbrust, A. Fox, R. Griffith, *et al.*, "A View of Cloud Computing," Communications of the ACM, vol. 53, no. 4, 2010, pp. 50–58.

[7] K. Gai, "Towards Cloud Computing: A Literature Review on Cloud Computing and its Development Trends," 2012 Fourth Int. Conf. Multimed. Inf. Netw. Secur., 2012, pp. 142–146.

[8] A. Botta, W. de Donato, V. Persico, and A. Pescapé, "On the Integration of Cloud Computing and Internet of Things," 2014 International Conference on Future Internet of Things and Cloud, Barcelona, 2014, pp. 23–30.

[9] R. Shanbhag and R. Shankarmani, "Architecture for Internet of Things to Minimize Human Intervention," 2015 Int. Conf. Adv. Comput. Commun. Informatics, 2015, pp. 2348–2353.

[10] S. M. Babu, A. J. Lakshmi, and B. T. Rao, "A Study on Cloud Based Internet of Things: Cloud IoT," 2015 Global Conference on Communication Technologies (GCCT), 2015, pp. 60–65.

[11] B. B. P. Rao, P. Saluia, N. Sharma, A. Mittal, and S. V. Sharma, "Cloud Computing for Internet of Things & Sensing Based Applications," 2012 Sixth International Conference on Sensing Technology (ICST), Kolkata, 2012, pp. 374–380.

[12] J. Zhou, T. Leppänen, E. Harjula *et al.*, "Cloud Things: A Common Architecture for Integrating the Internet of Things With Cloud Computing," Proceedings of the 2013 IEEE 17th International Conference on Computer Supported Cooperative Work in Design (CSCWD), 2013, pp. 651–657.

[13] K. Ashton, "That 'Internet of Things' Thing," RFID Journal, 2009, pp. 49–86.

[14] G. Joshi and S. Kim, "Survey, Nomenclature and Comparison of Reader Anti-Collision Protocols in RFID," IETE Technical Review, vol. 25, no. 5, 2013, pp. 285–292.

[15] ITU, "The Internet of Things," ITU Internet Rep., 2005, pp. 114–137.

[16] ITU, "Overview of the Internet of things," 2012, pp. 22–40.

[17] F. Kawsar, G. Kortuem, and B. Altakrouri, "Supporting Interaction With the Internet of Things across Objects, Time and Space," 2010.

[18] A. Botta, W. De Donato, V. Persico, and A. Pescapé, "Integration of Cloud Computing and Internet of Things: A survey," Future Generation Computing Systems, vol. 56, 2016, pp. 684–700.

[19] S. K. Dash, S. Mohapatra, and P. K. Pattnaik, "A Survey on Applications of Wireless Sensor Network Using Cloud Computing," International Journal of Computer science & Engineering Technologies, 2010, pp. 50–55.

[20] Open Cirrus. Cloud Computing. Open Cirrus: Why is cloud computing important? 2018. https://opencirrus.org/cloud-computing-important/.

[21] Y. Son, J. Jeong, Y. Lee *et al.*, "An Adaptive Offloading Method for an IoT-Cloud Converged Virtual Machine System Using a Hybrid Deep Neural Network," Sustainability, vol. 10, no. 11, 2018, p. 3955. MDPI AG, doi:10.3390/su10113955.

[22] Knud Lasse Lueth. IoT Analytics: The 10 most popular Internet of Things applications right now, 2015. https://iot-analytics.com/10-internet-of-things-applications/.

[23] P. Mishra, S. Kumar, and S. Mishra, "Significance of Fog Computing in IoT," Proceedings of 3rd International Conference on Internet of Things and Connected Technologies (ICIoTCT), 2018, pp. 26–27.

[24] M. Frigo, P. Hirmer, A. C. Franco da Silva, and L. Heloisa Thom. "A Toolbox for the Internet of Things – Easing the Setup of IoT Applications". In ER Forum, Demo and Posters. J. Michael and V. Torres (eds.), 2020.

[25] F. Bonomi, R. Milito, J. Zhu, and S. Addepalli, "Fog Computing and Its Role in the Internet of Things," Proceedings of the First Edition of the MCC Workshop on Mobile Cloud Computing. ACM, 2012, pp. 13–16.

[26] Cisco White Paper, "Fog Computing and the Internet of Things: Extend the Cloud to Where the Things Are," 2015.

[27] IBM, "What Is Fog Computing?," Sep 2016.

[28] Cisco Systems, "Fog Computing and the Internet of Things: Extend the Cloud to Where the Things Are," 2016, p. 6.

[29] R. K. Naha, S. Garg, D. Georgekopolous, *et al.*, "Fog Computing: Survey of Trends, Architectures, Requirements, and Research Directions," 2018.

[30] K. Jain and S. Mohapatra, Taxonomy of Edge Computing: Challenges, Opportunities, and Data Reduction Methods. In Edge Computing; Springer: Berlin, Germany, 2019; pp. 51–69.

[31] Z. Á. Mann, Optimization Problems in Fog and Edge Computing. In Fog and Edge Computing: Principles and Paradigms; John Wiley & Sons: Hoboken, NJ, USA, 2019; pp. 103–121.

[32] R. A. Cherrueau, A. Lèbre, D. Pertin, F. Wuhib, and J. Soares, "Edge Computing Resource Management System: A Critical Building Block! Initiating the Debate via Open Stack," Proceedings of the USENIX Workshop on Hot Topics in Edge Computing (HotEdge'18), Boston, MA, USA, 10 Jul 2018.

[33] S. A. Mostafavi, M. A. Dawlatnazar, and F. Paydar. "Edge Computing for IoT: Challenges and Solutions," Journal of Communications Technology, Electronics and Computer Science, Issue 26, 2019. ISSN 2457-905X.

[34] W. Shi, J. Cao, S. Member, Q. Zhang, Y. Li, and L. Xu, "Edge Computing: Vision and Challenges," IEEE Internet of Things Journal, vol. 3, no. 5, 2016.

[35] F.-J. Ferrández-Pastor, H. Mora, A. Jimeno-Morenilla, and B. Volckaert, "Deployment of IoT Edge and Fog Computing Technologies to Develop Smart Building Services," Sustainability, vol. 10, 2018, p. 3832.

Chapter 9

Fog computing framework for Big Data processing using cluster management in a resource-constraint environment

Srinivasa Raju Rudraraju[1], Nagender Kumar Suryadevara[1] and Atul Negi[1]

Cloud computing plays a vital role in processing an outsized quantity of data. The immense data generated from the net of things cannot be effectively realized into knowledge in real time if the data were to be processed by cloud computing. There is the requirement for transferal characteristics of cloud nearer to the request generator, so that processing of those immense data takes place at a one-hop distance nearer to the user. Fog computing technology helps one to overcome the challenges of huge data processing with the help of cluster management. The fog environmental setup consists of resource-constrained devices with minimal computational and storage capabilities. A fog computing framework augmented with cluster management can take the limitations of the resource-constrained devices for effective Big Data processing.

This chapter presents the implementation details related to the distributed storage and processing of big datasets in fog computing cluster environment. The implementation details of fog computing framework using Apache Spark for big data applications in a resource-constrained environment are given. The results related to Big Data processing, modeling, and prediction in a resource-constraint fog computing framework are presented by considering the evaluation of case studies using the e-commerce customer dataset and bank loan credit risk datasets. The chapter provides an arrangement of a distinctive fog cluster deployment. It elucidates the proposed framework and the results of the assessment of the proposed arrangement. Two case studies portraying how the proposed thought works for Big Data applications using fog cluster are described.

9.1 Introduction

The Internet of Things (IoT) and Big Data technologies have progressed enormously in recent years. The primary sources of Big Data are social data, transactional data,

[1]School of Computer and Information Sciences, University of Hyderabad, Hyderabad, India

IoT, etc. Big Data analytics provides competitive advantages in businesses, and the challenges include storing and analyzing large, rapidly growing, diverse data stores. Cloud computing provides a cost-effective and flexible solution to handle Big Data. However, it may not be useful for applications that require real-time response. The substantial processing capabilities of devices between cloud and source of data in the IoT environment paved the way to a new paradigm, fog computing, wherein a portion of the computation is shifted toward the origin of data from the traditional cloud-centric computation. In fog computing, computation occurs using the infrastructure on the way to the cloud from the source of data [1,2]. It offers several benefits like improved response time, data protection and security, reduced bandwidth consumption, and context- and location-aware service provisioning [3,4]. The performance of fog computing could be further improved by leveraging the processing capabilities of several fog nodes, by establishing a cluster and utilizing aggregated computing and storage capabilities of the cluster.

The *cluster computing* is a form of work out procedure in which a set of computational nodes is connected together to solve complex tasks more efficiently than a single node. Clusters improve availability and performance over that of a single computer. Parallel processing is a compelling and useful application of cluster computing. When a single processor executes one large task, it takes more time, whereas in cluster computing, a large task can be divided into smaller subtasks, and each connected node will execute one subtask, and the result will be collected at the master node. The processing time and burden of a single processor can be reduced by dividing the task among several processors [5]. Cluster computing harnesses the aggregated computing power of multiple devices in the cluster. A cluster can be categorized into high-availability, load-balancing, and high-performance clusters [6]. High-availability clusters are implemented primarily to improve the availability of services and usually employ redundancy to eliminate single point of failure. Load balancing clusters operate by having all workload come through one or more load-balancing front ends, which then distribute it to a collection of back-end servers. Although they are implemented primarily for improved performance, they commonly include high-availability features as well. High-performance clusters are implemented primarily to improve performance by dividing the computational task and distributing the execution across different nodes in the cluster.

The control of a cluster can be centralized or distributed [7]. In a centralized cluster, users submit jobs to a central node. The other nodes are processing nodes. The central node allocates user processes to processing nodes. The central node controls the cluster by collecting system state information and making all scheduling decisions. In a distributed cluster, a user can interact with any node in the cluster directly and submit the job. There is no master node in this configuration, and each node is considered as a local controller. Each node makes its own scheduling decisions for the processes submitted by its users and for accepting remote processes. The algorithms used in the load balancing clusters can be classified as either static or dynamic [8]. Static algorithms only use the given process and node information in making load balancing decisions. They do not adapt to fluctuations in the workload of the system. On the other hand, dynamic load balancing algorithms improve cluster performance by balancing the workload dynamically based on the current system state. However, dynamic algorithms are usually more complex than static algorithms. Performance benefits can be obtained by balancing the load among the nodes of a fog cluster [9].

In this chapter, a fog computing cluster is implemented using commodity hardware—Raspberry Pi to provide high performance and parallel processing for applications utilizing Big Data. The Apache-Spark-distributed processing environment is created in the fog cluster to realize the real-time large-scale data processing. To evaluate the functionality of the fog cluster, linear regression and logistic regression machine learning algorithms are run on different datasets in the distributed environment. The proposed system could be used in several application domains such as health care, smart home to get performance benefits compared to the traditional cloud-computing environment.

The rest of this chapter is organized as follows: Section 9.2 describes about the existing computational tasks that have been implemented for processing the Big Data using distributed frameworks. In Section 9.3, system description of the proposed framework is provided, and implementation details of the proposed system are given in Section 9.4. The results of the evaluation of the proposed system are provided in Section 9.5. In Section 9.6, we conclude this chapter and briefly discuss the possible future work directions.

9.2 Literature survey

This section presents related work done in the areas of distributed data processing in IoT and Big Data environment. Figure 9.1 depicts the taxonomy of distributed data processing considered in this chapter. Cluster computing supports parallel processing of a large task by making use of several computational nodes in the cluster. Utility computing provides computing resources to the customer based on demand and uses pay-per-use billing method [10]. Peer-to-peer (P2P) computing makes use of computer resources in a network. Several distributed computing frameworks such as Apache Hadoop, Apache Spark, and Microsoft's DMTK (Distributed Machine Learning Toolkit) and CNTK (Cognitive Toolkit) are available for processing Big Data. A brief

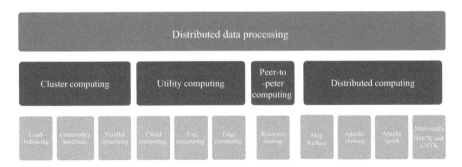

Figure 9.1 Taxonomy of distributed data processing

description about these computing models and frameworks is provided in the following subsections.

9.2.1   Cluster computing

9.2.1.1   Cluster computing using commodity hardware (Raspberry Pi)

Doucet and Zhang presented a study on cluster computing using Raspberry Pi [11]. The data collected from experiments running on the cluster computer are compared to those from a single Raspberry Pi. Diwedi and Sharma developed a cluster computer using five Raspberry Pis and used message passing interface for sharing the task among various nodes in the cluster for parallel processing [5]. The developed cluster has been tested using simple programs in C and Python. N. Ha presented work on parallel and distributed computing in the Raspberry Pi cluster [12]. Monte Carlo simulation to calculate Pi is used to investigate various aspects of the distribution of tasks and data within the cluster. Singer *et al.* presented a cheap, practical, and portable Raspberry Pi cluster called Pi Stack in their work [13]. The work also presented potential use cases for commodity single-board computer cluster architectures.

9.2.1.2   Load balancing algorithms

Load balancing aims to share the load between the available nodes. Several research works have focused on load balancing in cloud computing, but only a few works focused on fog computing. Prevost *et al.* presented a multi-tenant prediction model for predicting future workload for multiple services [14]. Round Robin load balancing algorithm is considered in the multi-tenant nature of cloud computing systems. The work does not consider resource utilization requirements of multi-tenants while balancing the load. Chien *et al.* presented a load balancing strategy for cloud environments on the basis of estimating the end of service time that reduces response and processing times [15]. This load balancing strategy optimizes resource utilization but does not consider multi-tenant applications of IoT architectures. W. Yong *et al.* presented a dynamic load balancing method of cloud center based on Software-defined networking (SDN) [16]. OpenFlow protocol, used in SDNs, offers task scheduling flexibility, real-time monitoring of the service node flow, and load condition. However, this work does not take into account fog computing and IoT, as well as multitenancy load balancing.

Xu *et al.* proposed a dynamic resource allocation method for load balancing in the fog environment [17]. This work proposed a framework for fog computing and the load-balance analysis for various types of computing nodes. Then, a corresponding resource allocation method in the fog environment is designed through static resource allocation and dynamic service migration to achieve the load balance for the fog computing systems. Neto *et al.* proposed a multi-tenant load distribution algorithm in fog computing environment for sharing the load among nodes considering specific tenants' requirements [18]. This work considers tenant maximum acceptable delay and tenant priority requirements that are used to sort the tenants according to their importance for the system. Werstein *et al.* proposed a load balancing algorithm for a cluster computer environment [19]. The proposed method considers CPU utilization, CPU queue length, network traffic, and memory utilization to determine the load of each node instead of traditional CPU queue length.

9.2.2 Utility computing

Utility computing is a service provisioning model that provides computing resources to the customer based on demand [10]. It uses *pay-per-use* billing method. Utility computing requires a cloud infrastructure backbone and focuses on business model for the services offered to the customer. Cloud computing relates to the underlying architecture in which services are designed. Cloud offers various services such as data storage, servers, software, and networking. Fog computing extends the concept of cloud computing to the network edge that makes it ideal for the deployment of latency-aware-distributed applications [4]. Fog computing brings down part of computation and storage from cloud to the network edge. Edge computing performs a part of the processing locally on the sensor or device itself. The difference among cloud, fog, and edge computing lies on where the computation happens on the continuum from end device (that generates data) to the cloud.

9.2.3 Peer-to-peer computing

P2P network consists of nodes where the communication and data sharing is carried on directly between nodes, rather than being arbitrated by an intermediary node. Each node in the P2P network acts as both a client and a server. The computing power of P2P network helps solving complex problems that require powerful computers using commodity hardware [20]. P2P computing uses distributed application architecture that divides the workload among peers in the network.

9.2.4 Distributed computing frameworks

9.2.4.1 MapReduce

The MapReduce framework and its algorithms are developed to process large-scale data applications in clusters. MapReduce uses two kernel elements: mappers and reducers in the programming model. The map function will generate a set of temporary key/value pairs, and the reduce function is used to merge/combine all the intermediate values of the key. The main idea of MapReduce algorithms is every job node of map and reduce is independent of other parallel job nodes that use different data and key to perform its operations [21]. MapReduce application is very useful if the algorithm is divided into mappers and reducers to work with large datasets.

9.2.4.2 Apache Hadoop

The Apache Software Foundation developed Hadoop as a top-level Apache project and it is written in Java. Hadoop is designed specifically to handle very large scale data operations, and its computing environment is built on top of the distributed clustered file system. MapReduce is used to manipulate data that are stored on a cluster of servers, and the work is broken down into mapper and reducer jobs to achieve massive parallelism. For a wider set of use cases and datasets, Hadoop has made it practical and applied for more applications. Unlike traditional transactional systems, Hadoop was developed and designed to scan through large datasets and produce its results using a highly scalable, distributed batch processing system. Hadoop works as a function to the data model and not as a data to the function model since it handles so much of data for analysis. Hadoop has two fundamental parts: a Hadoop distributed file system (HDFS) and a MapReduce programming framework [22,23].

9.2.4.3   Apache Spark

Spark is an open-source platform that defines a set of general-purpose APIs for Big Data processing. The key feature of Spark is its Resilient Distributed Datasets (RDDs), which can be represented by the nodes in a data processing graph. The edges represent the corresponding transformation that the RDDs will go through. In spirit, the RDD-based programming model is quite similar to Hadoop MapReduce and supports functional-style manipulations on RDDs via "transformations" and "actions." The difference between Spark and Hadoop lies in that Spark can cache the intermediate computation results in memory rather than dumping all results to the disk that involves much slower disk I/O [24]. Since Spark can also dump the result to the disk, it is strictly a superset of Hadoop MapReduce, leading to much faster speed especially after the first iteration. Spark is based on data parallelism paradigm [25] with the following features:

• low latency because of in-memory computation,
• speed: fast for large-scale data processing, and
• polyglot: we can write applications in Java, Scala, Python, and R.

Spark has two machine learning libraries—Spark MLlib and Spark ML—with very different APIs, but similar algorithms. These machine learning libraries inherit many of the performance considerations of the RDD and Dataset APIs, which they are based on, but also have their own considerations. MLlib is the first of the two libraries and is entering a maintenance/bug-fix only mode. Spark ML is the newer, scikit-learn inspired, and machine learning library and is where new active development is taking place.

9.2.4.4   Microsoft's DMTK and CNTK

DMTK is a platform designed for distributed machine learning [26]. "In recent years, practices have demonstrated the trend that more training data and bigger models tend to generate better accuracies in various applications. However, it remains a challenge for common machine learning researchers and practitioners to learn big models from the huge amount of data, because the task usually requires a large number of computation resources. To tackle this challenge, Microsoft has released DMTK, which contains both algorithmic and system innovations. These innovations make machine-learning tasks on big data highly scalable, efficient, and flexible. The algorithms released in DMTK are mostly non-deep learning algorithms." For state-of-the-art deep learning tools, Microsoft has released CNTK, which provides asynchronous parallel training functionalities [27]. "CNTK describes neural networks as a series of computational steps via a directed graph. It allows the user to easily realize and combine popular model types such as feed-forward deep neural networks (DNNs), convolutional neural networks (CNNs) and recurrent neural networks (RNNs/ LSTMs). CNTK implements stochastic gradient descent (SGD, error backpropagation) learning with automatic differentiation and parallelization across multiple GPUs and servers."

9.2.5 *Gaps identified in the existing research work*

The following are the gaps identified in the existing research work for processing Big Data in IoT environment:

- Processing the large amounts of data generated by IoT devices in the cloud environment introduces several disadvantages such as delayed response, excessive bandwidth utilization, and security concerns.
- Existing research work on cluster computing using commodity hardware has not focused on distributing the workload and performing machine learning tasks among several nodes in the cluster.
- Existing distributed computing frameworks use data parallel, model parallel mechanism for distributing the work load on resource-rich devices. Those frameworks are not directly adoptable to IoT environments with heterogeneous devices and different forms of data.

9.2.6 *Objectives of the chapter*

The following are the objectives of the chapter to address the earlier shortages with existing research work:

- Propose fog cluster environment that has distributed storage and processing capabilities of IoT data using commodity hardware nodes in the cluster.
- Augment fog computing with cluster management to address the effective Big Data processing on the resource-constrained devices.

9.3 System description

The proposed system contains a cluster of three Raspberry Pi fog nodes that are connected using a router, as shown in Figure 9.2(a). Out of these three nodes, one node acts as the master node and the other two nodes act as workers. Apache Hadoop is installed in all the nodes in the cluster. Hadoop is composed of the HDFS that handles scalability and redundancy of data across nodes and Hadoop YARN, a framework for job scheduling that executes data processing tasks on all nodes. Spark has been installed on top of the Hadoop Yarn cluster for scheduling the spark jobs submitted to the cluster.

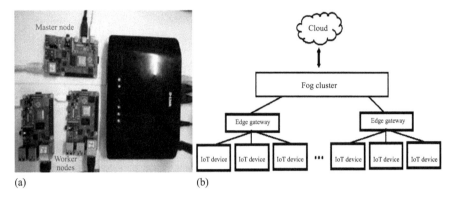

(a)   (b)

Figure 9.2   (a) Experimental setup of fog cluster with one master node and two worker nodes; (b) generic architecture of the proposed system

The generic architecture of the proposed system is shown in Figure 9.2(b). At the lower level of the hierarchy, IoT devices generate large amounts of data. Traditionally, Big Data analytics is performed in the cloud, which has few disadvantages such as more bandwidth consumption, delayed response, and data security concerns. Fog computing helps in addressing the problems related to cloud Big Data processing. As the resource capabilities (processing, memory, etc.) of fog nodes are limited in nature, our research work proposed a fog cluster architecture for processing Big Data in IoT setup. In the proposed architecture, the gateway devices aggregate data from several IoT devices and send it to the fog cluster for processing. These data could be processed by making the use of distributed processing and storage capabilities of the nodes in the fog cluster. The cluster manager distributes the load among several nodes in the cluster for the effective utilization of resources and better response times. The summary information from the fog cluster could be optionally sent to the cloud for further storage and analysis. The distributed storage and processing capabilities of fog cluster lends itself well to handle voluminous data generated in the IoT environment and offers various benefits such as improved response time, scalability, and data security.

9.4   Implementation details

9.4.1   *Using resource constraint device (Raspberry Pi)*

Initially, Raspberry Pi cluster is a set up with three nodes (Raspberry Pi 4B with 4GB RAM) in our experimentation [28,29]. The nodes in the cluster are given hostnames (node1, node2, and node3) by editing the information in the /etc/hosts file. This facilitates communication among the nodes by using names. As the nodes use Secure Shell (SSH) connection with key-pair authentication to connect with other nodes, each node generates keys (private key and public key) and the public keys of all nodes are shared among the nodes. Care should be taken about suitable Java version for the successful installation of Spark in the cluster. Hadoop

Table 9.1   Hadoop configuration parameters

Configuration file	Parameter name	Value
hdfs-site.xml	dfs.replication	2*
mapred-site.xml	yarn.app.mapreduce.am.resource.mb	1,024 MB
mapred-site.xml	mapreduce.map.memory.mb	512 MB
mapred-site.xml	mapreduce.reduce.memory.mb	512 MB
yarn-site.xml	yarn.nodemanager.resource.memory-mb	3,072 MB
yarn-site.xml	yarn.scheduler.maximum-allocation-mb	3,072 MB
yarn-site.xml	yarn.scheduler.minimum-allocation-mb	256 MB

*The value 2 indicates the replication factor. By default, HDFS replication factor is 3, but in the experimentation the factor was set to 2, because there is one master node and two worker nodes.

binaries (version 3.2.0) are downloaded from the Hadoop project page [23] and environment variables such as PATH and HADOOP_HOME are set properly in all the nodes in the cluster.

The configuration files *core-site.xml, hdfs-site.xml, mapred-site.xml,* and *yarn-site.xml* are edited appropriately to get the HDFS configuration properly [30]. The values set for important Hadoop configuration parameters are given in Table 9.1. The parameter *dfs.replication* specifies the replication factor of the data stored in HDFS. The remaining rows in Table 9.1 specify memory allocation (in MB) for YARN containers, mapper tasks, and reducer tasks. The *yarn.app.mapreduce.am. resource.mb* parameter specifies memory allocation to MapReduce application manager. The *mapreduce.map.memory.mb* and *mapreduce.reduce.memory.mb* specify the memory limits for the map and reduce processes, respectively. Resource manager allocates memory to containers in increments of the parameter value *yarn. scheduler.minimum-allocation-mb* and will not exceed *yarn.scheduler. maximum-allocation-mb* parameter value.

In our experimental setup, *node1* is the master node (runs the daemons HDFS NameNode and YARN ResourceManager), *node2 and node3* are the worker nodes (runs the daemons HDFS DataNode and YARN NodeManager). After the Hadoop cluster is established successfully, Spark has been installed on top of Hadoop. Spark binaries are downloaded into the master node from the Apache Spark download page [31] and SPARK_HOME environment variable value is set properly. Spark driver program declares transformations and actions on RDD and these requests are submitted to the master. The worker nodes execute these tasks (called *executors*). The information about these Spark memory settings is specified (in MB) in *spark-defaults.conf* file. The parameter *spark.executor.cores* specifies the number of cores used by the driver program. Table 9.2 gives information about the parameter values specified in our experimental setup (with 4GB RAM in each node).

The master node maintains knowledge about the distributed file system and schedules resource allocation. It hosts two daemons:

- the NameNode manages the distributed file system and knows where stored data blocks inside the cluster are, and

Table 9.2   Spark configuration parameters

Parameter name	Value
spark.driver.memory	1,024 MB
spark.yarn.am.memory	1,024 MB
spark.executor.memory	1,024 MB
spark.executor.cores	2[*]

[*]The value 2 indicates the number of concurrent tasks an executor can run.

- the ResourceManager manages the YARN jobs and takes care of scheduling and executing processes on worker nodes.

Worker nodes store the data and provide processing power to run the jobs and will host two daemons:

- the DataNode manages the physical data stored on the node, and
- the NodeManager manages the execution of tasks on the node.

Figure 9.3 shows the web user interface (UI) for monitoring the cluster (http://node1:9870). It provides information about the NameNode (master node) and various data nodes in the cluster (live nodes and dead nodes) and memory information.
The information provided by the web UI about data nodes is shown in Figure 9.4.
We can even use web UI for viewing the data nodes volume information (shown in Figure 9.5 for *node2* which is one of the data nodes in the cluster).

9.4.2   Spark fog cluster evaluation

The functionality of the Spark fog cluster has been tested by running linear regression and logistic regression machine learning algorithms using the API from *spark.ml* library. Scala programming language is used for developing applications. e-Commerce customer dataset [32] and bank loan credit risk dataset from UCI machine learning repository [33] are used in the experimentation. Figure 9.6 shows the storage of the dataset files in HDFS with a replication factor of two.
e-Commerce customer dataset contains eight attributes (such as Avg. Session Length, Time on App, Time on Website, Length of Membership, and Yearly Amount Spent) with 500 instances. Linear regression algorithm is used on this dataset to predict the value of Yearly Amount Spent attribute (dependent variable). Bank loan credit risk dataset contains 24 attributes (such as limit balance, bill amount, and payment amount) with 30,000 instances. Here, logistic regression is used for the binary classification task to determine whether payment will be done for the next month or not (dependent variable—*default_payment_next_month*).
Various steps followed for constructing *linear regression model* on e-commerce customer dataset on the cluster established in Section 9.4.1 are given next:

1. Construct data frame by reading the e-commerce customer dataset (.csv file downloaded from kaggle.com [32]).

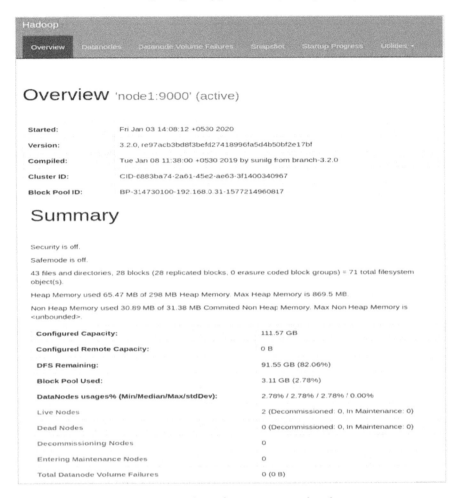

Figure 9.3   Web UI for monitoring the cluster

2. Add feature vector as a column to the data frame using *VectorAssembler* that allows the machine learning algorithm to use the features.
3. Add label column to the data frame with the values of *Yearly Amount Spent* column.
4. Dataset is split into training (80%) and test (20%) datasets by using *randomSplit()* function.
5. Create an object on *LinearRegression( )* class and train the model using function *fit( )* on the training dataset.
6. Run the model on test dataset to get the predictions. The trained model is also used for prediction on a new set of data.

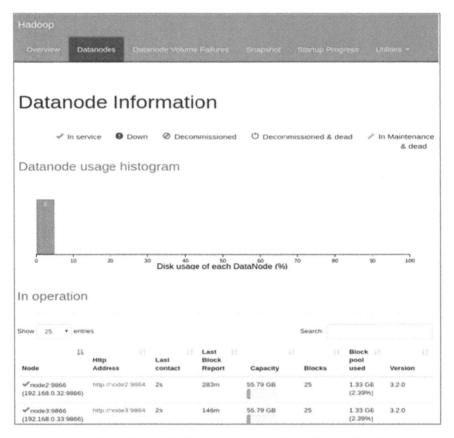

Figure 9.4   Web UI provided by master node about data node information

Various steps followed for constructing *logistic regression classifier* on bank loan credit risk dataset on the cluster established in Section 9.4.1 are given next:

1. Construct data frame by reading the bank loan credit risk data set [33].
2. Add feature vector as a column to the data frame using *VectorAssembler* that allows the machine learning algorithm to use the features.
3. Add label column to the data frame with the values of *Creditability* column.
4. Dataset is split into training (70%) and test (30%) datasets by using *randomSplit()* function with a *seed* value of 5,043.
5. Create an object on *LogisticRegression( )* class by setting *max iteration* value with 100 and train the model using *fit( )* function on the training dataset.
6. Run the model on test dataset to get the predictions. Prediction data frame is constructed using *transform()* function on logistic regression model.
7. An object on *BinaryClassificationEvaluator()* class is created by using the metric *areaUnderROC* to obtain the accuracy of the logistic regression model.

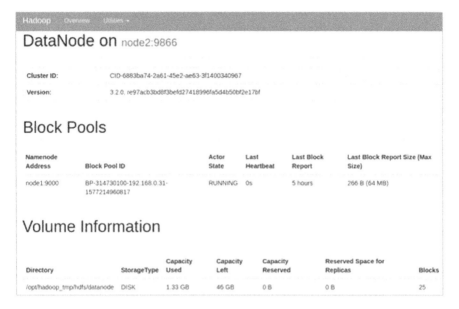

Figure 9.5   Web UI providing volume information for data node (node2)

Figure 9.6   Storage of datasets in HDFS with a replication factor of 2

9.5   Results and discussion

The proposed system makes use of the distributed storage and processing capabilities of Spark cluster to execute the machine learning algorithms on large datasets in the resource-constrained environment augmented with cluster management. The performance metrics such as *root mean square error*, *mean square error*, and *R-squared* for the linear regression model on e-commerce customer dataset are given in Table 9.3.

Table 9.3   Performance metric values for
linear regression model

Metric name	Value
Root mean square error	9.9232567
Mean square error	98.4710252
R-squared	0.9843155

Table 9.4   New data items used for testing linear regression model on e-commerce
customer dataset

Avg. Session Length	Time on App	Time on Website	Length of Membership	Yearly Amount Spent
40.49727	12.65565	39.57767	3.082621	687.9511
31.92627	20.10946	37.26896	2.664034	492.2049
33.00091	11.33028	17.1106	4.104543	487.5475

```
+----------------+--------------------+-------------------+
|           label|            features|         prediction|
+----------------+--------------------+-------------------+
|687.951053968401|[40.4972677251123...|687.5675908115015|
|492.204933444326|[31.9262720263602...|728.7461891763403|
|487.547504867472|[33.0009147556427...|496.4653551642202|
+----------------+--------------------+-------------------+
```

Figure 9.7   Prediction result of the model given by master node for a new set of
data (given in Table 9.4)

The prediction results of the model on a new set of data (given in Table 9.4) are shown in Figure 9.7. In this result, the first column of the table is the actual value of the dependent variable (*Yearly Amount Spent*) and the second column (features) is the feature vector prepared with the independent variable values. The model for prediction uses this feature vector. The last column (*prediction*) indicates the prediction made by the model.

The execution of spark application on e-commerce customer dataset created three containers in the cluster (two on node2 and one on node3), shown in Figure 9.8. The fog computing cluster can handle processing large datasets efficiently because of performing operations on RDDs using executors on several worker nodes in the cluster.

Figure 9.9 shows information about the execution of tasks by executors in the fog cluster environment. An instance of the creation of executors for doing the job submitted to the cluster is shown in Figure 9.10. As the fog devices are typically resource-constrained, the configuration of parameters related to memory and CPU is

Figure 9.8   *Containers created as part of the execution of spark application on e-commerce customer dataset*

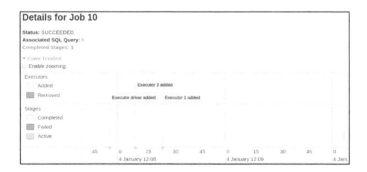

Figure 9.9   *Execution of various tasks by executors in the fog cluster environment*

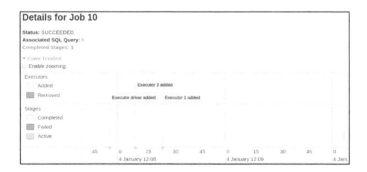

Figure 9.10   *Executors information for a particular job execution in the cluster*

very important for successfully establishing the cluster and making use of resources in the cluster for Big Data processing tasks.

The classification *accuracy* of the binary classifier on the credit risk dataset is 82% using *area under ROC curve (AUC)* metric (given in Table 9.5).

Table 9.5   *Performance metric values for logistic
regression*

Metric name	Value
Accuracy	0.8204
Area under ROC curve (AUC)	0.6332

9.6   Conclusion and future work

The IoT devices generate large amounts of data and are typically the sources of Big Data. Fog computing helps in addressing some of the issues related to processing the IoT data where the traditional cloud computing approaches have limitations. This chapter proposed a fog computing cluster environment for processing Big Data using distributed storage and processing capabilities. The implementation details about the setting up of fog computing clusters are presented in this chapter. The results related to processing, modeling, and predictions of Big Data on the proposed fog computing cluster are shown using two datasets. The proposed framework is useful for processing Big Data in several application domains such as health care, smart home, and smart building environments. It reveals the feasibility of processing Big Data in a resource-constraint environment. The present work will be extended to enable intelligence through federated learning in fog computing framework for IoT Big Data theme.

References

[1]   W. Shi, J. Cao, Q. Zhang, Y. Li and L. Xu, "Edge Computing: Vision and Challenges", IEEE Internet of Things, vol. 3, pp. 637–646, 2016.

[2]   S. R. Sahith, S. R. Rudraraju, A. Negi and N. K. Suryadevara, "Mesh WSN Data Aggregation and Face Identification in Fog Computing Framework", International Conference on Sensing Technology (ICST), Sydney, Australia, 2019, pp. 1–6, DOI: 10.1109/ICST46873.2019.9047708.

[3]   M. Aazam, S. Zeadally and K. A. Harrass, "Fog Computing Architecture, Evaluation, and Future Research Directions", IEEE Communications Magazine, 2018.

[4]   S. Sarkar, R. Wankar, S. Srirama and N. K Suryadevra, "Serverless Management of Sensing Systems for Fog Computing Framework", IEEE Sensors Journal, vol. 20, no. 3, pp. 1564–1572, 2020, DOI: 10.1109/JSEN.2019.2939182.

[5]   D. V. Diwedi and S. J. Sharma, "Development of a Low Cost Cluster Computer Using Raspberry Pi", IEEE Global Conference on Wireless Computing and Networking (GCWCN), Nov. 2018.

[6]   P. Sharma, B. Kumar and P. Gupta, "An Introduction To Cluster Computing using Mobile Nodes", IEEE International Conference on Emerging Trends

in Engineering and Technology (ICETET), Dec. 2009, DOI: 10.1109/ICETET.2009.28.

[7] P. Warstein, H. Situ and Z. Huang, "Load Balancing in a Cluster Computer", IEEE International Conference on Parallel and Distributed Computing, Applications and Technologies, 2010.

[8] A. Garg, "A Comparative Study of Static and Dynamic Load Balancing Algorithms", IJARCSMS, vol. 2, pp. 386–392, 2014.

[9] Q. Fan and N. Ansari, "Towards Workload Balancing in Fog Computing Empowered IoT", IEEE Transactions on Network Science and Engineering, vol. 7, no. 1, pp. 253–262, 2020, DOI: 10.1109/TNSE.2018.2852762.

[10] I. I. Ivanov, "Utility Computing: Reality and Beyond", ICETE 2007, Communications in Computer and Information Science, vol 23, Springer, 2007.

[11] K. Doucet and J. Zhang, "Learning Cluster Computing by Creating a Raspberry Pi Cluster", ACM SE '17 Proceedings of the SouthEast Conference, 2017, pp. 191–194.

[12] N. Ha, "Raspberry Pi Cluster for Parallel and Distributed Computing", MS Project Report, Montana Technological University, 2019.

[13] J. Singer, H. Herry, P. J. Basford, *et al.*, "Next Generation Single Board Clusters", IEEE/IFIP Network Operations and Management Symposium, Apr. 2018.

[14] J. J. Prevost, K. Nagothu, B. Kelley and M. Jamshidi, "Load Prediction Algorithm for Multi-Tenant Virtual Machine Environments", World Automation Congress (WAC), Puerto Vallarta, Mexico, 2012.

[15] N. K. Chien, N. H. Son and H. Dac Loc, "Load Balancing Algorithm Based on Estimating Finish Time of Services in Cloud Computing", 18th IEEE International Conference on Advanced Communication Technology (ICACT), Pyeongchang Kwangwoon Do, South Korea, 2016, pp. 228–233.

[16] W. Yong, T. Xiaoling, H. Qian and K. Yuwen, "A dynamic Load Balancing Method of Cloud-Center Based on SDN", China Communications, vol. 13, no. 2, pp. 130–137, 2016.

[17] X. Xu, S. Fu, Q. Cai, *et al.*, "Dynamic Resource Allocation for Load Balancing in Fog Environment", Wireless Communications and Mobile Computing, 2018.

[18] E. C. P. Neto, G. Callou and F. Aires, "An Algorithm to Optimize the Load Distribution of Fog Environments", IEEE International Conference on Systems, Man, and Cybernetics (SMC), Banff, Canada, October 2017.

[19] P. Werstein, H. Situ and Z. Huang, "Load Balancing in a Cluster Computer", IEEE International Conference on Parallel and Distributed Computing, Applications and Technologies (PDCAT), 2006.

[20] J. Mishra and S. Ahuja, "P2P Compute: A Peer-to-Peer Computing System", 2007 International Symposium on Collaborative Technologies and Systems, Orlando, FL, 2007, pp. 169–176, DOI: 10.1109/CTS.2007.4621754.

[21] P. R. Merla and Y. Liang, "Data Analysis Using Hadoop MapReduce Environment", IEEE International Conference on Big Data (Big Data), Dec. 2017, DOI: 10.1109/BigData. 2017.8258541.

[22] S. G. Manikandan and S. Ravi, "Big Data Analysis Using Apache Hadoop", International Conference on IT Convergence and Security (ICITCS), Oct. 2014, DOI: 10.1109/ ICITCS.2014.7021746.

[23] Apache Hadoop, Last accessed on 25 Nov 2019, https://hadoop.apache.org/.

[24] M. Zaharia, M. J. Franklin, A. Ghodsi, *et al.*, "Apache Spark", Communications of the ACM, 2016.

[25] J. Fu, J. Sun and K. Wang, "SPARK—A Big Data Processing Platform for Machine Learning", IEEE International Conference on Industrial Informatics – Computing Technology, Intelligent Technology, Industrial Information Integration, 2016.

[26] Distributed Machine Learning Toolkit, Last accessed on 18 Oct 2019, URL: http://www.dmtk.io/.

[27] Cognitive Toolkit, Last accessed on 18 Oct 2019, URL: https://docs.microsoft.com/en-us/cognitive-toolkit/.

[28] K. Doucet and J. Zhang, "Learning Cluster Computing by Creating a Raspberry Pi Cluster", ACM SE '17 Proceedings of the SouthEast Conference, 2017, pp. 191–194.

[29] G. Mills, Building a Raspberry Pi Cluster, Last accessed on 20 Nov 2019, URL: https://medium.com/@glmdev/building-a-raspberry-pi-cluster-784f0df9afbd.

[30] F. Houbart, Establishing a Hadoop Cluster, Last accessed on 30 Oct 2019, URL: https://www.linode.com/docs/databases/hadoop/how-to-install-and-set-up-hadoop-cluster/.

[31] Apache Spark, Last accessed on 20 Nov 2019, URL: https://spark.apache.org/downloads.html.

[32] Ecommerce Customer dataset, Last accessed on 25 Nov 2019, URL: https://www.kaggle.com/ksarafrazi/linear-regression-e-commerce-customers.

[33] Credit Card dataset, Last accessed on 25 Nov 2019, URL: https://archive.ics.uci.edu/ml/ datasets/default+of+credit+card+clients#.

Chapter 10

Role of artificial intelligence and big data in accelerating accessibility for persons with disabilities

Kundumani Srinivasan Kuppusamy[1]

Artificial intelligence (AI) and big data have emerged into mainstream tools from being niche tools in the recent past. These technological improvements have changed the manner in which software tools are designed and have provided unprecedented benefits to the users. This chapter analyses the impact of both of these technologies through the lens of accessibility computing which is a sub-domain of human–computer interaction. The rationales for incorporating accessibility for persons with disabilities in the digital ecosystem are illustrated. This chapter proposes a key term 'perception porting' which is aimed towards converting of data suitable for one sense through another with the help of AI and big data. The specific tools and techniques that are available to assist persons with specific disabilities such as smart vision, smart exoskeletons, captioning techniques, Internet of Things-based solutions are explored in this chapter.

10.1 Introduction

With the evolution of the knowledge-based economy that we are living in, data has become the most important asset. Access to this important resource decides the quality of life; hence, it becomes very important to keep this resource inclusive. Constructing a digital ecosystem that caters to the needs of a diverse population is a critical component. The emergence of artificial intelligence (AI) and big data has made a huge impact on the daily lives of each one of us. This chapter focusses on the impact of AI and big data on a special group of users, persons with disabilities. As per the World Health Organization's report, there are more than 1 billion persons with disabilities in the world who constitute 15% of the world population [1]. This means that one in seven persons in the world has some sort of disability. Hence it becomes inevitable to build the software applications in such a manner that everyone can get benefitted

[1]Department of Computer Science, School of Engineering and Technology, Pondicherry University, Pondicherry, India

irrespective of their physical disabilities. The founder of the World Wide Web, Tim Berners-Lee has popularly stated that 'The power of the Web is in its universality. Access by everyone regardless of disability is an essential aspect' [2]. Though Tim Berners-Lee has stated this about the web, it shall be very well extended to powerful technologies such as AI. Various incarnations of AI have made a ubiquitous impact on our lives. When we compare the impact of AI on persons with disabilities and on general users, it shall be observed that for general users it has made many tasks simpler whereas for persons with disabilities it has made them do or access things which were earlier not at all possible for them. In that perspective, the impact of AI on persons with disabilities is much larger than the general users.

With the prolific explosion in data, we have moved from the world of uniformly structured data. In the current scenario, we have a huge amount of data which has the following attributes: volume, variety, velocity and veracity [3]. In the perspective of persons with disabilities, each of these dimensions can cause certain barriers and hence efforts must be taken to build their impact universal.

This chapter attempts to provide an overview of the life-changing effects these technological developments have on persons with disabilities. With the acceptance of United Nations Conventions on Rights of Persons with Disabilities by many countries across the globe, the accessibility of information technology and its benefits to persons with disabilities has become mandatory. Persons with disabilities is an umbrella term that includes various types of disabilities. The requirements and impacts of specific types of disabilities are unique. This chapter explores the implications that these modern technologies have rendered to persons with disabilities. The primary objective of this chapter is to explore the life-changing impacts that AI has brought into the lives of persons with disabilities. Another objective is to explore the potential focus points which can be explored further to carry out extensive research.

10.2 Rationale for accessibility

Accessibility is emerging into an active sub-domain of human–computer interaction (HCI). There are works carried out in multiple dimensions in the accessibility domain such as web accessibility, mobile accessibility, accessible digital security, Internet of Things (IoT) accessibility [4–7]. In each of these dimensions, the role of big data and AI is there. Before exploring that, let us first identify the reasons or needs for incorporating accessibility in our digital ecosystem with the help of AI and big data:

- From the ethical perspective, accessibility is important because leaving out a large chunk of the human population from the positive impact of AI and big data would be unfair ethically.
- From a business perspective, it is not a wise decision to leave out a large customer base from accessing your business. Hence from the business perspective as well, accessibility is a critical factor.
- From the legal perspective, accessibility has been made compulsory by governments across the world. For example, in India, with the recent 'Rights of

Persons with Disabilities Act 2016', it is compulsory for organizations to keep their digital services and interfaces accessible to persons with disabilities [8]. Not only in India, but similar regulations are also available across various countries. Hence when building big data- or AI-based applications that would be used by users across the globe the developers need to be made aware of such regulations so that they will be in a position to build better accessible solutions [9].

• From the universal design perspective, it has to be understood that building accessible applications is not going to be useful only for persons with disabilities. There are certain situational disabilities such as while driving one cannot use hands. When an application is designed with considering the needs of such persons, it can be utilized by everyone.

From the aforementioned dimensions, it shall be understood that building an application with accessibility features is not a choice anymore. It is mandatory. AI and big data are no exceptions. So when building applications that utilize the features of AI and big data, accessibility should be made compulsory. This would enrich the overall user experience and increase the reach of the application across a spectrum of users.

One of the key challenges of accessibility is that it is not one-size-fits-all solution. What may be accessible for one group of persons may not be accessible for another group. In this dimension, AI and analytics can be adopted to measure, improve and monitor the accessibility of digital products to persons with disabilities. Through this persons belonging to various types of disabilities such as visual impairments, hearing impairments, locomotor disabilities, cognitive disabilities can all be benefitted with AI algorithms. The rationale is AI has made inferring of visual data, audio data and multimedia data better which might assist to cope up with the challenge in the specific sense such as vision, hearing and understanding.

10.3   Artificial intelligence for accessibility

The phenomenal adoption of AI across various domains has created unprecedented benefits to the end-users. The persons with disabilities as stated earlier are one of the most important groups that have gained benefits from AI. It is evident from the fact that leading IT majors have set up specialized research groups for carrying out accessibility research with AI. For example, Microsoft has set up a dedicated research group specializing in AI for accessibility [10]. Google has set up a state-of-the-art accessibility research group to enhance the accessibility of their entire product line-up [11]. IBM is giving a greater emphasis on accessibility and has contributed to enhance the technology-based accessibility to persons with disabilities [12]. With the emergence of trends such as machine learning, computer vision, there is an increased interest in providing accessibility for persons with disabilities.

10.3.1   *Perception porting*

Our day-to-day life decisions are taken by consuming data. Persons with disabilities have issues in consuming the data in the form which is suitable for particular senses. When the data gets presented through another channel of perception it becomes accessible. To say it simply, a person with visual impairment cannot see the world with his/her eyes. However, the environment becomes accessible to him/ her when the environment is presented through the auditory channel. This translation of visual perception to auditory perception shall be termed perception porting. AI has huge potential in performing this perception porting.

Perception porting requires AI and big data because of the following reasons:

- The perception porting has to happen in real time. For example, a user who wants to know what is around him through a mobile app should receive the responses reasonably immediately.
- The data inputs are of a wide variety, velocity and volume. For example, if we are building an app for narrating the objects around a user with visual impairment, the input data cannot be restricted, it would be noisy, sub-standard due to varying lighting conditions, etc. So such an application cannot be designed efficiently without incorporating AI and big data features.
- Perception porting requires continuous improvement through learning because of the aforementioned reasons. AI and its specialized sub-domains such as machine learning can be utilized for such purposes.

One of the important milestones in the perception porting happened with the parallel improvement in both AI and smartphone capabilities. The following are the important AI-based talking camera solutions:

- Seeing AI: It is an important project from Microsoft which can narrate the environment to users with visual impairments [13]. Some of its major capabilities are as follows: identify person, locate light, identify currency, read handwriting (with reasonable accuracy), read a scene. From the perspective of a person with visual impairments, these features would reduce the major barriers that they come across day-in, day-out.
- Lookout: The contribution from Google to narrate the environment around is termed Lookout [14]. Lookout uses computer vision and AI algorithms to narrate the visual world with auditory cues. It has specific modes such as work, home, scan and experimental. These modes can be used in coherence with the current place where the user is presently in.

10.3.2 Assisting deaf and hard of hearing

One of the primary complexities of accessibility is that it differs from one group to another or at times from one person to another person. For example, a solution which is accessible for persons with visual impairments may not be accessible for persons with hearing impairments. With the massive improvements in AI and big data, there are solutions which have emerged to assist the deaf and hard of hearing.

Live captions: The live captions from the Google accessibility research team are an important solution that is aimed towards adding text captions to a media which contains audio. This would assist the persons with hearing impairments [15]. It can be inferred that this solution is not assisting only the user with hearing impairments but anyone in a noisy ambiance. In this manner, many accessibility tools have helped one to improve the overall quality of user experience.

SignWriting: This solution is aimed towards converting multimedia captions written in oral language to sign language. As the sign language is the first language for trained persons with hearing impairments, they can perceive it in an easier and effective manner [16].

10.3.3   AI-based exoskeletons

One of the important applications of AI in the rehabilitation process is the development of smart exoskeletons [17,18]. In these solutions, the computational intelligence and machine learning algorithms are employed to detect user intention in the movement and provide better control to the user. The wearable robotics shall further emerge into an affordable accessibility solution and benefit the rehabilitation of mobility-restricted users. There are research studies on the development of exoskeletons to assist elderly [19]. Touch control-based robotic arms were developed by researchers to assist people to control a robotic arm with a simple touch screen-based interface [20]. The improvements which need to be incorporated in the currently available exoskeletons were also proposed by studies [21].

These AI-based exoskeletons need constant enhancement through learning which shall be enabled through a better understanding of the sensor data and efficient control algorithms.

10.3.4   Accessible data visualization

Along with the emergence of big data applications, data visualization techniques have also evolved to an advanced state. Visualization makes the consumption of data simpler for users. However, for persons with visual impairments, the consumption of these data visualizations is challenging. To solve this problem, there are solutions built that would use the other senses of data consumption such as auditory channels [22–24]. One such recent solution is Sonify which is aimed towards making the graphs accessible to persons with visual impairments [22].

The accessible data visualization is one of the important research domains in which there are still many challenging problems such as making the visualization universally accessible. As the accessibility needs each of the users, the type of visualization differs, so this problem is very challenging and requires the attention of researchers working in big data, AI and HCI domains.

10.3.5   Enabling smart environment through IoT for persons with disabilities

The workplace, home and public environments are evolving into a smarter landscape. The IoT along with AI, big data is facilitating this smart environment. Persons with disabilities and the elderly are two important groups of users who would get maximum benefits from this environment if implemented properly [25–28]. These smart environments can be used to guide the persons with visual impairments in proper navigation, can assist the mobility impaired, can help one to improve the overall interfacing of the persons with disabilities to the environment. The massive data gathered through these IoT sensors can be analysed through big data techniques, and smart solutions shall be provided through learning algorithms with the help of approaches such as machine learning. The emerging idea of smart cities has great potential in making the lives of persons with disabilities more independent with the application of AI [29]. To assist persons with mobility challenges, intelligent wheelchairs have been proposed, which shall be controlled with the help of facial expressions [30]. The roles of wearables in assisting the persons with disabilities are explored by research studies across various dimensions such as education [31]. Overall, the home where they live, the public spaces they navigate and the workplaces where they work all can be enhanced by ergonomic upgrading leading to improvements in ease-of-life for persons with disabilities [32].

10.4   Conclusions

This chapter has explored the potential impact of AI and big data techniques from the lens of accessibility computing. The power of these technologies becomes manifolds when it gets applied to persons with disabilities as it brings life-changing impacts to them. The rationale for providing accessibility is presented through four different dimensions. An important term perception porting is proposed in this chapter which deals with converting the data suitable for one sense into another with the help of AI algorithms. Specific benefits to individual types of disabilities are narrated and the state-of-the-art tools available are presented. The objective of this article is to bring the attention of researchers working in various domains such as big data, AI and HCI to consider the needs of these special groups of significantly sized users which would, in turn, benefit the overall humanity.

References

[1]   WHO. World Report on Disability [Internet]. WHO. 2020 [cited 2020 Jan 14]. Available from: http://www.who.int/disabilities/world_report/2011/report/en/.

[2]   Accessibility – W3C [Internet]. 2020 [cited 2020 Jan 14]. Available from: https://www.w3.org/standards/webdesign/accessibility.

[3]   Buhl HU, Röglinger M, Moser F, and Heidemann J. Big data. Business & Information Systems Engineering. 2013;5(2):65–9.

[4]   Foley AR and Masingila JO. The use of mobile devices as assistive technology in resource-limited environments: access for learners with visual impairments in Kenya. Disability and Rehabilitation: Assistive Technology. 2015;10(4):332–9.

[5]   Hanson VL and Richards JT. Progress on website accessibility? ACM Transactions on the Web. 2013;7(1):2:1–2:30.

[6]   Kuppusamy KS. PassContext and PassActions: transforming authentication into multi-dimensional contextual and interaction sequences. Journal of Ambient Intelligence and Humanized Computing [Internet]. 2019 [cited 2020 Jan 14]. Available from: https://doi.org/10.1007/s12652-019-01336-9.

[7] Mascetti S, Bernareggi C, and Belotti M. TypeInBraille: Quick Eyes-Free Typing on Smartphones. In: Computers Helping People with Special Needs [Internet]. Berlin Heidelberg: Springer; 2012 [cited 2014 Jul 31]. p. 615–22. (Lecture Notes in Computer Science). Available from: http://link.springer.com/chapter/10.1007/978-3-642-31534-3_90.

[8] Rights of Persons with Disabilities Bill – 2016 Passed by Parliament [Internet]. 2016 [cited 2020 Jan 14]. Available from: https://pib.gov.in/newsite/printrelease.aspx?relid=155592.

[9] w3c_wai. Web Accessibility Laws & Policies [Internet]. Web Accessibility Initiative (WAI). 2019 [cited 2020 Jan 14]. Available from: https://www.w3.org/WAI/policies/.

[10] AI for Accessibility – Microsoft AI [Internet]. 2020 [cited 2020 Jan 14]. Available from: https://www.microsoft.com/en-us/ai/ai-for-accessibility.

[11] Initiatives and Research [Internet]. Google Accessibility. [cited 2020 May 11]. Available from: https://www.google.com/accessibility/initiatives-research/.

[12] IBM Accessibility [Internet]. [cited 2020 May 11]. Available from: https://www.ibm.com/able/.

[13] Seeing AI | Talking Camera App for Those With a Visual Impairment [Internet]. 2020 [cited 2020 Jan 14]. Available from: https://www.microsoft.com/en-us/ai/seeing-ai.

[14] Clary P. Lookout: An App to Help Blind and Visually Impaired People Learn About Their Surroundings [Internet]. Google. 2018 [cited 2020 Jan 14]. Available from: https://blog.google/outreach-initiatives/accessibility/lookout-app-help-blind-and-visually-impaired-people-learn-about-their-surroundings/.

[15] Kemler B. If It Has Audio, Now It Can Have Captions [Internet]. Google. 2019 [cited 2020 Jan 14]. Available from: https://blog.google/products/android/live-caption/.

[16] Verdú E, Pelayo García-Bustelo BC, Martínez Sánchez MÁ, and González-Crespo R. A System to Generate SignWriting for Video Tracks Enhancing Accessibility of Deaf People. 2017 [cited 2020 Jan 14]. Available from: https://reunir.unir.net/handle/123456789/6383.

[17] Meng W, Liu Q, Zhou Z, Ai Q, Sheng B, and Xie S (Shane). Recent development of mechanisms and control strategies for robot-assisted lower limb rehabilitation. Mechatronics. 2015;31:132–45.

[18] Zaroug A, Proud JK, Lai DTH, Mudie K, Billing D, and Begg R. Overview of Computational Intelligence (CI) Techniques for Powered Exoskeletons. In: Mishra BB, Dehuri S, Panigrahi BK, Nayak AK, Mishra BSP, and Das H, editors. Computational Intelligence in Sensor Networks [Internet]. Berlin, Heidelberg: Springer; 2019 [cited 2020 Jan 14]. p. 353–83. (Studies in Computational Intelligence). Available from: https://doi.org/10.1007/978-3-662-57277-1_15.

[19] Hyun DJ, Lim H, Park S, and Jung K. Development of ankle-less active lower-limb exoskeleton controlled using finite leg function state machine. International Journal of Precision Engineering and Manufacturing. 2017; 18(6):803–11.

[20] Quiñonez Y, Zatarain O, Lizarraga C, Peraza J, and Mejía J. Algorithm Proposal to Control a Robotic Arm for Physically Disable People Using the LCD Touch Screen. In: Mejia J, Muñoz M, Rocha Á, and Calvo-Manzano J, editors. Trends and Applications in Software Engineering. Cham: Springer International Publishing; 2020. p. 187–207. (Advances in Intelligent Systems and Computing).

[21] Baratto M, Ceresi C, and Longatelli V. Upper Limb Exoskeletons for a Better Quality of Life: What Is Currently Available, and What Is Missing in the Market. In: Henriques J, Neves N, and de Carvalho P, editors. XV Mediterranean Conference on Medical and Biological Engineering and Computing – MEDICON 2019. Cham: Springer International Publishing; 2020. p. 1734–40. (IFMBE Proceedings).

[22] Ali S, Muralidharan L, Alfieri F, Agrawal M, and Jorgensen J. Sonify: Making Visual Graphs Accessible. In: Ahram T, Taiar R, Colson S, and Choplin A, editors. Human Interaction and Emerging Technologies. Cham: Springer International Publishing; 2020. p. 454–9. (Advances in Intelligent Systems and Computing).

[23] Chew YC, Davison B, and Walker BN. From design to deployment: an auditory graphing software for math education. In: Proceedings of the 29th Annual International Technology & Persons With Disabilities Conference (CSUN2014). 2014.

[24] Choi SH and Walker BN. Digitizer Auditory Graph: Making Graphs Accessible to the Visually Impaired. In: CHI '10 Extended Abstracts on Human Factors in Computing Systems [Internet]. Atlanta, GA, USA: Association for Computing Machinery; 2010 [cited 2020 Jan 13]. p. 3445–3450. (CHI EA '10). Available from: https://doi.org/10.1145/1753846.1753999.

[25] Abou-Zahra S, Brewer J, and Cooper M. Web Standards to Enable an Accessible and Inclusive Internet of Things (IoT). Association for Computing Machinery (ACM), New York, USA; 2017.

[26] Haouel J, Ghorbel H, and Bargaoui H. Towards an IoT Architecture for Persons with Disabilities and Applications. In: International Conference on IoT Technologies for HealthCare. Springer; 2016. p. 159–161.

[27] Hollier S and Abou-Zahra S. Internet of Things (IoT) as Assistive Technology: Potential Applications in Tertiary Education. In: Proceedings of the Internet of Accessible Things. ACM; 2018. p. 3.

[28] Misbahuddin S, Orabi H, Fatta R, Al-Juhany M, and Almatrafi A. IoT Framework Based Health Care System for Elderly and Disabled People. In: International Conference on Recent Advances in Computer Systems. Atlantis Press; 2015.

[29] de Oliveira Neto JS and Kofuji ST. Inclusive Smart City: An Exploratory Study. In: Antona M and Stephanidis C, editors. Universal Access in Human-Computer Interaction Techniques and Environments. Cham: Springer International Publishing; 2016. p. 456–65. (Lecture Notes in Computer Science).

[30] Rabhi Y, Mrabet M, and Fnaiech F. A facial expression controlled wheel-chair for people with disabilities. Computer Methods and Programs in Biomedicine. 2018;165:89–105.

[31] Anderson CL and Anderson KM. Wearable Technology: Meeting the Needs of Individuals with Disabilities and Its Applications to Education. In: Buchem I, Klamma R, and Wild F, editors. Perspectives on Wearable Enhanced Learning (WELL): Current Trends, Research, and Practice [Internet]. Cham: Springer International Publishing; 2019 [cited 2020 May 11]. p. 59–77. Available from: https://doi.org/10.1007/978-3-319-64301-4_3.

[32] Nevala-Puranen N, Seuri M, Simola A, and Elo J. Physically disabled at work: need for ergonomic interventions. Journal of Occupational Rehabilitation. 1999;9(4):215–25.

Overall conclusions

Vadlamani Ravi and Aswani Kumar Cherukuri

This volume discussed, at length, various aspects of big data, including all the dimensions, viz. five Vs. These aspects encompass data ingestion, metamorphosis in the database design, data storage, cloud/fog environment, various frameworks, parallelization, and scaling out various analytical/machine learning models and human–computer interaction in the big data analytics era, and finally streaming data analytics. This is one compendium that brought out all those important concepts under one roof. Future directions include performing edge intelligence in IoT at scale, large-scale time series data mining, anomaly detection in big datasets involving volume, velocity and variety aspects, hybridizing horizontal and vertical parallelism, i.e. a cluster of GPU-based servers, developing parallel and distributed versions of several evolutionary computing algorithms and finally developing fully automated algorithms that detect and eliminate noise in big data and thereby churning out the signal, i.e. important part of the big data, which will have several ramifications in many domains. Concerted efforts are also needed in the direction of increasing convergence speeds of deep learning architectures using the hybrid parallelization and distributed paradigm of big data. Even though this is achieved now using a cluster of GPU-based servers, a lot is left to be desired because they typically consume huge training times in domains like climate modelling, molecular modelling, etc.

Index

accessibility, rationale for 336–7
accessible data visualization 339
Accidents 221
AdaBoost 182
Adaptive Distributed Extreme
    Learning Machine (A-ELM*)
    228
aggregate-oriented NoSQL databases
    12–13
Airline on-time dataset 226
Alluxio 88
Amazon Dynamo 88–9
Amazon kinesis 111
Amazon Simple Storage Services,
    S3 88
Amazon Web Services (AWS) 115
ANOVA 228
ant colony optimization (ACO)
    algorithm 227
Apache Flink 92–3, 164–7, 177
  Apache Kafka 93
  Architecture of Kafka 93–4
Apache Flume 63, 168–9
  advantages of 63–4
  architecture of 65
  components of 64
  data flow model in 65
  features of 64
Apache Hadoop 319, 321–3
Apache Hadoop framework and
    Hadoop Ecosystem 39
  architecture of 39
  MapReduce, application
    implemented using 46–53
  MapReduce, architecture of 39–42
    executing map phase 42–3

reduce phase execution 45–6
  shuffling and sorting 43–5
Apache Hadoop MapReduce 212
Apache Kafka 111, 169–72, 192
Apache Mahout 61
  applications of 61–2
  features 61
Apache Oozie 66
Apache Pig 59
  characteristics of 59
  components of 59
  pig data model 60
  word count application using 60–1
Apache Samza 167
Apache Spark 67–8, 163–4, 177, 220,
    319, 322
  broadcast variables in spark 71–2
  caching RDDs 71
  concept generation in formal
    concept analysis using Spark
    82–5
  data processing in Spark 75
    example of GraphX 77–8
    features of Spark GraphX 76–7
    Spark GraphX 76
    Spark streaming 75–6
  driver program 69
  fault tolerance optimization 74
  I/O optimization 74
    data compression and sharing 74
    data shuffling 74
  memory optimization 73–4
  programming layer in Spark 80
    DataFrames in Spark SQL 81–2
    PySpark 80
    SparkR 80–1

Spark SQL 81
Spark cluster manager 70
Spark Context 69
Spark Core 69
Spark Datasets 72
Spark deep learning support 79–80
  CaffeOnSpark 80
  Deeplearning4j (DL4j) 80
Spark machine learning support 78
  example of MLlib 79
  keystone ML 79
  Spark MLlib 78–9
Spark resilient distributed datasets
  (RDDs) 70–1
Spark System optimization 73
  decentralized task scheduling 73
  scheduler optimization 73
Spark worker node 70
Apache-Spark-distributed processing
  environment 319
Apache Spark framework 212
Apache Sqoop 62
  export from Sqoop 63
  Sqoop import 62–3
Apache Storm 90, 167–8, 177
  architecture of 90–2
Apache Zookeeper 94
  ZDM—access control list 96–7
  Zookeeper data model 95–6
approximate kernel fuzzy *c*-means
  (akFCM) 238
approximate kernel possibilistic
  c-means (akPCM) 238
AprioriPMR 220
artificial immune system (AIS) 246
artificial intelligence (AI) 335
  for accessibility 337
    accessible data visualization 339
    AI-based exoskeletons 339
    assisting deaf and hard of
      hearing 338–9
    enabling smart environment
      through IoT for persons with
      disabilities 339–40
    perception porting 337–8

artificial neural network (ANN) 182
ARtool 221
association rule mining/pattern mining
  Hadoop MapReduce-based
    conference papers 220–3
  Hadoop MapReduce-based journal
    papers 217–19
  Spark-based conference papers
    223–4
  Spark-based journal papers 219–20
Auto-Associative Extreme Learning
  Machine (AAELM) 225
auto-associative neural network
  (AANN) 236
autoregressive integrated moving
  average (ARIMA) 178–9
Azure data lake environment 114–15

backpropagation neural network
  (BPNN) 225
batched online sequential ELM
  (BPOS-ELM) training 229
batch processing 166
Bayesian network (BN) classifiers 230
Bayesian predictive methods 177
best practices for data lakes 117–18
BigAnt 221
BIGCONNECT data lake 116–17
BigCross dataset 250
big data 298–9
  in cloud computing 299
  merits and demerits 299
Big Data Analytical 3–5
big data fabric 109–10
Big Data Operational 3–5
Big Data phenomenon 2–5
big data processing platforms 210
Big data storage systems 85
  Alluxio 88
  Amazon Dynamo 88–9
  Amazon Simple Storage Services,
    S3 88
  Cassandra 89
  Hadoop distributed file system 86–7
  HBase 88

Hive 89–90
Microsoft Azure Blob Storage-
WASB 88
binary Θ-join 135–7
BirdVis 194
BMSWebView2 224
bounded data streams 166
Brinkhoff 239
broadcast variables in spark 71–2
BSON 13
budgeted mini-batch parallel gradient
descent algorithm (BMBPGD)
235

CaffeOnSpark 80
CAIDA UCSD dataset 227
canopy-FCM 241
Car Evaluation 249
Cassandra 14–15, 89
categorical data 183
CDMC2012 246, 252
Celestial Spectral Dataset 217
CFI-Stream 189
CFS 251
change point detection (CPD) 186
Chebyshev function link ANN
(CFANN) 182
Chest-clinic network 250
Chi-FRBCS-BigData 233
Chi-FRBCS-BigData-Ave. 233
Chi-FRBCSBigData-Max 233
classification
Hadoop MapReduce-based
conference papers 231–5
Hadoop MapReduce-based journal
papers 227–30
Spark-based conference papers
235–7
Spark-based journal papers 230–1
Cleveland Heart Disease 252
Client document 29
Closed Enumerated Tree (CET) 189
closed frequent item sets (CFIs) 189
CloStream 189

cloud, fog and edge computing with the
IoT application
architectural view of 312–14
cloud computing with IoT
applications 299
applications of IoT 303–5
cloud computing importance 302–3
cloud offloading strategies 303
merits and demerits 305
ClueWeb dataset 250
cluster computing 318
distributed computing frameworks
Apache Hadoop 321–2
Apache Spark 322
MapReduce 321
Microsoft's DMTK and CNTK
322–3
gaps identified in the existing
research work 323
peer-to-peer computing 321
using commodity hardware
(Raspberry Pi)
load balancing algorithms 320–1
utility computing 321
clustering
Hadoop MapReduce-based
conference papers 239–44
Hadoop MapReduce-based journal
papers 237–9
Spark-based conference papers
244–6
Spark-based journal papers 239
clustering toolkit (CLUTO) 238
CNTK (Cognitive Toolkit) 319, 323
commercial-based data lakes 114
Amazon Web Services (AWS) 115
Azure data lake environment
114–15
developing data lake with IBM 115
Galaxy data lake (GDL) 115–16
computational approach to models 176
computational paradigm 191–6
concept adapting VFDT (CVFDT) 186
concept drift detection 177–9, 183–7

concept generation in formal
     concept analysis using Spark
     82–5
Connect-4 221, 223, 249
connected car 304
connected health 304
Connectionist 247
connectivity-based marketing 304
Connector API 172
Consumer API 172
cooperative PSO 250
counting triangles 138–40
Covertype 238, 249
Cubes document 28
cyber security, challenges of 313–14

DARPA 246
databases, impact of Big Data on 1
  Big Data phenomenon 2–5
  data distribution models 15
    combining sharding and
       replication 18–19
    replication 17–18
    sharding 15–16
  design examples using NoSQL
       databases 19–30
  NoSQL databases 9
    aggregate-oriented 12–13
    Cassandra 14–15
    disadvantages of 11–12
    MongoDB 13–14
  scalability in relational databases 6
    limitations of relational
       databases 7–9
    relational databases 6–7
data cataloging 114
data distribution models 15
  combining sharding and replication
       18–19
  replication 17–18
  sharding 15–16
data lake, architecture of 110
  data cataloging 114
  data ingestion layer 111
  data lake governance 113–14

data scientists responsibilities in data
     lakes 112–13
  ingress layer 112
  metadata management 113
  process layer 111–12
  raw data layer 110–11
data lake challenges 120
data lake in big data analytics 105
  architecture of data lake 110
    data cataloging 114
    data ingestion layer 111
    data lake governance 113–14
    data scientists responsibilities in
       data lakes 112–13
    ingress layer 112
    metadata management 113
    process layer 111–12
    raw data layer 110–11
  commercial-based data lakes 114
    Amazon Web Services (AWS)
       115
    Azure data lake environment
       114–15
    developing data lake with IBM
       115
    Galaxy data lake (GDL) 115–16
  data lakes pitfalls 108
  data warehouses and data lakes,
       differences between 107–8
  open source-based data lakes 116
    best practices for data lakes
       117–18
    BIGCONNECT data lake 116–17
    Delta lake 116
  taxonomy of data lakes 108
    big data fabric 109–10
    data reservoirs 109
    data silos 108–9
    data swamps 109
data lakes (DLs)
  Big data fabric 109–10
  data reservoirs 109
  data silos 108–9
  data swamps 109
  pitfalls 108

taxonomy of 108
data processing infrastructure 159
    analytics layer 159
    filtering layer 159
    formality layer 159
    storing layer 160
data processing in Spark 75
    example of GraphX 77–8
    features of Spark GraphX 76–7
    Spark GraphX 76
    Spark streaming 75–6
data reservoirs 109
data scientist 112–13
data scientists responsibilities in data
        lakes 112–13
data silos 108–9
data stream analytics (DSA) 175
    computational paradigm 191–6
    concept drift detection 183–7
    mining frequent item sets in data
        stream 187–91
    outlier detection 180–3
    prediction and forecasting 178–80
    scope and approach 177–8
data stream ingestion (DSI) 192
data streaming processing approaches,
        evaluation of 172
data stream models 176
data stream processing (DSP) 192–3
data stream processing systems
        (DSPSs) 177, 191–2
data stream resource management
        (DSRM) 193–4
Data Stream Resource Manager 193
data stream storage (DSS) 194
data swamps 109
data transport (DT) 192
data visualization tools 3
data warehouses and data lakes,
        differences between 107–8
deaf and hard of hearing, assisting
        338–9
deep learning (DL) 178, 182
Deeplearning4j (DL4j) 80
Delta lake 116

density-based forecasting 177
Design examples using NoSQL
        databases 19–30
directed acyclic graph (DAG) 191–2
DIrect Update (DIU) tree 189
disaster recovery data centre (DR-
        DC) 194
distributed computing frameworks
        319, 321–3
distributed data processing 319
distributed density-based clustering
        (DDC) algorithm 243
distributed density peaks clustering
        algorithm with locality-sensitive
        hashing (LSH-DDP) 238
distributed ELM (DELM) 228
distributed grid-based clustering
        (DGC) algorithm 243
distributed keyword search (DKS) 252
distributed processing 183
distributed stream processing engines
        90
    Apache Flink 92–3
        Apache Kafka 93
        Architecture of Kafka 93–4
    Apache Storm 90–2
distribution of papers 269
DMTK (Distributed Machine Learning
        Toolkit) 319, 322–3
drift adaptation 185
drift detection 183, 185
    in rule-based systems 187
drift understanding 185, 187
Driver program 69
dynamic neighborhood selection
        (DNS) clustering algorithm
        242

ECBDL'14 235
e-Commerce customer dataset 326
ECUESpam 235
edge computing 297
    benefits of 310–11
    future of 312
    in IoT applications 311–12

EdgeJoin 141–2
efficient parallel ELM (PELM) 224
ego-Facebook dataset 222
ego-Twitter dataset 222
Elapsed-Time-based Dynamic Passes
    Combined-counting 219
Electrical 240
EMSPOS 223
Enron dataset 238
Ensemble KF 179
Epsilon 235, 251
Erdõs–Rényi algorithm 231
estDec 188
Euclidean distance 181
extended Fiduccia–Mattheyses
    algorithm 238
extended Kalman filter (EKF) 178
extreme learning machine (ELM) 226

failure recovery 97–8
fast-mRMR 251
Fault Tolerance and Recovery 194
fault tolerance optimization 74
feature extraction 176
FedCSIS AAIA'14 DM competition
    dataset 234
FiDoop-HD 217
field grouping 168
field-programmable gate array
    (FPGA) 215
filtering procedure for the selection of
    articles to review 216
"5Vs" 2
Flink 194
Flink model 166
Flink zkNN (F-zkNN) algorithm 233
Flixster dataset 248
FLOating Rough Approximation
    (FLORA) 186
Flume 111
fog computing 297, 305
    definition 307
    layered architecture
        gateway 310
        monitoring layer 309

physical and virtualisation layer
    308–9
preprocessing layer 309
security layer 309
transport layer 310
network architecture 308
fog computing framework for Big Data
    processing 317
future work 332
implementation details
    Spark fog cluster evaluation 326–9
    using resource constraint device
        (Raspberry Pi) 324–6
literature survey 319
    cluster computing 320–1
    distributed computing
        frameworks 321–3
    gaps identified in the existing
        research work 323
    peer-to-peer computing 321
    utility computing 321
results and discussion 329–32
system description 323–4
fog–IoT–cloud architecture 313
fog nodes 297
forecasting 177–80
formal concept analysis (FCA)
    concept generation in 46–53
Fourier Inspired Windows for Concept
    Drift (FIWCD) 186
frequent item-set mining (FIM) 182,
    187–8, 190–1, 219
frequent item sets (FIS) mining
    187–91
frequent patterns (FPs) 217
Frequent Patterns Mining (FPM) 221
Friedman test 228
FRULER 225
FSM-H 217, 221
future directions 260–8
fuzzy-based clustering algorithms 245
fuzzy clustering 161
fuzzy *c*-means clustering algorithm
    implemented with MapReduce
    framework (MR-FCM) 238

fuzzy rule-based classification system (FRBCS) 228

Galaxy data lake (GDL) 115–16
GA optimized DT algorithm (MR-GAOT) 234
Gauss Distribution Set 238
general-purpose graphics processing unit (GPGPU) 215
genetic algorithms (GAs) 222
genome-sequence-encoding schema 236
Gisette 235
global grouping 168
glowworm swarm optimization (GSO) 241
Google 240
Google MillWheel 194
Google Search 299
GraphGen 217, 221
graph queries using MapReduce 138
    counting triangles 138–40
    subgraph enumeration 140–1
        EdgeJoin 141–2
        SEED Join 145–6
        Star Join 143–4
        TwinTwig Join 144–5
graph visualization tools 194
GraphX 164

Hadoop 2 66–7
Hadoop-based implementation of the *k*-NN (H-zkNN) 233
Hadoop-based KFCM (H-KFCM) 245
Hadoop distributed file system 86–7
Hadoop MapReduce-based conference papers 251–2
Hadoop MapReduce-based journal papers 249–50
HaLoop framework 53
    caching in HaLoop 55
    concept generation in FCA using HaLoop 56
    fault tolerance 55
    programming model of HaLoop 54

task scheduling in HaLoop 54–5
Handwritten dataset 251
hard clustering 161
HBase 88
Heart-Statlog 251
Hepatitis 252
Higgs 251
high-availability clusters 318
high-performance clusters 318
high utility itemset (HUI)-Miner algorithm 219
Hill Valley 247
Hitachi LDL 118
Hive 89–90
HK-medoids 241
Hoeffding-based decision trees 186
horizontal scaling 210
human–computer interaction (HCI) 336
Hypercube 240
Hypothesis testing (HT) 186

i^{2}MapReduce 250
IaaS (infrastructure as a service) model 300
IBM Quest Dataset Generator 221
IBM WebSphere MQ (IBM MQ) 192
IDS-MRCPSO 247
imbalanced classes 177
IM-K-means algorithm 241
Improved MapReduce Apriori (IMRApriori) algorithm 220
Improved Parallel Association Rule Based on Combination 223
incremental algorithms 159
incremental learning algorithm for ESVM (IESVM) 227
industrial Internet 304
InfoGain 251
InputSplit 43
Internet of Things (IoT) 297
    devices 210
intrusion detection (ID) 227
intrusion detection system (IDS) 246
Ionosphere 247

I/O optimization 74
    data compression and sharing 74
    data shuffling 74
Isolet 251

JAWBONE 303
join tree algorithm 238

Kalman filter (KF) 178
Karp–Papadimitriou–Shenker (KPS)
    algorithm 189
KDD99 240, 251
KDDB 251
KDD Cup 1999 dataset 228
KDDCUP99 246
Kent Ridge Breast Cancer 223
K-means clustering algorithm 243–4
K-medoids clustering 240
K-modes 243
k-nearest neighbor (*k*-NN) 226
k-NN algorithm 233
Kosarak dataset 224
Kruskal–Wallis test 228
Kyoto 246, 252

lambda architecture 162–3
Lambda Architecture (LA) 191
LC-CloStream algorithm 190
Letter Recognition dataset 234
linear regression algorithm 326
literal FCM (LFCM) 245
live captions 338–9
load balancing algorithms 320–1
load balancing clusters 318
logistic regression machine learning
    algorithm 326
Lookout 338
LOSSY COUNTING 188, 190
Lumada data lake (LDL) 105

machine cluster 6
machine learning (ML) 209
    in data lakes 120
    models 176
MapReduce 211–12, 321

application implemented using
    46–53
architecture of 39
    executing map phase 42–3
    reduce phase execution 45–6
    shuffling and sorting 43–5
preliminaries 127
MapReduce, and Voting-based
    instance selection (MRVIS)
    229
MapReduce-based Apriori algorithms
    219
mass processing systems 3
master–slave model 17–18
MATLAB 7.0 246
maximal frequent item sets (MFI) 189
Medical Expenditure Panel Survey
    226
medium window (MW) 186
memory management 97
memory optimization 73–4
Mesos 194
metadata management 113
MicroBlog-Latent Dirichlet Allocation
    (MB-LDA) 251
Microsoft Azure Blob Storage-WASB
    88
Microsoft Message Queuing 192
Microsoft's DMTK and CNTK 322–3
mining frequent item sets 177–8
MixSim R Package 241
MOMENT 189
MongoDB 13–14
Movielens dataset 248
MrAdam 221
MRK-means 239
MR-PFP 222
MRQAR 220
MR-Rocchio algorithm 234
MRSMRS 222
multi-label *k*-NN (ML-*k*-NN) 231
multi-objective ABC (MOABC)
    algorithm 252
multiple linear regression (MLR)
    225–6

multi-way joins using MapReduce
    127–8
  sequential join 129–30
  shares approach 130–2
  sharesSkew 132–5
  Θ-Join 135
    binary Θ-join 135–7
    multi-way Θ-join 137–8
multi-way spatial join 147–52
multi-way Θ-join 137–8
Mushroom 221, 223
Mushrooms 249
Musk 247
mutual information feature selection
    method based on spark
    framework (sf-MIFS) 236

Netflix competition dataset 251
neural network (NN) 179, 182
NewMOMENT 189
NewSQL databases 8
*1998 DARPA Intrusion Detection
    Evaluation Set* 219
NoSQL databases 9
  aggregate-oriented 12–13
  Cassandra 14–15
  disadvantages of 11–12
  MongoDB 13–14
NSL-KDD 246, 252

one-hot-encoding 183
OpenFlow protocol 320
OpenPlanet 225
Open source-based data lakes 116
  best practices for data lakes 117–18
  BIGCONNECT data lake 116–17
  Delta lake 116
outlier and anomaly detection 162
outlier detection 180–3
outlier detection/intrusion detection
    system
  Hadoop MapReduce-based
    conference paper 247
  Hadoop MapReduce-based journal
    paper 246

Spark-based conference papers
    247–8
Spark-based journal papers 246
Oxford Buildings Dataset 238

PaaS (platform as a service) model
    300
PaMPa-HD 223
Pampas 223
parallel backpropagation neural
    network (PBPNN) 230
Parallel Binary Bat Algorithm 246
Parallel Block FP-Growth
    (PBFP-Growth) 222
parallel ensemble of online sequential
    ELM (PEOS-ELM) algorithm
    229
parallel feature reduction algorithm
    250
parallel genetic algorithm based on
    Spark (PGAS) 250
Parallel Highly Informative *k*-ItemSet
    (PHIKS) 217, 222
parallel high utility itemset (PHUI)-
    Miner algorithm 219
parallelized version of extreme SVM
    (PESVM) 227
parallel methods of FIM (PARMA)
    219
parallel mining algorithm for the
    constrained FP (PACFP) 219
parallel processing 318
parallel PSO (PPSO) 243
parallel random forest (PRF)
    algorithm 230
Parallel Weighted Itemset (PaWI)
    Mining algorithm 223
particle swarm optimization (PSO)
    236
partition key 15
PatchWork 245
Patient Treatment Time Prediction
    algorithm 225
peer-to-peer (P2P) computing 319,
    321

PELT (pruned exact linear time)
    algorithm 186
perception porting 337–8
Phrase Nets 194
Pig data model 60
Pima Indian Diabetes 251
Pi Stack 320
Poker 251
PokerHand 228, 233, 249
PostgreSQL 194
prediction and forecasting 178–80
primary key 15
processing high-dimensional data 182
Producer API 170
production data centre (PR-DC) 194
Programming layer in Spark 80
    DataFrames in Spark SQL 81–2
    PySpark 80
    SparkR 80–1
    Spark SQL 81
proximal SVM 228
PSOAANN 236
PubChem 217, 221
PubChem website 220
public cloud 299
PySpark 80

quantitative analysis of drift 184
query optimization strategies for big
    data 125
    graph queries using MapReduce
        138
        counting triangles 138–40
        subgraph enumeration 140–6
    MapReduce preliminaries 127
    multi-way joins using MapReduce
        127–8
        sequential join 129–30
        shares approach 130–2
        sharesSkew 132–5
        Θ-Join 135–138
    multi-way spatial join 147–52

RabbitMQ. 192
Raspberry Pi 320, 324–6

reading quorum 19
real-time data processing 157
    data streaming processing
        approaches, evaluation of 172
    lambda architecture 162–3
    real-time data processing topology
        159
        choosing platform 159
        data processing infrastructure
            159
        entry points 159
    streaming processing 160–1
    stream mining 161
        classification 161
        clustering 161
        frequent 162
        outlier and anomaly detection
            162
    stream processing approach for Big
        Data 163
        Apache Flink 164–7
        Apache Flume 168–9
        Apache Kafka 169–72
        Apache Samza 167
        Apache Spark 163–4
        Apache Storm 167–8
real-time data processing topology
    159
    choosing platform 159
    data processing infrastructure 159
        analytics layer 159
        filtering layer 159
        formality layer 159
        storing layer 160
    entry points 159
recommendation
    Hadoop MapReduce-based
        conference papers 248–9
    Hadoop MapReduce-based journal
        paper 248
    Spark-based conference papers 249
Record Linkage Comparison Patterns
    (RLCPs) dataset 228
RecordReader 43
recurrence of drift 187

Redis 194
Reduced-Apriori (R-Apriori) 224
regression-based prediction and
      forecasting systems 179
regression/prediction/forecasting
   Hadoop MapReduce-based
      conference papers 225–6
   Hadoop MapReduce-based journal
      papers 224–5
   Spark-based conference papers
      226–7
   Spark-based journal papers 225
relational databases 6–9
   vs NoSQL databases 11
RELIEF-F 251
replication 17–18
   combining sharding and 18–19
resilient distributed datasets (RDDs)
      70–1, 164, 322
   caching 71
restricted Boltzmann machines
      (RBMs) 182
Retail dataset 224
Reuters dataset 238
review methodology 214–17
Round Robin load balancing
      algorithm 320
R programming language 3
RuleMR 233

SaaS (software as a service) model
      300
scalability in relational databases 6
   limitations of relational databases
      7–9
   relational databases 6–7
scalable fast evolutionary algorithm for
      clustering (SF-EAC) 243–4
Scalable Random Sampling with
      iterative optimization FCM
      algorithm (SRSIO-FCM) 245
Scala programming language 326
scale up 210
scaling 210
SDSS star spectrum datasets 219

Secure Shell (SSH) connection 324
SEED Join 145–6
Seeing AI 338
self-organizing map (SOM) clustering
      244
semantic-driven subtractive clustering
      method 238
semi-supervised learning 180–1
sequential join 129–30
sequential minimal optimization
      (SMO) 233
S-FRULER 225
sharding 15–16
   combining replication and 18–19
shares approach 130–2
sharesSkew 132–5
shuffle grouping 168
Shuttle dataset 251
SignWriting 339
SIMPLifying and Ensembling
      (SIMPLE) framework 239
Sina Weibo dataset 250
singular value decomposition with
      stochastic gradient descent
      (SVD-SGD) 248
16S rRNA dataset 237
SKIP-LCSS 190
small window (SW) 186
smart city 303
smart environment, enabling
   through IoT for persons with
      disabilities 339–40
smart farming 304–5
smart gateway 310
smart grids 303
smart homes 303
smart retail 304
smart supply chain 304
SMOTE algorithm 235
SMRF algorithm 231
SMR-*K*means 242
Snort logs 219
social media sites 298
soft clustering 161
software-defined networking (SDN) 320

SPAB-DKMC algorithm 243
SpamBase 227, 246, 252
SPARK 191
Spark-based conference paper 252
Spark-based journal papers 250–1
Spark-based KFCM (S-KFCM) 244–5
Spark cluster manager 70
Spark Context 69
Spark Core 69
Spark Datasets 72
Spark deep learning support 79–80
  CaffeOnSpark 80
  Deeplearning4j (DL4j) 80
Spark fog cluster evaluation 326–9
Spark-gram 224
Spark GraphX 76
Spark machine learning support 78
  example of MLlib 79
  keystone ML 79
  Spark MLlib 78–9
Spark ML 322
Spark MLlib 78–9, 164, 322
SparkR 80–1
Spark SQL 81, 164
Spark Streaming 164
Spark System optimization 73
  decentralized task scheduling 73
  scheduler optimization 73
Spark worker node 70
specific programming languages 3
splitting-based data balancing method
    (SplitBal) 230
Sqoop 111
Stanford Network Analysis Project
    (SNAP) 222
Star Join 143–4
static algorithms 318
statistical models 176, 180
STORM 191
StoryFlow 194
stream grouping 168
streaming processing 160–1
stream mining 161
  classification 161

clustering 161
frequent 162
outlier and anomaly detection 162
STREAM MINING 189
stream processing approach for Big
    Data 163
  Apache Flink 164–7
  Apache Flume 168–9
  Apache Kafka 169–72
  Apache Samza 167
  Apache Spark 163–4
  Apache Storm 167–8
Streams API 172
subgraph enumeration 140–1
  EdgeJoin 141–2
  SEED Join 145–6
  Star Join 143–4
  TwinTwig Join 144–5
summarization 176
summingbird framework 163
supervised learning 180
support vector machine (SVM) 182
SVM-RFE 251

T10I4D100K 224
T25I10D10K 224
TDL for digital banking 118–19
Temenos data lake (TDL) 105
text visualization 194
Θ-Join 135
  binary Θ-join 135–7
  multi-way Θ-join 137–8
time-sensitive computing 307
time-series data 178
top-*k* CFIs 189–90
TreeNetViz 194
20NewsGroup 235
TwinTwig Join 144–5
Twister framework 56
  architecture of 57–8
  fault tolerance 58–9
Twitter dataset 231, 248
Twitter Search API 236
TWMINSWAP-IS 190

UML diagram 22, 26
unbounded data streams 165
unsupervised learning 180–1
URL-Reputation 235
user BN (UBN) 250
USPS 251
utility computing 321

value 2
Variable Size-based Fixed Passes
    Combined-counting 219
variety 2
velocity 2
veracity 2
Vertical-Apriori MapReduce
    (VAMR) 222
vertical scaling 210
very fast decision tree (VFDT) 186
VoltDB 194
volume 2

Washington State Inpatient Database
    226

WBDC 247
wearable robotics 339
wearables 303
weighted ensemble classifier based on
    DELM (WE-DELM) 228
Weighted Label Propagation
    Algorithm with Probability
    Threshold (P-WLPA)
    algorithm 235
Wikipedia articles collection dataset 224
WikiTalk dataset 250
windowing technique 186
Wine 247
Wisconsin Breast Cancer 251
Word Clouds 194
writing quorum 19

Yet Another Resource Negotiator
    (YARN) 194
YouTube Faces dataset 245

ZooKeeper 194